Economic History of Europe:
Twentieth Century

DOCUMENTARY HISTORY OF WESTERN CIVILIZATION
Edited by Eugene C. Black and Leonard W. Levy

ANCIENT AND MEDIEVAL HISTORY OF THE WEST

Morton Smith: ANCIENT GREECE

A. H. M. Jones: A HISTORY OF ROME THROUGH THE FIFTH CENTURY
Vol. I: The Republic   TB/1364
Vol. II: The Empire

Deno Geanakoplos: BYZANTINE EMPIRE

Marshall W. Baldwin: CHRISTIANITY THROUGH THE CRUSADES

Bernard Lewis: ISLAM THROUGH SULEIMAN THE MAGNIFICENT

David Herlihy: HISTORY OF FEUDALISM

William M. Bowsky: RISE OF COMMERCE AND TOWNS

David Herlihy: MEDIEVAL CULTURE AND SOCIETY   TB/1340

EARLY MODERN HISTORY

Hanna H. Gray: CULTURAL HISTORY OF THE RENAISSANCE

Florence Edler de Roover: MONEY, BANKING,
AND COMMERCE, THIRTEENTH THROUGH SIXTEENTH CENTURIES

V. J. Parry: THE OTTOMAN EMPIRE

Ralph E. Giesey: EVOLUTION OF THE DYNASTIC STATE

J. H. Parry: THE EUROPEAN RECONNAISSANCE: *Selected Documents*   TB/1345

Hans J. Hillerbrand: THE PROTESTANT REFORMATION   TB/1342

John C. Olin: THE CATHOLIC COUNTER-REFORMATION

Orest Ranum: THE CENTURY OF LOUIS XIV

Thomas Hegarty: RUSSIAN HISTORY THROUGH PETER THE GREAT

Marie Boas-Hall: THE SCIENTIFIC REVOLUTION

Barry E. Supple: HISTORY OF MERCANTILISM

Arthur J. Slavin: IMPERIALISM, WAR, AND DIPLOMACY, 1550-1763

Herbert H. Rowen: THE LOW COUNTRIES

C. A. Macartney: THE EVOLUTION OF THE HABSBURG
AND HOHENZOLLERN DYNASTIES   TB/1400

Lester G. Crocker: THE ENLIGHTENMENT

Robert and Elborg Forster: EUROPEAN SOCIETY IN THE EIGHTEENTH CENTURY   TB/1404

REVOLUTIONARY EUROPE, 1789-1848

Paul H. Beik: THE FRENCH REVOLUTION
David L. Dowd: NAPOLEONIC ERA, 1799-1815
René Albrecht-Carrié: THE CONCERT OF EUROPE   TB/1341
John B. Halsted: ROMANTICISM   TB/1387
R. Max Hartwell: THE INDUSTRIAL REVOLUTION
Mack Walker: METTERNICH'S EUROPE   TB/1361
Douglas Johnson: THE ASCENDANT BOURGEOISIE
John A. Hawgood: THE REVOLUTIONS OF 1848

NATIONALISM, LIBERALISM, AND SOCIALISM, 1850-1914

Eugene C. Black: VICTORIAN CULTURE AND SOCIETY
Eugene C. Black: BRITISH POLITICS IN THE NINETEENTH CENTURY
Denis Mack Smith: THE MAKING OF ITALY, 1796-1870 TB/1356
David Thomson: FRANCE: *Empire and Republic*, 1850-1940   TB/1378
Theodore S. Hamerow: BISMARCK'S MITTELEUROPA
Eugene O. Golob: THE AGE OF LAISSEZ FAIRE
Roland N. Stromberg: REALISM, NATURALISM, AND SYMBOLISM:
Modes of Thought and Expression in Europe, 1848-1914   TB/1355
Melvin Kranzberg: SCIENCE AND TECHNOLOGY
Jesse D. Clarkson: TSARIST RUSSIA: *Catherine the Great to Nicholas II*
Philip D. Curtin and John R. W. Smail: IMPERIALISM
Massimo Salvadori: MODERN SOCIALISM   TB/1374

THE TWENTIETH CENTURY

Jere C. King: THE FIRST WORLD WAR
S. Clough and T. & C. Moodie: ECONOMIC HISTORY OF EUROPE:
Twentieth Century   TB/1388
W. Warren Wagar: SCIENCE, FAITH, AND MAN:
European Thought Since 1914   TB/1362
Paul A. Gagnon: INTERNATIONALISM AND DIPLOMACY BETWEEN THE WARS, 1919-1939
Henry Cord Meyer: WEIMAR AND NAZI GERMANY
Michal Vyvyan: RUSSIA FROM LENIN TO KHRUSHCHEV
Charles F. Delzell: MEDITERRANEAN TOTALITARIANISM, 1919-1945
———————: THE SECOND WORLD WAR

A volume
in
DOCUMENTARY HISTORY
of
WESTERN CIVILIZATION

Economic History of Europe: Twentieth Century

edited by

SHEPARD B. CLOUGH
THOMAS MOODIE
CAROL MOODIE

Maps by Willow Roberts

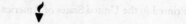

HARPER TORCHBOOKS

Harper & Row, Publishers, New York, Evanston, and London

To the memory of
WILLIAM T. GAYLE

ECONOMIC HISTORY OF EUROPE:
TWENTIETH CENTURY

Preface, Chronology, Introduction, editorial notes, translations by the editors, and compilation copyright © 1968 by Shepard B. Clough, Thomas Moodie, and Carol Moodie.

Printed in the United States of America.

All rights reserved.

First HARPER TORCHBOOK edition published 1968 by Harper & Row, Publishers, Incorporated, New York, N.Y. 10016.

A clothbound edition of this book is published in the United States and Canada by Walker and Company.

Library of Congress Catalog Card Number: 68-27379.

Contents

Maps to follow page viii

PART III: THE POSTWAR CRISIS

PART IV: RECOVERY AND STAGNATION, 1924–29

PART V: SOVIET ECONOMIC POLICY IN THE 1920'S

Maps

I EUROPE BEFORE WORLD WAR I (1914)

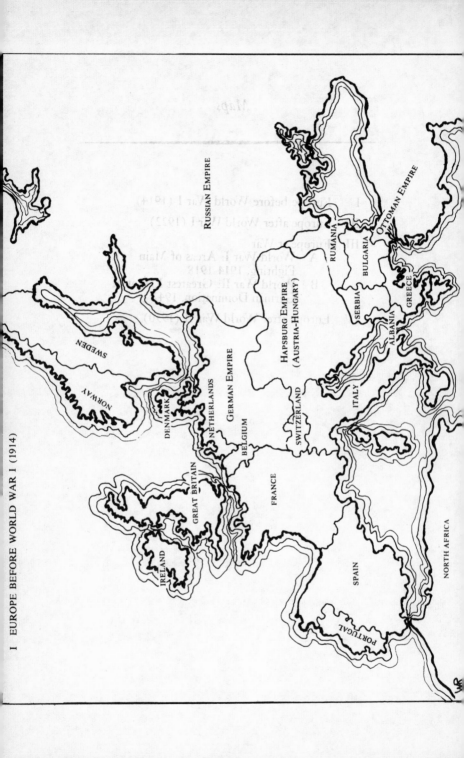

II EUROPE AFTER WORLD WAR I (1922)

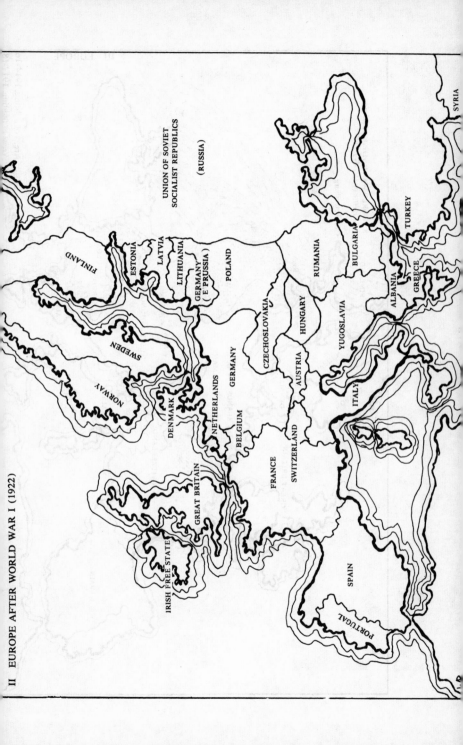

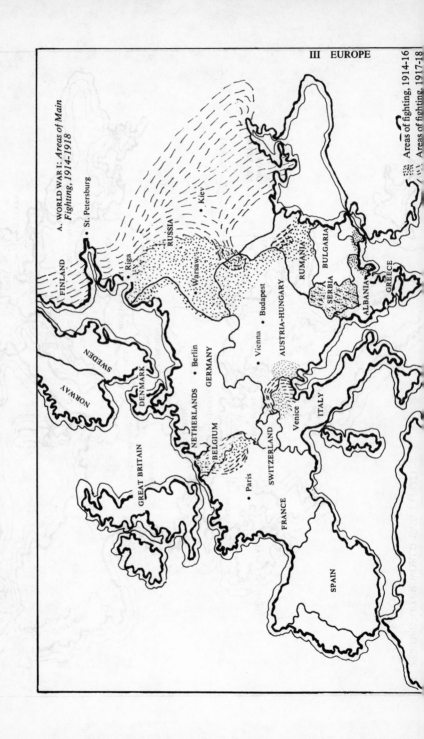

III EUROPE

A. WORLD WAR I: *Areas of Main Fighting, 1914-1918*

Areas of fighting, 1914-16
Areas of fighting, 1917-18

NORWAY
SWEDEN
FINLAND
St. Petersburg
DENMARK
GREAT BRITAIN
NETHERLANDS
Berlin
RUSSIA
BELGIUM
GERMANY
Riga
Warsaw
Kiev
Paris
SWITZERLAND
Vienna
Budapest
AUSTRIA-HUNGARY
FRANCE
Venice
ITALY
RUMANIA
SERBIA
BULGARIA
ALBANIA
GREECE
SPAIN

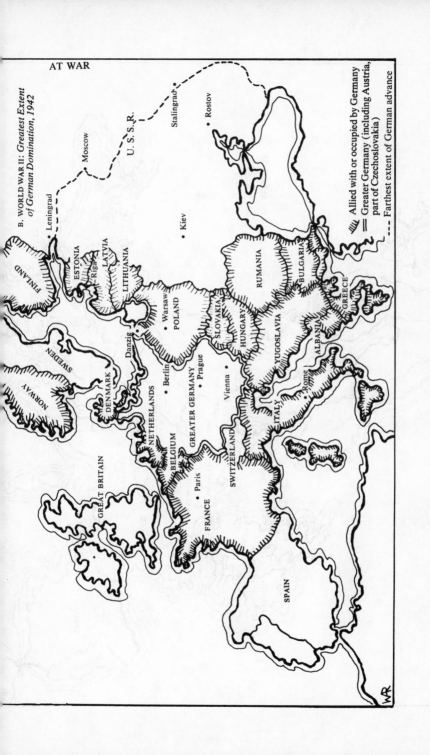

B. WORLD WAR II: *Greatest Extent
of German Domination, 1942*

Allied with or occupied by Germany

Greater Germany (including Austria,
part of Czechoslovakia)

Farthest extent of German advance

FINLAND

NORWAY

SWEDEN

GREAT BRITAIN

Leningrad

ESTONIA

Riga

LATVIA

LITHUANIA

Moscow

U. S. S. R.

Stalingrad

Rostov

Kiev

Danzig

Warsaw

POLAND

Berlin

DENMARK

NETHERLANDS

BELGIUM

GREATER GERMANY

Prague

SLOVAKIA

Vienna

HUNGARY

RUMANIA

BULGARIA

YUGOSLAVIA

ALBANIA

GREECE

Paris

FRANCE

SWITZERLAND

Rome

ITALY

SPAIN

W·R

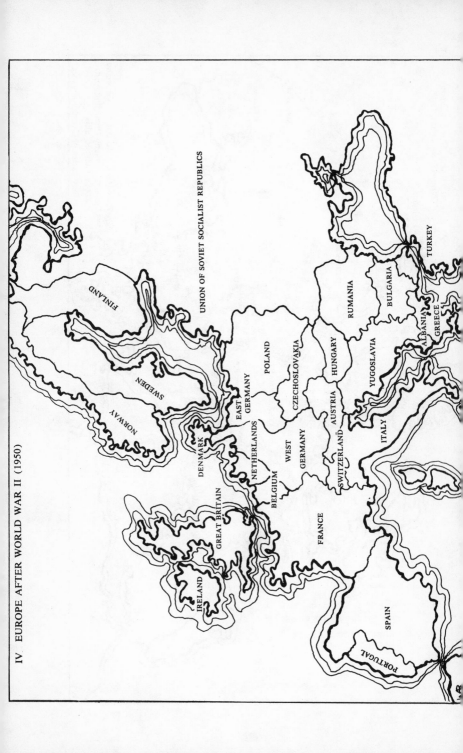

IV EUROPE AFTER WORLD WAR II (1950)

UNION OF SOVIET SOCIALIST REPUBLICS

FINLAND

NORWAY

SWEDEN

DENMARK

EAST GERMANY

POLAND

CZECHOSLOVAKIA

HUNGARY

RUMANIA

BULGARIA

YUGOSLAVIA

ALBANIA

GREECE

TURKEY

ITALY

AUSTRIA

SWITZERLAND

WEST GERMANY

NETHERLANDS

BELGIUM

FRANCE

GREAT BRITAIN

IRELAND

SPAIN

PORTUGAL

Preface

THERE IS an embarrassingly rich supply of documentary material for the study of Europe's economic history in the twentieth century. Any number of agencies, both public and private, gather and preserve all kinds of information relevant to economic life. Confronted with such wealth and variety of material, we were required to limit the scope of this collection in a number of ways. First of all, we omitted some topics that might ordinarily be included in economic history. Probably most notable is the absence of any attention to economic theory, and the absence of coverage of trade-union activity and labor history in general. Secondly, the primary focus has been on the major industrial countries—Britain, France, Germany, the Soviet Union and, to a lesser extent, Italy. This is not to deny that economic life goes on in smaller nations or agricultural countries, but only to bow to the exigencies of space.

The organization of the material reflects our assumptions about the significance of short-term economic change and about the relationship between economic and political life. It would have been possible to pursue broad secular lines of development (such as changing patterns of European and world trade, demographic change, growth and capital formation, technological advance) in a way that largely ignored the numerous and frequently violent short-term economic fluctuations. But to do so, we felt, would have limited too severely the definition of economic history and would have obscured one of the most characteristic features of the twentieth century, the tremendous extent to which economic life has been affected by the external factors of war and political upheaval. Thus, our chapters follow divisions that will not be unfamiliar to the political historian.

Our account starts with 1914 rather than the turn of the century because we believe that the First World War was the beginning of the catastrophic course of twentieth-century European history, in economic as well as political life. By contrast, the general

economic experience of Europe before 1914 displayed the nineteenth century's traits of stability and optimism. We have made no
attempt to give full coverage to the years following the Second
World War because of the limited perspective upon this period.
Instead, we have taken the account to the later 1950's by sketching
out three trends that seem to us of special importance: new ap-
proaches to problems of postwar recovery; the radical reconstruction of the economies of eastern European states; and the
development of regional economic cooperation.

The distinction between "documents" and "secondary sources"
is frequently fuzzy, and this is particularly true of twentieth-century history. In order to establish a clear separation between secondary and documentary materials of economic history we have
relied heavily upon public documents—on speeches, legislation, international agreements, official inquiries—that deal with important
economic issues or problems. Especially in official reports, the
language has that faceless and dispassionate quality that has become
the badge of impartiality, although such verbal timidity should not
be allowed to obscure the importance of the information presented
or the issues involved. Another characteristic of official reports is
their great length. With few exceptions we have been forced to
cut the material, but we have always tried to give the reader a
sense of the entire document and to avoid paring it down to a few
lonely sentences. The diversity of sources from which the documents were assembled has raised serious problems of style. In translations by the editors, modern American usage has been followed.
In the case of translations not made by the editors, we have retained
the spelling and usage of the translation. However, we have taken
the liberty of making minor emendations in cases of dark obscurity
or to avoid confusion (for instance "billion" is used uniformly
throughout the text for a thousand millions, even when "milliard"
appeared in the original). For transliterating Russian titles and
names, we have used the Library of Congress system with some
simplifications, except where some other form of the name is
common.

It gives us great pleasure to acknowledge with gratitude the help
we received in compiling this book. We relied heavily upon the
resourcefulness and tried the patience of the librarians of Lake
Forest College; and we were generously allowed to use the resources of the libraries of the University of Chicago, Northwestern
University, and Columbia University, as well as those of the New

York Public Library. We are also indebted to our colleagues for
help on portions of the book. The Introduction benefited from the
criticism of Murray Herlihy and Arthur Zilversmit, both of Lake
Forest College. The translations have been improved by Gaida
Hughes of Lake Forest College and Eva Richter. We would also
like to thank Ludwig Kolman, Maria Kolman and Arthur Rohr for
work on the translations. And finally, we would like to thank the
Harper editors and readers, Hugh Van Dusen, Elisabeth Jakab,
Bonnie Anderson, and Ann Adelman, who have devoted much skill
to improving the manuscript and to guiding it through the stages
leading to publication. The errors or obscurities of the book are
ours alone.

Chronology

1924   Dawes Plan settled reparation problem temporarily; followed by flow of private American capital to Germany and Austria.

1925   Rough benchmark for recovery of prewar production levels; Britain returned to gold standard.

1927–30   Falling prices in world market for primary products.

1914–18   First World War: stalemate by end of 1914 made economic power crucial; required mobilization and control of national economic resources everywhere; 1917, collapse of Russia and eastern front balanced by U.S. entry.

1917   Under Provisional Government Russian economic dislocation and inflation became severe; after November Revolution, Bolsheviks decreed workers' control in factories, nationalized banks, repudiated foreign government debts (1918), tolerated peasant seizures of land.

1918–21   Creation of new states in eastern Europe; boundary conflicts, building new national economic institutions difficult; land reforms.

1918–21   Russian Civil War and economic policy of War Communism destroyed production and trade; March, 1921, New Economic Policy instituted.

1919   Paris Peace Conference: Treaty of Versailles.

1919–23   Postwar economic disorders: brief postwar boom followed by depression, unemployment and labor difficulties; impossible to re-establish old trade patterns; inflation in all countries, runaway inflations in eastern and central Europe.

1922   Fascist régime in Italy: extended state control over economy, especially labor (1926, Law on Corporations), and state responsibility for public welfare (1927, Labor Charter).

1923   French-Belgian occupation of Ruhr; German runaway inflation, halted in autumn of 1923 by establishment of Rentenbank.

1923–29   Increased cartelization of industry (especially in Germany).

1924   Dawes Plan: settled reparations problem temporarily; followed by flow of private American capital to Germany and Austria.

1925   Rough benchmark for recovery of prewar production levels; Britain returned to gold standard.

1927–29   Falling prices in world market for primary products.

1928   U.S.S.R. adopts First Five Year Plan; in 1929 industrialization speeded up, forcible and rapid collectivization begun; Plan declared complete in 1932; Second Five Year Plan (1933–38) stressed improved quality in production; use of income differentials as incentives.

1930   Impact of World Economic Depression felt in Europe: collapse of Austrian Creditanstalt and other central European banks followed October, 1929, collapse of New York stock market.

1931   Hoover moratorium on reparation and war-debt payments; Britain abandoned gold standard.

1932   Britain abandoned free trade with adoption of general *ad valorem* tariff.

1933   Nazi régime in Germany: wide government financing of public works to combat Depression; labor unions destroyed and Nazi-controlled National Labor Front created (1934); 1936, major rearmament begun.

1934–39   Eastern Europe brought increasingly into German commercial sphere.

1936   Popular Front Government elected in France, put through moderate economic and social reforms.

1939–45   Second World War: economic mobilization faster and more efficient than in 1914; warfare more mechanized, strategic bombing destroyed urban centers.

1941   Lend-Lease system of U.S. aid to European allies begun.

1944   Benelux customs union agreed on by Belgium, The Netherlands and Luxembourg.

1945   War's end left Europe divided between Western and Soviet occupation; devastation severe, production at standstill; emergency relief (through UNRRA) brought rapid but limited improvement.

1945–52 Recovery and establishment of Soviet-type economies in eastern European states.

1945 New British Labour Government; nationalized major industries and Bank of England; extended welfare system, instituted National Health Service.

1945–46 Some French industries, banks, and insurance companies nationalized; Monnet Plan for French reconstruction and modernization adopted in 1946.

1946 U.S.S.R. adopted Fourth Five Year Plan (1946–50), directed at recovery, but along lines of earlier Plans.

1947 Balance of payments crisis stalled recovery; U.S. offer of aid through Marshall Plan accepted by western European nations that formed (in 1948) the Committee of European Economic Cooperation.

1948 German inflation ended by currency reforms in Allied and then Soviet sectors of Occupied Germany, established two German currencies; provided sound basis for West German recovery; East Germany brought increasingly into Soviet economic pattern.

1949–50 Prewar levels of production achieved in western Europe and U.S.S.R.

1951 Treaty establishing European Coal and Steel Community signed.

1953 "New Course" in U.S.S.R. and eastern Europe after Stalin's death included economic reforms.

1957 Treaty of Rome establishing the Common Market signed.

Introduction

Europe Before 1914

To many who lived through the First World War and the chaos of the early 1920's, the decades just before 1914 seemed a golden age and the unified European economy an ideal construction of human effort. Economic stability, security, and progress, which were so lacking after 1914, stood out as the dominant characteristics of the earlier age. John Maynard Keynes's famous description of "Europe before the war" captures this attitude and many of the qualities of the economic life of that era.

> What an extraordinary episode in the economic progress of man that age was which came to an end in August 1914! . . . The [prosperous] inhabitant of London could order by telephone, sipping his morning tea in bed, the various products of the whole earth, in such quantity as he might see fit, and reasonably expect their early delivery upon his doorstep; he could at the same moment and by the same means adventure his wealth in the natural resources and new enterprises of any quarter of the world, and share, without exertion or even trouble, in their prospective fruits and advantages. . . . He could secure forthwith, if he wished it, cheap and comfortable means of transit to any country or climate without passport or other formality, could dispatch his servant to the neighboring office of a bank for such supply of the precious metals as might seem convenient, and could then proceed abroad to foreign quarters, . . . and would consider himself greatly aggrieved and much surprised at the least interference. But, most important of all, he regarded this state of affairs as normal, certain, and permanent, except in the direction of further improvement. . . .[1]

The remarkably free movement of persons, goods, and capital here described by Keynes is indicative of the great international economic interdependency of the decades before 1914. Especially

---

[1] John Maynard Keynes, *The Economic Consequences of the Peace* (New York: Harcourt, Brace and Howe, 1920), pp. 10–11. Used by permission of Harcourt, Brace and World.

among European countries, the extent of economic interaction was such that for many purposes national frontiers lost their significance and one may legitimately speak of a "European economy." This is not to deny disparities in the level of economic development and in the kind of production that prevailed from one country to another, or the great variety in the social and legal systems of European states. Nevertheless, many patterns prevailed throughout the entire continent. Financial and commercial practices had much in common from one country to another, and the common use of a gold standard for currency facilitated multilateral trade. Tariffs were generally at levels that did not seriously impede the international flow of goods. If all the continent was not industrialized to the same extent, well-established channels for exchanging primary products for industrial goods existed and allowed agrarian regions to share in the prosperity of industrial centers. And the industrialization of some backward countries—sometimes at a very rapid rate, as for example of Russia—was closing the gap between industrialized and backward countries. Steady and orderly progress was the common expectation.

Almost any measure one would choose points to growing wealth and prosperity for Europe in the two decades before 1914. Population rose steadily throughout the period. In 1890 the total population of Europe (excluding Russia, but including the rest of eastern Europe) stood at 265.9 million; by 1900 it had increased to 289.5 million and in 1913 reached 324 million. At the same time the growth of cities, characteristic of the entire nineteenth century, continued unabated. This great internal migration produced radical changes in the lives of the people. City life afforded a great variety of new comforts and conveniences. Many products formerly considered luxuries were available at moderate cost. Improved lighting and sewage systems made the cities safer and healthier. Even the less fortunate, crowded into the tenements of industrial suburbs, shared to a lesser degree in the greater comforts of urban life. Compared with those still living on the land in backward areas, their incomes were high and steadily improving, and reasonably steady work afforded a greater degree of economic security. For those with talent and ambition the opportunities for rising on the social and economic scale were greater than before. In eastern and southern Europe the bulk of the population still derived its living from the land, but the preponderance was shifting toward the cities in the industrialized countries of the West.

GROWTH OF URBAN POPULATION
(percentages)

Country	Year	Urban	Rural
England and Wales	1891	74.7	25.3
	1901	76.8	23.2
	1911	79.1	21.9
France	1896	39.1	60.9
	1906	42.1	57.9
	1911	44.1	55.9
Germany	1890	42.5	57.5
	1900	54.4	45.6
	1910	60.0	40.0

Note: "Urban" is here defined as towns with populations of 2,000 or more. This is at best a rough index of urbanization.

Sources: For England, W. Bowden, M. Karpovich, and A. P. Usher, *An Economic History of Europe Since 1750* (New York: American Book Company, 1937), p. 9; for France and Germany, J. H. Clapham, *The Economic Development of France and Germany, 1815–1914*, 4th edition (Cambridge, England: Cambridge University Press, 1963), pp. 159, 278.

In the decades before the war the European economy expanded at a rapid rate in spite of occasional downturns in the business cycle. This growth, and the prosperity it brought, derived largely from industrial expansion. The annual rate of growth of manufacturing output for Europe as a whole was about three and one-quarter per cent. Agricultural income and productivity rose in many places, but it was the large industrial states, particularly Great Britain and Germany, that enjoyed the highest national and per capita incomes.

The period from 1890 to 1914 was also one of great expansion of world trade and of European domination of that trade. On the eve of the First World War, Europe accounted for more than half of world trade; the value of both imports and exports was slightly over 50 per cent of the total in 1913.[2] Although some European countries exported substantial quantities of primary products, manufactured goods were the most important element in the expansion of European trade. The substantial and steady increase in both world trade and the trade of European states in manufactures is indicated in the tables below.

[2] Colin Clark, *The Conditions of Economic Progress* (London: Macmillan and Co., 1951), p. 300 (table A.64).

FIGURES RELATING TO NATIONAL INCOME FOR SELECTED EUROPEAN COUNTRIES
BEFORE THE FIRST WORLD WAR[1]

Country	Years	Net National Income		Number Employed[b] (millions)	Real Product in I.U.	
		Current Prices (billions)	I.U.[a] (billions)		Per Man Year	Per Man Hour
Great Britain	1894–1903	1.666 pounds	13.47	17.11	842	.301
	1904–10	1.940	17.27	18.38	1001	.360
	1911–13	2.241	19.27	20.00	1017	.365
	1913	2.339	19.70	20.36	1019	.366
France	1890–99	27.0 francs	7.45	15.6	555	.181
	1900–09	33.0	9.00	16.7	597	.197
	1911	36.0	10.05	17.4	627	.207
Italy	1893	7.0 lira	3.20	11.9	370	.101
	1901	9.3[c]	3.72	12.7	451	.135
	1914	19.0	4.52	13.5	399	.134
Germany	1894–1903	29.06 marks	14.57	18.21	820	.259
	1904–10	39.14	17.30	20.93	847	.278
	1911–13	47.77	19.28	22.38	881	.297
	1913	50.13	20.62	22.69	930	.314
Belgium	1895	3.28 francs	.892	2.95	351	.113
	1913	6.50	2.145	3.36	666	.222

[a] An I.U. (International Unit), developed by Colin Clark as a standard measure of purchasing power, is the amount of goods that could be purchased for $1 in the United States, averaged for the period 1925 to 1934.

[b] Occupied population less unemployed and excluding women engaged in agriculture.

[c] Includes indirect taxation, not included in figures for 1893 and 1914. A downward correction of between 5 and 10 per cent is suggested by figures for other years.

Source: Colin Clark, The Conditions of Economic Progress, tables in Chapter III.

[1] The figures in this table are not to be taken as precise. There are enormous difficulties in arriving at measures of national income that provide an accurate basis of comparison over time and from one country to another. This is particularly true of a period (such as the one considered here) where regularly collected and accurate data are lacking. For a thorough discussion of these problems, see Clark, op. cit., Chapter III.

GROWTH OF WORLD TRADE, 1891–1913
(annual averages)

Period	Actual values in dollars (millions)			Value in dollars at 1913 prices (millions)
	Imports	Exports	Total	Total
Manufactured Articles				
1891–95	2,890	2,720	5,610	6,960
1896–1900	3,370	3,230	6,600	7,285
1901–05	4,160	3,990	8,150	9,588
1906–10	5,620	5,400	11,020	11,824
1911–13	7,250	6,920	14,170	14,504
1913	7,720	7,450	15,170	15,170
Primary Products				
1891–95	5,500	4,650	10,150	13,013
1896–1900	6,440	5,460	11,900	15,256
1901–05	7,780	6,920	14,700	17,927
1906–10	10,030	8,920	18,950	21,056
1911–13	12,670	11,400	24,070	24,561
1913	13,330	12,000	25,330	25,330

Note: $1 = 1.50463 grams of fine gold.

Source: League of Nations, *Industrialization and Foreign Trade* (Geneva: League of Nations, 1945), p. 157.

The remarkable advance characteristic of the decades before 1914 supports the optimistic view of the future that Keynes noted in prewar Europe. Yet, many of the changes in Europe's economic position that became more pronounced after 1914 were already discernible. A careful observer in 1910 might have predicted that the European economy would soon face major difficulties requiring basic adjustments. By that time Europe's leadership in industrial production was already beginning to decline. In the years 1896 to 1900 the three leading industrial countries of Europe (Britain, France, and Germany) accounted for slightly more than 42 per cent of world manufacturing production, and for all of Europe (excluding Russia) the figure was well above 50 per cent. But the non-European share, and especially the United States share, was steadily rising, so that by 1913 those three European countries accounted for only 36.1 per cent of the world total.[3] Western

[3] League of Nations, *Industrialization and Foreign Trade*, p. 13.

GROWTH OF TRADE IN MANUFACTURED GOODS, SELECTED EUROPEAN STATES, JAPAN, AND THE UNITED STATES
(quantum indices, 1913 = 100)

Period	United States	United Kingdom	Germany	France	Russia	Austria-Hungary	Italy	Sweden	Nether-lands	Japan
Imports										
1891–95	61.1	57.5	51.2	48.3	28.0	51.0	38.1	60.5	39.5	24.8
1896–1900	52.6	64.0	54.1	48.8	44.8	51.0	37.6	68.4	46.3	50.7
1901–05	69.1	88.7	63.6	62.2	44.0	61.9	53.1	76.3	65.4	65.0
1906–10	87.6	80.9	84.6	82.0	62.9	84.0	96.5	85.5	81.7	84.7
1911–13	94.7	95.9	97.0	106.1	93.1	102.7	100.9	93.4	93.7	98.0
Exports										
1891–95	21.9	57.3	38.1	54.6	27.3	60.0	22.2	38.2	40.6	16.7
1896–1900	34.4	55.4	42.8	54.6	38.6	59.2	36.1	33.8	38.2	24.5
1901–05	52.1	67.9	58.3	69.9	61.4	75.7	52.6	48.5	55.5	47.1
1906–10	65.6	82.2	73.7	82.9	72.7	87.8	66.5	69.1	66.0	65.7
1911–13	90.2	96.0	93.7	95.7	90.9	96.8	96.9	92.6	91.4	88.2

Source: *Industrialization and Foreign Trade*, pp. 162–163.

Europe was no longer the "workshop of the world" it had once been.

Technological innovation required adjustments in the older industrial countries. The backbone of European industry in the latter half of the nineteenth century had been coal and steel, but by 1914 new industries based on the new technology were beginning to threaten their relative importance. Europe was certainly not incapable of producing the new goods or adopting the new technology (indeed, much of it was developed in Europe), but the transfer of resources to new lines of production using new techniques was bound to produce dislocation in older, heavily capitalized industries. Old industrial centers were likely to decline as the new sources of power, such as high voltage transmission of electricity, permitted a greater geographic dispersion of production.

When this transition came in the 1920's, it was marked by stagnation and unemployment in old industrial centers, dislocation of some markets as patterns of world production changed, and rapid expansion in other sectors. The pattern of growth in some industries and stagnation in others was set by economic changes that had their roots in the period before 1914. Yet the transformation called for was rendered far more difficult and the contrasts between dynamic and stagnating sectors were greatly accentuated by the First World War and the violent economic fluctuations of the interwar period. Indeed, the establishment of economic equilibrium was delayed until after the Second World War.

Europe After 1914

The contrast between the economic history of Europe before 1914 and after is so great that the two periods cannot be approached in the same way. Our habit of thinking that normally economic activity is carried on under conditions of relative peace and stability, that war and political disorder only rarely and for brief periods disrupt "normal" operations, must be abandoned. Except for a brief period in the late 1920's and in the years after 1950, there have been no "normal" times in the economic history of Europe since 1914. Under these circumstances it would be an error to examine the history of the twentieth century as if economic change were generated primarily from within the economy itself, by demographic factors, technological progress, improved methods of production, marketing, and the like. There were indeed some important changes of this sort already under way before the war, but war, revolution, and political change fundamentally altered the course of European economic development after 1914. Yet, one must guard against the dangers of overemphasizing the crisis atmosphere of twentieth-century economic life and thereby of losing sight of broad patterns of transformation not growing directly out of crisis.

From European Economy to National Economies

The economic experience of different nations diverged so radically after the First World War that the term "European economy," so apt for the years before 1914, cannot here be applied. The war and the Treaty of Versailles, by creating a division between victorious and defeated powers that carried long-range economic implications, had much to do with this. The collapse of the empires of eastern and central Europe—this, too, a result of the war—led to the creation of a group of successor states, which, in spite of abortive attempts at regional cooperation, tended to regard one another as economic rivals rather than partners. In general, recovery after the war was pursued within a national rather than regional or international context. This tendency toward economic nationalism was reinforced during the Great Depression of the 1930's, when many governments went even further to cordon off their economies and seek recovery in isolation. Finally, two economic systems, explicitly hostile to the economic liberalism that had prevailed in the West before 1914, were created in the interwar years—the Soviet system of planned state socialism and the Fascist economies of Italy and Germany. But these new economic systems were only the most extreme examples of the general trend toward the national organization of economic life that did much to obliterate the common experience of the earlier age.

To contemporaries, the "Great War" was the chasm separating one era from another in economic matters as in so many other spheres, and it remains so for the historian as well. Never before had Europe organized for conflict on such a vast scale. Between 1914 and 1918 some 65 million troops were mobilized by all belligerents, and combined government expenditures for military purposes reached a figure of about $200 billion. Quite obviously, the economic impact of this Armageddon was tremendous. Some economies collapsed, or very nearly, under the strain. The Central Powers, subject to Allied blockade, and the industrially weak and underdeveloped states of Italy and Russia were all in conditions approaching complete breakdown by the end of the war. But even in states not faced with imminent collapse it was idle to pretend that economic life would quickly return to normal. Everywhere governments had introduced rationing of strategic materials and food, control of foreign trade, and regulation of prices, wages, and use of manpower. Although the measures of control taken during the war were generally regarded as temporary, it proved difficult to dismantle wartime regulation speedily (see Part I, The First World War).

One reason for this was that the extraordinary demands of war had so thoroughly upset the operations of the market economy. Some activities, of which housing construction is a good example, had been almost completely neglected for four years. In view of the shortages that resulted, immediate abolition of rent controls would have created chaos in the housing market. Another serious upset to the market system resulted from the financial measures taken by the belligerent states. Gold payments were suspended and governments resorted to extensive borrowing and printing of paper money. Inflation, sometimes so extreme as to wipe out the value of the currency completely, was the inevitable result. Wartime and postwar inflation changed the distribution of income and wealth as savings were destroyed and the earnings of various groups responded more or less quickly to the inflationary spiral. Foreign trade and exchange were disrupted. In some extreme cases, such as that of Russia between 1918 and 1921 and Austria between 1919 and 1921, fiscal chaos contributed to a dangerous deterioration of internal trade between agriculture and industry because peasants refused to accept worthless paper money for their products and either produced less or consumed their crops (see Part III, The Postwar Crisis).

Even after the dislocations of the war and the postwar crisis had been surmounted (that is, by about 1924 or 1925), Europe did not return to the prewar economic pattern. Reparations and interallied debt payments continued to bedevil international finance and to reduce the purchasing power of some countries. Because governments had assumed greater responsibility for the welfare of their citizens, taxation and public expenditure remained high in order to cover the costs of war pensions, unemployment and sickness insurance, and heavier expenses for education, public housing, and other facilities. The wartime practices of regulating conditions of labor and of subsidizing certain industries were retained in many nations. Eastern European agriculture became heavily dependent on price subsidies or controls. The prosperity that returned in the later 1920's was therefore fragile and unevenly distributed among various sectors of the economy. In both agriculture and several important branches of industry, prosperity often depended on direct government support (see Part IV, Recovery and Stagnation, 1924–29).

This delicate European prosperity quickly collapsed in the 1930's. The bleak years of Depression brought mass unemployment and sharp declines in output and prices. In late 1932 registered unemployment for all of Europe reached 15 million,[4] while in Germany alone over 6 million were unemployed. The powers of government were eventually mobilized to deal with the Depression, although in most countries the initial response to the vast increase in the burden of unemployment relief was a deflationary policy and reduction of public expenditures. After this initial phase, most governments sought to stimulate employment either directly through public-works projects or by increased government spending to stimulate recovery of industrial production. Almost universally, tariff barriers were raised in an effort to protect national production. In spite of these measures, banking and industrial concerns continued to falter, and many governments found themselves forced to take over bankrupt enterprises in order to prevent further deterioration. This trend was strong in eastern Europe, where public enterprise was already familiar. In Poland in 1938 the government owned 100 per cent of the aircraft and automobile industries, 95 per cent of dyestuff production, 70 per cent of smelting, and 25 per cent of natural gas.[5] In Fascist Italy the government took over the assets and therefore the liabilities of

[4] Ingvar Svennilson, *Growth and Stagnation in the European Economy* (Geneva: United Nations, 1954), p. 30. As Svennilson points out, the statistics are incomplete. They are based on figures of trade unions and unemployment insurance and thus omit important sections of the labor force—agricultural workers in particular—as well as underemployment.

[5] Samuel L. Sharp, *Nationalization of Key Industries in Eastern Europe* (Washington, D.C.: Foundation for Foreign Affairs, 1946), p. 4.

a number of foundering banks and industrial establishments. In 1933 a kind of government holding company, the Institute for Industrial Recovery (*Istituto per la Ricostruzione Industriale*, IRI) was created to manage the growing portfolio of government-owned securities, which, it was hoped, could be marketed when conditions improved.[6] In fact, however, many important enterprises remained in government control. But despite the various measures adopted, recovery proved elusive in many countries (see Part VI, The Depression).

In contrast to the poor performance of the economies of western nations, the substantial growth of the Soviet economy was truly impressive. After reaching its nadir in 1920–21, when industrial production stood between 10 and 15 per cent of the 1913 level, output steadily grew during the interwar years and by 1938 had increased more than sevenfold over 1913 levels.[7] The old economic order had been wiped out in the years following the November Revolution as much by the continued warfare and runaway inflation as by Bolshevik policy. During the years of recovery after 1921, even before the adoption of over-all state planning, the role of the state in economic life was substantial. Basic industry and financial institutions were operated directly by the government, and foreign trade was a state monopoly. Beginning in 1927, the pattern of Soviet economic life broke entirely with that of western Europe. The First Five Year Plan called for substantial collectivization of agriculture, a large expansion in industrial output, and the elimination of private enterprise in light industry and domestic commerce. A high rate of growth was achieved through forced savings and heavy investment in basic industry. The costs of the program were extremely high, especially for the agrarian population, the techniques of the planners were often crude, and numer-

[6] On IRI see Andrew Shonfield, *Modern Capitalism: The Changing Balance of Public and Private Power* (London: Oxford University Press, 1965), pp. 178–179, and Shepard B. Clough, *The Economic History of Modern Italy* (New York: Columbia University Press, 1964), pp. 249–250.

[7] There are numerous disputes about the reliability of Soviet statistics and the proper correctives to be applied in order to get figures of international comparability. This labyrinth is best not entered into in a short introduction. The levels indicated here are based on *Industrialization and Foreign Trade*, p. 130. A good selection of articles on the problems of interpreting Soviet statistics is contained in Franklyn D. Holzman, ed., *Readings on the Soviet Economy* (Chicago: Rand McNally and Co., 1962).

ous bottlenecks appeared. Nevertheless, by the outbreak of the Second World War the Soviets had mastered the fundamentals of planning and demonstrated the basic viability of their system (see Part V, Soviet Economic Policy in the 1920's).

The Fascist régimes broke less completely than the Soviet Union with liberal economic traditions. Their economic program concentrated on two points: the elimination of economic conflict (chiefly that between industry and labor) in order to create an integral national economy or corporate state; and the augmenting of national production along autarchic lines, at first to eliminate economic distress, but later in preparation for war. Labor, and to a lesser extent industry, were brought under government control. Numerous public-works projects were undertaken, such as the highway construction program in Germany and land reclamation in Italy. Foreign trade and exchange received close government supervision. And from the mid-1930's huge government expenditures were being made for military purposes. Under the impact of these various measures, economic revival, less impressive than that of the Soviet Union to be sure but greater than that of the western democracies, was stimulated (see Part VII, The Economics of Fascism).

It was hard to deny, in view of the Soviet and Fascist experiments, that government intervention to develop national economies in relative isolation offered an effective road to recovery. Yet, with the significant exception of the Soviet Union, no European state in the interwar period developed a long-range economic policy designed to bring about basic changes in economic structure through government initiative. Intervention was directed toward more limited objectives—even in the Fascist states, where, in spite of the elaborate machinery of corporatism, measures to reduce unemployment and to restore production followed lines not unlike those taken by the western democracies. In general, it can be said that governments *reacted* to economic crisis or the requirements of war. In the process they introduced important changes in the organization of economic life and assumed greater responsibility for general economic well-being. But the conscious pursuit of basic transformation through nationalization and over-all economic planning, while rooted in the experience of the First World War and the years following, was delayed, except in Russia, until after the Second World War.

Europe and the World Economy between the Wars

The crises of twentieth-century Europe greatly accelerated the changes in Europe's position in the world economy. The increase in non-European manufacturing production, already under way before the war, quickened in the period from 1914 to 1938. The index of world manufacturing output (1913 = 100) rose to 138.9 for the years 1926 to 1929 and to 185 for 1936 to 1938. But the major industrial states of Europe did not fully share in this growth. On the same basis the index numbers for France, Germany, and the United Kingdom were as follows:[8]

Country	1926–29	1936–38
France	130.6	118.2
Germany	112.2	138.3
U.K.	92.6	121.5

The share of these three countries in world manufacturing output, which had been 36.1 per cent in 1913, declined to 27.6 per cent for 1926 to 1929 and to 24.4 for 1936 to 1938.[9]

The spread of industrialization to new parts of the world was a secular trend not likely to be reversed, but it hurt many European industries oriented toward export markets. The decline of the British cotton textile industry is a notable case in point. Throughout the decade before the war cotton yarn and textiles constituted roughly 20 per cent of the value of British exports,[10] and in 1913 about 75 per cent of the total output was exported.[11] A steady decline in the export of cotton piece goods (to less than one-quarter of the 1913 level by 1938) brought serious stagnation to the industry, and production fell by more than half in spite of increased domestic consumption.[12] Numerous less dramatic examples of the deterioration of Europe's position as a producer of

[8] *Industrialization and Foreign Trade*, p. 130.

[9] *Ibid.*, p. 13.

[10] William Woodruff, *The Impact of Western Man: A Study of Europe's Role in the World Economy* (New York: St. Martin's Press, 1967), p. 302 (table VII/1).

[11] Sidney Pollard, *The Development of the British Economy, 1914–1950* (London: Edward Arnold, 1962), p. 120.

[12] *Ibid.*, p. 121.

manufactured goods could be given to demonstrate that Europe in the twentieth century was required to accommodate its production to a world that had become increasingly industrialized.

If this process was irreversible, it was nevertheless speeded by the First World War. War mobilization called for increased production in industries whose relative importance was declining (shipbuilding, basic steel). New capacity was added at high cost, and much old, inefficient plant was kept in production. The result was that Europe emerged from the war with productive capacity in some industries tremendously out of proportion to peacetime demand and with other industries underdeveloped or run down through failure to install new equipment. Consequently, many European industries were placed at a competitive disadvantage in world markets. Stagnation became characteristic of the 1920's and 1930's, creating a relatively high level of unemployment.

European agriculture in the interwar period faced many of these same problems. The war of 1914 to 1918 disrupted the prewar network of European agricultural trade by cutting off supplies from eastern Europe. Non-European producers at the same time vastly expanded output to supply growing markets in the Allied countries. With the recovery of European agriculture this great overcapacity began, by the middle of the 1920's, to depress agricultural prices and incomes. Conditions were especially severe in eastern and southern Europe, where peasant production predominated and where there was a great expansion of rural population as a result of improved public health. Despite the fall in agricultural incomes, much of this increased population remained locked on the land. There was little industrial development to absorb excess rural population, and the mobility of labor was impeded by national regulation (including immigration barriers erected by the United States immediately after the war). Land reforms helped to redistribute agricultural income, but they did nothing to reduce the surplus of rural labor or to increase agricultural income.

Yet there were many dynamic and expanding sectors of the European economy in the interwar period. The first quarter of the twentieth century was rich in technological innovation, often leading to the development of entirely new industries. Some of these industries were greatly stimulated by wartime requirements, while for some others, expansion was delayed until after the war. New sources of power—electricity and petroleum—were increasingly substituted for coal. The first diesel-powered ship of large tonnage had been launched in 1912, and in the postwar years these began to replace the steamship. In the period just before the war a number of new techniques in metallurgy allowed the development of new alloys in both steel and nonferrous metals. Low-cost methods of producing aluminum made possible rapid expansion in its production. There was great progress in the chemical industry; during the war years cheap methods of nitrogen fixation and the production of many synthetics were either developed or greatly expanded. Artificial fibers came into general use. Perhaps the greatest changes resulted from the increased consumption of electricity for industrial and domestic use and the changes in transportation resulting from the rapid expansion of road traffic. The automobile, the electric light, and the radio helped spread the fruits of modern technology to the countryside as well as the city and to break down the differences between rural and urban life. The dynamism of these new industries is indicated by the figures that follow:

GROWTH OF PRODUCTION IN SOME NEW INDUSTRIES
European Totals (excluding USSR)

Product	1913	1922	1926–28	1936–37	1950
Chemical Nitrogen (thousands of tons)	278		1071	1415	2166
Rayon Filament Yarn and Staple Fiber (thousands of tons)	10.2		91.1	403.0[a]	785.5
Number of Registered Motor Vehicles (thousands)		1213	3138[b]	8381[c]	10097
Electricity (billions of kilowatt hours)		60.5	95.7[d]	171.5[e]	301.2

[a] 1936–38; [b] 1926; [c] 1938; [d] 1927; [e] 1937.

Source: Svennilson, *op. cit.*, Appendix A, Statistical Tables.

Partially as a result of the expansion of new industries, the indices of European manufacturing production were restored to prewar levels by the middle of the 1920's, but world trade and Europe's place in it did not experience a similar recovery. The interwar years were ones of general stagnation in the volume of international trade, during which the relative importance of European trade declined. The pattern is revealed by the following table:

VOLUME OF WORLD AND EUROPEAN EXPORTS,
1876–1938
(index numbers)

Year	World 1913 = 100	Europe 1913 = 100
1876–80	30	..
1881–85	38	45
1886–90	44	51
1891–95	48	51
1896–1900	57	61
1901–05	67	69
1906–10	81	81
1911–13	96	97
1913	100	100
1921	65	56
1922	75	70
1923	81	70
1924	90	74
1925	97	82
1926	98	84
1927	108	93
1928	113	98
1929	120	103
1930	113	93
1931	102	79
1932	89	64
1933	89	64
1934	91	65
1935	96	67
1936	102	70
1937	114	81
1938	103	75

Source: Svennilson, *op. cit.*, p. 292, table A.58.

Europe's declining role in world trade involved several factors. The increased industrialization of non-European areas caused losses to some of Europe's major export industries; Europe never fully adjusted to the changes in world demand thus produced. Disruptions of trade resulting directly from the war played an important role by speeding up the changes in the world market. The mobilization of European economies sharply reduced the amount of goods available for export and forced Europe's former customers to seek new sources of supply or to develop their own productive capacity. At the same time, the liquidation of much of the overseas capital assets held by Europeans broke one of the ties that had encouraged foreign purchases in Europe. In the interwar years financial instability and changes in the value of currency rendered international transactions difficult. In addition, a change in the terms of trade between primary and manufactured goods in favor of manufactures reduced the purchasing power of some of Europe's important customers. Finally, the introduction of high tariffs and import quotas, a process by no means confined to Europe, created artificial barriers to the international movement of goods, further diminishing world trade.

The Second World War and the Postwar Years

The Second World War called forth many of the same measures of economic mobilization as the First and caused similar dislocations. On all sides, vast numbers of men were called to military service, production and trade were disrupted and all economic resources mobilized to meet the economic burden of total warfare. Despite Germany's ability to occupy large areas of the European continent between 1939 and 1943, the balance of economic power lay with the Allies, in large measure because of the ability of the Soviet economy to withstand German invasion. Devastation was greater than in the first war and it was spread more widely, partly because the motorized armies fought across wider areas, but also because strategic bombing allowed both sides to inflict substantial damage on industrial and urban complexes behind the lines. After the war the now familiar disorders of inflation, shortages, and large population transfers further weakened Europe's economy. Although there were fewer boundary changes than in 1919, the structure of the European system was radically changed: eastern Europe fell under Soviet political and economic domination and was cut off from the West; German economic unity was destroyed as the country was divided along lines established by Allied and Soviet occupation forces; and for a decade this divided Europe was economically dependent upon the United States or the Soviet Union (see Part VIII, The Second World War).

But the Second World War did not have the same psychological impact as the First. European states were infinitely better prepared to organize their efforts for total warfare; in fact, planning for economic mobilization began before the war. More important, the war seemed to break the economic deadlock of Europe. Europeans did not look back with nostalgia on a past age of European dominance, but rather beyond the war toward an era of economic and social reorganization that would correspond to Europe's needs. Government wartime controls were regarded by many as preliminary steps to broader government intervention, to nationalization, and planning for economic development.

As a consequence of this changed attitude, elaborate programs for reform as well as recovery were developed. Reconstruction of damaged regions and conversion to peacetime production, it was believed, were not enough. More rapid growth, greater productivity, higher standards of living, and the channeling of more money into the public sector for such things as education and public services were also required. The elaboration of programs such as those embodied in the British Beveridge Report and the French Monnet Plan reflected the new attitude of relying upon governmental intervention in the economy to maintain public welfare and economic growth.

In many countries nationalization was one of the first steps taken to enlarge the role of the state in economic life. A foundation had been established by the close control over many industries during the war and by disruption of prewar property relations in German-occupied Europe. The British Labour Party was voted into power in 1945 with a program that called for nationalization of major sectors of the economy. Between 1945 and 1951 the Bank of England, utilities, most of transport, coal and steel were nationalized, and important welfare measures, such as that creating the National Health Service, were enacted. The return of the Conservatives to power in 1951 brought the denationalization of the steel and trucking industries, but with these exceptions the postwar Labour program was left largely intact.[13] In France, coal, utilities, and major banking and insurance companies were nationalized in 1946. The eastern European nations in the first years after the war proceeded along similar lines, although nationalization laws were

[13] On British nationalization and planning after the war, see Pollard, *op. cit.*, Chapter VII.

generally drawn to include more categories of industry. In Italy, the nationalized sector was largely a legacy of the Fascist era. The Institute for Industrial Recovery, reorganized in 1937 as a public corporation to consolidate the operations of the businesses under its control, was preserved in postwar Italy. IRI's activities increased until it became the largest business enterprise in the country, controlling a vast and diversified economic empire.

More significant, perhaps, than nationalization was the shift in government policy away from temporary and ill-coordinated measures toward long-range planning. Economic growth and full employment became central goals of all European governments, and planning was adopted to coordinate private as well as public enterprise. All of the western European states developed, often by trial and error, flexible systems of manipulating government expenditures, monetary policies, and taxation to direct investment, in order to control business cycles and to maintain economic growth and full employment. The difference between relieving unemployment and planning for full employment, between propping up declining industries and developing programs of modernization, did not necessarily extend the scope of government intervention greatly, but the change in approach was fundamental.

In eastern Europe the conversion to economic planning after the war was even more complete than in the West. Under the impact of Russian domination, the eastern European countries adopted development plans modeled rigidly on the early Soviet Five Year Plans. Centralized planning and allocation of resources, a high rate of savings, collectivization of agriculture, and heavy investment in basic industry radically reshaped the economic life of eastern Europe during the early 1950's. An industrial base was created in these formerly agrarian countries, and large elements of the population shifted from agricultural to industrial occupations. As had been true in the Soviet Union, the transformation involved many inefficiencies and was achieved at the expense of standards of living in the early years.[14]

Finally, Europe abandoned in large measure the economic nationalism of the interwar years. In western Europe, government

[14] A good account of the transformation of the eastern European countries after the war is Nicolas Spulber's, *The Economics of Communist Eastern Europe* (New York: John Wiley & Sons, 1957).

planning and intervention in national economic affairs did not divide Europe into closed national economies but rather developed simultaneously with increased international cooperation. The basis for this cooperation was laid in the years of recovery immediately following the war to meet the demands established by the United States for economic aid through the Marshall Plan. It had developed sufficiently by the later 1950's for a European Economic Community to be organized with the purpose of maximizing the free flow not only of goods but also of labor and capital across national lines. The economies of the eastern European states could not develop in isolation because of the important role of the Soviet Union in the economic relations within the Soviet bloc and because of the uniform pattern of economic development imposed by Soviet-type planning. Only toward the end of the 1950's, when the eastern European states were freed from extreme Soviet control and allowed to pursue more independent economic policies, was there any attempt at creating genuine economic integration of resources and production within the Soviet bloc, although with only limited success.

In spite of the enormous losses caused by the Second World War, especially in Germany and eastern Europe, and serious dislocations after the fighting had stopped, a remarkable revitalization of European economic life began in about 1949. High rates of savings and growth, and increases in productivity, have been characteristic of both eastern and western Europe. Thus, there has been a significant reversal of the patterns that prevailed in the interwar period, and, in spite of some temporary setbacks here and there, the prospect for continued expansion is good. The first table below provides some of the basic indicators of economic growth for western Europe. Growth rates in the Soviet bloc have been even more spectacular, as is shown by the second table below, but, because of different methods of computation, the figures in the two tables are not strictly comparable.

In the years after the Second World War, Europeans were able to recognize Europe's changed place in the world economy and to make the necessary accommodations. Industrial production was shaped to meet the needs of the world market and to provide better living conditions for the home population. Modern methods have revitalized European industry. Everywhere, even in the older industrial countries, economic expansion has brought more people

GROWTH OF OUTPUT, PRODUCTIVITY, AND INVESTMENT
IN SOME WESTERN EUROPEAN COUNTRIES, 1949–59
(annual averages in percentages)

Country	Growth in Gross Nat'l Product	Population Increases	Increases in Labor Productivity	Investment Ratio at Current Prices
Austria	5.7	0.2	4.8	16.7
Belgium	3.1	0.6	2.7	7.4
Denmark	3.5	0.7[d]	2.2	11.7
France	4.5	0.9	4.3	10.2
W. Germany[a]	7.4	1.1	5.7	15.2
Greece	5.2	0.9[b]	4.3	12.2[c]
Ireland	1.4	−0.5	2.4	—
Italy	6.1	0.5[a]	4.8	13.4
Netherlands	4.5	1.3	3.6	14.9
Norway	3.5	1.0	3.1	23.1
Spain	5.4	0.8[e]	4.3	—
Sweden	3.4	0.6[d]	2.9	11.2
Switzerland	5.1	1.4[d]	3.7	—
United Kingdom	2.5	0.4	1.8	8.0

[a] 1950–59; [b] 1951–61; [c] 1950–58; [d] 1950–60.

Source: United Nations, Economic Commission for Europe, *Economic Survey of Europe in 1961*, Part 2 (Geneva: United Nations, 1964), Chapter II, tables 1, 4, and 8.

into industrial work. Standards of living have been raised, more slowly to be sure in eastern Europe than in western Europe, but in general it is possible to say that the fruits of economic transformation have been widely distributed. Long-range economic planning has become a central feature in European economic life, whether in the socialist form of the Soviet Union and eastern Europe or the forms developed in the market economies of western Europe. In both East and West planning has become a more sophisticated and flexible instrument than seemed possible from the interwar Soviet model of the planned economy. This shift of control of economic policy from private to public authority, more than anything else, lies at the heart of the economic revolution Europe has experienced in the twentieth century.

GROWTH OF OUTPUT, PRODUCTIVITY, AND INVESTMENT
IN SOME EASTERN EUROPEAN COUNTRIES, 1949–59
(annual averages in percentages)

Country	Growth of NMP* at Constant Prices		Population Increases	Increases in Labor Productivity	Investment Ratio†	
	Prices of	Increase			I	II
Albania	1956	10.5[b]	2.9[b]	—	—	—
Bulgaria	1957	9.8	0.8	8.7	13.2[c]	13.5[c]
Czechoslovakia	1955	7.7	1.0	6.8[b]	—	—
Hungary	1954	7.0	0.7	5.0	17.1[d]	15.5[d]
Poland	1956	8.0[b]	1.9[b]	6.3[b]	14.5	—
Rumania	1950	10.3[b]	1.3[b]	—	—	—
Soviet Union	a	10.5[b]	1.7[b]	8.8[b]	22.7	16.6

[a] 1951 prices for the years 1951 to 1955; 1956 prices for 1956 to 1958; and 1958 prices for 1959 (combined by use of a chain index).

[b] 1950–59; [c] 1952 prices; [d] 1949 prices.

* NMP (Net Material Product) differs from Gross Domestic Product in that figures are not corrected for depreciation and exclude "nonproductive" services. If calculated on the basis of GDP, the figures in column 2 would in most cases be somewhat lower.

† Variant I of investment ratios is based on the volume of net investment obtained from investment outlays (investment outlays including capital repairs *plus* such part of the natural increase of livestock, standing timber, etc., as may be regarded as an addition to "fixed assets" rather than as a change in working capital *minus* amortization), whereas for Variant II net fixed investment is obtained from data on changes in the value of completed fixed assets.

Source: *Ibid.*, Chapter II, tables 3, 5, and 9.

PART I

The First World War

After the first few months of the hostilities, it became clear to many that, contrary to expectations, the First World War would not be a short and decisive war of movement, but rather a war of attrition in which continued military operations would depend on the ability of the belligerents to mobilize their economies as well as their armies. Because military and political leaders had seriously miscalculated the character of the war, few plans for economic mobilization had been developed before the conflict began. Only after some months of fighting did governments begin to elaborate the machinery of economic mobilization.

The need for maximum production of war material led logically to the extension of controls throughout the economies of the nations at war. Labor and raw materials had to be allocated according to wartime priorities. New industries were developed and others in their infancy greatly expanded under the direct stimulus of government intervention—chemicals, automobiles, wireless telegraphy (the early radio), and aircraft, to name but a few. New sources of raw materials, either at home or abroad, had to be found. In the case of Germany this led to a determined search for substitute materials, while Allied governments introduced controls on foreign purchases and shipping and, especially toward the end of the war, a degree of interallied economic cooperation. Thus, by the end of the conflict government control in one form or another had reached into nearly every sector of the economies of the nations at war. Although the wartime emergency measures were considered temporary, their impact was lasting; the extent to which governments regulated economic life was greatly and permanently increased.

Some countries—Italy and Russia most notably—were unable to bear the strain on their resources caused by the war and found their economic and social life severely shaken. But even states not threatened with collapse experienced serious dislocation. The astronomical cost of the military operations led everywhere to changes in the structure of taxation, to huge public debts, and to inflation. Four years of war production created grave imbalances in productive capacity; foreign markets were lost to neutral competitors; and changes occurred in the income, distribution, and organization of the labor force. War devastation called for major reconstruction efforts on the part of several countries. Europe, in short, emerged from the war with permanent changes in its economic structure and a host of problems of recovery to be dealt with.

1. Measures of Economic Mobilization: The British Example

All the belligerent powers faced three major and interrelated economic tasks: to secure sufficient raw materials to meet the ever-growing needs of war production, while at the same time providing for minimum civilian requirements; to expand rapidly certain key industries (such as armaments, shipbuilding, and chemicals); and to mobilize the labor force for a maximum effort in essential industries at a time when millions were diverted from productive employment to the trenches. The character of the problems and the means by which they were met differed from country to country. The reaction in Britain at the outbreak of the war was, in a phrase attributed to Winston Churchill, "business as usual." Only gradually, especially during 1916 and 1917, was a system of government economic control established in response to inflationary pressures, shortages of food and materials, and labor-management conflicts. A coalition government, led by David Lloyd George and established at the end of 1916, paid special attention to mobilizing the economy. Some of the basic difficulties of economic mobilization as well as its implications for the future were discussed in the report of the British War Cabinet for 1917. The selection that follows is taken from the introduction to that report.

Report of the British War Cabinet, 1917

A REPORT covering so great a field of political and administrative activity would seem to require a brief introduction, partly in order to draw attention to the more important events of the year, and partly in order to show their relation to the earlier history of the war. These events, indeed, can only be fully appreciated in the light of that history, for they are largely the outcome of the activities of the previous years. In 1914 the British Empire took up the challenge thrown down to Europe by the Governments of the Central Empires and entered the field in defence of national liberty and international right. When war was declared, neither Government nor people had any idea of the magnitude of the struggle to which they were then committed. For modern war, except in the naval sphere, they were almost wholly unprepared. Their military

Source: *The War Cabinet Report for 1917* (Cd. 9005) (London: His Majesty's Stationery Office, 1918), pp. iv–xvii, with deletions.

forces were designed not for use on the continent of Europe but to defend the outlying frontiers of a world-wide commonwealth. There was no effective organisation for bringing the overseas portions of the Empire into close and continuous touch with the realities of the international situation. The external policy of the Empire was rather concerned to preserve the peace by the maintenance of the balance of power than by promoting the active co-operation of all free nations for the defence of freedom and justice in international affairs. The ensuing years witnessed a period of activity unparalleled in British history. A vast army, mainly of volunteers, was enrolled and organised into a force fit to engage in battle with the most formidable and most highly organised military power in the world, and private industries throughout the length and breadth of the land were gradually converted to the production of munitions of war—a transformation which entailed far-reaching alterations in the status and methods both of management and labour. The Overseas Dominions raised national armies which at an early date took their place in the battle line. India, fired by the cause for which the Empire stood, flung its army at a vital moment into the war and thereafter set steadily to work to expand it. . . .

The first problem was that of man-power. During the preceding year [1916] all sources which could be tapped without trenching upon the essential supplies of the Allied armies and the nation had been exhausted, and the question had narrowed itself down to that of finding substitutes for fit men of military age still engaged in industry. An attempt was, therefore, made to enrol a large army of volunteers to take the place of the men called to the army. Partly owing to difficulties in withdrawing labour from the great war industries and partly owing to the limited supply of labour, great obstacles presented themselves in the execution of this scheme. But though the plan of enrolling an army of industrial volunteers had eventually to be abandoned, the system of dilution and substitution[1] was steadily carried out and 820,646 men of all categories were taken for the service of the army during the year. The needs of the army, however, were not the only drain. A large amount of additional labour was required for agriculture, timber production

[1] The system of "dilution" of labor involved the substitution of less skilled for skilled labor, especially by the introduction of women into the labor force.—Eds.

and iron ore mining, as well as for industrial purposes. The needs in these respects also were gradually supplied by reducing unessential industries and by organising supplies of soldier, civilian, and foreign labour. Investigations were carried out as to the use of labour in different trades, and trade committees representing employers and employed were organised to deal with economy of man-power in particular industries. The evidence so obtained, while it demonstrated clearly the complexity and difficulty of a system of compulsory national service in industry, made it clear that in order to effect the best strategic use of the man-power of the country, the National Service Department required extension. . . .

Notwithstanding the tremendous calls upon the man-power of the country for the ever-increasing needs of the army, the supply of munitions has steadily increased. In addition to large consignments to other fronts of the war, there has been an increase of 30 per cent in all kinds of guns and howitzers and of over 100 per cent in heavy guns and howitzers in the recent offensive in France as compared with those of last year. The weight of shell filled per month has been more than doubled since 1916. The output of high explosives has been sufficient to meet the increased demands of our armies, to build up stocks and to supply part of the needs of the Allies. There has been a steady improvement in the detonating value of gun ammunition and a continuous reduction in the number of premature explosions. In addition to guns, shells, and rifles the demands of the military and naval forces during the year for aircraft, tanks, mechanical transport, railway material, and equipment of every sort and kind have been endless. Despite the immensity of the demand it has, on the whole, been supplied. The British army is now probably the best provided of all the armies in the field, not only in technical equipment, but in clothing, food and similar provision. The tremendous reorganisation of the industrial life of the country which has been necessary in order to produce these supplies, a reorganisation which includes not only manufacturing industries, railways, mines and shipping, but an immense variety of lesser enterprises . . . amounts to a reconstruction of our economic life for the purposes of the war. . . .

The most difficult problems which confronted the administration in the early part of 1917 were those which arose from the growing inadequacy of the overseas communications of the Allies —problems which were aggravated by the introduction of the unlimited submarine campaign on February 1st. The expansion of

the armies, the ever-increasing demand for warlike material, the fall
in production, especially of foodstuffs in all Allied countries
through the calling of men to the Colours, and the decline in cultivation, coupled with the diversion of a large part of the shipping of
the Allies to purely military and naval transportation, had already
put a severe strain on the shipping resources of the country. The
immediate effect of the new campaign was to double the rate of
losses which had been incurred during 1916, and these losses rose
rapidly to a climax in March and April. . . .

There is a non-military aspect of the administrative developments of the year which it is important to note. In themselves these
developments have been the result of the determination of the
people to leave nothing undone which could contribute to the
winning of the war. None the less they are bound to produce
lasting and far-reaching effects on the social and economic life of
the community. No record of the year would be complete which
did not point out the changes which have been wrought in the
structure of society by the experiences of the war.

In the first place, the organic life of the community has been
greatly strengthened. On the one hand, not only have enormous
numbers of men, and latterly of women also, been mobilised for
military and naval purposes, but the vast majority of the people are
now working directly or indirectly on public service. If they are
not in the Army, the Navy or the Civil Service, they are growing
food, or making munitions, or engaged in the work of organising,
transporting or distributing the national supplies. On the other
hand, the State has taken control for the period of the war over
certain national industries, such as the railways, shipping, coal and
iron mines, and the great majority of engineering businesses. It has
also made itself responsible for the securing of adequate quantities
of certain staple commodities and services, such as food, coal,
timber and other raw materials, railroad and sea transportation, and
for distributing the available supplies justly as between individual
and individual in the national interest. The Government has further had to regulate prices and prevent profiteering. It has done so
partly by controlling freights, fixing maximum prices to the home
producer, and regulating wholesale and retail charges, and partly
by its monopoly of imported supplies. The information which the
Government has obtained as to sources of supply, consumption
and cost of production, and the relations it has entered into with
other Governments as to the mutual purchase of essential products

which they jointly control have, for the first time, brought within the sphere of practical politics the possibility of fixing relatively stable world prices for fundamental staples. The State has even taken the drastic step of fixing the price of the 1-lb. loaf [of bread] at 9d., at a considerable loss to itself. Thus the war, and especially the year 1917, has brought about a transformation of the social and administrative structure of the State, much of which is bound to be permanent. Owing to the imperative importance of speed there has perhaps been an undue expansion of the functions of the central Government. But a very large amount of work has been devolved on to local authorities and to new bodies such as the War Agricultural Executive Committees, or the Local Food Control Committees. Taking the year as a whole the Administration has been brought into far closer contact with every aspect of the life of the people, the provinces and the metropolis have been linked more closely together, and the whole community has received an education in the problems of practical democracy such as it has never had before.

In the second place, the war has profoundly altered the conditions of the industrial problem. Since 1914 the community itself has become by far the greatest employer of labour. It has assumed control for the duration of the war over a great number of the larger private undertakings, it has limited profits by imposing an 80 per cent excess profits tax, and it has intervened to prevent profiteering in the essential requirements of the nation. Further, the regulations of the trade unions have been suspended for the duration of the war, industry has been diluted throughout, new methods and new industries have been introduced, labour saving machinery has been everywhere installed, and the speed of production and the number and skill of workers has greatly risen. The nation today is far better organised and far more productive than it has ever been before. The effect of these changes on the supply of the national needs, on foreign trade, on employment, on the provision of capital after the war, is still quite incalculable. But it is bound to be enormous. The satisfactory settlement, however, of the tremendous problems which lie ahead will largely depend upon the mutual relations between employer and employed. Unless these improve, rapid and orderly progress will be almost impossible. With the advent of the new Government [under Lloyd George] at the end of 1916, a Ministry of Labour was created to deal with labour questions. . . .

In the third place, agriculture has been restored to its proper
position in the national economy. After long years of neglect, its
vital importance not only for the production of food, but for the
healthy balance of the life of the nation, has at last been recognised.
The guarantee of minimum prices for food products, the fixing of
a minimum wage of 25s. a week for agricultural labourers, and the
establishment of Agricultural Wages Boards for England and
Wales, Scotland and Ireland, coupled with the other measures of
the departments of Agriculture, mark a new era in the rural history
of the British Isles. . . .

2. The Problem of Essential Raw Materials in Germany

The procuring of essential raw materials was far more difficult in Germany than in Allied countries. The loss of overseas supplies resulting from the Allied blockade taxed the ingenuity of German science and industry to find substitutes and synthetics and led to a policy of rigid control of the limited supplies available. The architect of the German program was the industrialist Walther Rathenau. Here, in a speech delivered on December 20, 1915, is his account of the activities of the War Raw Materials Department of the War Office, which he established.

Address of Walther Rathenau on Germany's Provision for Raw Materials

THE OBJECT of my paper is to report to you a new departure in our economic warfare which has no precedent in history, which will have a decided influence on the war, and which in all probability is destined to affect future times. In its methods it is closely akin to communism and yet it departs essentially from the prophecies and demands resulting from radical theories. It is not my purpose to give an account of a rigid system based on theories, but I shall relate how this system grew out of our actual life, first taking concrete form in a small group, then affecting ever widening circles, and finally bringing about a complete change in our economic life. Its visible result is a new department attached to the War Office which places our whole economic life in the service of the war. . . .

When on August 4 of last year England declared war our country became a beleaguered fortress. Cut off by land and cut off by sea it was made wholly self-dependent; we were facing a war the duration, cost, danger, and sacrifices of which no one could foresee.

Source: Excerpted from *Fall of the German Empire, 1914–1918*, Vol. II, edited by Ralph Haswell Lutz, pp. 77–90. Hoover War Library Publications, No. 2, with the permission of the publishers, Stanford University Press. Copyright 1932 by the Board of Trustees of the Leland Stanford Junior University. Copyright renewed 1960 by Ralph Haswell Lutz.

When three days had passed after England had declared war I could no longer stand the agony. I called on the Chief of the War Department, Colonel Scheuch, and on the evening of the same day I was kindly received by him. I explained to him that I was convinced that the supply of the absolutely needed raw materials on hand could probably last only a limited number of months. Colonel Scheuch shared my opinion that the war would be one of long duration, and so I was forced to ask him, "What has been done and what can be done to avert the danger that Germany will be strangled?"

Very little had been done in the past, but much has been done since the interest of the War Department has been aroused. Returning home deeply concerned and worried I found a telegram from [General Erich] von Falkenhayn, then [Prussian] Minister of War, asking me to come to his office the next morning.

This was Sunday, August 9. I expressed my thanks to the Minister, telling him that I was astonished that he, at the time of mobilization, could afford to find leisure to acquaint himself with the thoughts of outsiders. Pointing to his desk he said: "The desk is cleared. The great work has been done, our mobilization has been carried out; not a single claim for exemption from military service has been made and I am free to receive visitors."

Our discussion lasted the greater part of the forenoon, and when it was ended the Minister of War had decided to establish an organization, no matter whether great or small, provided it had authority and was efficient and able to solve the problem which we were facing. In that moment the Prussian Minister of War was bold enough to take upon himself the responsibility for a decision which meant the turning-point in that matter which I am discussing here.

I was about to take leave, but the Minister detained me by making the unexpected demand that I should undertake to organize the work. I was not prepared for this; I asked for time to think the matter over, but my request was not granted; I had to consent, and a few days later I found myself installed at the War Office.

The *Kriegs-Rohstoff-Abteilung* (War Raw Materials Department) was established by ministerial decree. There were to be two directors: a retired colonel, a man of great experience, representing the War Office in matters demanding expert military knowledge; and myself, whose duty it was to create the organization. We were located in four small rooms, working with the assistance of a secretary whose practical experience was of great value. . . .

The first problem was the question of available supplies. It was necessary to ascertain the period of months for which the country was provided with the indispensable materials. Any further action depended on that. Opinions received from the great industries were quite contradictory. . . .

We were forced to take a daring step, namely, we had to rely on a hypothesis. And this hypothesis proved to be reliable. We started with the assumption that the store of supplies available for the whole country would be approximately equal to the available supply stored by any large group of industries. The War Office did business with some 900 or 1,000 concerns. If we found out to what extent these industries were supplied with the various materials needed by them, we might expect to ascertain data for the entire country. Fractions did not matter; what we wanted were round figures. The experiment was successful. After two weeks we saw light; after three weeks we were sure of our facts. Few of the materials needed for the army were available in quantities sufficient for a year (and since that time the yearly demands of the army have substantially increased); in most cases they were considerably less.

At first we were concerned with only a small number of materials. The whole fields of foodstuffs and of liquid fuel were excluded; included was everything called "raw materials." The official definition gave the following interpretation: "Such materials as are needed for the defense of the country and which cannot be produced within the country at all times and in sufficient quantities." At first hardly more than a dozen of such indispensable materials were enumerated; the number, however, increased from week to week and has now passed the hundred mark.

So far we had but little data, but we had a foundation to work on. We had learned to what extent the country was supplied, and by degrees we began to see the problem in its entirety. But we did not yet know how the problem was to be solved.

Four measures appeared feasible and worth trying out for reconstructing our economic policies so as to afford proper protection for the country.

First: Coercive measures had to be adopted regarding the use of all raw materials in the country. No material must be used arbitrarily, or for luxury, or for anything that is not absolutely needed. The needs of the army are of paramount importance and everything must be directed toward that ultimate end. That was our first and most difficult task.

Secondly: [Author's omission].

The third way of solving the problem was through manufacture. Anything indispensable and not procurable must be manufactured within the country. New methods of manufacture had to be invented and developed wherever the old technique was inadequate.

And now the fourth measure: Materials difficult to obtain must be replaced by others more easily procurable. It is not ordained that this or that object must be made of copper or of aluminum; it may be made of some other material. Substitutes must be found. Instead of using the time-honored materials for our household goods, etc., we must use new substances, and articles must be manufactured that do not require so much raw material.

Such were the measures that we seized upon; they were not solutions, yet were possibilities, and they gave us hope.

On the other hand, we faced insurmountable opposition.

Our laws regulating the economic and industrial life in war time had hardly been changed since the time of Frederick the Great. According to the letter of the law we were given about as much leeway as though the law, shorn of its theoretical terms, had said: if a captain of cavalry comes into a village, he may ask the chief magistrate of the place for barley, and if the magistrate should raise difficulties, he, under certain conditions, may take the barley himself. That, in a nutshell, is about all the law that we found. . . .

The very fact that the problem was not understood caused many difficulties. Up to the present the German people believe that the supply of raw materials takes care of itself. The food question is being discussed all day long; the question of raw materials is hardly mentioned. Even now it is hard for us to realize what the situation was at the beginning of the war. For the first six months no one had any idea what we were trying to do. The [Prussian] Diet, meeting in November 1914, considered us to be a kind of commercial agency charged to see that leather and wool became cheaper. That questions were at stake on which war and peace, victory or defeat depended, no one seemed to see and many fail to see today. We suffered under these conditions. In industrial circles our inquiries were sometimes considered to be offensive and unpleasant interference with the industrial situation. We were accused of injuring certain peace industries. . . .

We now come to the solution.

The first question was to establish a legal basis. I have already alluded to the defective and incomplete state of our laws. It was necessary to establish and formulate new and fundamental ideas upon which the reorganization of our economic life could rest. The term "sequestration" was given a new interpretation, somewhat arbitrarily, I admit, but supported by certain passages in our martial law. At a later period our interpretation was sanctioned by law.

"Sequestration" does not mean that merchandise or material is seized by the state but only that it is restricted, i.e., that it no longer can be disposed of by the owner at will but must be reserved for a more important purpose (or, that it must be put at the disposal of a higher authority). The merchandise must be used for war purposes only: it may be sold, manufactured, shipped, transformed; but no matter what is done to it, it always remains subject to the law that it must be used for war purposes only.

At first many people found it difficult to adjust themselves to the new doctrine. We were often told that we had made the great mistake of not confiscating everything. I do not mention this assertion with the idea of contradicting it, for it needs no contradiction. If we had requisitioned the goods of even a single branch of industry, e.g., of the metal industries (that is to say, if we had requisitioned all copper, tin, nickel, aluminum, antimony, wolfram, chrome) we should have become owners of millions of lots of goods and every day innumerable inquiries would have been received demanding to know what was to be done with this or that parcel of goods? Is it to be rolled, drawn, or cast? Who is to get it? There is much demand! On the other hand, all manufacturing would have come practically to a standstill until such a time as all goods could have been reapportioned. And the responsibility of accounting for goods worth many billions of marks would have rested on us.

The interpretation formulated by us for the term "sequestration" has stood the test and will remain a potent factor in our economic warfare. The new doctrine, however, entailed grave dangers. For when goods are sequestered, peace industries must come to a stop. A manufacturer of metal goods whose store of metals has been sequestered no longer can manufacture peace articles; he must depend on war work. His whole plant and his machinery, his methods, and his products must be readjusted. He has to begin all over again. Our industries underwent a terrible period of trial and hardship, especially those in the field of metallurgy, chemistry, and the textile materials.

In those trying weeks of 1915 when the new order had just gone
out, my colleagues of the General Electric Company came to me
and said: "Do you know what you have done? Sixty thousand men
will be without bread." . . .

Within two months German industrial life was readjusted. It
was done quietly, without a breakdown, with self-confidence and
energy, and with magnificent efficiency. That, gentlemen, speaks
highly for the German industries and must never be forgotten. Not
France, nor England, nor the United States, nor any of our
enemies or our quasi-enemies will ever do the same.

So much regarding sequestration. Its effect was the reorganization of our industries. And now I approach the second factor.

We were aware that our economic life had to be remade. We
knew that new forms and methods must be found for the distribution of materials. But how was that to be done?

The army and the navy must retain absolute freedom to do
business with whom they choose. We could not tell them: you will
receive orders from us as to with whom you may deal. On the
other hand, the concern receiving orders from the Government
must be furnished the needed material. New agencies had to be
created for gathering, storing, and distributing the material circulating in a new form through the arteries of German commerce. A
new system had to be created, that of the *Kriegswirtschafts-Gesell-
schaften* (War Industries Boards). Today we are as accustomed to
them as if they had been handed down from time immemorial. But
at first they appeared so paradoxical that, even in our intimate
circle, otherwise so harmonious, there was difference of opinion as
to the possibility and practicability of this new organ.

On the one hand, it meant a step in the direction of state
socialism. For commerce was no longer free, but had become
restricted.

On the other hand, it meant the attempt to encourage self-
administration of our industries. How were such contradictory
doctrines to be made to agree? . . .

The system of war boards is based upon self-administration; yet
that does not signify unrestricted freedom. The War Raw Materials Department was established under strict government supervision. The boards serve the interests of the public at large; they
neither distribute dividends nor apportion profits; in addition to
the usual organs of stock companies, a board of governors and a
supervising committee, they have another independent organ, a

committee of appraisement and distribution, made up of members selected from various chambers of commerce, or of government officials. This committee serves as intermediary between the stock companies, representing capitalism, and the Government—an economic innovation which may be destined to become generally accepted in future times.

Their duty is to amass raw materials and to direct the flow of supply in such a way that each manufacturing concern is furnished the needed materials in quantities corresponding to the orders it receives from the Government and at prices fixed for such materials.

These boards were not always kindly received by the industrialists.

The metal industries were comparatively friendly. They asked: "A stock company which makes no profits? What is the good of that? So far, we have attended to our business alone and we are quite able to do so in the future." Nevertheless, they acquiesced, partly to do me a personal favor and partly, I presume, because they thought that no harm was done.

It was different with the chemical industries. They are the great captains of industry along the Rhine, proud, charged with great responsibilities, commanders of whole armies of workingmen. One of them, a man of great influence, went about in the Rhenish provinces warning the people against new experiments. But finally a constituent assembly was held in the Hoffmannhaus, Berlin. At first everything went smoothly, but toward the end the discussion became heated. When the gentlemen saw that saltpeter would have to be restricted, a scene was enacted which reminded one somewhat of Paris in 1789. Nevertheless the board was founded, and today we must express our gratitude to the chemists for their efficient co-operation. This model German industry, which at first found it somewhat difficult to adjust itself to the new order, has, I venture to say, subsequently, by its initiative and inventive genius, by its courage and perseverance, reached the highest place in our economic warfare system. . . .

It is well known that the most important explosives used in warfare are nitrous compounds, that saltpeter is a nitrous compound, and that, consequently, war is, to a certain extent, a problem of nitrates.

At the beginning of the war our supply of nitrates was not unsatisfactory. I shall use fictitious figures selected to indicate proportions. Let us imagine that at the outbreak of the war we had in the country 90 tons of nitrogen, and let us further assume that 50 more tons were expected in Antwerp or Ostend; that would give us a total of 140 tons at our disposal. Supposing that we used 10 tons a month, we should thus have a supply sufficient for 14 months. I repeat that my figures are merely chosen to serve as proportional numbers. . . .

All of a sudden it dawned upon us: suppose the war at the eastern front assumes the same dimensions as the war in the West? Suppose the war will last longer and will surpass in magnitude anything that we are able to imagine at present? Will, under such conditions, the supply of nitrate suffice? There was no answer.

It was an anxious moment when I laid these considerations before the Minister of War requesting permission to build as many factories as the chemical industries were able to construct.

The Minister of War, von Wandel, always quiet, energetic, and farsighted, authorized me at once to take up negotiations with the chemical industries. . . .

The construction of a large number of factories was decided upon and the chemists, bold and confident, were willing to undertake actual construction work even before I could give them the contract authorized by the Treasury. Construction was finished before the contract was signed. That was about Christmas [1914]. Nitrates had now become a German product; we no longer needed the world. The most difficult technical danger of the war had been averted.

But while the factories were building the information came from the front: 10 tons no longer suffice, we need 16; 16 tons no longer are enough, we need 21, soon 27, and so on—I shall not give any more figures for fear that my proportional numbers might indicate to what extent the demands had increased. But I may say that the original store had by that time been reduced to insignificant proportions. Had we deferred building until the time when the situation had become critical, a dangerous point would have been reached and that at a time when the offensive in Galicia demanded enormous supplies of ammunition.

Chemical products, especially nitric acid, were and are by far the most important of our products. But a large number of other products were added to our department: factories for refining metals and for used materials were erected; methods for extracting metals from ore were improved; and electrolytic and electrothermic works were established or enlarged, partly by the War Raw Materials Department and partly by the War Industries Boards. . . .

. . . [Finally,] the question of obtaining and introducing substitutes and surrogates was taken up.

The materials used for the Prussian uniforms had to be changed. Worsted and other goods were added. Rare materials no longer could be used for helmets, buttons, and other accessories. In manufacturing ammunition zinc and steel were employed, replacing rare materials. Metals heretofore not used for such purposes were now introduced for the making of electrical apparatus. Many products thus became cheaper. New and large chemical works were constructed for the manufacture of known or hitherto unknown substitutes. Even the textile industries adopted the system of utilizing used materials. Today there are but few branches of industry using exclusively the same materials as before the war. Many have profited by the reorganization. . . .

When His Excellency von Falkenhayn came to Berlin this spring and asked after the state of our supplies, I was in a position to tell him: As far as the essentials are concerned our supplies are sufficient; the outcome of the war is not threatened by a lack of raw materials. . . .

Our methods will leave their impress on future times. I do not wish to take up the social question. Nor is it my intention to discuss to what extent our methods may affect the whole field of general economics, or whether they might possibly result in a reform of capitalism. One effect is felt even now: our valuation of political economy has changed—we have developed a new conception of raw materials. Many substitutes will continue to be used; home products will be employed where formerly we depended on imported materials; many foreign products we shall, I trust, no longer need, among them saltpeter; sulphur must no longer be imported. Our economic life will become more independent in a double sense: we shall no longer be obliged to rely on the good will of the vendors nor on that of our creditors whom we must pay and who, under certain conditions, by increasing their tariff rates, might have the power to depress the value of our payments, i.e., the value of our exported goods. . . .

The War Raw Materials Department will not cease to function in peace time; it will be made the nucleus of an Economic General Staff. Names will change. It is possible that the term War Economy

Department will be used, for it is that now. We cannot and must not be drawn again into a war without being economically prepared. The years of peace must be employed with utmost energy for this preparation. We must constantly keep informed of our supplies of essentials. Our stores must be equal to our needs. Depots of enormous size must be maintained. That will require considerable statistical and clerical work. Arrangements must be made for the smooth and automatic readjustment of these organizations in war time, whereas in this war coercion had to be employed. A general economic mobilization plan must be worked out. . . .

3. The Straining of Productive Capacity: The Russian Example

As the war dragged on it became clear that some of the belligerents were not able to meet the economic strains it imposed. Italy, Austria-Hungary, and Russia, all relatively underdeveloped economically, found their limited resources overtaxed by the war and had difficulties in organizing for total war. The problem was particularly acute in Russia where economic weakness was combined with the inability of the bureaucratic central government to recognize the need for economic mobilization and to carry out that mobilization effectively. The government acted belatedly to control allocation of materials or prices, a problem intensified by the fact that the Russian war effort was financed largely by increased issue of paper currency. The demands of the immense army absorbed the greater part of the production of both heavy and light industry and this starved the consumer market. The following report describes the serious problems of falling production and rising prices faced by the Russian metals industry.

Excerpts from a Russian Report on the Shortage of Metals, 1916

THE PURPOSE of this report is to draw the attention of the representatives of the Unions of Zemstvos and of Towns[1] to two pressing problems: on the one hand, the danger of a shortage of metals in Russia; on the other, an ever-increasing rise in the price of metals that has now reached bacchanalian proportions. These problems require the representatives of civic organizations to work actively to intensify the production of metals and to protect the consumer interest in their distribution.

Source: "Providing the Country with Metals in 1916," report by A. G. Khrushchov, member of the Main Committee of the All-Russian Unions of Zemstvos and Towns, published in Vserossiiskie Zemskii i Gorodskoi Soiuzy, *Izvestiia Glavnogo Komiteta po snabzheniiu armii*, No. 13 (March 1, 1916), pp. 7–16, with deletions. Translated by the editors.
[1] Zemstvos were organs of limited self-government. At the very onset of the war the provincial zemstvos created an All-Russian Union of Zemstvos for relief of the wounded. It was followed almost immediately by a Union of Towns. In July, 1915, the two groups formed a joint body, the Main Committee, to aid the bureaucratic central government in supplying the army and hence in improving industrial production.—Eds.

A most alarming symptom is the decline in the amount of iron produced in the country, despite an expanding need for iron for defense requirements. Compared with the [prewar] average annual iron production of 292 million puds,[2] the amount of iron smelted was, in 1913, 286.6 million puds; in 1914, 268.4 million puds; in 1915, 226.0 million puds. Consequently, in 1915, in comparison with 1913, output declined by 61 million puds, or by 21 per cent. In the foundries of [Russian] Poland, 1913 production was 25.5 million puds, while in 1914 it was 13.9 million.

Along with the decline in iron smelting there has been a decline in the supply of ore at the foundries. In 1915 stocks at foundries averaged three months' supply, that is, a quarter of yearly output. But at present, these stocks average no more than enough for two weeks' production. Thus, given their present ore reserves, the southern foundries, which in 1915 smelted only 158 million puds instead of 200 million, will have to cut back production even more sharply in the current year. . . .

Information on the situation at the end of January of this year [1916] shows that of 18 foundries of the South Russian Blast Furnace Company only 3 are operating at full capacity; all the others are producing at 20 to 25 per cent below normal. Of the company's 62 blast furnaces, 17 were completely shut down, although if they were put back to work they could produce 50 million puds of iron a year. The production of the Ural foundries has not declined so sharply, but many foundries report that they foresee a significant decline in iron smelting, or even a complete halt for lack of workers and ore. All the foundries of the Moscow region are also working at less than full capacity. We must admit that the situation is very serious. . . .

We will not dwell on the causes of the fall in the production of iron. They are generally known and can be reduced to three factors: 1. Shortage of raw materials (coke, ore, flux, coal); 2. Disruption of transport; 3. Lack of labor—the great decline in the number of Russian workers (for instance, while the mines of southern Russia usually employ 27,000 workers, at present they are using 7,000 Russian workers and 11,000 Austrians, whose labor, as is always true with forced labor, is only one-third as productive as normal labor). These are the factors that must be reckoned with, and it is necessary to face them squarely, to realize that if radical

[2] *Pud* (also transliterated "pood") is equal to 36 pounds.—Eds.

measures are not taken, the country will experience a metals famine this year, and it will not be possible to satisfy completely the needs of the private market.

What, then, are the demands of the country for iron? An attempt to calculate supply and demand of iron for the current year of 1916 was made by the Metallurgical Committee. This Committee has just been formed by the main governmental offices concerned with the distribution of Russian metals and is subordinate to the Conference for the Defense of the State, under the War Minister. Its calculations show that this year, after meeting the requirements of the military departments and the postal and telegraphic services, only an insignificant amount of iron will reach the private market, an amount far less than the demand. Thus, the civilian economy must get along on already exhausted stocks of iron from previous years and scrap from finished metal left over at the foundries after defense needs have been met. Unfortunately, the Metallurgical Committee so far has not been able to make precise calculation of nongovernmental demand for iron. . . .

The Metallurgical Committee, however, was created to meet the demands of foundries producing metal for defense needs and other needs of the State connected with defense, and at present it is limiting its activities to that area. As representatives of the Zemstvos and Towns our immediate task is to ensure at least a minimum supply of iron for private needs. Now all attention is directed at defense needs, but the peasant's cart without iron tires or hardware falls apart and cannot deliver grain to the army. Thus, we must meet the vital civilian needs for metal. . . .

As in the case of supplying the population with bread in a year of famine, there is a known minimum impossible to reduce. The necessary minimum of civilian iron consumption must be determined and supplies of iron must not be permitted to fall below it, for the success of the army depends upon the well-being of the home front. We suggest that it would be reasonable to set as the minimum norm the consumption level of iron on the private market in the second half of 1915. . . . Thus, we have set the famine minimum to which the requirements of the private market can be reduced at 26 million puds [annually]. We must point out that any reduction of supply below this minimum threatens the country with great dislocation, for it must not be forgotten that in the second half of 1915, despite the fact that the foundries provided the private market with iron in the quantity we have chosen

as the norm, civilian needs were met by drawing on the stocks of
iron in warehouses and that these are now exhausted. . . .

Furthermore, one has only to look at the accompanying table to
see how [even before the war] our country lagged behind its
neighbors in the amount of iron consumed per capita.

1911 Per Capita Consumption of Iron (in kilograms)

United States	285
Belgium	143
Germany	136
France	106
England	105
Austria	44
Russia	25
Spain	23

. . . We present a price table for ordinary metal products,
comparing prices before the war, in June, 1914, and wholesale
prices at present:

Product	Wholesale Prices, 1914 (prewar)	Wholesale Prices, 1916	Increase over 1914 (%)
Copper in bars	12 rubles	32 rubles	167
Horseshoe nails	5 rubles 80 kopecks	15 rubles	158
Wire nails	2 rubles 50 kopecks	6 rubles 50 kopecks	160
Wire	1 ruble 80 kopecks	3 rubles 75 kopecks	170
Sheet iron	1 ruble 80 kopecks	4 rubles	120
Cast iron	1 ruble 55 kopecks	2 rubles 50 kopecks	61

. . . The information in the table on the increase in the price of
metal products during the war (from 61 to 170 per cent) forces us
to confront squarely the question of the necessity of regulating the
prices of metals, setting fixed prices for them. And it is necessary to
do that quickly, or we have no protection against further increases.
The table gives wholesale market prices for metals, prices almost
unrelated to the consumer. In reality, the available goods get to the
man in the street at a price two or three times higher than the
wholesale price. . . .

On the basis of the foregoing, the following resolution is suggested to the congress of representatives of the Zemstvos and

Towns to be submitted to the State Duma and the Special Conference for the Defense of the State:

(1) It is necessary to adopt without delay the most energetic measures for increasing the smelting of iron, including restoring the factories that are not working. . . .

(2) It is necessary for the government to establish fixed prices for metals immediately.

(3) It is necessary to eliminate the duties on copper temporarily because they are a factor in the increase in domestic copper prices.

(4) It is necessary to assure the civilian population of a supply of iron in a quantity not less than 26 million puds, because without this minimum amount the country's economic life is threatened with complete dislocation. The distribution of this metal must involve the participation of and control by the civic organizations, the Unions of Zemstvos and Towns.

4. Labor Problems and the Employment of Women

Following an initial period of falling production and unemployment in the early months of the war, labor shortages began to appear in essential industries everywhere. Governments soon intervened to ensure an adequate labor supply: skilled workers who had been called to the colors were returned to their jobs and others were protected from conscription; workers in nonessential industries were encouraged, and sometimes compelled, to change their jobs; production techniques were simplified to allow greater use of unskilled labor; and efforts were made to recruit new sources of labor, especially from among the female population. The increased employment of women not only represented a substantial contribution to the war production effort, but also gave rise to a number of questions about the future status of women in society. The following selection, taken from a 1919 report by a British War Cabinet Committee created to investigate the wartime employment of women, raises, sometimes unwittingly, some of these issues.

Report on Wartime Employment of Women in Britain

Unemployment at the Beginning of the War. The outbreak of War was followed by the partial cessation of foreign orders and by a reduction of avoidable expenditure at home, and these resulted in a period of unemployment. Owing mainly to their absorption in the Army and in Government factories and workshops, men's unemployment had largely ceased by October, 1914, and entirely before the end of the year. The contraction of the employment of women in industry went down less rapidly. It was represented by 190,000 [unemployed] female workers in September, 136,000 in October, 77,000 in December and 39,000 in February . . . and there were still a number of women unemployed in the middle of 1915. Women's unemployment was most serious in the Cotton industry, which had been declining for some time before August, 1914, and suffered at once from stoppage in the import of raw

Source: *Report of the War Cabinet Committee on Women in Industry* (Cd. 135) (London: His Majesty's Stationery Office, 1919), pp. 79–159, with deletions.

material and difficulties in the export of manufactured goods as well as from contraction of demand. . . .

Increased Employment of Women during the War. In the second half of 1915 unemployed women were rapidly absorbed in munition factories, and in January, 1916, in industry proper the number of women had already increased by over a quarter of a million, of whom about one-half were employed in the Metal and Chemical trades. From this time onwards the figure of female employment rose steadily until in July, 1918, the total number of occupied women had, according to Board of Trade figures, increased by 22 ½ per cent, or from just under 6 million to nearly 7 ⅓ million as shown in the following table:

Numbers of Women Working	*In July, 1914*	*In July, 1918*	*Net Change*
On their own account or as employers	430,000	470,000	+ 40,000
In Industry	2,178,600	2,970,600	+ 792,000
In Domestic Service	1,658,000	1,258,000	− 400,000
In Commerce, etc.	505,500	934,500	+ 429,000
In National and Local Government, including Education	262,200	460,200	+ 198,000
In Agriculture	190,000	228,000	+ 38,000
In employment of Hotels, Public Houses, Theatres, etc.	181,000	220,000	+ 39,000
In Transport	18,200	117,200	+ 99,000
In other, including professional employment and as home workers	542,500	652,500	+ 110,000
Altogether in occupations	5,966,000	7,311,000	+1,345,000

. . . It will be seen that after industry the most important increases were in commerce—mostly clerks and shop assistants; in the National and Local Government—mainly the Civil Service, which took on some 168,000 women clerks, etc.; and in transport. The additions in the different branches of industry, their effect in altering the proportion of women to men in those branches and the extent to which females directly replaced males are shown in the following table:

Trades	Estimated Number of Females Employed in July, 1914	Estimated Number of Females Employed in July, 1918	Net Change	Percentage of Females in Total Workforce		Estimated Number of Females Directly Replacing Males in Jan., 1918
				July, 1914	July, 1918	
Metal	170,000	594,000	+ 424,000	9	25	195,000
Chemical	40,000	104,000	+ 64,000	20	39	35,000
Textile	863,000	827,000	− 36,000	58	67	64,000
Clothing	612,000	568,000	− 44,000	68	76	43,000
Food, Drink, and Tobacco	196,000	235,000	+ 39,000	35	49	60,000
Paper and Printing	147,500	141,500	− 6,000	36	48	21,000
Wood	44,000	79,000	+ 35,000	15	32	23,000
China and Earthenware	32,000 ⎫					
Leather	23,100 ⎬	197,100	+ 93,000	4	10	62,000
Other	49,000 ⎭					
Government Establishments	2,000	225,000	+ 223,000	3	47	197,000
Total	2,178,600	2,970,600	+ 792,000	26	37	704,000

Employment of Women during the War. Munition and Metal Trades. First and foremost the requirements of munitions brought women into the Metal trades, but down to the end of December, 1914, the special munition problem had not emerged and the female employees in these trades only increased by some 3,000. During the next six months the shortage of munitions was recognised, but the attempt was made to meet it by ordinary methods, by a speeding up of contracts and by a gradual development of the agencies of supply. During this period, some 26,000 women came in. Their increased employment, though not unimportant, was, however, confined to a few well-defined but unskilled processes. Then followed in the second half of 1915 the initial energies of the Ministry of Munitions when the engineering resources of the nation were mobilised and every possible step taken to expand them. Another 45,000 female workers were added to the Metal trades during this period, in which dilution became, as it continued up to the end of the war, a leading method of increasing the munitions labour supply. From the beginning of 1916 the forces set in motion gathered strength and produced results with uninterrupted acceleration. Between July, 1914, and July, 1918, the number of women rose from 170,000 to 594,000, or by 424,000, of whom about 90 per cent were employed on work customarily done by men. To this last figure must be added a large proportion of the 223,000 women employed, mostly on metal work, in National establishments where practically none had worked before, making a total addition to female metal workers of over 600,000. The most important single trade was shell-making. The women were soon some 60 per cent of the workers, and made the shell throughout from the roughing and turning of the bodies to the final gauging of the completed shell. In general engineering shops and ship-yards, foundries, gun and aircraft factories, women were introduced on most varieties of men's work. . . . In some munition factories the men's work was almost entirely carried out by women, but the processes were not generally the same as were the men's processes. In factories employing already semi-skilled workers, the job was sometimes identical, but in factories employing normally skilled tradesmen, either the machine was transformed by the adjustment of "jigs" or fool-proof appliances, or the women performed only a part of the man's job and were confined to one of a comparatively narrow range of operations. . . . The effect of the war was, in fact, to hasten greatly the division of process. The Amalgamated

Society of Engineers[1] were, however, of opinion, as they informed the Committee, that the extent of subdivision and standardisation adopted during the war could not be taken as at all indicative of its probable extent after the war. They thought that it had not always been economical even with low rates of wages for the women employed. . . .

Speaking generally of women employed on men's work, members of the Engineering and National Employers' Federation placed the women's productive value at about two-thirds of the men's. "Where a woman is paid more than 66 per cent of a man she ceases to be profitable as a producer." Beyond this point, the employers would prefer to employ boys. The employers laid stress on the high proportionate overhead charges, caused by reduction of output. The cost of shop supervision was again variously estimated at 30 per cent and 50 per cent higher where women were employed and one additional supervisor was said to be required for each 100 women. . . .

Domestic Service. It is estimated that displacement from domestic service and from very small workshops and workrooms in the dressmaking trade taken together amounted to 400,000. Skilled domestic servants, because of their generally superior intelligence and physical fitness, were in high demand in munition factories. For this reason, and owing to attractive openings in other occupations depleted of male workers, the falling off in the supply of servants, especially of young servants, which had begun before the war owing to the increase in clerical and other positions admitting of living-out, was greatly accelerated. The shortage of cook-generals and house-parlour-maids was even more seriously felt and aggravated by the increased number of households requiring general servants. "Inefficients" readily secured employment, while mistresses were compelled to make good the shortage by their own labour. Many of the girls are, moreover, not expected to return, at least to living-in service, except as a last resort. They want more freedom and limited hours of work.

Commercial Occupations. Including wholesale and retail shops, the percentage of females to all workpeople engaged in commerce rose during the same period from 29 to 54 per cent, or by 364,000 women, of whom the large body replaced men. . . . Apart from

[1] The Amalgamated Society of Engineers, one of the most important trade unions in the munitions field.—Eds.

the employment of women in managerial posts, displacement took place chiefly in grocery, fish and provision shops and in hardware. The general opinion of employers was that three women were efficient when taking the place of two men, while the cost was further increased by the higher percentage of wastage. . . .

Clerical Work. In *Finance and Banking* the proportion of females to all workpeople rose from 5 per cent in July, 1914, to 42 per cent in July, 1918, and the number by 65,000 women. . . .

Employment of Women in Men's Occupations. From the foregoing examination of the evidence and returns submitted to the Committee, it appears that the principal changes made by the war in the direction of introducing women into men's occupations have been:

(1) To bring or bring back women into manual labour and outdoor occupations, viz., agriculture, transport, chemical manufacture.

(2) To admit women into skilled trades of an apprenticeship or "craft" character, e.g., "all round" engineering and woodworking, and scientific instrument making.

(3) To hasten the normal movement of women into "repetition" and routine processes of trades or other occupations, such as specialised engineering, wood-working, or clerical work.

These changes resulted from shortage of male labour, and were rendered possible by the patriotic enthusiasm of women and, in the case of the organised trades, by the relaxation of Trade Union restrictions. . . .

Relaxation of Trade Union Restrictions in Employment of Women. The additional number of women employed in industry proper at the end of the war was not far short of the number that were directly replacing men. The arrangements by which the substitution of women for men were allowed by the Trade Unions were thus of vast importance in securing the necessary war output. The Engineering Unions, whose rules prohibited female labour, were chiefly concerned. At first, the women were confined to simple automatic operations, or merely replaced boys and youths up-graded to work of higher quality. In November, 1914, an agreement was drawn up between the Amalgamated Society of Engineers and the Engineering Employers' Federation, known as the "Crayford Agreement," relating to the establishment of Messrs.

Vickers, which provided that female labour should be restricted to purely automatic machines used for the production of repetition work, and that all such automatic machines should be set up by fully-skilled mechanics. In February, 1915, the Committee on Production in Engineering and Shipbuilding Establishments, appointed to enquire and report as to the best means of making fully available the productive power of the workers, made a strong suggestion to employers and workpeople that female labour should be further utilised under proper and suitable conditions, on the production of shells and fuzes, and accordingly, on the 5th March, the Engineering Employers' Federation, and the Amalgamated Society of Engineers made an agreement known as the "Shells and Fuzes Agreement." This provided that semi-skilled and female labour might be admitted to operations on which skilled men were at present employed, subject to their being paid "the usual rates of the district obtaining for the operations performed." . . .

Regulation of Wages by Collective Bargaining. One of the most conspicuous features of the war period has been the growth in organisation both among employers and employed. Trades such as chemicals, explosives, rubber, brick and clay have formed employers' associations or federations in the course of the war, largely in order to deal with problems arising out of wages, and in other cases federations which previously did not deal with wages have been compelled to do so. But it is rather in the strengthening of existing associations and federations of employers that the war has had its most marked effect. On the other side also a powerful impetus has been given to the organisation of women in Trade Unions. According to figures supplied by the Ministry of Labour, there were, at the end of 1917, nearly 660,000 female members of Trade Unions in the United Kingdom against some 350,000 before the war. . . . But, as before, the great bulk of organised women are to be found in the textile trades—approximately 350,000. . . . It is, of course, too early at present to say whether the extension of trade unionism among women which has been caused by the war will be permanent or not. It seems probable that a decline will follow the cessation of munitions work. . . .

5. *Mobilization of Private Capital*

A problem that affected the Allied Powers in particular was how to pay for the purchase of increased quantities of essential foreign products at a time when their export business had fallen off sharply. Both France and Britain had invested huge amounts of capital in overseas territories before the war. By 1914 British-held foreign assets, it is estimated, were worth about 4 billion pounds, while the figure for France in the same year was about 45 billion francs.[1] Certainly not all of these vast amounts were or could have been liquidated to provide foreign exchange for purchases abroad, but both countries did draw on this reserve. The liquidation of foreign-held assets combined with the great increase in foreign indebtedness substantially reduced the net British overseas investment and converted France into a debtor nation. The selection that follows represents the important articles of the French decree establishing the machinery for tapping the resource of private foreign investments.

French Decree on the Loan of Foreign Securities to the State, 1916

ARTICLE 1. The [foreign] securities of which a list is given below[2] can be made, under the conditions herein indicated, the object of a loan of securities to the state, which reserves to itself the right to appropriate them as a pledge on exchange operations to which it has given consent or on credits it has opened.

ARTICLE 2. Borrowed securities are to be made to bearer. The nominal value of the securities delivered by a single lender is not to be less than five hundred francs.

ARTICLE 3. The loan will be made for one year, from the 16th day of the month in which the securities were delivered by the lenders if this was done before the 15th day, and from the first day of the

Source: *Journal Officiel de la République française* (May 5, 1916), p. 3907. Translated by the editors.

[1] Values of currencies in 1913 (annual average): Great Britain, £1 = $4.86; France, 1 franc = $0.19.—Eds.

[2] The list, which appears on pp. 3908–3909 of the *Journal Officiel*, is not reproduced here. It contains, for the most part, long-term loan issues of neutral states. A few railroad stocks and bonds and Suez Canal stocks and bonds were included. The price offered was the market price.—Eds.

next month for those delivered after the 15th. It may be extended at the discretion of the Treasury from year to year for three years.

Lenders will have the right to request certificates, negotiable on the stock exchange, that permit them to dispose of the lent securities, with reservation of the rights conferred on the state by the loan.

ARTICLE 4. In the event the Treasury judges it necessary to sell any or all of the securities lent, it will pay their value at prices indicated in lists established by the Ministry of Finance, or, if the seller prefers, at the highest price quoted in the quarter preceding the announcement of sale.

ARTICLE 5. The lenders will have the right to the entire income from their securities under the normal conditions including profits from exchange, if there are any. In addition, they will receive each year a bonus equal to one-quarter (25 per cent) of the annual gross revenue without profits from exchange. This bonus is payable for the first year at the time the securities are delivered and for both the following years when the first coupons fall due in each of those years.

For stocks the bonus will be equal to one-quarter of the dividends of the previous year.

ARTICLE 6. The loan may be terminated before the end of the third year: a) by a notice of termination of the contract by the Treasury, which has reserved the right to do so at any time, in whole or in part with one month's notice, the bonus paid remaining in full the property of the lender; b) by the purchase by the Treasury of all or part of the securities lent, on condition of one month's notice, the price being fixed according to the provisions indicated above; c) by the amortization or the redemption of the securities according to the terms of their issue; these securities or their equivalent will be returned to the lenders within three months. . . .

6. Interallied Cooperation

The long duration of the war with its ever-rising requirements of supply drove the Allied Powers to coordinate their economic activities in many spheres. The toll of merchant shipping taken by the German submarines, for example, produced shortages necessitating cooperation in the allocation of shipping tonnage. Similarly, cooperation in foreign purchasing helped to assure that the requirements of all were reasonably well met and that competitive bidding for scarce products did not needlessly drive up prices. One example of interallied cooperation is provided by the activities of the Wheat Executive, created in November, 1916. The text of the agreement establishing the Wheat Executive is given below.

The Wheat Executive, November, 1916

As a result of the Conference of the representatives of the Allied governments held in Paris on November 15 and 16, 1916, and in conformity with the general agreement reached at that conference, His Excellency Mr. Clémentel, Minister of Commerce, representing the French government, His Excellency Mr. Raineri, Minister of Agriculture, representing the Italian government, and the Right Honorable Walter Runciman, President of the Board of Trade, representing the British government, have reached the following agreement regarding the supplying of wheat.

1. The Allies will make a common effort for the purpose of:
a) calculating the amounts of various grains they require according to needs determined by inventories;
b) purchasing abroad and importing the amounts of grain required by the inventory.

2. Wheat (including flour) is submitted to inventory under the present agreement and henceforth will be regulated according to the plan set forth in the present agreement.

3. France and Italy shall each appoint without delay a representative in London who, joined by a member of the Royal Com-

Source: Etienne Clémentel, *La France et la politique économique interalliée* (Paris: Presses Universitaires de France, 1931), pp. 330–333, with deletions. Translated by the editors. Used by permission of the Carnegie Endowment for International Peace.

mission on Wheat, will form the Wheat Executive which will begin to operate at once in the manner of a trading company. Within the limits and conditions imposed on the use of funds available to the respective representatives of France, Italy and Great Britain, the Wheat Executive will have full power to meet the needs of the Allies by the purchase and allocation of grains included in the inventory and will provide for their shipment. The Wheat Executive will establish whatever regulations and keep whatever records seem necessary for the conduct of its business. The absence of unanimous decision will in no way prevent the Wheat Executive from acting, but in cases of clear difference of opinion the respective governments are to be consulted on the point in question.

4. The Wheat Executive shall submit to inventory and shall regulate grains other than wheat, if it regards this as necessary.

5. The Wheat Executive shall take into consideration the import requirements of wheat of each Ally beginning November 1, 1916, and the dates by which time the supplies are necessary. It shall reduce these requirements to the lowest point compatible with assuring the necessary supplies. The proportions in which the above figures are fixed shall be called hereafter the "fixed proportion" for each Ally.

6. The Wheat Executive shall assemble from its members each month complete information as to existing stocks and consumption in each of the Allied nations. The fixed proportions are subject to periodic revision. In evaluating needs, the home-produced supplies available for consumption in each country, as well as imports, are to be taken into consideration.

7. The Wheat Executive shall make an estimate of the wheat surplus available for export to the Allies as it is shipped from each exporting country (including shipments not yet received [in Allied countries]), which shall be called the available surplus. The amount of wheat purchased by each Ally in each exporting country shall be indicated, as well as any probable balance available for purchase in common. . . .

Unless a contrary arrangement is made, payment shall be made by the British government which shall be reimbursed by the Allied powers to which the wheat is allocated, according to arrangements agreed to by the Allied finance ministers. . . .

10. An average price for available wheat shall be established independently for each exporting country. . . . The Wheat Ex-

ecutive shall fix periodically the approximate price of the available wheat allotted to each Ally, and a final accounting shall take place as soon as possible after the end of the harvest year.

11. The shipping of that wheat allocated to each Ally . . . is the responsibility of the Ally concerned, and each one shall make immediately every effort to furnish the Wheat Executive with the necessary ships. The Wheat Executive shall establish a common program for the purpose of tonnage and to facilitate the chartering of ships . . . for any Ally not able with his own ships completely to fulfill his obligation. . . .

12. The Wheat Executive shall have a free hand to use the tonnage furnished by the Allies for the purposes indicated in this agreement and to charter whatever neutral tonnage is necessary. . . .

13. In order to economize on tonnage, it is understood that wheat available in various exporting countries is only provisionally divided among the Allies. This allocation shall establish the amount of wheat purchased by each Ally and the costs and obligations of shipping, but not the actual destination of the wheat. This shall be determined as quickly as possible by the Wheat Executive according to the principle that each exporting country is to provide wheat for the nearest Allied consumer, always with the reservation that these shipping arrangements never constitute an advantage for one Ally at the expense of the others, either in wheat supply or shipping.

14. The Wheat Executive must always bear in mind the advantages of centralizing all wheat purchases and shipping arrangements made for its transport on the accounts of the Allies. . . .

7. War Devastation

The costs of the First World War were staggering. For more than four years some of the wealthiest and most highly developed industrial countries in the world had devoted their resources, both human and material, to total war. The casualties (10 million known dead and twice that number wounded), the destruction, the indebtedness, and the inflation that resulted were unparalleled. Attempts to calculate the total costs of the war have had only limited success. What was spent for military purposes by the belligerent governments—and that is a figure in the vicinity of $200 billion—is only part of the total. It is far more difficult to arrive at an accurate figure for the destruction of life and property. Efforts have been made, but the issue has been seriously complicated by controversies over reparation payments (see Part III: The Postwar Crisis). The selection below is taken from a report prepared in December, 1918, by the American Red Cross, which makes a preliminary estimate of the war damage in France. It was approved by the French government, but is not to be taken as a definitive statement of the amount of destruction.

The Devastated Area of France, December, 1918

THE DEVASTATED area in France covers approximately 6,000 square miles in all, about 2 per cent of France, with a total population of nearly 2,000,000 people. This is about equal to the area of Connecticut and Rhode Island. . . .

The hasty investigation since the signing of the armistice shows that [compared with the estimates of earlier reports] the total destruction in France has been quintupled, with something like 500,000 buildings damaged, and at least 250,000 completely destroyed.

The average cost of these buildings before the war was nearly $5,000. As the present cost of a building is about two and a half times greater than it was then, we can say that the total destruction in France of the buildings alone is today over $6,000,000,000, as estimated by the Government engineers, and $4,000,000,000 as estimated by the architects and constructors' associations.

Source: Report prepared by George B. Ford, head of the Research Department of the American Red Cross, *Current History*, Vol. IX, Part II, No. 3 (March, 1919), pp. 516–519, with deletions.

The total cost of repairing and replacing the used or destroyed public works is estimated at about $2,000,000,000, of which $200,-000,000 is for the Nord Railroad, $150,000,000 for the East, $50,000,000 for the other railroads, $200,000,000 to cover the rebuilding of the canals. The Nord alone has lost 1,731 bridges and 338 stations.

In 1917 there were 527 communes in which over half of the buildings had been completely destroyed. This number has probably reached today something like 1,500 communes in all. In 1917, in 400 communes, over 80 per cent of the buildings had been damaged, and this proportion probably reaches today over 1,000 communes in all. In the summer of 1917 they counted over 435 town halls destroyed, 600 schools, 472 churches, and 377 other public buildings, and it could be safely said today that there are over 1,200 churches destroyed and over 1,500 schools in all.

In 1917 they counted over 414 industrial plants destroyed, which supported 105,000 persons. It can probably be said today that there are in all over 1,000 plants destroyed, supporting at least 500,000 persons.

On Oct. 25, 1916, a report was made by the Minister of the Interior on the building materials destroyed which would have to be replaced. It was made for 790 communes, or for 41,223 buildings totally or approximately destroyed, and it comprises the destruction of 1,700,000 cubic yards of stone masonry, 600,000 cubic yards of brick masonry, 300,000 tons of lime. The largest part of this destruction was in the Pas-de-Calais, and the next larger in the Meurthe-et-Moselle. It also showed the destruction of 200,-000,000 feet of lumber and 33,000 tons of iron and steel, with 91,-000,000 roof tiles destroyed and 32,000,000 roofing slates. It can be probably said today that the total destruction would be at least five times the amount given in the above figures.

The total cost of furniture and furnishings today, exclusive of machinery, amounts to at least $2,225,000,000, as estimated by the Government engineers, and over $1,000,000,000, as estimated by the insurance companies.

According to a report made by the Office de Reconstitution Agricole to the Minister of Liberated Regions in May, 1918, it was reckoned that at that time about 8,000 square miles of French land was in the hands of the Germans. About three-quarters of that area is tillable, and a large proportion of the rest is good for hay or pasturage. This is some of the very best and richest agricultural land in Europe. The ten invaded and liberated departments produced in 1913 nearly $400,000,000 worth of crops. The average yield of this land is about 32 bushels of wheat to the acre, and in the Meuse and Meurthe-et-Moselle it drops down to about 17 bushels to the acre. In the Marne this drops down to about 22 bushels to the acre. These regions constitute about 15 per cent of the total tillable area of France, and the crops constitute about 20 per cent of the total for France. The agricultural population here is about 807,000, or about 10 per cent of the working agricultural population of France. It is estimated that 250,000 acres are now rendered uncultivable by the war. . . .

With regard to the cattle lost, it is hard to get at the exact figures, but in these ten departments in 1913 there were 607,000 horses, whereas in 1915 there were only 242,000, or a loss of 60 per cent. Of cattle of all kinds there was a loss of 850,000, or 55 per cent; of pigs there was a loss of 380,000, or about 55 per cent. The loss in wheat amounts to about 1,300,000 acres. The loss in hay amounts to about 850,000 acres. The total damage to the soil, to live stock, to crops, to forests, tools, etc., is estimated at $2,000,-000,000.

. . . In all something over 70 per cent of the total coal supply of France came from the invaded regions, and very much the best quality of coal at that. About 140,000 men were employed in these mines in the invaded regions out of 203,208 coal miners for all of France. This means, with their families, three-quarters of a million people were largely dependent on the coal mines. Over $200,000,-000 of machinery has probably been destroyed.

Before the war the total production of iron ore in France was about 21,918,000 tons, of which 19,629,000 tons came from the Briey and Longwy basins in the Meurthe-et-Moselle; that is, 90 per cent of the total, of which 16,500,000 tons were in the hands of the Germans. The miners who were employed in these invaded mines, with their families, represented at least 150,000 people out of employment. . . . More than $500,000,000 worth of machinery has been destroyed, including that of steel and iron mills.

Before the war 3,000,000 tons of steel were manufactured in the region invaded by Germany out of 4,686,000 tons for all of France, or nearly 65 per cent. The same percentage holds for cast iron.

The effect of the German invasion on other metals has not been so serious, as most of them come from the interior of France. The chemical industries have proportionally suffered very little from the invasion.

The textile industry consisted before the war of about 7,530,000 cotton spindles throughout France, of which 4,500,000 were in the region invaded by Germany and of which almost all were either destroyed or carried into Germany. Out of 2,365,000 wool spindles, 2,000,000 were in the invaded districts. Out of 550,000 linen spindles, 500,000 were in the invaded regions and destroyed or removed. The same is true of looms, of which there were 140,000 in France, and over 81,000 of these were in the invaded districts. Over $120,000,000 worth of machinery has been destroyed.

Of 210 sugar refineries in France, 140 have been destroyed by the Germans. Of 3,000 brush factories, more than 2,000 have been destroyed. Over $25,000,000 worth of machinery has been destroyed. Electric power stations, totaling 300,000 kilowatts, have been destroyed with an equipment loss of $50,000,000. Breweries have lost more than $250,000,000 worth of machinery. In machine shops $100,000,000 worth of machinery has been destroyed. In foundries, etc., $60,000,000 worth of machinery is gone.

None of these damages include land or buildings. Furthermore, almost all of this machinery costs three times as much to replace today, so that it can safely be said that $4,000,000,000 worth of machinery will be needed to replace that destroyed or carried away. This includes the stock and raw materials damaged and damage done to the mines.

Before the war France used to manufacture 3,000,000 tons of cement a year. In February, 1918, it was manufacturing only 400,000 tons. . . .

Before the war there were about 750,000 men in the various building trades, of whom about 75,000 were in the invaded departments. The total building done throughout France before the war in any one year was less than 7 per cent of the building that would have to be done to replace what has been destroyed in the invaded departments. Therefore if no building were to be done elsewhere in France after the war, and reckoning that 500,000 of the building tradesmen of France would be available to work in the devastated regions, it would take over twenty years to rebuild.

The total damage in the north of France, including buildings, agriculture, industry, furniture, and public works, is estimated at

64,500,000,000 francs, or about $13,000,000,000. These were the
figures reported by M. Dubois for the Committee on Budget in the
Chamber of Deputies, December, 1918. We have checked most of
these figures from various official and private sources and believe
they are somewhat high. . . .

PART II

The Peace Settlement

In January, 1919, the Peace Conference convened in Paris. It was a meeting of the victors only; Germany was excluded from the negotiating table, as was Bolshevik Russia. Among the victors, the crucial decisions were made by the Big Four, Georges Clemenceau of France, David Lloyd George of Britain, Woodrow Wilson of the United States, and Vittorio Orlando of Italy. As well as ending the state of war between the Central Powers and the Allied Powers, these men faced the immense task of restoring order to war-torn Europe. The reconstruction of Europe raised economic as well as political issues, or, more accurately, economic and political problems were hopelessly knotted together. For example, the creation of a number of new states in eastern Europe carried tremendous economic implications that were only partially perceived in 1919 and that were inadequately dealt with in the treaties.

The results of the Conference were embodied in five treaties, but the focus of attention and the model for the other treaties was that with Germany, the Treaty of Versailles, signed on June 28, 1919. The Treaty affected German economic life in many ways. It imposed significant territorial cessions, especially in the east, and the loss of colonies and foreign economic rights; it included clauses that amounted to unilateral limitations upon economic sovereignty. Of particular importance were the clauses on the reparation of war damage. Except for Britain, none of the European belligerents had succeeded in financing any major portion of the war effort out of current income, and all were anxious to transfer to Germany some of the burden of debt they had built up. France claimed full reparation for the property damage wrought by four years of fighting on French soil. Britain, which had not suffered significant civilian property damage, insisted upon including in the reparation bill costs of war pensions and other charges that went far beyond the traditional definitions of indemnifiable war damage. The result was to require of Germany monetary reparation in gold and bonds (to an amount to be determined), reparation by deliveries out of current production, and the loss of its merchant marine.

The Treaty of Versailles, and the Peace Conference in general, failed to provide solutions to the economic problems created by the war and the peace settlement, largely because few realized in 1919 the degree to which the war had unhinged the economic system of prewar Europe. Although the judgment is harsh, it is worth considering the indictment of one of the most famous of the contemporary critics of the Treaty of Versailles, John Maynard Keynes:

> The Treaty includes no provisions for the economic rehabilitation of Europe—nothing to make the defeated Central Empires into good neighbors, nothing to stabilize the new States of Europe, nothing to reclaim Russia; nor does it promote in any way a compact of economic solidarity amongst the Allies themselves; no arrangement was reached at Paris for restoring the disordered finances of France and Italy, or to adjust the systems of the Old World and the New.
>
> The Council of Four paid no attention to these issues. . . . It is an extraordinary fact that the fundamental economic problems of a Europe starving and disintegrating before their eyes, was the one question in which it was impossible to arouse the interest of the Four. Reparation was their main excursion into the economic field, and they settled it as a problem of theology, of politics, of electoral chicane, from every point of view except that of the economic future of the States whose destiny they were handling.[1]

[1] John Maynard Keynes, *The Economic Consequences of the Peace* (New York: Harcourt, Brace and Howe, 1920), pp. 226–227. Used by permission of Harcourt, Brace and World.

8. The Treaty of Versailles

The Treaty of Versailles is a lengthy document of almost 450 articles and numerous annexes. It is divided into fifteen parts: The Covenant of the League of Nations; Boundaries of Germany; Political Clauses for Europe; German Rights and Interests Outside Germany; Military, Naval, and Air Clauses; Prisoners of War and Graves; Penalties; Reparation; Financial Clauses; Economic Clauses; Aerial Navigation; Ports, Waterways and Railways; Labor; Guarantees; and Miscellaneous Provisions. It is difficult to separate out the purely economic clauses. Many of the articles concerning economic matters were tailored to fit political ends. Most of the territorial changes were of economic importance, depriving Germany of about 15 per cent of her arable land, three-quarters of her iron ore and one-quarter of her coal production. The excerpts presented below include two examples of territorial change (the Saar Basin and Danzig), along with representative clauses from the financial and economic sections and the section on German interests abroad. All of the articles of Part VIII, concerning the much-debated issue of reparation, have been included as has much of the material in the related annexes (only one of the seven annexes has been entirely omitted). The clauses on transport, however, have been omitted.

Excerpts from the Treaty of Versailles, June, 1919

Part III: Political Clauses for Europe

SECTION IV: SAAR BASIN

ARTICLE 45. As compensation for the destruction of the coal mines in the north of France and as part payment towards the total reparation due from Germany for the damage resulting from the war, Germany cedes to France in full and absolute possession, with exclusive rights of exploitation, unencumbered and free from all debts and charges of any kind, the coal-mines situated in the Saar Basin as defined in Article 48 [which describes the boundaries of the Saar Basin].

ARTICLE 46. In order to assure the rights and welfare of the population and to guarantee to France complete freedom in work-

Source: *The Treaty of Peace Between the Allied and Associated Powers and Germany* (London: His Majesty's Stationery Office, 1919).

ing the mines, Germany agrees to the provisions . . . of the
Annex hereto. . . .

ANNEX

In accordance with the provisions of Articles 45 to 50 of the
present Treaty, the stipulations under which the cession by Germany to France of the mines of the Saar Basin will be effected, as
well as the measures intended to ensure respect for the rights and
well-being of the population and the government of the territory,
and the conditions in which the inhabitants will be called upon to
indicate the sovereignty under which they may wish to be placed,
have been laid down as follows:

1. From the date of the coming into force of the present Treaty,
all the deposits of coal situated within the Saar Basin as defined in
Article 48 of the said Treaty, become the complete and absolute
property of the French State.

The French State will have the right of working or not working
the said mines, or of transferring to a third party the right of
working them, without having to obtain any previous authorisa-
tion or to fulfil any formalities.

The French State may always require that the German mining
laws and regulations referred to below shall be applied in order to
ensure the determination of its rights.

2. The right of ownership of the French State will apply not
only to the deposits which are free and for which concessions have
not yet been granted, but also to the deposits for which concessions
have already been granted, whoever may be the present proprietors, irrespective of whether they belong to the Prussian State,
to the Bavarian State, to other States or bodies, to companies or to
individuals, whether they have been worked or not, or whether a
right of exploitation distinct from the right of the owners of the
surface of the soil has or has not been recognised.

3. As far as concerns the mines which are being worked, the
transfer of the ownership to the French State will apply to all the
accessories and subsidiaries of the said mines, in particular to their
plant and equipment both on and below the surface, to their
extracting machinery, their plants for transforming coal into electric power, coke and by-products, their workshops, means of
communication, electric lines, plant for catching and distributing
water, land, buildings such as offices, managers', employees' and
workmen's dwellings, schools, hospitals and dispensaries, their

stocks and supplies of every description, their archives and plans, and in general everything which those who own or exploit the mines possess or enjoy for the purpose of exploiting the mines and their accessories and subsidiaries.

The transfer will apply also to the debts owing for products delivered before the entry into possession by the French State, and after the signature of the present Treaty, and to deposits of money made by customers, whose rights will be guaranteed by the French State.

4. The French State will acquire the property free and clear of all debts and charges. Nevertheless, the rights acquired, or in course of being acquired, by the employees of the mines and their accessories and subsidiaries at the date of the coming into force of the present Treaty, in connection with pensions for old age or disability, will not be affected. In return, Germany must pay over to the French State a sum representing the actuarial amounts to which the said employees are entitled.

5. The value of the property thus ceded to the French State will be determined by the Reparation Commission referred to in Article 233 of Part VIII (Reparation) of the present Treaty.

This value shall be credited to Germany in part payment of the amount due for reparation.

It will be for Germany to indemnify the proprietors or parties concerned, whoever they may be.

6. No tariff shall be established on the German railways and canals which may directly or indirectly discriminate to the prejudice of the transport of the personnel or products of the mines and their accessories or subsidiaries, or of the material necessary to their exploitation. Such transport shall enjoy all the rights and privileges which any international railway conventions may guarantee to similar products of French origin. . . .

15. The French State shall enjoy complete liberty with respect to the distribution, despatch and sale prices of the products of the mines and their accessories and subsidiaries.

Nevertheless, whatever may be the total product of the mines, the French Government undertakes that the requirements of local consumption for industrial and domestic purposes shall always be satisfied in the proportion existing in 1913 between the amount consumed locally and the total output of the Saar Basin. . . .

31. The territory of the Saar Basin as defined by Article 48 of the present Treaty shall be subjected to the French customs

régime. The receipts from the customs duties on goods intended for local consumption shall be included in the budget of the said territory after deduction of all costs of collection.

No export tax shall be imposed upon metallurgical products or coal exported from the said territory to Germany, nor upon German exports for the use of the industries of the territory of the Saar Basin.

Natural or manufactured products originating in the Basin in transit over German territory and, similarly, German products in transit over the territory of the Basin shall be free of all customs duties.

Products which both originate in and pass from the Basin into Germany shall be free of import duties for a period of five years from the date of the coming into force of the present Treaty, and during the same period articles imported from Germany into the territory of the Basin for local consumption shall likewise be free of import duties.

During these five years the French Government reserves to itself the right of limiting to the annual average of the quantities imported into Alsace-Lorraine and France in the years 1911 to 1913 the quantities which may be sent into France of all articles coming from the Basin which include raw materials and semi-manufactured goods imported duty free from Germany. Such average shall be determined after reference to all available official information and statistics. . . .

36. If [after a plebiscite to be held in 15 years] the League of Nations decides in favour of the union of the whole or part of the territory of the Saar Basin with Germany, France's rights of ownership in the mines situated in such part of the territory will be repurchased by Germany in their entirety at a price payable in gold. The price to be paid will be fixed by three experts, one nominated by Germany, one by France, and one, who shall be neither a Frenchman nor a German, by the Council of the League of Nations; the decision of the experts will be given by a majority.

The obligation of Germany to make such payment shall be taken into account by the Reparation Commission, and for the purpose of this payment, Germany may create a prior charge upon her assets or revenues upon such detailed terms as shall be agreed to by the Reparation Commission.

If, nevertheless, Germany after a period of one year from the date on which payment becomes due shall not have effected the said payment, the Reparation Commission shall do so in accordance with such instructions as may be given by the League of Nations, and, if necessary, by liquidating that part of the mines which is in question.

37. If, in consequence of the repurchase provided for in paragraph 36, the ownership of the mines or any part of them is transferred to Germany, the French State and French nationals shall have the right to purchase such amount of coal of the Saar Basin as their industrial and domestic needs are found at that time to require. An equitable arrangement regarding amounts of coal, duration of contract, and prices will be fixed in due time by the Council of the League of Nations. . . .

Section XI: Danzig

Article 100. Germany renounces in favour of the Principal Allied and Associated Powers all rights and title over the territory [of Danzig, the boundaries of which are defined in the rest of the article]. . . .

Article 102. The Principal Allied and Associated Powers undertake to establish the town of Danzig, together with the rest of the territory described in Article 100, as a Free City. It will be placed under the protection of the League of Nations. . . .

Article 104. The Principal Allied and Associated Powers undertake to negotiate a Treaty between the Polish Government and the Free City of Danzig, which shall come into force at the same time as the establishment of the said Free City, with the following objects:

(1) To effect the inclusion of the Free City of Danzig within the Polish Customs frontiers, and to establish a free area in the port;

(2) To ensure to Poland without any restriction the free use and service of all waterways, docks, basins, wharves and other works within the territory of the Free City necessary for Polish imports and exports;

(3) To ensure to Poland the control and administration of the Vistula and of the whole railway system within the Free City, except such street and other railways as serve primarily the needs of the Free City, and of postal, telegraphic and telephonic communication between Poland and the port of Danzig;

(4) To ensure to Poland the right to develop and improve the waterways, docks, basins, wharves, railways and other works and

means of communication mentioned in this Article, as well as to lease or purchase through appropriate processes such land and other property as may be necessary for these purposes. . . .

ARTICLE 108. All property situated within the territory of the Free City of Danzig belonging to the German Empire or to any German State shall pass to the Principal Allied and Associated Powers for transfer to the Free City of Danzig or to the Polish State as they may consider equitable. . . .

Part IV: German Rights and Interests Outside Germany

SECTION I: GERMAN COLONIES

ARTICLE 119. Germany renounces in favour of the Principal Allied and Associated Powers all her rights and titles over her oversea possessions.

ARTICLE 120. All movable and immovable property in such territories belonging to the German Empire or to any German State shall pass to the Government exercising authority over such territories. . . .

Part VIII: Reparation

SECTION I: GENERAL PROVISIONS

ARTICLE 231. The Allied and Associated Governments affirm and Germany accepts the responsibility of Germany and her allies for causing all the loss and damage to which the Allied and Associated Governments and their nationals have been subjected as a consequence of the war imposed upon them by the aggression of Germany and her allies.

ARTICLE 232. The Allied and Associated Governments recognize that the resources of Germany are not adequate, after taking into account permanent diminutions of such resources which will result from other provisions of the present Treaty, to make complete reparation for all such loss and damage.

The Allied and Associated Governments, however, require, and Germany undertakes, that she will make compensation for all damage done to the civilian population of the Allied and Associated Powers and to their property during the period of the belligerency of each as an Allied or Associated Power against Germany by such aggression by land, by sea and from the air, and in general all damage as defined in Annex I hereto.

In accordance with Germany's pledges, already given, as to

complete restoration for Belgium, Germany undertakes, in addition to the compensation for damage elsewhere in this Part provided for, as a consequence of the violation of the Treaty of 1839, to make reimbursement of all sums which Belgium has borrowed from the Allied and Associated Governments up to November 11, 1918, together with interest at the rate of five per cent (5%) per annum on such sums. This amount shall be determined by the Reparation Commission, and the German Government undertakes thereupon forthwith to make a special issue of bearer bonds to an equivalent amount payable in marks gold, on May 1, 1926, or, at the option of the German Government, on May 1 in any year up to 1926. Subject to the foregoing, the form of such bonds shall be determined by the Reparation Commission. Such bonds shall be handed over to the Reparation Commission, which has authority to take and acknowledge receipt thereof on behalf of Belgium.

ARTICLE 233. The amount of the above damage for which compensation is to be made by Germany shall be determined by an Inter-Allied Commission, to be called the *Reparation Commission* and constituted in the form and with the powers set forth hereunder and in Annexes II to VII inclusive hereto.

This Commission shall consider the claims and give to the German Government a just opportunity to be heard.

The findings of the Commission as to the amount of damage defined as above shall be concluded and notified to the German Government on or before May 1, 1921, as representing the extent of that Government's obligations.

The Commission shall concurrently draw up a schedule of payments prescribing the time and manner for securing and discharging the entire obligation within a period of thirty years from May 1, 1921. If, however, within the period mentioned, Germany fails to discharge her obligations, any balance remaining unpaid may, within the discretion of the Commission, be postponed for settlement in subsequent years, or may be handled otherwise in such manner as the Allied and Associated Governments, acting in accordance with the procedure laid down in this Part of the present Treaty, shall determine.

ARTICLE 234. The Reparation Commission shall after May 1, 1921, from time to time, consider the resources and capacity of Germany, and, after giving her representatives a just opportunity to be heard, shall have discretion to extend the date, and to modify the form of payments, such as are to be provided for in accordance with Article 233; but not to cancel any part, except with the specific authority of the several Governments represented upon the Commission.

ARTICLE 235. In order to enable the Allied and Associated Powers to proceed at once to the restoration of their industrial and economic life, pending the full determination of their claims, Germany shall pay in such instalments and in such manner (whether in gold, commodities, ships, securities or otherwise) as the Reparation Commission may fix, during 1919, 1920 and the first four months of 1921, the equivalent of 20,000,000,000 gold marks.[1] Out of this sum the expenses of the armies of occupation subsequent to the Armistice of November 11, 1918, shall first be met, and such supplies of food and raw materials as may be judged by the Governments of the Principal Allied and Associated Powers to be essential to enable Germany to meet her obligations for reparation may also, with the approval of the said Governments, be paid for out of the above sum. The balance shall be reckoned towards liquidation of the amounts due for reparation. Germany shall further deposit bonds as prescribed in paragraph 12 (c) of Annex II hereto.

ARTICLE 236. Germany further agrees to the direct application of her economic resources to reparation as specified in Annexes III, IV, V and VI, relating respectively to merchant shipping, to physical restoration, to coal and derivatives of coal, and to dyestuffs and other chemical products; provided always that the value of the property transferred and any services rendered by her under these Annexes, assessed in the manner therein prescribed, shall be credited to her towards liquidation of her obligations under the above Articles.

ARTICLE 237. The successive instalments, including the above sum, paid over by Germany in satisfaction of the above claims will be divided by the Allied and Associated Governments in proportions which have been determined upon by them in advance on a basis of general equity and of the rights of each.

For the purposes of this division the value of property transferred and services rendered under Article 243, and under Annexes III, IV, V, VI and VII, shall be reckoned in the same manner as cash payments effected in that year.

ARTICLE 238. In addition to the payments mentioned above Germany shall effect, in accordance with the procedure laid down by

[1] The gold mark, the prewar currency of Germany, had a dollar value at prewar exchange rates of roughly 25 cents.—Eds.

the Reparation Commission, restitution in cash of cash taken away, seized or sequestrated, and also restitution of animals, objects of every nature and securities taken away, seized or sequestrated, in the cases in which it proves possible to identify them in territory belonging to Germany or her allies.

Until this procedure is laid down, restitution will continue in accordance with the provisions of the Armistice of November 11, 1918, and its renewals and the Protocols thereto.

ARTICLE 239. The German Government undertakes to make forthwith the restitution contemplated by Article 238 and to make the payments and deliveries contemplated by Articles 233, 234, 235 and 236.

ARTICLE 240. The German Government recognizes the Commission provided for by Article 233 as the same may be constituted by the Allied and Associated Governments in accordance with Annex II, and agrees irrevocably to the possession and exercise by such Commission of the power and authority given to it under the present Treaty.

The German Government will supply to the Commission all the information which the Commission may require relative to the financial situation and operations and to the property, productive capacity, and stocks and current production of raw materials and manufactured articles of Germany and her nationals, and further any information relative to military operations which in the judgment of the Commission may be necessary for the assessment of Germany's liability for reparation as defined in Annex I.

The German Government will accord to the members of the Commission and its authorised agents the same rights and immunities as are enjoyed in Germany by duly accredited diplomatic agents of friendly Powers.

Germany further agrees to provide for the salaries and expenses of the Commission and of such staff as it may employ.

ARTICLE 241. Germany undertakes to pass, issue and maintain in force any legislation, orders and decrees that may be necessary to give complete effect to these provisions.

ARTICLE 242. The provisions of this Part of the present Treaty do not apply to the property, rights and interests referred to in Sections III [Debts] and IV [Property, Rights and Interests] of Part X (Economic Clauses) of the present Treaty, nor to the product of their liquidation, except so far as concerns any final balance in favour of Germany under Article 243 (a).

ARTICLE 243. The following shall be reckoned as credits to Germany in respect of her reparation obligations:

(a) Any final balance in favour of Germany under Section V (Alsace-Lorraine) of Part III (Political Clauses for Europe) and Sections III and IV of Part X (Economic Clauses) of the present Treaty;

(b) Amounts due to Germany in respect of transfers under Section IV (Saar Basin) of Part III (Political Clauses for Europe), Part IX (Financial Clauses), and Part XII (Ports, Waterways and Railways);

(c) Amounts which in the judgment of the Reparation Commission should be credited to Germany on account of any other transfers under the present Treaty of property, rights, concessions or other interests.

In no case however shall credit be given for property restored in accordance with Article 238 of the present Part.

ARTICLE 244. The transfer of the German submarine cables which do not form the subject of particular provisions of the present Treaty is regulated by Annex VII hereto. [Annex VII has been omitted. It specifies some dozen cables which Germany was to renounce in favor of the Allied and Associated Powers, the original cost minus depreciation being credited to Germany in the reparation account.]

ANNEX I

Compensation may be claimed from Germany under Article 232 above in respect of the total damage under the following categories:

(1) Damage to injured persons and to surviving dependents by personal injury to or death of civilians caused by acts of war, including bombardments or other attacks on land, on sea, or from the air, and all the direct consequences thereof, and of all operations of war by the two groups of belligerents wherever arising.

(2) Damage caused by Germany or her allies to civilian victims of acts of cruelty, violence or maltreatment (including injuries to life or health) as a consequence of imprisonment, deportation, internment or evacuation, of exposure at sea or of being forced to labour, wherever arising, and to the surviving dependents of such victims.

(3) Damage caused by Germany or her allies in their own territory or in occupied or invaded territory to civilian victims of

all acts injurious to health or capacity to work, or to honour, as well as to the surviving dependents of such victims.

(4) Damage caused by any kind of maltreatment of prisoners of war.

(5) As damage caused to the peoples of the Allied and Associated Powers, all pensions and compensation in the nature of pensions to naval and military victims of war (including members of the air force), whether mutilated, wounded, sick or invalided, and to the dependents of such victims, the amount due to the Allied and Associated Governments being calculated for each of them as being the capitalised cost of such pensions and compensation at the date of the coming into force of the present Treaty, on the basis of the scales in force in France at such date.

(6) The cost of assistance by the Governments of the Allied and Associated Powers to prisoners of war and to their families and dependents.

(7) Allowances by the Governments of the Allied and Associated Powers to the families and dependents of mobilised persons or persons serving with the forces, the amount due to them for each calendar year in which hostilities occurred being calculated for each Government on the basis of the average scale for such payments in force in France during that year.

(8) Damage caused to civilians by being forced by Germany or her allies to labour without just remuneration.

(9) Damage in respect of all property wherever situated belonging to any of the Allied or Associated States or their nationals, with the exception of naval and military works or materials, which has been carried off, seized, injured or destroyed by the acts of Germany or her allies on land, on sea or from the air, or damage directly in consequence of hostilities or of any operations of war.

(10) Damage in the form of levies, fines and other similar exactions imposed by Germany or her allies upon the civilian population.

ANNEX II

1. The Commission referred to in Article 233 shall be called "The Reparation Commission" and is hereinafter referred to as "the Commission."

2. Delegates to this Commission shall be nominated by the United States of America, Great Britain, France, Italy, Japan, Belgium and the Serb-Croat-Slovene State. . . .

12. The Commission shall have all the powers conferred upon it, and shall exercise all the functions assigned to it, by the present Treaty.

The Commission shall in general have wide latitude as to its control and handling of the whole reparation problem as dealt with in this Part of the present Treaty and shall have authority to interpret its provisions. Subject to the provisions of the present Treaty, the Commission is constituted by the several Allied and Associated Governments referred to . . . above as the exclusive agency of the said Governments respectively for receiving, selling, holding, and distributing the reparation payments to be made by Germany under this Part of the present Treaty. The Commission must comply with the following conditions and provisions:

(*a*) Whatever part of the full amount of the proved claims is not paid in gold, or in ships, securities and commodities or otherwise, Germany shall be required, under such conditions as the Commission may determine, to cover by way of guarantee by an equivalent issue of bonds, obligations or otherwise, in order to constitute an acknowledgment of the said part of the debt.

(*b*) In periodically estimating Germany's capacity to pay, the Commission shall examine the German system of taxation, first, to the end that the sums for reparation which Germany is required to pay shall become a charge upon all her revenues prior to that for the service or discharge of any domestic loan, and secondly, so as to satisfy itself that, in general, the German scheme of taxation is fully as heavy proportionately as that of any of the Powers represented on the Commission.

(*c*) In order to facilitate and continue the immediate restoration of the economic life of the Allied and Associated countries, the Commission will as provided in Article 235 take from Germany by way of security for and acknowledgment of her debt a first instalment of gold bearer bonds free of all taxes and charges of every description established or to be established by the Government of the German Empire or of the German States, or by any authority subject to them; these bonds will be delivered on account and in three portions, the marks gold being payable . . . as follows:

(1) To be issued forthwith, 20,000,000,000 Marks gold bearer bonds, payable not later than May 1, 1921, without interest. There shall be specially applied towards the amortisation of these bonds the payments which Germany is pledged to make in conformity with Article 235, after deduction of the sums used for the re-

imbursement of expenses of the armies of occupation and for payment of foodstuffs and raw materials. Such bonds as have not been redeemed by May 1, 1921, shall then be exchanged for new bonds of the same type as those provided for below (paragraph 12, c, 2).

(2) To be issued forthwith, further 40,000,000,000 Marks gold bearer bonds, bearing interest at 2½ per cent per annum between 1921 and 1926, and thereafter at 5 per cent per annum with an additional 1 per cent for amortisation beginning in 1926 on the whole amount of the issue.

(3) To be delivered forthwith a covering undertaking in writing to issue when, but not until, the Commission is satisfied that Germany can meet such interest and sinking fund obligations, a further instalment of 40,000,000,000 Marks gold 5 per cent bearer bonds, the time and mode of payment of principal and interest to be determined by the Commission.

The dates for payment of interest, the manner of applying the amortisation fund, and all other questions relating to the issue, management and regulation of the bond issue shall be determined by the Commission from time to time. . . .

(e) The damage for repairing, reconstructing and rebuilding property in the invaded and devastated districts, including re-installation of furniture, machinery and other equipment, will be calculated according to the cost at the dates when the work is done. . . .

16. Interest shall be debited to Germany as from May 1, 1921, in respect of her debt as determined by the Commission, after allowing for sums already covered by cash payments or their equivalent, or by bonds issued to the Commission, or under Article 243. The rate of interest shall be 5 per cent, unless the Commission shall determine at some future time that circumstances justify a variation of this rate.

The Commission, in fixing on May 1, 1921, the total amount of the debt of Germany, may take account of interest due on sums arising out of the reparation of material damage as from November 11, 1918, up to May 1, 1921.

17. In case of default by Germany in the performance of any obligation under this Part of the present Treaty, the Commission will forthwith give notice of such default to each of the interested Powers and may make such recommendations as to the action to be taken in consequence of such default as it may think necessary.

18. The measures which the Allied and Associated Powers shall have the right to take, in case of voluntary default by Germany, and which Germany agrees not to regard as acts of war, may include economic and financial prohibitions and reprisals and in general such other measures as the respective Governments may determine to be necessary in the circumstances. . . .

Annex III

1. Germany recognises the right of the Allied and Associated Powers to the replacement, ton for ton (gross tonnage) and class for class, of all merchant ships and fishing boats lost or damaged owing to the war.

Nevertheless, and in spite of the fact that the tonnage of German shipping at present in existence is much less than that lost by the Allied and Associated Powers in consequence of the German aggression, the right thus recognised will be enforced on German ships and boats under the following conditions:

The German Government, on behalf of themselves and so as to bind all other persons interested, cede to the Allied and Associated Governments the property in all the German merchant ships which are of 1,600 tons gross and upwards; in one-half, reckoned in tonnage, of the ships which are between 1,000 tons and 1,600 tons gross; in one-quarter, reckoned in tonnage, of the steam trawlers; and in one-quarter, reckoned in tonnage, of the other fishing boats.

2. The German Government will, within two months of the coming into force of the present Treaty, deliver to the Reparation Commission all the ships and boats mentioned in paragraph 1.

3. The ships and boats mentioned in paragraph 1 include all ships and boats which (a) fly, or may be entitled to fly, the German merchant flag; or (b) are owned by any German national, company or corporation or by any company or corporation belonging to a country other than an Allied or Associated country and under the control or direction of German nationals; or (c) are now under construction (1) in Germany, (2) in other than Allied or Associated countries for the account of any German national, company or corporation. . . .

5. As an additional part of reparation, Germany agrees to cause merchant ships to be built in German yards for the account of the Allied and Associated Governments as follows:

(a) Within three months of the coming into force of the

present Treaty, the Reparation Commission will notify to the German Government the amount of tonnage to be laid down in German shipyards in each of the two years next succeeding the three months mentioned above.

(b) Within two years of the coming into force of the present Treaty, the Reparation Commission will notify to the German Government the amount of tonnage to be laid down in each of the three years following the two years mentioned above.

(c) The amount of tonnage to be laid down in each year shall not exceed 200,000 tons, gross tonnage.

(d) The specifications of the ships to be built, the conditions under which they are to be built and delivered, the price per ton at which they are to be accounted for by the Reparation Commission, and all other questions relating to the accounting, ordering, building and delivery of the ships, shall be determined by the Commission. . . .

8. Germany waives all claims of any description against the Allied and Associated Governments and their nationals in respect of the detention, employment, loss or damage of any German ships or boats. . . .

Annex IV

1. The Allied and Associated Powers require, and Germany undertakes, that in part satisfaction of her obligations expressed in the present Part she will, as hereinafter provided, devote her economic resources directly to the physical restoration of the invaded areas of the Allied and Associated Powers, to the extent that these Powers may determine.

2. The Allied and Associated Governments may file with the Reparation Commission lists showing:

(a) Animals, machinery, equipment, tools and like articles of a commercial character, which have been seized, consumed or destroyed by Germany or destroyed in direct consequence of military operations, and which such Governments, for the purpose of meeting immediate and urgent needs, desire to have replaced by animals and articles of the same nature which are in being in German territory at the date of the coming into force of the present Treaty;

(b) Reconstruction materials (stones, bricks, refractory bricks, tiles, wood, window-glass, steel, lime, cement, etc.), machinery, heating apparatus, furniture and like articles of a commercial character which the said Governments desire to have produced and manufactured in Germany and delivered to them to permit of the restoration of the invaded areas. . . .

5. The Commission shall determine the value to be attributed to the materials, articles and animals to be delivered in accordance with the foregoing, and the Allied or Associated Power receiving the same agrees to be charged with such value, and the amount thereof shall be treated as a payment by Germany to be divided in accordance with Article 237 of this Part of the present Treaty.

In cases where the right to require physical restoration as above provided is exercised, the Commission shall ensure that the amount to be credited against the reparation obligation of Germany shall be the fair value of work done or materials supplied by Germany, and that the claim made by the interested Power in respect of the damage so repaired by physical restoration shall be discharged to the extent of the proportion which the damage thus repaired bears to the whole of the damage thus claimed for.

6. As an immediate advance on account of the animals referred to in Paragraph 2 (a) above, Germany undertakes to deliver in equal monthly instalments in the three months following the coming into force of the present Treaty, the following quantities of live stock:

(1) *To the French Government:* 500 stallions (3 to 7 years); 30,000 fillies and mares (18 months to 7 years), type: Ardennais, Boulonnais or Belgian; 2,000 bulls (18 months to 3 years); 90,000 milch cows (2 to 6 years); 1,000 rams; 100,000 sheep; 10,000 goats.

(2) *To the Belgian Government:* 200 stallions (3 to 7 years), large Belgian type; 5,000 mares (3 to 7 years), large Belgian type; 5,000 fillies (18 months to 3 years), large Belgian type; 2,000 bulls (18 months to 3 years); 50,000 milch cows (2 to 6 years); 40,000 heifers; 200 rams; 20,000 sheep; 15,000 sows.

The animals delivered shall be of average health and condition.

To the extent that animals so delivered cannot be identified as animals taken away or seized, the value of such animals shall be credited against the reparation obligations of Germany in accordance with paragraph 5 of this Annex. . . .

Annex V

1. Germany accords the following options for the delivery of coal and derivatives of coal to the undermentioned signatories of the present Treaty.

2. Germany undertakes to deliver to France seven million tons of coal per year for ten years. In addition, Germany undertakes to deliver to France annually for a period not exceeding ten years an amount of coal equal to the difference between the annual production before the war of the coal mines of the Nord and Pas de Calais, destroyed as a result of the war, and the production of the mines of the same area during the years in question: such delivery not to exceed twenty million tons in any one year of the first five years, and eight million tons in any one year of the succeeding five years.

It is understood that due diligence will be exercised in the restoration of the destroyed mines in the Nord and the Pas de Calais.

3. Germany undertakes to deliver to Belgium eight million tons of coal annually for ten years.

4. Germany undertakes to deliver to Italy up to the following quantities of coal: July 1919 to June 1920, 4½ million tons; July 1920 to June 1921, 6 million tons; July 1921 to June 1922, 7½ million tons; July 1922 to June 1923, 8 million tons; July 1923 to June 1924, and in each of the following five years, 8½ million tons. . . .

Annex VI

1. Germany accords to the Reparation Commission an option to require as part of reparation the delivery by Germany of such quantities and kinds of dyestuffs and chemical drugs as the Commission may designate, not exceeding 50 per cent of the total stock of each and every kind of dyestuff and chemical drug in Germany or under German control at the date of the coming into force of the present Treaty.

This option shall be exercised within sixty days of the receipt by the Commission of such particulars as to stocks as may be considered necessary by the Commission.

2. Germany further accords to the Reparation Commission an option to require delivery during the period from the date of the coming into force of the present Treaty until January 1, 1920, and during each period of six months thereafter until January 1, 1925, of any specified kind of dyestuff and chemical drug up to an amount not exceeding 25 per cent of the German production of such dyestuffs and chemical drugs during the previous six months period. If in any case the production during such previous six months was, in the opinion of the Commission, less than normal,

the amount required may be 25 per cent of the normal production. . . .

Part IX: Financial Clauses

ARTICLE 248. Subject to such exceptions as the Reparation Commission may approve, a first charge upon all the assets and revenues of the German Empire and its constituent States shall be the cost of reparation and all other costs arising under the present Treaty or any treaties or agreements supplementary thereto or under arrangements concluded between Germany and the Allied and Associated Powers during the Armistice or its extensions.

Up to May 1, 1921, the German Government shall not export or dispose of, and shall forbid the export or disposal of, gold without the previous approval of the Allied and Associated Powers acting through the Reparation Commission.

ARTICLE 249. There shall be paid by the German Government the total cost of all armies of the Allied and Associated Governments in occupied German territory from the date of the signature of the Armistice of November 11, 1918, including the keep of men and beasts, lodging and billeting, pay and allowances, salaries and wages, bedding, heating, lighting, clothing, equipment, harness and saddlery, armament and rolling-stock, air services, treatment of sick and wounded, veterinary and remount services, transport service of all sorts (such as by rail, sea or river, motor lorries), communications and correspondence, and in general the cost of all administrative or technical services the working of which is necessary for the training of troops and for keeping their numbers up to strength and preserving their military efficiency.

The cost of such liabilities under the above heads so far as they relate to purchases or requisitions by the Allied and Associated Governments in the occupied territories shall be paid by the German Government to the Allied and Associated Governments in marks at the current or agreed rate of exchange. All other of the above costs shall be paid in gold marks.

ARTICLE 250. Germany confirms the surrender of all material handed over to the Allied and Associated Powers in accordance with the Armistice of November 11, 1918, and subsequent Armistice Agreements, and recognises the title of the Allied and Associated Powers to such material. . . .

ARTICLE 251. The priority of the charges established by Article 248 shall, subject to the qualifications made below, be as follows:

(*a*) The cost of the armies of occupation as defined under Article 249 during the Armistice and its extensions;

(*b*) The cost of any armies of occupation as defined under Article 249 after the coming into force of the present Treaty;

(*c*) The cost of reparation arising out of the present Treaty or any treaties or conventions supplementary thereto;

(*d*) The cost of all other obligations incumbent on Germany under the Armistice Conventions or under this Treaty or any treaties or conventions supplementary thereto.

The payment for such supplies of food and raw material for Germany and such other payments as may be judged by the Allied and Associated Powers to be essential to enable Germany to meet her obligations in respect of reparation will have priority to the extent and upon the conditions which have been or may be determined by the Governments of the said Powers. . . .

ARTICLE 254. The Powers to which German territory is ceded shall, subject to the qualifications made in Article 255, undertake to pay:

(i) A portion of the debt of the German Empire as it stood on August 1, 1914, calculated on the basis of the ratio between the average for the three financial years 1911, 1912, 1913, of such revenues of the ceded territory, and the average for the same years of such revenues of the whole German Empire as in the judgment of the Reparation Commission are best calculated to represent the relative ability of the respective territories to make payment;

(ii) A portion of the debt as it stood on August 1, 1914, of the German State to which the ceded territory belonged, to be determined in accordance with the principle stated above.

Such portions shall be determined by the Reparation Commission. . . .

ARTICLE 255. (1) As an exception to the above provision and inasmuch as in 1871 Germany refused to undertake any portion of the burden of the French debt, France shall be, in respect of Alsace-Lorraine, exempt from any payment under Article 254.

(2) In the case of Poland that portion of the debt which, in the opinion of the Reparation Commission, is attributable to the measures taken by the German and Prussian Governments for the German colonisation of Poland shall be excluded from the apportionment to be made under Article 254. . . .

ARTICLE 256. Powers to which German territory is ceded shall acquire all property and possessions situated therein belonging to the German Empire or to the German States, and the value of such acquisitions shall be fixed by the Reparation Commission, and paid by the State acquiring the territory to the Reparation Commission for the credit of the German Government on account of the sums due for reparation. . . .

ARTICLE 258. Germany renounces all rights accorded to her or her nationals by treaties, conventions or agreements, of whatsoever kind, to representation upon or participation in the control or administration of commissions, state banks, agencies or other financial or economic organisations of an international character, exercising powers of control or administration, and operating in any of the Allied or Associated States, or in Austria, Hungary, Bulgaria or Turkey, or in the dependencies of these States, or in the former Russian Empire. . . .

Part X: Economic Clauses

SECTION I: COMMERCIAL RELATIONS

ARTICLE 264. Germany undertakes that goods the produce or manufacture of any one of the Allied or Associated States imported into German territory, from whatsoever place arriving, shall not be subjected to other or higher duties or charges (including internal charges) than those to which the like goods the produce or manufacture of any other such State or of any other foreign country are subject.

Germany will not maintain or impose any prohibition or restriction on the importation into German territory of any goods the produce or manufacture of the territories of any one of the Allied or Associated States, from whatsoever place arriving, which shall not equally extend to the importation of the like goods the produce or manufacture of any other such State or of any other foreign country.

ARTICLE 265. Germany further undertakes that, in the matter of the régime applicable on importation, no discrimination against the commerce of any of the Allied and Associated States as compared with any other of the said States or any other foreign country shall be made, even by indirect means, such as customs regulations or procedure, methods of verification or analysis, conditions of payment of duties, tariff classification or interpretation, or the operation of monopolies.

ARTICLE 266. In all that concerns exportation Germany undertakes that goods, natural products or manufactured articles, exported from German territory to the territories of any one of the Allied or Associated States, shall not be subjected to other or higher duties or charges (including internal charges) than those paid on the like goods exported to any other such State or to any other foreign country.

Germany will not maintain or impose any prohibition or restriction on the exportation of any goods sent from her territory to any one of the Allied or Associated States which shall not equally extend to the exportation of the like goods, natural products or manufactured articles, sent to any other such State or to any other foreign country.

ARTICLE 267. Every favour, immunity or privilege in regard to the importation, exportation or transit of goods granted by Germany to any Allied or Associated State or to any other foreign country whatever shall simultaneously and unconditionally, without request and without compensation, be extended to all the Allied and Associated States.

ARTICLE 268. The provisions of Articles 264 to 267 inclusive . . . are subject to the following exceptions:

(a) For a period of five years from the coming into force of the present Treaty, natural or manufactured products which both originate in and come from the territories of Alsace and Lorraine reunited to France shall, on importation into German customs territory, be exempt from all customs duty. . . .

(b) During a period of three years from the coming into force of the present Treaty natural or manufactured products which both originate in and come from Polish territories which before the war were part of Germany shall, on importation into German customs territory, be exempt from all customs duty. . . .

SECTION IV: PROPERTY, RIGHTS AND INTERESTS

ARTICLE 297. The question of private property, rights and interests in an enemy country shall be settled according to the principles laid down in this Section and to the provisions of the Annex hereto.

(a) The exceptional war measures and measures of transfer . . . taken by Germany with respect to the property, rights and interests of nationals of Allied or Associated Powers, including companies and associations in which they are interested, when liquidation has not been completed, shall be immediately discontinued or stayed and the property, rights and interests concerned restored to their owners, who shall enjoy full rights therein. . . .

(*b*) Subject to any contrary stipulations which may be provided for in the present Treaty, the Allied and Associated Powers reserve the right to retain and liquidate all property, rights and interests belonging at the date of the coming into force of the present Treaty to German nationals, or companies controlled by them, within their territories, colonies, possessions and protectorates, including territories ceded to them by the present Treaty. . . .

(*c*) The price or the amount of compensation in respect of the exercise of the right referred to in the preceding paragraph (*b*) will be fixed in accordance with the methods of sale or valuation adopted by the laws of the country in which the property has been retained or liquidated. . . .

(*e*) The nationals of Allied and Associated Powers shall be entitled to compensation in respect of damage or injury inflicted upon their property, rights or interests, including any company or association in which they are interested, in German territory as it existed on August 1, 1914, by the application either of the exceptional war measures or measures of transfer. . . .

9. German Reaction to the Economic Demands of the Treaty

The German delegation that was called to Paris on April 25 to "receive" the Treaty was aghast at many of the demands it contained, especially the economic demands. At the beginning of May an economic commission of the German delegation set forth its view of the broad economic impact the Treaty would have upon German life. The declaration was transmitted to the Allies on May 13, 1919, in a note from the head of the German delegation, the Foreign Minister, Count Ulrich von Brockdorff-Rantzau, to Clemenceau, President of the Conference.

German Declaration on the Economic Provisions of the Treaty, May, 1919

IN THE course of the last two generations, Germany has changed from an agricultural to an industrial state. As an agricultural state, Germany could support 40 million inhabitants. As an industrial state, she could assure the maintenance of a population of 67 million. In 1913, the importation of food amounted in round numbers to 12 million tons. Before the war, about 15 million persons in Germany owed their existence to foreign trade and to shipping—either directly or indirectly through the consumption of foreign raw materials.

In accordance with the provisions of the Treaty of Peace, Germany is to surrender its serviceable merchant tonnage and that under construction, in so far as these are designed for commerce overseas. In the same way, the shipyards are to construct as their first work for a period of five years tonnage for the Allied and Associated Governments. Besides this, Germany gives up her colonies; all her overseas possessions, all her interests and titles in the Allied and Associated countries and in their colonies, dominions and protectorates will be, as a partial payment on the reparation account, subjected to liquidation and will be exposed to all other

Source: The full note appears in Philip Mason Burnett, ed., *Reparation at the Paris Peace Conference From the Standpoint of the American Delegation*, Vol. II (New York: Columbia University Press, 1940), pp. 7–9. Used by permission.

measures of economic war the Allied and Associated Powers may decide to maintain or to introduce during the years of peace.

With the execution of the territorial clauses of the Treaty of Peace, the regions in the east most important for the production of grain and potatoes would be lost; that would be equivalent to a falling-off of 21 per cent of the total yield of these foodstuffs. Moreover, the intensity of our agricultural production will be considerably decreased. If, on the one hand, the importation of certain raw materials for the German fertilizer industry, such as phosphates, would be made more difficult, so, on the other, this industry would suffer, like every other, from the scarcity of coal, since the Treaty provides for the loss of almost one-third of our coal production; besides this decrease, Germany is burdened for the first ten years with enormous deliveries of coal to various Allied countries. What is more, in accordance with the Treaty, Germany is to cede to its neighbors nearly three-quarters of its production of iron ore and more than three-fifths of its production of zinc.

After this deprivation of specific products, after the economic crippling caused by the loss of her colonies, of her merchant fleet and of her foreign possessions, Germany would not be any longer in a condition to import from abroad sufficient raw material. German industry would then have to die out on a large scale. At the same time, the need of importing food would increase considerably, while the possibility of satisfying that need would diminish extraordinarily.

At the end of a very short time, Germany would then no longer be in a condition to give bread and work to the many millions of persons dependent for their living upon shipping and upon commerce. These people would then have to leave the country; but that is technically impossible, all the more since many of the most important countries of the world are opposed to a German immigration. Besides, hundreds of thousands of Germans expelled from the territories of the Powers at war with Germany as well as from the territories that Germany is to cede, will stream back again into the remaining German territory.

If the Conditions of Peace are put into force, it simply means that many millions in Germany will perish. This process would develop quickly since the health of the population has been broken during the war by the blockade and during the armistice by its increased severity.

No aid, important and of long duration as it might be, could bring a halt to this wholesale death. The peace would demand of Germany a greater human sacrifice than the war devoured in four years and a half (1¾ million fallen in the field, almost 1 million as victims of the blockade).

We do not know—and we doubt—whether the Delegates of the Allied and Associated Powers realize the consequences that would be inevitable if Germany, an industrial state with a dense population, tied to a world economy and dependent upon an enormous importation of raw materials and foodstuffs, finds itself all at once pushed back into a phase of its development that would correspond to her economic position and population of half a century ago. Those who sign the Treaty will pass a sentence of death upon many millions of German men, women and children.

10. The Reparation Bill

The Treaty of Versailles required Germany to make immediate payments of 20 billion gold marks ($5 billion), the rest of the reparation debt to be calculated by the Reparation Commission and announced in 1921. In working out the total debt, the sum initially suggested by the Allies was nearly eight times that proposed by Germany, and there was disagreement on the valuation of deliveries in kind already made. At the beginning of May, 1921, the Reparation Commission presented the final bill in an ultimatum to Germany, setting the sum at 132 billion gold marks ($33 billion) plus interest, and establishing a complicated schedule of payments extending over an undefined period. Because of the uncertainty of how the Commission would value nonmonetary deliveries, and because the sum of 132 billion gold marks was to bear interest, the final bill did not establish definitively the total burden on Germany.

Schedule of Reparation Payments, May, 1921

THE REPARATION COMMISSION has, in accordance with Article 232 of the Treaty of Versailles, to define the time and manner for securing and discharging the entire obligation of Germany for reparation under Articles 231, 232 and 233 of the Treaty, as follows:

This determination is without prejudice to the duty of Germany to make restitution under Article 238 or to other obligations under the Treaty.

1. Germany will perform in the manner laid down in this schedule her obligation to pay the total fixed in accordance with Articles 231, 232 and 233 of the Treaty of Versailles by the Commission, viz., 132,000,000,000 gold marks less (a) the amount already paid on account of reparation; (b) sums which may from time to time be credited to Germany in respect of State properties in ceded territory, etc.; and (c) any sums received from other enemy or ex-enemy Powers in respect of which the Commission may decide that credit should be given to Germany, plus the amount of the Belgian

Source: *International Conciliation*, Series 11, No. 184 (March, 1923), pp. 194–201, with deletions. Used by permission of the Carnegie Endowment for International Peace.

debt to the Allies, the amounts of these deductions and additions to be determined later by the Commission.

2. Germany shall create and deliver to the Commission in substitution for bonds already delivered or delivered under paragraph 12(c) of Annex II, Part VIII, Treaty of Versailles, bonds hereafter described:

(A) Bonds for the amount of 12,000,000,000 gold marks. These bonds shall be created and delivered at the latest on July 1, 1921. There shall be an annual payment from funds to be provided by Germany as prescribed in this schedule in each year from May 1, 1921, equal in amount to 6 per cent of the nominal value of the issued bonds, out of which there shall be paid interest at 5 per cent per annum, payable half-yearly on the bonds outstanding at any time, and the balance to a sinking fund for redemption of bonds by annual drawings at par. These bonds are hereinafter referred to as bonds of Series "A."

(B) Bonds for a further amount of 38,000,000,000 gold marks. These bonds shall be created and delivered at the latest on November 1, 1921. There shall be an annual payment from funds to be provided by Germany as prescribed in this schedule in each year from November 1, 1921, equal in amount to 6 per cent of the nominal value of the issued bonds, out of which there shall be paid interest at 5 per cent per annum, payable half-yearly, on the bonds outstanding at any time and the balance to a sinking fund for the redemption of the bonds by annual drawings at par. These bonds are hereinafter referred to as bonds of Series "B."

(C) Bonds for 82,000,000,000 gold marks, subject to such subsequent adjustment by creation or cancellation of bonds as may be required under the first paragraph. These bonds shall be created and delivered to the Reparation Commission, without coupons attached, at the latest on November 1, 1921. They shall be issued by the Commission as and when it is satisfied that the payments which Germany is required to make in pursuance of this schedule are sufficient to provide for the payment of interest and sinking fund on such bonds. There shall be an annual payment from funds to be provided by Germany as prescribed in this schedule in each year from the date of issue by the Reparation Commission equal in amount to 6 per cent of the nominal value of the issued bonds, out of which shall be paid interest at 5 per cent per annum, payable half-yearly, on the bonds outstanding at any time, and the balance to a sinking fund for redemption of the bonds by annual drawings at par. The German Government shall supply to the Commission coupon sheets for such bonds as and when issued by the Commission. These bonds are hereinafter referred to as bonds of Series "C."

3. The bonds provided for in Article 2 shall be signed by the German Government as bearer bonds, in such form and in such denominations as the Commission shall prescribe for the purpose of making them marketable and shall be free of all German taxes and charges of every description, present or future.

Subject to the provisions of Articles 248 and 251, Treaty of Versailles, these bonds shall be secured on the whole assets and revenues of the German Empire and the German States, and in particular on the assets and revenues specified in Article 7 of this schedule. The service of bonds "A," "B," and "C" shall be a first, second and third charge, respectively, on said assets and revenues, and shall be met by payments to be made by Germany under this schedule.

4. Germany shall pay in each year until the redemption of bonds provided for in Article 2 by means of a sinking fund attached thereto:

(1) The sum of 2,000,000,000 gold marks;

(2) (a) A sum equivalent to 25 per cent of the value of her exports in each period of twelve months, starting from May 1, 1921, as determined by the Commission, or

(b) alternately an equivalent amount as fixed in accordance with any other index proposed by Germany and accepted by the Commission;

(3) A further sum equivalent to 1 per cent of the value of her exports, as above defined, or, alternatively, an equivalent amount fixed as provided in Article 2, paragraph (B) above. Provided always that when Germany shall have discharged her obligations under this schedule, other than her liability in respect of outstanding bonds, the amount to be paid in each year under this paragraph shall be reduced to the amount required in that year to meet the interest and sinking fund on the bonds then outstanding. . . .

5. Germany shall pay within twenty-five days from this notification 1,000,000,000 gold marks, in gold or approved foreign currencies or approved foreign bills or in drafts at three months on the German Treasury, endorsed by approved German banks and payable in pounds sterling in London, in francs in Paris, in dollars in New York or any currency in any other place designated by the Commission. These payments will be treated as the two first

quarterly instalments of payments provided in Article 4, paragraph (1).

6. The Commission will, within twenty-five days from this notification, in accordance with paragraph 12(a), Annex II, of the Treaty as amended, establish a special sub-commission to be called the Committee of Guarantees. The Committee of Guarantees will consist of representatives of the Allied Powers now represented on the Reparation Commission, including a representative of the United States in the event of that Government desiring to make an appointment. The Committee shall comprise not more than three representatives of nationals of other Powers whenever it shall appear to the Commission that a sufficient portion of the bonds to be issued under this schedule is held by nationals of such Powers to justify their representation on the Committee of Guarantees.

7. The Committee of Guarantees is charged with the duty of securing the application of Articles 241 and 248 of the Treaty of Versailles.

It shall supervise the application to the service of the bonds provided for in Article 2 of the funds assigned as security for the payments to be made by Germany under Article 4. The funds to be assigned shall be:

(a) The proceeds of all German maritime and land customs and duties, and in particular the proceeds of all import and export duties;

(b) Proceeds of a levy of 25 per cent on the value of all exports from Germany. . . .

(c) The proceeds of such direct or indirect taxes or any other funds as may be proposed by the German Government and accepted by the Committee of Guarantees in addition to, or in substitution for, the funds specified in (a) or (b) above. . . .

8. In accordance with paragraph 19, clause 2 of Annex II, as amended, Germany shall on demand, subject to prior approval of the Commission, provide such material and labor as any of the Allied Powers may require toward restoration of the devastated areas of that Power, or to enable any Allied Power to proceed with the restoration or the development of its industrial or economic life. The value of such material and labor shall be determined in each case by a valuer appointed by Germany and a valuer appointed by the Power concerned and, in default of an agreement, by a referee nominated by the Commission. This provision as to valuation does not apply to deliveries under Annexes III, IV, V and VI to Part VIII of the Treaty. . . .

PART III

The Postwar Crisis

After more than four years of war, Europe experienced a period nearly as long of economic, social, and political dislocation, sometimes marked by violent upheaval. Nearly everywhere wages and prices were seriously maladjusted, and strikes were frequent. Unemployment rose and output fell off as industries converted to peacetime production. And everywhere the difficulties of adjustment were increased by inflation.

While these problems were common to all the belligerent states, and felt to a lesser degree by neutrals, the disorder was most intense in central and eastern Europe. It was significantly worsened there by the redrawing of frontiers and by political ferment of which the Russian revolutions of 1917 were only the most dramatic examples. In the East the front lines had moved across a much wider area than in the West, producing a larger swath of destruction, and the world war was followed by several years of continued hostilities in the form of civil war and border conflicts. Finally there were the special problems of creating new states. New boundaries broke up old trading patterns, particularly in the former Habsburg and Russian Empires; railroad systems had to be reorganized, often by sewing together the pieces of several former systems; new currencies had to be created and old ones retired. Land reforms carried out in the new states significantly reshaped agricultural production. Under these conditions normal economic activity came nearly to a halt, and eastern Europe faced famine and disease.

Some of the dislocation of the immediate postwar years was produced by basic and long-term changes in the European economy, but a good deal resulted from temporary if nevertheless severe ailments. The most serious and general of these was inflation. The currencies of France and Italy lost about three-quarters of their prewar value; those of central and eastern Europe lost nine-tenths or more. In Russia, Hungary, Austria, and Germany, the old currencies were entirely destroyed by runaway inflation. Inflation hurt those on fixed incomes and those who held cash assets or promises to pay. It was advantageous to those with outstanding debts or who had products of real value to sell. It also had the effect of reducing the burden of national debts.

However, inflation did not reduce the size of the foreign debts governments had contracted during the war because creditors required payment in gold or hard currencies. Thus, interallied debts and Germany's reparation obligation remained as harsh reminders of the war costs yet to be paid. Although there was no formal connection between the two, they became informally linked as the Allies looked to reparations as a means of meeting their war-debt obligations. Thus a vicious cycle developed in which some states counted on the receipt of assets beyond the capability of others to provide in order to meet their own obligations. Recovery seemed choked by the tangle of war debts, reparations, and financial chaos.

11. Economic Chaos in Eastern Europe

Almost every element of the prewar economic life of central and eastern Europe seemed to have disintegrated during the war and the years immediately following. What caught the attention of western Europeans was the intensity of famine and disease in the region; relief missions were dispatched and conditions improved somewhat, particularly in Vienna, as a result. A British mission to central Europe, headed by Sir William Goode, arrived at the beginning of 1919. Goode's reports on the general activities of the mission during 1919 and its work in Poland in that year indicate the extent of suffering. But they also reflect many other aspects of economic dislocation arising from the creation of new states.

Report of British Relief Mission to Central Europe, January, 1920

1. General Summary of the Situation During 1919

THE QUESTIONS of transport and coal are so interlocking that I have classed them together. Everywhere I went I found chaos on the railways. In the earlier part of the year it was impossible to rely upon any relief supplies reaching their destination by land unless the trains were not only started on their way, but "nursed" at frontier points by allied soldiers. To some extent this was due to political causes and to the technical continuance of hostilities as between the various countries, but in the main this escort was necessary merely from the point of view of railway dislocation. . . . In all the economic welter of Europe there is no more perplexing vicious circle than that of coal and railways. In countries where I found wagons [freight cars] I found, almost invariably, a shortage of locomotives; where there were locomotives there was a shortage of wagons; where coal lay at the pithead awaiting transport there were no wagons; and where wagons waited, men were not available to work the coal. For want of coal in Austria whole

Source: This selection is taken from two reports by Sir William Goode, British Director of Relief, published in *Economic Conditions in Central Europe, I* (Cd. 521) (London: His Majesty's Stationery Office, 1920), pp. 7–10, and *Economic Conditions in Central Europe, II* (Cd. 641) (London: His Majesty's Stationery Office, 1920), pp. 27–33, with deletions.

trains of wagons stood idle on the tracks. There were locomotives, but you cannot get up steam without fuel. In Yugo-Slavia and Hungary the lines were congested with empty wagons for want of locomotives. In Poland, where efforts were made to stimulate the production of oil fuel, there were not enough tank wagons to carry the increased quantity of oil. . . .

The latest reports show a tendency to increased coal production throughout Europe—it is now about 80 per cent of the 1913 production—but the natural tendency of the coal-producing countries to retain the pre-war quantities for their own consumption, will result for some time to come in a continued under-supply to non-coal-producing countries. Up to the date of this report it has been found almost impossible, despite entreaty and pressure, to carry into effect the arrangements made under allied intervention for supplying Austria with coal from Czecho-Slovakia, Poland and Upper Silesia. . . .

. . . As a profession of policy there is probably no one of these governments [Czechoslovakia, Poland, Yugoslavia, Hungary, and Austria] that will not adhere to the principle that it is to their own interest to trade freely amongst themselves, but there is a natural disinclination to put such a policy into execution when it involves taking bad money in exchange for good food or coal. An example in point is the contract between Yugo-Slavia and Austria. The former country, one of the few with a surplus of food products, undertook to deliver 160,000 tons of food to Austria in exchange for manufactured articles, Austrian currency, foreign exchange, etc. Meantime, the Austrian krone depreciated to between 500 and 600 kronen to the £1 sterling, as compared with a pre-war basis of 25 to the £1, with the result that it became practically worthless to the Yugo-Slavs, who, themselves in need of raw material, desired to sell their crops to countries where they required credits with which to purchase wool, cotton, etc. Up to the middle of December 1919, only 4,000 tons of food supplies had been delivered to Austria on account of the 160,000 tons contracted for with the Yugo-Slavian government. Again, in the case of sugar, the Czecho-Slovakian government had an exportable surplus of sugar. They were under contract to the Austrian government to deliver an amount which would have met Austria's minimal requirements. On the other hand, the Czecho-Slovakian government, like that of Yugo-Slavia, is dependent for its national welfare upon imports of raw material, but has no credits with which to buy them. Practically its only security for loans or credits is its sugar crop, and a large quantity of this has now been pledged in return for external loans. Austria is therefore likely to have to obtain sugar by arrangement with the allied governments if she gets it at all. These two instances—typical of similar incidents in other countries—are sufficient to show the economic misdirection which is occurring in the exchange of fundamental commodities. . . .

. . . Vienna, perhaps more than any city in Europe, visualises the misery that arises from want of food and coal and from the cumulative effects of over four years of ruinous war. Here, in a city of 2½ million inhabitants, the sharp contrasts between pre-war prosperity and present-day insolvency, between the nervous rich and the starving poor, between the relics of ill-fated monarchy and a revolutionary, but rather desperate, government, stand out with brutal appeal to the imagination. . . .

Hand in hand with the disease and distress due to the cumulative effects of war and to the immediate lack of food and warmth is the spectre of unemployment. In all these relief countries[1] a considerable percentage of the industrial population is in receipt of unemployment pay. President Masaryk, of the Czecho-Slovak Republic, whom I saw at Prague on the 10th October, 1919, pointed out that it was impossible to put his people to work without wool and cotton for the factories, and that the problem of this new state resolved itself into a question of the export of merchandise or of population. If raw material were not forthcoming, the industrial population would have to leave the country, and, unlike Great Britain or France, they had no colonies of their own to which they could go. As regards the agricultural population of this republic, President Masaryk told me that the land had lost at least one-third of its productivity owing to the war losses of cattle and the consequent loss of manure. In the train of this vicious circle there had come a shortage of milk and consequent malnutrition of thousands of children. What President Masaryk said of his own country might, with little or worse variation, be said of every country where relief missions were stationed. . . .

2. Report on Poland During 1919

The situation in Poland was serious. The German occupation and administration of Poland had ceased on the 10th November, 1918,

---

[1] I.e., countries receiving aid.—Eds.

the majority of the German army of occupation having been disarmed by the Poles with no resistance. The Germans during the war had followed the example of the Russians and kept all administration in their own hands, and had only allowed Poles a very limited authority. The Poles were then suddenly faced with the necessity of forming, without notice, some kind of government. . . . This government had naturally found it impossible to secure immediately officials who had the necessary administrative experience to fill the important posts. Information, even on the most essential matters, was lacking, and in any case the authority of the central government was at first of very limited extent.

Poland at this time was fighting on four fronts against the Ukrainians, the Bolsheviks, the Czechs and the Germans, and the military situation was not good. Lemberg in the south-east was practically invested by the Ukrainians and was starving. There was a shortage of munitions and military equipment, and even women and boys of twelve were fighting in the trenches. In many parts of Poland there was a complete lack of essential foods. Children were dying for want of milk, and adults were unable to obtain bread or fats. In the eastern districts, towards Pinsk, Baranowice, Slonim and Wilno there was virtually a state of famine. The country there had undergone four or five occupations by different armies, each of which had combed the land for supplies. Most of the villages had been burnt down by the Russians in their retreat [of 1915]; land had been uncultivated for four years and had been cleared of cattle, grain, horses and agricultural machinery by both Germans and Bolsheviks. The population here was living upon roots, grass, acorns and heather. The only bread obtainable was composed of these ingredients, with perhaps about 5 per cent of rye flour. Their clothes were in the last stages of dilapidation; the majority were without boots and shoes, and had reached the lowest depths of misery and degradation. The distribution of food in the towns was very unequal. It was possible to buy almost anything in the restaurants at a price, and cafes and cake shops were well supplied, but in other parts of the same towns it was impossible to obtain any food. The industrial towns in the coal and cotton areas were especially badly off for food, and the inhabitants suffered greatly from lack of flour and fats.

The above conditions were greatly aggravated by unemployment. Half the population of Warsaw was in receipt of out-of-work pay from the government, while nearly the whole population of Lodz was in a similar plight. This was largely due to the wholesale requisitions which the Germans made of plant and raw materials. At the same time about 700,000 Polish labourers who had been in Germany at the outbreak of the war and had remained there during the war began to flock into Poland after the armistice. They were naturally in very bad physical condition and in want of clothing and boots. It was impossible to find any work for them, and they had to be maintained by the government as soon as they arrived. The number of unemployed was also swelled by the stream of prisoners and deportees continually arriving from Russia. As a rule these unfortunate people found nothing left of their former houses, and had to live where they could find any kind of shelter, in old trenches or dug-outs or holes in the ground. Some of them made pitiful attempts to begin cultivation, using anything which they could find to dig with, such as old bits of scrap iron or broken shovels or bits of wood.

Under these conditions disease was unavoidably widespread. The returned prisoners, especially those from Russia, carried typhus with them wherever they went, and in some areas as much as 60 per cent of the total population was affected by typhus. Consumption and the effects of malnutrition further increased the mortality rate, which rose to over 40 per thousand, while the birth rate in Warsaw had fallen to 11.9 per thousand. There were far too few doctors in Poland to cope with the situation. In the absence of railways, motor cars and horses, they had no means of getting about the country, and, most important of all, soap and all essential drugs and medical appliances were either totally lacking or utterly insufficient to meet the needs of the population. The currency of Poland was in an exceedingly chaotic condition. The following notes were in circulation—Russian rouble notes of various issues; German mark notes; Austrian kronen notes; Ukraine notes (Karbowance); Polish mark notes issued by the Germans during their occupation, and Polish mark notes issued by the new Polish government. Exchange was immensely complicated not only by the great variety of notes current, but also by the prejudices of the peasant population, who would not accept rouble notes if they were damaged even in the slightest degree; while in certain districts particular issues only would be regarded as valid. In general German mark notes were at a premium owing to the fact that they could be used for purchase from the Germans, and were also accepted by the Swiss, and it was also possible by this means to obtain a certain amount of sterling in London. Sterling could be obtained in small amounts, mostly £1 notes filtering through from Germany. The price for the pound sterling in February was 42, in October 180–200 [marks?]. . . .

In general, trade is reviving, especially with Germany, German Austria, and Czecho-Slovakia, whose exchanges are more or less in the same plight as that of Poland. Tea, coffee, soap, etc., are finding their way in through Norway, Sweden, and Italy, while tobacco —a government monopoly—has been obtained through Holland, where the Polish government have placed large orders on long credit.

New railway lines are being constructed in various parts, especially to the north and west of Warsaw, in order to link up Posnania [Posen, formerly German] with the other parts of Greater Poland. Several carriage and wagon [passenger and freight car] factories are in course of construction, the steel and rolled plates for which will be obtained from Czestochowa. Schemes are being devised by the Ministry of Public Works for road construction, barge ports on the Vistula, etc. The more ambitious scheme for the regulation of the Vistula for steamer and barge traffic is for the time being too big to be undertaken. . . .

Among the difficulties which obstruct the restarting of Polish industry the following have to be faced:

1. Complete lack of fluid capital. Most Polish capital was locked up in Russian concerns, and at present, while much of the fixed industrial capital is intact, there is no means of paying for raw materials nor for the replacement of necessary parts of machinery.
2. Currency disorganisation.
3. Lack of fuel and transport.
4. Small efficiency of labour, owing to the exceedingly hard conditions to which the Poles have been subjected during the war.

Efforts towards reconstruction should primarily be directed towards restarting the textile industry. This would have a very great effect on the well-being and morale of the Polish nation, mainly because work could thus be found for perhaps 120,000 to 150,000 of the unemployed, whose numbers are steadily recruited by Poles returning from Germany and Russia; but also on account of the extreme shortage of clothing. About six million sterling liquid capital on long term credit would probably be required to restart this industry, which formerly sent 70 per cent of its output to Russia, but is now unable to supply home demands. At the same time, it is probable that Poland could reopen her former export trade with neighbouring states to their mutual advantage.

Much will depend on the financial policy pursued by Poland. Her budget for the period of the 1st January 1919 to the 30th June 1919 showed a deficit of 2,030 million marks, and the continuance of very heavy military expenditure will inevitably increase this deficit and necessitate the issue of more paper money to finance these operations. Poland is a State with great natural wealth, but raw material must be imported in order that the export industries may be set going again, and this involves credit from the raw material-owning countries, which will in turn depend largely upon the general economic and financial policy of the Polish government. . . .

12. Peasant Agriculture and Land Reform in Eastern Europe

Toward the end of the war and in the years immediately following, peasant unrest became significant throughout eastern Europe, manifesting itself in the withholding of produce from the market as well as in political disorders. In economic terms, the problems of peasant agriculture arose from the fact that it was undercapitalized, labor intensive and low in productivity. But to the peasant the problem seemed to lie entirely in his lack of enough land to farm, and he looked enviously at the land of large estates. Assuaging this land hunger became the conditon for retaining peasant loyalty. In July, 1917, when German armies overran Rumania, and neighboring Russia was torn apart by revolution, the Rumanian government committed itself to a radical measure of land reform. This called for the expropriation of large holdings and distribution of land to peasants on easy terms. Other eastern European states soon adopted land reforms. In Russia the Bolsheviks found it necessary to ratify wholesale land seizures; Czechoslovakia in 1919 and Poland in 1925 carried out expropriations of large holdings, although these were less extreme than in Rumania. The direct economic effect of the reforms is not at all clear, although probably they tended to reduce productivity by increasing the number of inefficient small holdings. In any case land reform did not touch the fundamental problems of limited capital, low levels of technology, and rural overpopulation in eastern Europe.

The Rumanian Land Reform, 1917–18

I. In the national interest the rural property of the peasants shall be augmented by the expropriation of arable land, to the extent of and under the conditions indicated below. It shall be sold to peasant cultivators, with preference being given to peasants of this category in military service or to their families if they have died as a result of and during the war.

Source: The Rumanian land reform involved three legal steps: an amendment to Article 19 of the Constitution, which forbade interference with private property; a law of December, 1918, carrying out the expropriation; and a law of 1921 providing greater detail. The above document is the constitutional amendent passed in July, 1917, setting out the broad lines of the reform. It is reprinted in Mitiță Constantinesco, *L'Evolution de la propriété rurale et la réforme agraire en Roumanie* (Bucharest: Cultura Natională, 1925), pp. 307–309, translated by the editors.

The following shall be expropriated in entirety:

(a) arable lands of the royal domain, of the Rural Office [a state-supported peasant land bank], and of public and private legal persons, endowed institutions, etc., even if by the terms of the endowment, gift, bequest, or by other dispositions of any sort whatever, their alienation shall be directly forbidden, or if by prohibitive clauses of any sort they shall be assigned to some particular use;

(b) all rural properties of foreign subjects, whether they be foreigners by birth or have become foreigners by marriage or some other means;

(c) all rural properties of absentee landlords.

From among all these properties, and also from among the properties of the State—which likewise shall be sold to peasant cultivators—the State may exempt those arable lands that serve a special function in the public interest, or even those that might in the future serve some special function.

II. A total of 2,000,000 hectares[1] of arable land shall be expropriated from private properties. This expropriation shall be made on the basis of a progressive scale to be fixed by the law on expropriation, but which shall begin with properties consisting of more than the exempt minimum of 100 hectares of arable.

The size of holdings shall be defined in accordance with their legal status as of August 15, 1916, but taking into account direct inheritances between that date and the promulgation of the general law of expropriation.

The total of 2,000,000 hectares shall not include properties that are to be totally expropriated in accordance with Paragraph I, Sections (a) and (b), but only the arable portion of those properties covered by Section (c).

Land declared to be petroleum-bearing shall be exempt from expropriation, up to a total amount of 12,000 hectares throughout the entire country, on the condition that the owner of a piece [of petroleum-bearing] land that would be subject to expropriation substitute a piece of arable land of equal size in the same district or in a neighboring district.

III. In addition to the expropriation of land indicated in Paragraph I, Sections (a), (b), and (c), and Paragraph II, the law of expropriation must include measures to create communal pastures in the

---

[1] One hectare equals 2.47 acres.—Eds.

mountain regions. These shall be formed by the expropriation of the necessary amount of private property not included in the above categories.

IV. The price of land expropriated in the national interest shall be set, in the last instance, by the Courts of Appeal, and payment shall be made in redeemable bonds issued by the State bearing interest at 5 per cent a year, the nominal value being identical with the real value.

V. The drafting of the general and specific legislation for this expropriation in the national interest shall begin at once. At the latest, the laws shall be promulgated within six months after the liberation of the country.

13. Postwar Inflation

Of all the aspects of the postwar crisis, monetary inflation was most keenly felt by the population at large. It wiped out savings, but also wiped out debts. Farmers found their burden of debt lightened while prices for their products rose. People who had bought war bonds suffered because inflation diminished the value of these bonds, while governments were relieved of much of the domestic debt they had built up during the war—it amounted to unannounced repudiation. The imbalances created by inflation were so widespread that in 1920 the League of Nations convened an International Financial Conference in Brussels to discuss the matter. The following document, from the introduction to the report of the Conference, indicates some of the general aspects of the postwar inflation.

Report of the International Financial Conference, 1920

SOME OF the financial ills from which the world is suffering are common to all nations. But the severity of the malady and the effects which it has produced on the body politic have varied immensely in proportion to the degree in which each nation has been immersed in the maelstrom of the war. . . .

Certain of the belligerent countries of Europe (Belgium, Bulgaria, France, Germany, Great Britain, Greece, Italy and Portugal), unable to cover the expenses of the war from their national current revenue, find their balance sheet burdened with an enormous volume of both internal and external debt, the amount of the latter being still undetermined in the case of Germany. The total external debt of the European belligerents converted into dollars at par amounts to about $155,000,000,000 compared with about $17,000,000,000 in 1913, which, even when full allowance is made for the depreciation of money, represents a tremendous burden in proportion to the total national income of the belligerent countries. The external debt, amounting to about $11,000,000,000 due to the United States, to 1,750,000,000 pounds sterling due to Great Britain, presents an even more difficult financial problem because in

Source: *World Peace Foundation Pamphlets*, Vol. III (1920), No. 5, pp. 226–30.

nearly every case it is payable in a currency which is less depreciated than that of the country concerned.

The Government expenditure of these belligerent countries has
increased in proportions which vary between 500 and 1500 per
cent, the present figures amounting to between 20 and 40 per cent
of the total national income. The higher of these percentages represents the expenditure of France, which includes in her budget a
very large sum for the restoration of her devastated provinces.

In all cases vigorous efforts have been made to introduce an
orderly fiscal system into state finance by the imposition of fresh
taxation—mostly in the form of direct taxes, and the ordinary
revenues are in most cases now equal to or not far short of the
ordinary expenditure. But except in the case of Great Britain, there
is still a very large gap between the total income and expenditure.

These countries together have lost a very large proportion of
their pre-war holdings of gold and have enormously increased their
paper currencies. This process of inflation, which has been reduced
by Great Britain and checked by France, still continues in other
countries. Except in the case of Germany and her allies, whose
imports were prevented by the blockade, all these countries have
during the war had an enormous excess of imports over exports.
This excess increased in some cases after the Armistice, but is now
diminishing. Indeed in almost every case there is now a perceptible
growth of exports.

During the war the exchanges of these countries did not reflect
their real economic position, as artificial measures were in most
cases taken to stabilize them; but the exchanges rapidly deteriorated when these measures were given up in 1919. This depreciation continued for twelve months. Since the spring of this year
there have been appreciable variations, but on the balance the net
movement has been toward improvement.

As a result of the war a number of new states have been created,
while certain existing states, some of which were belligerents, have
had their territories profoundly modified. Among these are
Austria, Czecho-Slovakia, Esthonia, Finland, Hungary, Latvia,
Lithuania, Poland, Rumania and Serbia. For none of these countries, except Finland, is there a definite basis of comparison. All of
them have received as a legacy of the war extremely depreciated
currencies. In most cases the machinery of an orderly state revenue
system is not yet in operation, and with enormous expenditure
upon food relief, armaments, and in some cases actual war, there is

no sign yet of any possibility of a budget equilibrium. In many of these countries the printing press is still in operation. On the other hand several of them are predominantly agricultural. Their productive powers may recover rapidly, and a single good harvest—especially with the present high price of food—is likely to strengthen both their financial and their economic position. In the case of Austria, whose economic life has been more completely disintegrated than elsewhere, the situation is peculiarly difficult.

In the countries of Europe which were neutral during the War, including Denmark, Sweden, Holland, Luxemburg, Norway, Spain and Switzerland, the position is essentially different; but the financial difficulties are also serious. In some cases heavy expenditure was incurred by these countries directly in consequence of the War and they have had largely to increase their internal debt. But in most cases the budget difficulties are due to the growth of Government expenditure caused by the rise of prices and the provision of subsidies to prevent this rise pressing too heavily on the general population. This expenditure has in some cases been met by increased taxation, but in the case of Holland, Switzerland and Spain there are considerable deficits and in the two latter cases no equilibrium is yet in sight. The trade position of these countries also presents peculiar difficulties. During the War their trade balances were very favorable owing to the demand for their products from the belligerent nations and the stoppage of their imports. The result was an accumulation of gold which led to an expansion of currency and a rise of prices almost as serious as that which for entirely different reasons took place in the belligerent countries. Since the War, the trade situation has been reversed, as these countries have been importing the goods required to replenish stocks and, owing in part to the premium to which their exchanges have risen, as compared with the depreciated currencies of the belligerent nations, the maintenance of their exports has become difficult. To some extent therefore the favorable factors in the situation of these countries are actually an embarrassment.

The countries outside Europe have on the whole the most favorable economic position. Though special conditions affect certain of them, especially China, in general it may be said that they have benefited by the ready disposal of their products to the nations of Europe. Their trade balances have been very favorable and their exchanges have improved relatively to those of European countries. They have in many cases been able to pay off a large proportion of their external debts and, on the other hand, have made large loans to their former creditors. This is particularly the case with the United States, to whom most of the countries of Europe are now heavily indebted. But as in the case of European neutrals, their accumulation of gold has led to a rise in prices and has rendered more difficult the maintenance of their exports. Their future economic position, therefore, is vitally dependent on the restoration of the purchasing power of their European customers. It must also be kept in view that many of these countries, especially in the new hemisphere, have immense unfulfilled demands for capital expenditure, and the world-wide shortage of capital at the present time constitutes a serious handicap to their development.

It is noteworthy, however, that, different as are the conditions in these different groups of countries, certain features are common to practically every country of the world as a consequence of the destruction and dislocation of the War. In every country the purchasing power of the national currency has diminished, and the cost of living in terms of that currency has increased. With few exceptions, neutral as well as belligerent countries suspended the gold basis of their currency. Even where the gold basis has been retained, the purchasing value of the currency has declined, for the value of gold itself in terms of commodities has diminished to about one-half.

In every country international trade has been impeded, dislocated and diverted from its normal channels. The inability of Europe to export during the War forced the normal purchasers of her goods to look elsewhere for their requirements, to develop production in unaccustomed channels at home or in other countries overseas. Simultaneously Europe's need for imports compelled the sale of her capital holdings abroad, which are not therefore now available for her present needs. The instability and depreciation of exchanges resulting from these and other causes have impeded the trade of both seller and buyer. Countries with unfavorable exchanges have found it difficult to buy raw materials and those with favorable exchanges have found in them an obstacle to the sale of their exports. With half the world producing less than it consumes and having insufficient exports to pay for its imports, credits alone can bridge the gulf between seller and buyer, and credits are rendered difficult by the very causes which make them necessary. Finally, every country finds impediments to its international trade in the new economic barriers which have been imposed during and since the war.

14. The Russian Runaway Inflation

Arising out of general inflation came a new phenomenon, runaway inflation. In a runaway inflation a high proportion of state expenditures are covered by the printing of new currency, and as the volume of notes in circulation increases, they lose value by the day or hour, the currency turns into worthless bits of paper, and trade is destroyed. Two famous examples are the Austrian inflation in 1922, when the krone fell from 11,000 to the dollar on May 31 to 22,000 to the dollar on June 13; and the German inflation of 1923 (see document 17). The first of the runaway inflations, however, was in Russia in the years following the Bolshevik Revolution, although this has been obscured by the political isolation of the Soviet régime. Inflation was well advanced by the time of the Revolution, but in 1918, as the Soviet government faced huge expenses arising from the Civil War and the costs of nationalized industry, vast quantities of currency were printed and the ruble began to fall precipitously. By January, 1920, it took more than 2,400 rubles to buy what a single ruble had bought in 1913; by January, 1921, it took almost 17,000; and by January, 1922, almost 290,000. The following description of the Russian inflation at the end of 1919 is from the preliminary report prepared for the International Financial Conference.

Survey of the Russian Inflation, 1919

OWING TO the well-known but exceptional violence of the political changes which have taken and are taking place in what before the War was the Russian Empire, a summary of the financial measures taken on behalf of the Government cannot be scientific. From August, 1914, to March, 1917, the political condition of the country was, broadly, unaltered. But the Empire had lost by invasion the industrially advanced province of Poland, and by the decision to suspend the sale of vodka the State lost a valuable source of revenue from this monopoly, which in 1911 produced nearly 28 per cent of the Budget receipts. During the War, there were some attempts to raise internal loans, and large sums were borrowed from abroad. Thus the State debt had risen from 9.3 billions of roubles in 1914 to 16.7 billions in January, 1916, and to

Source: *Currencies After the War: A Survey of Conditions in Various Countries, Compiled Under the Auspices of the International Secretariat of the League of Nations* (London: Harrison & Sons [1919]), pp. 91–99, with deletions.

33.6 billions by the beginning of 1917. At the latter date the gold
reserve had fallen to 1,175 million roubles, while the note circulation (always the stand-by of Russian finance during a war) had
increased to 9,103 millions; i.e., it had roughly been multiplied by
five; further, the balance of trade had become unfavourable to
Russia to the extent, in 1916, of 75 millions sterling. The rate of
exchange had, however, not depreciated proportionately at this
date, thanks in part to the pre-existent Chancery of Credit system
(under which Russians selling goods abroad had to accept payment
in roubles from the Russian government, to which they handed the
foreign monies they had received in the first instance). Other
factors which helped to sustain the exchange value of the rouble
were the credits given to the Russian Government abroad by the
Allied Governments (including £568 millions by England) and
some private credits arranged by bankers abroad for the Russian
banks, including about £8 millions drawn on London accepting
houses and banks. These factors had largely neutralised the effect
of the inflation of the rouble circulation and the closing of the
Dardanelles to Russia's principal export, wheat from the South.
Thus the price paid for £1 sterling had in this time only risen from
about 10 to about 20 roubles.

In March, 1917, came the first revolution, which was marked,
financially, by more rapid inflation of the currency and a great deal
of domestic speculation. In November, 1917, the Bolsheviks obtained supreme power. Various portions of the old Russian Empire,
representing, with Siberia, about one-quarter of the whole population, broke away from the centre (now, after many years, once
more Moscow), and round the White and Black Seas, as well as in
Siberia, Governments hostile to Moscow were established. The
Bolshevik rulers, first from weakness and finally out of set purpose,
pursued a policy of rapid inflation of the currency, and all connection with a gold standard was completely abolished—part of what
gold remained having been removed by the Germans after [the
Treaty of] Brest-Litovsk.[1] By the terms of the Armistice of 1918,
Germany was compelled to hand over this stolen gold, which had

---

[1] Treaty of Brest-Litovsk, imposed by Imperial Germany on the new
Soviet government in March, 1918. By it Russia gained peace at the ex-
pense of substantial territorial cessions (including the Ukraine, Russian
Poland, the Baltic provinces and Finland) which represented the most eco-
nomically advanced and productive areas of the former Russian Empire.
—Eds.

already figured in the Reichsbank's weekly returns, to the Allies for safe custody on behalf of a reconstituted Russia. The present position in regard to this gold, the remains of the Russian State Bank's own gold reserve, a small amount of Roumanian gold, and the foreign balances claimed by the Russian State Bank from pre-Bolshevik times, is a legal question of some obscurity.

The circulation of Russian roubles, which at 9 billions at the beginning of 1917 had caused alarm, was largely increased during the Kerensky regime,[2] so that the rate of exchange fell from 20 to 35, and the circulation had risen to 18 billions. On 31st October, 1918, it was 50 billions, and on 1st January, 1919, the Bolsheviks officially gave the figure as 55 billions. On 30th June, 1919, it was officially given as 70 billions, and unofficially but competently estimated at 85 to 100 billions, including forgeries. It is now increasing at the rate of 40 billions a year. Nor does this give a full account of what has taken place. For, according to the Bolshevik organ *Pravda*, economy of notes has been rendered necessary by the perpetual absorption of the output of notes by the peasant sellers of foodstuffs, who can buy hardly any of the tools which they need owing to the breakdown of importation, transport and domestic production, and this economy has been obtained by the "partial abolition of money payments between Government Departments, and the partial payment of State employees in kind."

Further, there are numerous issues of local currency in addition to those made by the various anti-Bolshevik Governments at Omsk, Tiflis, Archangel and elsewhere. Coupons of War Loans are also legal tender, and even the scrip of these loans may be used to make settlements between Governmental and semi-Governmental institutions. . . .

For a short time after the Bolsheviks came into power scarcity of actual rouble notes in foreign centers and certain operations, political in origin, by foreign Governments in Russia itself, maintained the rate of exchange at about 40 to £1, though the real value was not half that. Thereafter, economic laws asserted themselves, and, though in certain places a buyer of Tsar notes (on which sentiment has placed a premium) will only be able to get 120 such roubles for £1, transactions have taken place in Kerensky "beer labels" [as the

[2] That is, the Provisional Government, which governed Russia between the March and November Revolutions of 1917. Alexander Kerensky was Premier of the Provisional Government from July.—Eds.

notes issued by the Provisional Government were called] at 1,600 to the pound.

As was indicated above, this depreciation of the currency is now regarded with favour by the Bolshevik Government, which in June, 1919, decided to introduce a new note issue of its own (having hitherto relied on the reproduction of old types of notes). According to the latest available reports, these notes are regarded by the populace as even more worthless than their predecessors, which are in consequence being driven out of active circulation to some extent. These notes are apparently little different from food tickets, and it is the policy of the Government to educate the proletariat to dispense with money, the symbol of capitalism, altogether. Meanwhile, budgets are introduced half-yearly which are admittedly unreliable, and each of which is about double its predecessor. That for the first half of 1919 showed estimates of expenditure amounting to 50 billions of roubles and revenue amounting to 20 billions including about 4 billions from taxes. The balance was to be met by the printing of notes. . . .

The foreign trade of Soviet Russia can hardly be considered here, owing to the political anomalies of the relationship of that country to the rest of the world; broadly speaking, barter is the only basis. Within the Soviet area barter fails, because the towns have nothing to offer the peasants. The latter no longer come into the towns looking for work and offering goods, but remain at home and grow what food they need themselves. Their stockings are filled with unprecedented quantities of notes, received as compensation for their property expropriated in the earlier days of the Revolution. Examples of barter need not be given; it is sufficient to refer to the appeals officially issued by Lenin to the industrialists of the "Centro-Textile" and other State trusts to increase production in order to provide a stock of manufactured goods to barter against the peasants' wheat. The experience of the Allied troops in North Russia in regard to the uselessness of ordinary currency and the value of cigarettes, etc. only confirms what is admitted by the Bolshevik Government. . . .

Tremendous costs were connected with reconstructing the battle zones in northern France. Within six months after the end of hostilities, the French government decided to support reconstruction with the full resources of public finance, and the Law on the Reparation of Damages Caused by Acts of War of 1919 is evidence of the broad manner in which that task was defined. By the end of 1924 the total cost of reconstruction in the devastated region had been estimated at 80 billion francs, based on claims for damage to 3.3 million hectares of land, 23,000 factories, 5,000 kilometers of railroad, 200 mine shafts, and 742,000 houses, as well as other damages, and the state had by that date already paid out some 60 billion francs in indemnity. Although this injection of public credit into the French economy helped to lengthen the period of postwar inflation, it also stimulated significant economic growth during the decade of the 1920's. Not surprisingly, the French government continued to insist rigidly upon forcing Germany to meet its reparation payments in order to cover these outlays.

Titles I and II of the Law on the Reparation of Damages Caused by Acts of War, April, 1919

Title I: General Provisions

ARTICLE 1. The Republic proclaims the equal and mutual responsibility of all Frenchmen in meeting the costs of the war.

ARTICLE 2. Complete reparation, according to Article 12 of the law of December 26, 1914, is due for all definite, material, and direct damages to real and personal property in France and Algeria caused by acts of war, without prejudice to the right of the French State to claim payment of them from the enemy.

The following are to be considered damages resulting from acts of war:

1. All requisitions made by the authorities or troops of the enemy, appropriations in kind, in whatever manner or form, including occupation, lodging or billeting of troops, as well as taxes, war contributions, and fines to which individuals or groups have been subject;

Source: *Journal Officiel de la République française* (April 18, 1919), pp. 4050–4053, with deletions. Translated by the editors.

2. The removal of all objects, such as harvests, animals, trees and wood, raw materials, merchandise, movable furniture, stocks, and securities; damage to or partial or complete destruction of harvests, merchandise, all personal property, regardless of who was responsible for the removal, damage, or destruction; losses of personal property whether in France or abroad caused by evacuation or repatriation;

3. Damages to real property, improved or unimproved, including woods and forests, partial or total destruction of buildings, damages or partial or total destruction caused by the removal of machinery, equipment, or animals of commercial, industrial, or agricultural enterprises, which under the terms of the present law will be considered real property, whether they belong to the user or the owner of the property, without his having to determine who was responsible for the damages indicated in the present paragraph;

4. All damages indicated in the preceding paragraphs caused in the border defense zone as well as in the vicinity of fighting or fortifications, as long as they are not contrary to the exceptions made in the laws and decrees governing military service. In any case, the Evaluation Commissions[1] must take into account the precarious nature of buildings constructed in the military zones in violation of the laws and regulations, or under an authorization requiring their demolition on request;

5. All damages to armed boats of the fishing fleet. An administrative regulation will set forth the procedure to be followed in declaring and evaluating the damage.

Included in the damages covered by the preceding paragraphs are those caused by French or Allied armies, either because of preparations for attack or defense, because of necessities of battle or of evacuation of threatened positions, or because of the requirements of occupation in territories included in the military zone, especially the requisition of lodgings and billets. . . .

ARTICLE 3. The rights defined above may be employed by in-

---

[1] The law established a hierarchy of bodies to handle the assessment of damages. The primary body was the cantonal Evaluation Commission, headed by a judge or lawyer appointed by the Minister of Justice, and including one other member appointed by the government as well as a number of men of the locality of different occupations. Above the Commissions were established War Damages Tribunals in each *arrondissement*. The War Damages Tribunal of the Paris region also functioned as the court of final appeal for all disputes.—Eds.

dividual persons or their heirs, companies, public establishments or public services, municipal and departmental governments. . . .

The right to indemnification extends to foreigners in France and to naturalized citizens whose French citizenship has been derived under conditions established by treaties to be concluded between France and the nation from which the naturalized citizen has or will transfer his allegiance. . . .

Title II: The Indemnity

ARTICLE 4. The indemnity, in cases of real property, includes the amount of the damage caused, evaluated as of the eve of mobilization, and the additional costs necessary to replace or repair the property.

The granting of these two elements of indemnity is conditional on its being used in accordance with the articles to follow.

In cases where the property is not to be re-employed, the claimant will receive only the amount of the damage suffered.

ARTICLE 5. The amounts for damage caused and for additional costs for reconstruction are to be determined separately by the Commissions. . . .

For buildings and equipment, the amount of the loss is to be determined on the basis of the cost of construction, installation, or repair on the eve of mobilization with a deduction for depreciation resulting from deterioration, and, in cases where reconstruction or repair took place after mobilization, on the day when they were repaired or reconstructed. . . . The additional costs are equal to the difference between the cost of construction, installation, or repair on the eve of mobilization and that of the reconstruction of identical buildings at the time the assessment is made.

On the condition that the property is returned to use, the sum for depreciation is allowed for all the property of an owner to a total of ten thousand francs (10,000 fr.). To cover additional depreciation, further sums may be advanced to the owner at his request. These are to be repaid to the State within twenty-five years, beginning with the year following the last payment to the owner and carry interest of three per cent. . . .

The reinvestment is to be in properties having the same purpose as those destroyed or in industrial, commercial, or agricultural enterprises within the municipality in which the damage took place or within a radius of 50 kilometers, but is not to be made outside the devastated area. However, in the case of expropriation or purchase of land by the State the reinvestment may be made anywhere in the devastated regions. . . .

For unimproved property the amount of the loss inflicted is to be determined on the basis of the deterioration of the soil, the deterioration or destruction of walls, of trees of all kinds, of vines, plants, copses, and forests. In cases where the land is returned to use, the owner has the right, in addition, to the amount necessary to restore the land to its previous condition or productivity by the repair of walls, the clearing of stumps, replanting, and reforestation. . . .

ARTICLE 7. In cases where properties are not restored, the indemnity is nevertheless to be calculated for both the amount of the loss sustained and the additional costs. The damaged party receives the amount for the loss sustained.

A sum equal to the additional costs of reconstruction will be placed in a common fund under circumstances to be determined by a financial law. The fund is to be employed for the benefit of the damaged regions. . . .

16. Interallied Debts

Allied borrowing to prosecute the war left a complicated network of debts that became closely bound up with the matter of German reparation. Britain and the United States were the main lenders. Britain lent roughly 1.7 billion pounds ($8 billion) to its European Allies, and in turn borrowed some 1.4 billion pounds ($6.4 billion), most from the United States. The United States steadfastly refused to bow to Allied pressure for a general cancellation of all Allied debts in the name of the common victory, and all of the borrowers intended that German reparations should help repay their loans. By 1922 the British no longer believed that Germany could be made to pay in full, and so they sought to encourage a reduction in reparation demands. This they did by proposing to collect from their debtors only enough to meet their American debt. The following document, the note of August 1, 1922, addressed to the French Ambassador and signed by the Foreign Secretary, Lord Balfour, reviews the network of debts and outlines this proposal.

The Balfour Note, August, 1922

YOUR EXCELLENCY: As your excellency is aware, the general question of the French debt to this country has not as yet been the subject of any formal communication between the two Governments, nor are His Majesty's Government anxious to raise it at the present moment. Recent events, however, leave them little choice in the matter, and they feel compelled to lay before the French Government their views on certain aspects of the situation created by the present condition of international indebtedness.

Speaking in general terms, the war debts, exclusive of interest, due to Great Britain at the present moment amount in the aggregate to about £3,400,000,000 of which Germany owes £1,450,-000,000, Russia £650,000,000, and our allies £1,300,000,000. On the other hand, Great Britain owes the United States about a quarter of this sum—say, £850,000,000 at par of exchange, together with interest accrued since 1919.

No international discussion has yet taken place on the unex-

Source: *Federal Reserve Bulletin*, Vol. VIII, No. 9 (September, 1922), pp. 1047–1048.

ampled situation partially disclosed by these figures; and, pending a settlement which would go to the root of the problem, His Majesty's Government have silently abstained from making any demands upon their allies, either for the payment of interest or the repayment of capital. But if action in the matter has hitherto been deemed inopportune, this is not because His Majesty's Government either underrate the evils of the present state of affairs, or because they are reluctant to make large sacrifices to bring it to an end. On the contrary, they are prepared, if such a policy formed part of a satisfactory international settlement, to remit all the debts due to Great Britain by our allies in respect of loans, or by Germany in respect of reparations.

Recent events, however, make such a policy difficult of accomplishment. With the most perfect courtesy, and in the exercise of their undoubted rights, the American Government have required this country to pay the interest accrued since 1919 on the Anglo-American debt, to convert it from an unfunded debt to a funded debt, and to repay it by a sinking fund in 25 years. Such a procedure is clearly in accordance with the original contract. His Majesty's Government make no complaint of it; they recognize their obligations and are prepared to fulfill them. But evidently they can not do so without profoundly modifying the course which in different circumstances they would have wished to pursue. They can not treat the repayment of the Anglo-American loan as if it were an isolated incident in which only the United States of America and Great Britain had any concern. It is but one of a connected series of transactions in which this country appears sometimes as debtor, sometimes as creditor, and, if our undoubted obligations as a debtor are to be enforced, our not less undoubted rights as a creditor can not be left wholly in abeyance.

His Majesty's Government do not conceal the fact that they adopt this change of policy with the greatest reluctance. It is true that Great Britain is owed more than it owes, and that, if all inter-allied war debts were paid, the British treasury would, on balance, be a large gainer by the transaction. But can the present world situation be looked at only from this narrow financial standpoint? It is true that many of the allied and associated powers are, as between each other, creditors or debtors, or both. But they were, and are, much more. They were partners in the greatest international effort ever made in the cause of freedom; and they are still partners in dealing with some, at least, of its results. Their debts were incurred, their loans were made, not for the separate advantage of particular States, but for a great purpose common to them all, and that purpose has been, in the main, accomplished.

To generous minds it can never be agreeable, although, for reasons of State, it may perhaps be necessary, to regard the monetary aspect of this great event as a thing apart, to be torn from its historical setting and treated as no more than an ordinary commercial dealing between traders who borrow and capitalists who lend. There are, moreover, reasons of a different order, to which I have already referred, which increase the distaste with which His Majesty's Government adopt so fundamental an alteration in method of dealing with loans to allies. The economic ills from which the world is suffering are due to many causes, moral and material, which are quite outside the scope of this dispatch. But among them must certainly be reckoned the weight of international indebtedness, with all its unhappy effects upon credit and exchange, upon national production and international trade. The peoples of all countries long for a speedy return to the normal. But how can the normal be reached while conditions so abnormal are permitted to prevail? And how can these conditions be cured by any remedies that seem at present likely to be applied?

For evidently the policy hitherto pursued by this country of refusing to make demands upon its debtors is only tolerable so long as it is generally accepted. It can not be right that one partner in the common enterprise should recover all that she has lent, and that another while recovering nothing, should be required to pay all that she has borrowed. Such a procedure is contrary to every principle of natural justice and can not be expected to commend itself to the people of this country. They are suffering from an unparalleled burden of taxation, from an immense diminution in national wealth, from serious want of employment, and from the severe curtailment of useful expenditure. These evils are courageously borne. But were they to be increased by an arrangement which, however legitimate, is obviously one-sided, the British taxpayer would inevitably ask why he should be singled out to bear a burden which others are bound to share.

To such a question there can be but one answer, and I am convinced that allied opinion will admit its justice. But while His Majesty's Government are thus regretfully constrained to request the French Government to make arrangements for dealing to the best of their ability with Anglo-French loans, they desire to explain that the amount of interest and repayment for which they ask depends not so much on what France and other allies owe to Great Britain as on what Great Britain has to pay America. The policy favored by His Majesty's Government is, as I have already observed, that of surrendering their share of German reparation, and writing off, through one great transaction, the whole body of interallied indebtedness. But, if this be found impossible of accomplishment, we wish it to be understood that we do not in any event desire to make a profit out of any less satisfactory arrangement. In no circumstances do we propose to ask more from our debtors than is necessary to pay to our creditors. And, while we do not ask for more, all will admit that we can hardly be content with less. For it should not be forgotten, though it sometimes is, that our liabilities were incurred for others, not for ourselves. The food, the raw material, the munitions required by the immense naval and military efforts of Great Britain and half the £2,000,000,000 advanced to allies were provided not by means of foreign loans, but by internal borrowing and war taxation. Unfortunately, a similar policy was beyond the power of other European nations. Appeal was therefore made to the Government of the United States; and under the arrangement then arrived at the United States insisted, in substance if not in form, that, though our allies were to spend the money, it was only on our security that they were prepared to lend it. This cooperative effort was of infinite value to the common cause, but it can not be said that the role assigned in it to this country was one of special privilege or advantage.

Before concluding I may be permitted to offer one further observation in order to make still clearer the spirit in which His Majesty's Government desire to deal with the thorny problem of international indebtedness.

In an earlier passage of this dispatch I pointed out that this, after all, is not a question merely between allies. Ex-enemy countries also are involved; for the greatest of all international debtors is Germany. Now, His Majesty's Government do not suggest that, either as a matter of justice or expediency, Germany should be relieved of her obligation to the other allied States. They speak only for Great Britain; and they content themselves with saying once again, so deeply are they convinced of the economic injury inflicted on the world by the existing state of things, that this country would be prepared (subject to the just claims of other parts of the empire) to abandon all further right to German reparation and all claims to repayment by allies, provided that this renunciation formed part of a general plan by which this great problem could be dealt with as a whole and find a satisfactory solution. A general settlement would, in their view, be of more value to mankind than any gains that could accrue even from the most successful enforcement of legal obligations.

17. The German Inflation of 1923

French and Belgian occupation of the Ruhr in 1923 coincided with the worsening of a major inflation of the German currency into a runaway inflation. The mark had depreciated substantially during the war, falling to barely half its prewar value by 1918. Inflation increased throughout 1921 as the heavy demands of reparations upon the state budget were covered by the printing of currency rather than revenues. During 1922 the mark fell precipitously. In January 1922 the gold mark was worth 48 paper marks; in July it was worth 160; and by December, 1,750. When the Ruhr was occupied, the German government lost the revenue of that rich industrial area. Because it also took upon itself the support of the population in passive resistance to the occupying armies, its outlays increased enormously. These costs, mainly unemployment insurance, were covered by astronomical issues of currency. By May, 1923, a gold mark equaled 16,556 paper marks; by the end of August it equaled 2,453,595; on October 11, 1,205,358,227; and by November over 1 trillion. Currency lost value by the hour, payments and purchases became impossible. Small businesses collapsed, and people on fixed incomes were ruined, but people with debts or those who held real assets gained, and many large industrial organizations profited amid the chaos.

The inflation was halted in the fall of 1923, when a new government abandoned the policy of supporting passive resistance in the Ruhr and faced the necessity of stopping the currency presses. A unique currency reform provided for a new medium of exchange, the Rentenmark, theoretically secured upon all agricultural and industrial property by the device of a mortgage held by a new institution, the Rentenbank. With the issue of Rentenmarks in November, the period of runaway inflation was ended; as part of the Dawes Plan of 1924 (see document 18) a new currency, the Reichsmark, replaced the Rentenmark and the Rentenbank was in turn abolished.

The first of the documents below is a description of the runaway inflation as it entered its worst phase. It is taken from a speech by the newly appointed Minister of Economics, Hans von Raumer, on August 31, 1923. The second document is the decree establishing the Rentenbank, promulgated on October 15, 1923.

A. The Worst Phase of the Inflation, August, 1923

THE ECONOMY has been wounded by the catastrophic collapse of the currency. The mark's value has decreased fifteen-hundredfold since the Ruhr invasion. Everyone tries—and, indeed, from his own point of view, justifiably—to protect himself from the consequences of this inflation. Everyone carries a table [projecting further depreciation of the mark]. He gets bonuses or surcharges to cover depreciation on wages or sales; but the increase in purchasing power or selling price does not last. These gains are only fictions, for there is no corresponding increase in the supply of goods. Thus, higher wages and prices enrich no one. On the contrary, they lead only to more inflation and a greater fall in purchasing power. In this race against depreciation, wages and prices have outstripped the world market and the gold standard. But that works only for a certain period of time. The runaway rate of exchange brings wages and prices back below the world level one day, but on the next they rise above it. Exchange rates dance up and down. The result of this process is a thorough destruction of business, of employer and worker. Everyone has only one thought —to protect himself against depreciation; constructive work is pushed into the background, and thus we see a complete deterioration of production in all fields.

Markets contract daily. Orders hardly come in any more. Those that do are only for replacement parts. Simultaneously, there is a dreadful shortage of working capital. Businesses can no longer meet wage bills. From the end of June to about August 29 wages have climbed three or four times faster than the mark has depreciated. Consequently, the receipts from the sale of goods no longer cover wage payments. Credit terms have become exceedingly onerous; the interest demanded is enormous. No depreciation surcharge that may be placed on goods can even approximately keep up with the inflation between billing time and receipt of payment.

The only way to change this would be to stop the currency

Source: Excerpts from the speech of the Reich Minister of Economics to the Economic Policy Committee of the Economic Council of the Reich, *Ursachen und Folgen vom deutschen Zusammenbruch 1918 und 1945*, Vol. V (Berlin: Dokumenten-Verlag Dr. Herbert Wendler & Co., [1960?]), pp. 186–190, with deletions. Translated by the editors. Used by permission.

presses. Stopping the currency presses would presuppose balancing the budget. This cannot be done so long as the struggle in the Ruhr devours enormous sums. No sort of tax receipts can fill this gap. From the financial side, at the moment, one can only create the basis for reorganization toward the time when the currency presses can be shut down. However, even at present, one can begin on the expenditures side. The Minister of Finance, Dr. Hilferding, has shown in the Reichstag Main Committee how everything today depends on public payments. We have reached the point where not only the costs of the states and municipalities, but even the wage bills of private industry are being paid by the Treasury. Measures of the most rigorous severity will be necessary here. Everyone must be clear about the fact that we are not in a position to run things as we have. Public means will soon no longer be available as relief to anyone.

Until finances are brought under control, i.e., until the currency presses are stopped, we can only, in my opinion, make the attempt to keep the economy above water with makeshifts. It is these makeshifts that I would like to discuss with you and for which I ask your support.

The root of the evil is the depreciation adjustment. Inflation goes on unchecked because one must add enormous increments for depreciation on wages and prices alike, and these in their turn work in such a manner that the depreciation provided for actually occurs through the inflation thus caused.

How can I create a means of payment of stable value, one for both big and small businesses? We must understand that the solution to this question becomes one of public security, the preservation of public order, and that in view of this questions of principle and of economics must give way. Recall how it was in Vienna [during the Austrian inflation] when one fine day shops declined to accept the krone. If something like that should occur here, it would be impossible to maintain peace and order; for an economy and a social organization based on legal tender are destroyed on the day that a generally accessible means of payment no longer exists. . . . The most normal solution would be to set up a *Goldnoten-bank*, as in Austria, in which the Reichsbank could have a controlling share and which could, under the protection of total independence and total separation from the finances of the Reich, put gold notes into circulation. I would, for my part, have absolutely no objection to some participation of international capital; for the essential thing is that we get out of this deadlock. . . .

The other question that will concern us here is the expansion of exports. The seriousness of the situation is evident from the figures. The Statistics Office's figures on exports are not sufficiently up to date. I give you export figures taken from export licenses granted, in order to give a characteristic picture of the orders received. The licenses amount to 614 million gold marks in May, 380 million gold marks in June, and 105 million gold marks in July. There is nothing to add to these figures. They indicate the actual ability of our industry to compete and to export. The economy can no longer survive by the depreciation of the currency. This advantage has been exhausted. At first we got by on foreign losses on our mark. Then we drew on the capital of our pensioners and citizens on fixed incomes. Next we consumed the reserves of the economy itself. There are no more reserves available. . . .

B. The Rentenbank, October, 1923

ON THE basis of the Enabling Act of October 13, 1923, the Government decrees:

1. The German Rentenbank shall be established by representatives of agriculture, and of industry, business, and commerce, including the banks. The Rentenbank shall have its seat in Berlin. In civil law it shall have the attributes of a juridical person.

2. The capital and reserve of the Rentenbank shall amount to 3.2 billion Rentenmarks, the sum to be subscribed in equal parts by agriculture (paragraph 6) on the one hand, and by industry, business, and commerce, including banks (paragraph 9) on the other. In order to strengthen the resources of the Rentenbank, any properties covered neither by paragraph 6 nor paragraph 9 shall be included by virtue of the appropriate suspension of government economic control.

3. (1) The Charter of the Rentenbank shall be drawn up by the founders. It requires the approval of the Government. . . .

4. Unless otherwise specified in this decree or in the Charter, the Rentenbank shall be autonomous in matters of the administration

Source: *Reichsgesetzblatt* (Jahrgang 1923), Part I, No. 100, pp. 963–966, with deletions. Translated by the editors.

and management of its affairs as well as in the appointment of personnel. The election of the President of the Bank requires the approval of the Government. . . .

5. The Rentenbank shall be free from all taxes of the Reich, the states, and the municipalities, upon property or upon income from either real property or business activity. Because the purpose of its establishment is an expansion of capital, the Reich, the states, and the municipalities shall not be permitted to levy any sort of tax or charge on the issue of Renten annuity bonds [*Rentenbriefe*] or on the exchange of Rentenbank notes [*Rentenbankscheine*] against such Renten bonds.

6. (1) The Rentenbank shall acquire a mortgage upon all landed property regularly used for agricultural or forestry purposes. This mortgage shall be expressed in gold marks and shall amount to 4 per cent of the value of the property as assessed for the Defense Levy[1] and on the taxes due from it in accordance with the law of August 11, 1923, on the taxation of enterprises. . . . Insofar as it does not conflict with agreements involving other states, the mortgage takes precedence over all other obligations. . . .

(4) The mortgage shall bear interest at 6 per cent annually. The interest from the effective date of this law shall be payable on April 1 and October 1, beginning April 1, 1924, and shall be due within a week after that date. The Rentenbank shall determine the system of payment.

(5) For the Rentenbank, the capital of the mortgage is non-negotiable. But property owners may redeem [the mortgage] after a period of five years has elapsed.

(6) The interest, section (4), and the capital, section (5), shall be paid in Rentenmarks at their gold value at the time of payment. . . .

(7) The claims arising from the mortgage shall come into legal force immediately upon notice by the Rentenbank. The notice replaces the executable title. At the request of the Rentenbank sequestration must be undertaken by local agricultural banks . . . or, in case these do not exist, by another authority designated by the Government in conjunction with the state government. . . .

9. (1) The industrial, business, and commercial enterprises, including banks, existing at the time this decree comes into force

---

[1] *Wehrbeitragswert*, a 1913 property tax whose proceeds were initially to be devoted to meeting the costs of defense.—Eds.

insofar as they are taxed according to the law on the taxation of enterprises of August 11, 1923 . . . shall owe the Rentenbank the same total amount in gold marks as is charged against agricultural land as a whole. This charge shall be apportioned among the individual enterprises according to the determination of the Government and shall bear interest. Section (4) of paragraph 6 shall apply.

(2) If the assets of a business include land, the Rentenbank shall acquire a mortgage on that land expressed in gold marks to the amount of 4 per cent of the value as assessed for the Defense Levy, but not above this valuation. Insofar as it does not conflict with agreements involving other states, the mortgage takes precedence over all other obligations. The prescriptions of paragraph 6 . . . apply.

(3) Insofar as that share of the charge falling to an individual entrepreneur is not met by a mortgage, the entrepreneur must draw up in favor of the Rentenbank a bond expressed in gold marks. The claim arising from the bond takes precedence over all other claims against the assets of the debtor, insofar as agreements involving other states do not exist. If the entrepreneur does not meet his obligation to issue the bond within a period of two weeks after it is demanded, then on the request of the Rentenbank, the Government, or a representative designated and empowered to act in its stead, shall make out a bond in favor of the Rentenbank and binding upon the entrepreneur. . . .

11. (1) The owners of the mortgaged land and the owners of the pledged enterprises shall have a share in the capital of the Rentenbank in proportion to the mortgage, bonds, gold, and foreign currency they contribute.

(2) No stock certificates shall be distributed. The shares shall be negotiable only with the approval of the Rentenbank. The representation of shareholders' rights will be regulated by the Rentenbank Charter.

12. (1) On the basis of this mortgage and the bonds drawn in its favor, the Rentenbank shall issue Renten annuity bonds [*Rentenbriefe*]. The Renten bonds shall be issued in denominations of 500 gold marks or multiples thereof.

(2) The Renten bonds bear interest at 5 per cent annually, and after five years may be recalled by the Rentenbank, in their entirety or by series, for redemption at face value. They may be recalled earlier only in the case of liquidation.

(3) As to demands against the bonds drawn in favor of the Rentenbank, the claims of holders of Renten bonds take precedence over the claims of all other creditors of the Rentenbank.

(4) If assets of the Rentenbank should diminish, a corresponding amount in Renten bonds shall be cancelled.

13. (1) The Renten bonds serve as security for Rentenbank notes [*Rentenbankscheine*] issued by the Rentenbank.

(2) The unit of value of these Rentenbank notes is the Rentenmark, which is divided into 100 Renten pennies.

14. (1) Special bills in the amount of 500 Rentenmarks may be issued on the basis of one for every Renten bond of 500 gold marks. These shall be designated Rentenbank notes. The total issue may not exceed the capital and reserve.

(2) Insofar as the security provided for in section (1) is not available, no Rentenbank notes may be issued.

(3) The Rentenbank notes are to be accepted as legal tender for all public debts; the detailed regulations shall be issued by the Minister of Finance. . . .

15. The Rentenbank shall be obliged, at any time, upon demand, to redeem the Rentenbank notes against its Renten bonds so that there shall be granted for 500 Rentenmarks a Renten bond of 500 gold marks with current interest from the end of the next interest period.

16. (1) The Rentenbank may operate as a bank only in dealings with the Reich, the Reichsbank, and with private banks of issue.

(2) During the next two years it will grant to the Reich credits payable in Rentenmarks and, except as stipulated in paragraph 17, interest-bearing loans up to the total of 1.2 billion Rentenmarks at the fixed interest rate of 6 per cent. The interest is payable on April 1 and October 1 of every year. The Rentenbank is not permitted to stand security for the Reich.

(3) For the purpose of supplying credit to private enterprise, the Rentenbank is further authorized, in accordance with the Charter, to grant to the Reichsbank and the private banks of issue loans up to the amount of 1.2 billion Rentenmarks. The division of this loan among the Reichsbank and the individual private banks of issue shall be made in accordance with the proportion of notes issued by each on July 31, 1914. The limit on the amount of notes that may be issued by the private banks of issue without special authorizing legislation shall be reduced by the actual value in marks of the loan to which they are entitled.

17. (1) As part of the maximum sum stipulated in paragraph 16, section (2), the Rentenbank shall immediately place at the disposal of the Reich an interest-free loan of 300 million Rentenmarks. The Reich will use this sum for the redemption or partial redemption of its discounted Treasury bills from the Reichsbank.

(2) If the sum of 300 million Rentenmarks is not sufficient to redeem entirely the discounted Treasury bills from the Reichsbank, then, at the request of the Reich, in accordance with paragraph 16, section (2), an interest-bearing supplementary loan shall be applied for and granted. The amount of the supplementary loan is to be negotiated between the Reich and the Rentenbank. . . .

19. As soon as the Rentenbank has begun to issue Rentenbank notes, the Reichsbank shall no longer be permitted to discount Treasury bills. Until redemption has been completed on Treasury bills previously discounted by the Reichsbank on behalf of the Reich, extensions on such Treasury bills are permissible. . . .

PART IV

Recovery and Stagnation, 1924-29

For most western Europeans, "recovery" meant returning to the pattern of economic life that had prevailed before 1914. At first, few understood clearly the impossibility of a simple return to the former system. The foundations of the European economy had been significantly reshaped by the emergence of new patterns of world trade, by the rise of new industries and the relative decline in importance of older ones, and by the provisions of the peace settlement. Yet, in spite of all these changes, and the difficulties both psychological and real of adjusting to them, Europe managed to achieve considerable economic stability and prosperity in the second half of the 1920's. By 1925 industrial production had returned to prewar levels, and it continued to climb until 1930. In most western European countries real wages were higher by 1925 than before the war. Construction of housing and also of public works, especially in Germany, seemed the outward signs of prosperity. To politicians and the common man, economic conditions appeared good.

Yet, to generalize in this fashion for the whole of Europe is to ignore specific difficulties. There were many regions and many sectors of production that did not share in the recovery recorded in the general indexes. A significant increase in total European population, despite the high casualties during the war, meant that returning to prewar production levels would not provide prewar standards for everyone. The problem was especially acute in the less-developed countries, where population expanded most rapidly and where agricultural production did not participate in the boom of the second half of the decade. But even in the industrial nations, lagging or stagnating sectors acted to retard general European recovery. This was reflected in an over-all rate of economic growth that was lower than before the war and in high levels of unemployment. Capital investment was generally inadequate. Much of the apparent expansion was generated by public-works projects—municipal buildings and the like. This heavy investment in nonproductive assets, frequently financed by short-term borrowing, endangered financial stability, especially in Germany. In addition, the relative decline in Europe's position in world trade and manu-

facturing output came at a time when, because of the liquidation of
foreign assets during the war, European countries were heavily dependent on exports to pay for purchases abroad and to service foreign
debts. Thus the recovery of the 1920's, while it seemed bright, was
brittle and pitted with weak spots.

18. The Dawes Plan

Given the position Germany had occupied in the prewar European economy, recovery depended to a considerable degree upon the return of more stable conditions there. After the calamities of the period from 1919 to 1923 this fact was more widely recognized. The key to recovery in Germany lay in the restoration of fiscal stability, and this question in turn was bound up with Germany's reparation obligations. At the end of 1923 a committee of economic and financial experts, headed by the American banker Charles Dawes, was appointed by the Reparation Commission to investigate Germany's financial situation and to make proposals for financial recovery and future reparation payments. The committee submitted its report on April 9, 1924, and the recommendations it contained, generally called the Dawes Plan, were accepted. The Dawes Plan did nothing to reduce the total reparation obligation, but by devising a system of annual payments that could be adjusted to Germany's capacity to pay and by greatly reducing the problem of the transfer of these amounts to recipient countries it set the stage for the remarkable German economic recovery that followed. This document, taken from Part I of the lengthy Dawes Committee Report, contains the basic provisions of the Plan.

The Dawes Committee Report, 1924

WE HAVE approached our task as business men anxious to obtain effective results. We have been concerned with the technical, and not the political, aspects of the problem presented to us. We have recognized indeed that political considerations necessarily set certain limits within which a solution must be found if it is to have any chance of acceptance. To this extent, and to this extent only, we have borne them in mind. . . .

The Committee has had to consider to what extent the balancing of the budget and the stabilization of the currency could be reestablished permanently in Germany as she actually is at the present moment, with limitations as to her fiscal and economic rights over part of her area.

We should say at the outset that we have been unable to find any practical means of ensuring permanent stability in budget and

Source: "Text of the Dawes Committee Report," *World Peace Foundation Pamphlets,* Vol. VII (1924), No. 5, pp. 364–385, with deletions.

currency under these conditions, and we think it unlikely that such means exist. The solution of the double problem submitted to us implies indeed the restoration of Germany's credit both externally and internally, and it has appeared to us impossible to provide for this restoration under the conditions mentioned. We have, therefore, been compelled to make the assumption that the fiscal and economic unity of the Reich will be restored and our whole report is based on this hypothesis. . . .

The task [of the committee] would be hopeless if the present situation of Germany accurately reflected her potential capacity; the proceeds from Germany's national production could not in that case enable her both to meet the national needs and to ensure the payment of her foreign debts.

But Germany's growing and industrious population; her great technical skill; the wealth of her material resources; the development of her agriculture on progressive lines; her eminence in industrial science; all these factors enable us to be hopeful with regard to her future production.

Further, ever since 1919 the country has been improving its plant and equipment; the experts specially appointed to examine the railways have shown in their report that expense has not been spared in improving the German railway system; telephone and telegraph communications have been assured with the help of the most modern appliances; harbors and canals have likewise been developed; lastly, the industrialists have been enabled further to increase an entirely modern plant which is now adapted in many industries to produce a greater output than before the war.

Germany is therefore well equipped with resources; she possesses the means for exploiting them on a large scale; when the present credit shortage has been overcome, she will be able to resume a favored position in the activity of a world where normal conditions of exchange are gradually being restored.

Without undue optimism, it may be anticipated that Germany's production will enable her to satisfy her own requirements and raise the amounts contemplated in this plan for reparation obligations. The restoration of her financial situation and of her currency, as well as the world's return to a sound economic position, seem to us essential but adequate conditions for obtaining this result.

We propose to deal in the first place with the currency problem. . . . By means of the Rentenmark, stability has been attained for a few months, but on a basis which, in the absence of other measures, can only be temporary.

The Committee proposes the establishment of a new bank of issue in Germany, or, alternatively, a reorganization of the Reichs-bank, as an essential agency for creating in Germany a unified and stable currency. Such a currency, the Committee believes, is neces-sary for the rehabilitation of Germany's finances, the balancing of her budget and the restoration of her foreign credit. The principal features of the bank plan . . . are as follows: —

The Bank is to have the exclusive right (with certain minor qualifications) to issue paper money in Germany for the period of its charter, fifty (50) years. All of the many kinds of paper money now circulating in Germany (except limited note issues of certain State banks) are to be gradually withdrawn from circulation, giving place to a single uniform paper currency, the bank-notes of the new bank. These bank-notes will be protected by a normal legal reserve of thirty-three and one-third per cent, and by other liquid assets. The reserve will be held largely in the form of deposits in foreign banks.

The plan contemplates that as a permanent policy the notes of the Bank shall be redeemable in gold, but the Committee is of the opinion that at the time of the inception of the Bank the situation will temporarily not allow of the application of the rule of con-vertibility. It therefore suggests that a currency should be created which will be kept stable in relation to gold and as soon as condi-tions permit be placed on a convertible basis.

Like the present Reichsbank, the new bank will serve as a bankers' bank, rediscounting the safest category of short-term bills, etc., and so establishing the official rate of discount. . . .

The Bank will deal with the public, making short-time com-mercial loans and discounts, effecting transfers and receiving deposits.

It will be the depository and the fiscal agent of the German Government. It may make short-term loans to the Government, but the amount and character of these loans are strictly limited, and the granting of such loans is carefully safeguarded. The German Government is to participate in the profits of the Bank, but the Bank is to be entirely free from Governmental control or inter-ference.

Treaty funds [i.e., for reparation] collected in Germany are all to be deposited in the new bank to the credit of a special account and are only to be withdrawable by the creditor nations under conditions and safeguards which will adequately protect the German exchange market and the interests of the creditor nations and the German economy.

The new bank will have a capital of four hundred million (400,000,000) gold marks, part to be subscribed in Germany and part abroad. It is to be administered by a German President and a German Managing Board, which can have the assistance, as in the case of the Reichsbank, of a consultative committee. Alongside of this German Managing Board there is to be another Board, called the "General Board," which will consist of seven Germans and seven foreigners, one each of the following nationalities: British, French, Italian, Belgian, American, Dutch and Swiss. This General Board is given broad powers in such matters of bank organization and operation as might affect the interests of the creditor nations. . . .

We repudiate, of course, the view that Germany's full domestic demands constitute a first charge on her resources and that what is available for her Treaty obligations is merely the surplus revenue that she may be willing to realize. But at the same time, if the prior obligation for reparation that is fixed for Germany to pay, together with an irreducible minimum for her own domestic expenditure, make up in a given year a sum beyond her taxable capacity, then budget instability at once ensues and currency stability is also probably involved. In that event, an adjustment of the Treaty obligations of the year is obviously the only course possible. The amount that can safely be fixed for reparation purposes tends therefore to be the difference between the maximum revenue and minimum expenditure for Germany's own needs. . . .

. . . We fully recognize both the necessity and the justice of maintaining the principle embodied in the Treaty that Germany's payments should increase with what may prove to be the increase in her future capacity.

We also recognize that an estimate now made once for all might well underestimate this, and that it is both just and practicable that the Allies should share in any increased prosperity. All that we regard as essential as a condition of stabilization is that any such increased demands to correspond with increasing capacity should be determined by a method which is clearly defined in the original settlement, and which is capable of automatic, or at least professional, impartial, and practically indisputable application.

This requirement we have tried to meet, as will be seen, by providing that in addition to a fixed annual payment, there shall be a variable addition dependent upon a composite index figure [the index of prosperity] designed to reflect Germany's increasing capacity. . . .

After a short period of recovery we believe that the financial and economic situation of Germany will have returned to a normal state, after which time the index will begin to operate.

The system of a variable annuity has the sanction of usage in the schedule of payments. But we venture to suggest for most careful consideration the advisability of altering the existing index, constituted by the value of exports. This index appears to us to be imperfect.

We are aware that there are cogent reasons both for and against any test which may be suggested, and we do not propose to examine them in detail. We are of opinion that the undoubted shortcomings of particular indices are neutralized to a large extent if a composite index is chosen, and we have a reasonable assurance that a fair measure of Germany's increasing prosperity will be obtained. . . .

We propose that an average of years (chiefly 1926, 1927, 1928, and 1929) should be taken as the base; that the percentage increase shown by each of six sets of representative statistics (railway traffic, population, foreign trade, consumption of tobacco, etc., budget expenditure and consumption of coal) should be ascertained; and that the average of these six percentages should be taken as indicating the proportionate increase to be added to the Treaty sums demanded in a given future year.

Under this system Germany will retain her incentive to develop, as she retains the major part of the advantage of any increase in prosperity, while the Allies obtain a reasonable share in this increase and avoid the risk of losing through a premature estimate of future capacity.

At the same time, the adoption of a method involving not discretionary but automatic application, gives the necessary assurance from the commencement both to Germany and the world that Treaty demands will not, in the period to which the settlement relates, be again the subject of negotiation and dispute.

There has been a tendency in the past to confuse two distinct though related questions, *i.e.*, first, the amount of revenue which Germany can raise available for reparation account, and, second, the amount which can be transferred to foreign countries. The funds raised and transferred to the Allies on reparation account cannot, in the long run, exceed the sums which the balance of payments makes it possible to transfer, without currency and budget instability ensuing. But it is quite obvious that the amount of budget surplus which can be raised by taxation is not limited by the entirely distinct question of the conditions of external transfer. We propose to distinguish sharply between the two problems, and first deal with the problem of the maximum budget surplus and afterwards with the problem of payment to the Allies. In the past, the varying conclusions formed as to Germany's "capacity" have often depended upon which of these two methods has been chosen.

As a first method of approach the budgetary criterion has obvious advantages and attractions. Reparation must first be provided for as an item in the budget. . . .

But the limits set by the economic balance, if impossible of exact determination, are real. For the stability of a country's currency to be permanently maintained, not only must her budget be balanced, but her earnings from abroad must be equal to the payments she must make abroad, including not only payments for the goods she imports, but the sums paid in reparation. Nor can the balance of the budget itself be permanently maintained except on the same conditions. Loan operations may disguise the position—or postpone its practical results—but they cannot alter it. If reparation can, and must, be provided by means of the inclusion of an item in the budget—*i.e.*, by the collection of taxes in excess of internal expenditure—it can only be paid abroad by means of an economic surplus in the country's activities.

We have, it will be seen, attempted to give effect to both these sets of considerations by a method we believe to be both logical and practical. We estimate the amount which we think Germany can pay in gold marks by consideration of her budget possibilities; but we propose safeguards against such transfers of these mark payments into foreign exchange as would destroy stabilization and thereby endanger future reparation. . . .

Above all, we recommend our proposal for these reasons: it adjusts itself automatically to realities; the burden which should rest upon the German taxpayer should, in justice, so obviously be commensurate with that borne by the Allied taxpayer that, in our view, nothing but the most compelling and proved necessity should operate to make it lighter. It would be both speculative and unjust to attempt to forecast the possibilities of the future exchange position and to determine Germany's burden in advance with reference to a problematic estimate of it. Experience, and experience alone, can show what transfer into foreign currencies can in practice be made. Our system provides in the meantime for a proper charge upon the German taxpayer, and a corresponding deposit in gold marks to the Allies' account; and then secures the maximum conversion of these mark deposits into foreign currencies which the actual capacity of the exchange position at any given time renders possible.

With these principles in mind, we recommend that Germany should make payment from the following sources:

    (a) From her ordinary budget.
    (b) From Railway Bonds and Transport Tax.
    (c) From Industrial Debentures.

We proceed to consider each of these in turn.

To recommend what payments Germany can make from her ordinary budget, and from what dates, is in effect to answer the first of the two specific questions put to us, *i.e.,* how to "balance the German Budget." For, in our view, if the economic and fiscal unity of the Reich is restored, if a stable currency is established, and if the budget is given temporary relief from Treaty payments, Germany should balance her budget from her own resources by a vigorous internal effort supported by the confidence which a general and stable settlement may be expected to give, and she should thereafter be able to maintain it in equilibrium, if the future charge for Treaty payments is determined by a method which assures that it will not exceed her capacity.

In other words, we do not consider that an external loan is needed—as in the case of Austria and Hungary—to be devoted specifically to meeting ordinary deficits during a transition period. External money is indeed an essential part of our scheme, in part for the establishment of a new Bank of Issue; in part to prevent an interruption of deliveries in kind during the transition period; and essentially, to create the confidence upon which the whole success of the scheme depends. But we do not propose that it should be confined, or devoted specially, to meeting deficits on ordinary expenditure even during a transition period. On the contrary, as will be seen, we think that, from the beginning, internal resources should meet internal ordinary expenditure, and at a very early date should suffice in addition to make substantial contributions towards the external debt. . . .

(1) *1924–25 Budget*. In the first year (1924–25) we consider that the ordinary budget may balance. Even if there is a deficit we are confident that it should not be such as to endanger the stability of the currency, and that at the worst the Government can meet it by the orthodox expedients—increases of existing taxation, further emergency taxes and internal loans.

Even if energetic measures are taken to obviate any deficit in 1924–25, we are satisfied that neither by reduction of expenditure nor by an increase in receipts can Germany be expected to provide out of budget resources for any Peace Treaty payments to the Allies, and that any demand for their payment would imperil both the structure of the budget and the stability of the currency. How relief can be otherwise provided for the reparation creditors will be considered separately. . . .

(2) *1925–26 Budget*. . . . On the revenue side, the lapse of a whole year of currency stability and readjustment should, of itself, increase receipts. . . . On the expenditure side it may be hoped, with some degree of confidence, that expenditure on unemployment will exhibit a notable decrease. The expenditure on the Army is capable of reduction. An automatic decrease will make itself felt in the pension charge. It is not to be expected on the other hand that sums thus saved on these or other heads will represent a net benefit to the budget. . . .

(3) *The Budget of Later Years*. As we have said already, Germany's credit cannot rest upon the mere establishment of budget equilibrium. It must be clear that it can be permanently maintained. It is therefore necessary for us to consider what burden Germany can bear in the near future without danger to that equilibrium. In this connection, certain assumptions have necessarily been made. It has been considered that if for two years the budget is relieved from Peace Treaty charges and a stable currency is re-established, Germany ought in 1926 to be making rapid strides towards complete recovery, and should in three years, by 1928, reach a normal economic condition. We have taken into account the probable yield of her several taxes and her taxable capacity as a whole and the probable changes in expenditure under these improving conditions, and after making full allowance for error, we have reached

definite conclusions as to the sums which can be fixed for Peace Treaty charges, without endangering the stability of the budget. These results we have considered in relation to the maximum probable rate at which the national income can be expected to grow from its present point and the maximum proportion of that growth which can successfully be absorbed in taxation.

We draw the conclusion that, allowance being made for some inevitable growth in expenditure, the Budgets for the three subsequent years can safely provide for the following maximum sums:

1926–27	110 million gold marks
1927–28	500 million gold marks
1928–29	1,250 million gold marks

On the other hand, regard being had to the fact that it is difficult to estimate the recuperative power of Germany in 1926–27 and 1927–28, we would propose that these amounts should be regarded as subject to modification by a sum not exceeding 250 million gold marks on the following plan: if the aggregate controlled revenues . . . exceed 1 billion in 1926–27 or 1,250 million in 1927–28, an addition shall be made to the above contributions equal to one-third of such excess. Conversely, if those aggregate revenues fall short of 1 billion in 1926–27 or 1,250 million in 1927–28, the total contributions shall be diminished by an amount equal to one-third of the deficiency.

We believe that at the end of the fiscal year 1928–29, the financial and economic situation of Germany will have returned to a normal state, and that in this and subsequent years the ordinary budget should support the inclusion of a sum of 1,250 million gold marks. The total sums therefore to be provided from *ordinary budget resources* would be the standard payment of 1,250 million plus the additional sum (already referred to) computed upon the Index of Prosperity, as from 1929–30 onwards.

We have considered carefully the question of the amount to which the index should be applied and, as we are desirous that in the earlier years of her recovery German progress shall not be unduly handicapped by shortage of new capital, we think that it will be desirable to apply it to the purely budget contribution 1,250 million (or one-half of the total standard payment) for the first five years of the application of the index, *viz.*, 1929–30 to

1933-34. After that date, 1934-35, the index should apply on the full amount of the contribution, namely, 2,500 million gold marks.

We have conducted, with the assistance of two eminent railway experts, a close examination of the situation of the German railways. The subject is an important one, for the railways have been operated since the Armistice at a constantly increasing loss, which has involved heavy burdens upon the German budget.

Most, if not all, railways systems have passed through a period of great difficulty since the war from causes which were largely beyond their control. It is clear, however, from a study of the report drawn up by the experts . . . that the greatest difficulties were of the Germans' own making. The German railway administration cannot but plead guilty to two serious charges. In the first place, as is proved by the reduction which it is now possible to make, they have been enormously overstaffed, even when all account is taken of the introduction of an eight-hour day and of Peace Treaty charges justifying temporary disorganization. In the second place, the administration has indulged in extravagant capital expenditure for which the official excuse is that construction was largely undertaken to ward off unemployment.

It is only just to observe that the situation has now improved out of recognition, though more remains to be done. The German Government have separated the railways from the ordinary administration and assimilated them in form, so far as is possible, to a business concern. Capital construction has been slackened and fares have at any rate been raised to a point where the railways are not only self-supporting, but can provide some profit.

These measures are, however, insufficient. The capital value of the railways is estimated by the experts on a conservative basis at 26 billions. They are unencumbered with old debts, for their prior charges were extinguished by the depreciation of the mark, and these prior charges absorbed half the gross profits in the pre-war period, which amounted to approximately 1 billion gold marks, in spite of the fact that it was the custom to include in operating and maintenance charges large expenditures which might properly have been charged to capital account.

The railway experts are convinced, and we share their conviction, that under proper management, under unified control, and with a proper tariff policy, the railways can without difficulty earn a fair return upon their present capital value. . . .

The railway experts arrived, however, with considerable reluctance at the conclusion that it would be useless to expect anything approaching the full measure of improvement which is possible, so long as the railways remain in the control of the Government. The whole spirit of the Government's ownership in the past has been directed to running the railways primarily in the interest of German industry, and only secondarily as a revenue-producing concern, and in their opinion a complete break with old traditions is essential.

We accept their conclusions and we recommend the conversion of the German railways into a joint stock company. It is not our intention thus to deprive Germany of the administration of her railways in favor of the Allies; on the contrary, our plan demands only a modest return on the capital cost, and so long as this return is forthcoming we do not anticipate any interference in the German management of the undertaking. . . .

The Committee recommends that there should be paid from the German railways, 11 billion gold marks to be represented by first mortgage bonds bearing 5 per cent interest and 1 per cent sinking fund per annum. The capital cost of the German railways computed on a gold mark basis is estimated by our experts at 26 billions. The net earnings of these railways before the war, after liberal and indeed exaggerated charges to operating and maintenance, were as high as 1 billion. The interest and sinking fund on these debentures represents less than 3 per cent of the capital cost, which is a very modest charge on the capital investment compared with that required in many other countries of the world.

Realizing that during the period of reorganization of the railways, full interest and sinking fund charges should not be required, we think payments on account of interest should be as follows:

1924–25: three hundred and thirty million gold marks;
1925–26: four hundred and sixty-five million gold marks;
1926–27: five hundred and fifty million gold marks;
1927–28 and thereafter: six hundred and sixty million gold marks.
    This is regarded as a normal year. . . .

The Committee has been impressed with the fairness and desirability of requiring as a contribution to reparation payments from German industry, a sum of not less than 5 billions of gold marks, to be represented by First Mortgage bonds bearing 5 per cent interest and 1 per cent sinking fund per annum. This amount of bonds is less than the total debt of industrial undertakings in Germany before the war. Such indebtedness has for the most part been discharged by nominal payments in depreciated currency, or practically extinguished. In addition the industrial concerns have profited in many ways through the depreciated currency, such as the long delayed payment of taxes, by subsidies granted and advances made by the German Government, and by depreciation of emergency money which they have issued. On the other hand it is incontestably true that there have also in many instances resulted losses, through the depreciation of currency, from the sale of output at fixed prices and in other ways. . . .

Realizing the depletion of the liquid capital supply in Germany, and that a period should be provided for its recuperation, we recommend that the interest on the 5 billions of debentures above referred to be waived entirely during the first year, that the interest during the second year be 2½ per cent, during the third year 5 per cent, and thereafter 5 per cent plus 1 per cent sinking fund. . . .

We are now in a position to summarize the full provision we contemplate for Treaty payments:

	Million gold marks
Budget Moratorium Period:	
First year: from foreign loan and part interest (200 millions) on railway bonds;	
Total of	1,000
Second year: from interest on railway bonds (including 130 millions balance from first year) and interest on industrial debentures and budget contribution, including sale of railway shares;	
Total of	1,220
Transition Period:	
Third year: from interest on railway bonds and industrial debentures, from transport tax and from budget;	
Total of	1,200
subject to contingent addition or reduction not exceeding 250 [million] gold marks.	
Fourth year: from interest on railway bonds and industrial debentures, from transport tax and from budget;	
Total of	1,750

subject to contingent addition or reduction not exceeding
250 million gold marks.

Standard Year:

Fifth year: from interest on railway bonds and industrial debentures, from transport tax and from budget;

Total of   2,500

The first year will begin to run from the date when the plan shall
have been accepted and made effective. . . .

19. Britain's Return to the Gold Standard

Before the war the monetary system of Europe had been based on gold. That is, each national treasury on demand bought and sold gold at a specified price so that currencies were freely convertible into gold or other currencies, and no restrictions upon the import or export of gold impeded its international movement. The period from the late 1890's to 1914 had been, in general, one of remarkable financial stability, and the gold standard had greatly facilitated multilateral trade and foreign investment. During the war and the immediate postwar period, gold payments were suspended, and restrictions were placed upon the export of gold. A return to the gold standard and the monetary stability it would provide was regarded as a key step in recovery. This was especially true in Britain, the financial center of the world before the war, where restoration of the pound to gold took on symbolic importance because it was hoped that would re-establish Britain's prewar financial dominance. With fairly wide public support, the Chancellor of the Exchequer, Winston Churchill, announced the return to gold during his budget speech on April 28, 1925. By this means the value of the pound was stabilized, but at the high prewar rate of $4.86, which had the effect of raising the price of British goods to foreign buyers. The following selection is from Churchill's speech.

Churchill's Budget Speech Announcing Britain's Return to the Gold Standard, April, 1925

BUT BEFORE I come to the prospects of 1925 I have an important announcement to make to the Committee.[1] It is something in the nature of a digression, and yet it is an essential part of our financial policy. Ever since the Spring of 1919, first under War powers and later under the Gold and Silver (Export Control) Act, 1920, the export of gold coin and bullion from this country, except under licence, has been prohibited. By the express decision of the Parliament of 1920 the Act which prohibits the export was of a temporary character. That Act expires on the 31st December of the present year, and Great Britain would automatically revert to the

Source: Great Britain, *Parliamentary Debates: House of Commons*, Fifth Series, Vol. 183, columns 52–58, with deletions.
[1] That is, the House of Commons meeting as a Committee of the Whole.—Eds.

pre-War free market for gold at that date. Now His Majesty's Government have been obliged to decide whether to renew or prolong that Act on the one hand, or to let it lapse on the other. That is the issue which has presented itself to us. We have decided to allow it to lapse. . . .

A return to an effective gold standard has long been the settled and declared policy of this country. Every Expert Conference since the War—Brussels, Genoa—every expert Committee in this country, has urged the principle of a return to the gold standard. No responsible authority has advocated any other policy. No British Government—and every party has held office—no political party, no previous holder of the Office of Chancellor of the Exchequer has challenged, or so far as I am aware is now challenging, the principle of a reversion to the gold standard in international affairs at the earliest possible moment. It has always been taken as a matter of course that we should return to it, and the only questions open have been the difficult and the very delicate questions of how and when. . . . This is the moment most favourable for action. Our exchange with the United States has for some time been stable, and is at the moment buoyant. We have no immediate heavy commitments across the Atlantic. We have entered a period on both sides of the Atlantic when political and economic stability seems to be more assured than it has been for some years. If this opportunity were missed, it might not soon recur, and the whole finance of the country would be overclouded for a considerable interval by an important factor of uncertainty. Now is the appointed time.

We have therefore decided, although the prohibition on the export of gold will continue in form on the Statute Book until the 31st December, that a general licence will be given to the Bank of England for the export of gold bullion from to-day. We thus resume our international position as a gold standard country from the moment of the declaration that I have made to the Committee. That is an important event, but I hasten to add a qualification. Returning to the international gold standard does not mean that we are going to issue gold coinage. That is quite unnecessary for the purpose of the gold standard, and it is out of the question in present circumstances. It would be an unwarrantable extravance which our present financial stringency by no means allows us to indulge in. Indeed, I must appeal to all classes in the public interest to continue to use notes and to make no change in the habits and

practices they have become used to for the last ten years. The
practice of the last ten years has protected the Bank of England
and other banks against any appreciable demand for sovereigns or
half-sovereigns. But now that we are returning publicly to the gold
standard in international matters with a free export of gold, I feel
that it will be better for us to regularise what has been our practice
by legislation. I shall therefore propose to introduce a Bill which,
among other things, will provide the following:

First, That until otherwise provided by Proclamation the Bank of
England and Treasury Notes will be convertible into coin only at
the option of the Bank of England;
Secondly, That the right to tender bullion to the Mint to be coined
shall be confined in the future by law, as it has long been confined in
practice, to the Bank of England.

Simultaneously with these two provisions, the Bank of England
will be put under obligations to sell gold bullion in amounts of not
less than 400 fine ounces in exchange for legal tender at the fixed
price of £3 17s. 10½ d. per standard ounce. If any considerable sum
of legal tender is presented to the Bank of England the bank will be
under obligation to meet it by bullion at that price. . . .

The Bill also has another purpose. We are convinced that our
financial position warrants a return to the gold standard under the
conditions that I have described. We have accumulated a gold
reserve of £153,000,000. That is the amount considered necessary
by the Cunliffe Committee,[2] and that gold reserve we shall use
without hesitation, if necessary with the Bank Rate, in order to
defend and sustain our new position. To concentrate our reserves
of gold in the most effective form, I have arranged to transfer the
£27,000,000 of gold which the Treasury hold against the Treasury
Note issue to the Bank of England in exchange for bank notes. The
increase of the gold reserve of the Bank of England will, of course,
figure in their accounts.

Further, the Treasury have succeeded in discreetly accumulating
dollars, and we have already accumulated the whole of the 166
million dollars which are required not only for the June payment
but also for the December payment of our American debt and for
all our other American debt obligations this year. Therefore—and

[2] A Treasury Committee, headed by Lord Cunliffe, the Governor of the
Bank of England, which reported in 1918 that Britain's adverse balance of
trade could be solved only by restoration of the gold standard and by
establishing the pound at the prewar rate.—Eds.

it is important—the Treasury will have no need to go on the market as a competitor for the purchase of dollars. Finally, although we believe that we are strong enough to achieve this important change from our own resources, as a further precaution and to make assurance doubly sure, I have made arrangements to obtain, if required, credits in the United States of not less than 300 million dollars, and of course there is the possibility of expansion if need be. These credits will only be used if, as, and when they are required. . . .

These matters are very technical, and, of course, I have to be very guarded in every word that I use in regard to them. I have only one observation to make on the merits. In our policy of returning to the gold standard we do not move alone. Indeed, I think we could not have afforded to remain stationary while so many others moved. The two greatest manufacturing countries in the world on either side of us, the United States and Germany, are in different ways either on or related to an international gold exchange. Sweden is on the gold exchange. Austria and Hungary are already based on gold, or on sterling, which is now the equivalent of gold. I have reason to know that Holland and the Dutch East Indies—very important factors in world finance—will act simultaneously with us to-day. As far as the British Empire is concerned—the self-governing Dominions—there will be complete unity of action. The Dominion of Canada is already on the gold standard. The Dominion of South Africa has given notice of her intention to revert to the gold standard as from 1st July. I am authorised to inform the Committee that the Commonwealth of Australia, synchronising its action with ours, proposes from to-day to abolish the existing restrictions on the free export of gold, and that the Dominion of New Zealand will from to-day adopt the same course as ourselves in freely licensing the export of gold. . . .

Thus over the wide area of the British Empire and over a very wide and important area of the world there has been established at once one uniform standard of value to which all international transactions are related and can be referred. That standard may, of course, vary in itself from time to time, but the position of all the countries related to it will vary together, like ships in a harbour whose gangways are joined and who rise and fall together with the tide. I believe that the establishment of this great area of common arrangement will facilitate the revival of international trade and of inter-Imperial trade. Such a revival and such a foundation is important to all countries and to no country is it more important than to this island, whose population is larger than its agriculture or its industry can sustain . . . which is the centre of a wide Empire, and which, in spite of all its burdens, has still retained, if not the primacy, at any rate the central position, in the financial systems of the world.

20. Lingering Problems of Recovery

To outward appearance recovery seemed well under way by 1925. Stability had returned to Germany, which was making an effort to meet her reparation obligations under the Dawes Plan; with the assistance of lavish foreign credit—largely from private American sources—industrial expansion and numerous public-works projects were being carried out. In France the reconstruction of the devastated regions provided a powerful stimulus to economic activity; new plants and equipment made the north of France one of the most thoroughly modern industrial areas of Europe. Elsewhere, too, by 1925, many of the prewar indexes of production had been matched or surpassed. Yet, nagging problems remained. These were not merely below the surface to be unearthed by historians in the light of the Depression of the 1930's, but were apparent to contemporaries as well. The convening of a World Economic Conference in 1927 under the auspices of the League of Nations provides clear evidence of concern. Its voluminous publications provide much information on the European economy in the 1920's and indicate, as does the selection from the Conference's final report given below, the special concern with international exchange. In his closing speech the president of the Conference stressed the general conclusion of the discussions:

> The eight years of post-war experience have demonstrated the outstanding fact that, except in the actual fields of conflict, the *dislocation* caused by the war was immensely more serious than the actual *destruction*. . . . It is all in one form or another a maladjustment—not an insufficient productive capacity but a series of impediments to the full utilisation of that capacity. The main obstacles to economic revival have been the hindrances opposed to the free flow of labour, capital and goods.[1]

Report of the World Economic Conference, 1927

In its resolution of September 24th, 1925, relating to the summoning of a World Economic Conference, the Assembly of the League of Nations declared itself "firmly resolved to seek all

Source: League of Nations, Economic and Financial Section, *The World Economic Conference: Final Report* (Geneva: League of Nations, 1927), pp. 10–29, with deletions.

[1] Closing speech of M. Theunis, in League of Nations, Economic and Financial Section, *The World Economic Conference: Final Report*, p. 9.

possible means of establishing peace throughout the world" and affirmed its conviction that "economic peace will largely contribute to security among the nations." It further emphasised the "necessity of investigating the economic difficulties which stand in the way of the revival of general prosperity and of ascertaining the best means of overcoming these difficulties and of preventing disputes."

The Economic Conference has constantly kept these general directions in view. At the end of nearly nine years after the war, during which the disturbances resulting from that unprecedented catastrophe have had time to reveal their permanent effects, the Conference has used its best endeavours to discover and analyse the fundamental causes of the troubles from which the world is at present suffering, and to find remedies which, if they will not effect a complete cure, will at least afford some of the relief for which the civilised world is so insistently calling.

The documentation prepared by the Secretariat under the direction of the Preparatory Committee, to which many commercial and industrial organisations in various countries and many individual experts have contributed, presents a picture of the economic condition of the world with a fullness and authority which has probably never hitherto been attained. It is only possible to refer in the briefest way to the results shown in these reports.

A general impression of the change which has taken place since the war can be gathered from the statistics which have been compiled of the world's production of foodstuffs and raw materials. The figures show that, whereas in 1925 the world's population was about 5 per cent greater than in 1913, production of foodstuffs and of raw materials was from 16 to 18 per cent greater. In other words, production and consumption, both in total and per head of the world's population, are greater than before the war.

This increased production of food and raw materials has, however, not been accompanied by a corresponding increase of international commerce, for the volume of trade in 1925 was only 5 per cent higher than before the war.

But these statistics relate to the world as a whole. They do not represent the position of each continent. While certain parts of the world have progressed considerably more than these average figures indicate, there are other continents, notably Europe, which are far behind. The production of Europe, whose population has increased by 1 per cent, was in 1925 about 5 per cent greater than in 1913, an increase materially slower than in pre-war years, while its international trade was only 89 per cent of the pre-war volume. Further illustration of the fact that the economic difficulties are most acute in Europe is to be found in the volumes on special industries. Its most distressing symptom is the abnormal degree of unemployment which still obtains in certain countries, while its financial reactions are shown in the burdensome taxation and inadequate savings of Europe.

It would, however, be a mistake to assume that the economic condition of Europe could be so seriously disorganised without affecting that of the rest of the world. Other countries certainly feel the effects of Europe's reduced consuming power. There also is no doubt that the world is affected by the fact that Europe has been compelled for the time being to renounce several of the functions in world economy which had previously been hers.

But neither in Europe nor in the rest of the world is the economic position uniformly good or bad. On the contrary, the depression is clearly concentrated in certain main trades. Some of these, such as the iron and steel industry, shipbuilding, and the chemical trades, were artificially expanded to meet war needs. Demand has, however, been restricted by the fact that lack of capital resulting from diminished savings has prevented economic development on the same scale as before the war. The iron and steel industry, which is largely concerned with providing fixed capital in various forms, is particularly affected by this fact. Other industries, of which the cotton industry is a notable example, have had to adapt themselves to a very considerable increase in productive capacity in distant countries. Others, again, like the coal trade—the demand for whose product has been considerably checked by alternative sources of power and by economies in the use of fuel—have suffered, while the petroleum and electric power industries have prospered. But perhaps the most extreme example of dislocation is that of shipping, for, whereas the world's total mercantile tonnage has increased by 38 per cent, the volume of goods to be carried by sea has hardly increased at all. The condition of these trades is in sharp contrast to that of many industries providing articles of immediate consumption or even of luxury. The production of motor-cars, artificial silk, and rubber goods may be taken as examples.

But though the harmful effects of the war have been concentrated on a few special trades, the depression has inevitably limited the expansion that would have taken place in other directions, for by creating complete or partial unemployment it has diminished the purchasing power of a large industrial population.

Moreover, the troubles of industry have an even wider repercussion, since they affect in a similar way the whole of the world's agriculture. Agriculture, which is daily becoming more industrial in its processes and methods, suffers directly from the fact that the prices of industrial products in certain countries have for some years remained relatively high, while those of agricultural products have been on a comparatively lower level. The agriculturist complains that he buys the manufactures which he needs at high prices, but sells at low prices the products of the soil. The documentation of the Conference indicates that, if agricultural prices are low and the agricultural community in many countries in a state of depression, it is not because there has been any abnormal increase in the production of foodstuffs but because the demand from certain manufacturing communities in Europe is inadequate.

Thus, while the documentation of the Conference serves on the one hand to pick out the darkest spots in the present situation, it also emphasises on the other the interdependence of nations, of industries and of classes. During the great war, the nations were driven temporarily to live to a quite abnormal extent on their own resources, but this condition of self-sufficiency—incomplete though it was—was only attained at the cost of hardships which tended rapidly to become almost intolerable. The attempts after the war to seek prosperity by a policy of economic isolation have, after an experience of nearly nine years, proved a failure. The opinion of the world is beginning to understand that prosperity is not something which can be enjoyed in small compartments.

Immediately after the war, many people naturally assumed that the war and the war alone was the reason for the dislocation that emerged in the economic relations of individuals, of nations and of continents. A simple return to pre-war conditions seemed in the circumstances the appropriate objective of economic policy which would be sufficient to cure the current difficulties. It is an instinctive tendency of mankind to turn to the past rather than to the future and, even at a moment when an old order is being displaced by a new, to revert to former ideas and to attempt to restore the traditional state of affairs. Experience has shown, however, that the problems left by the war cannot be solved in so simple a manner.

At first, this desire to return to the pre-war regime was a wise as well as a natural instinct; for the first and most urgent task after the war was to re-start the economic life of the world which had been so sharply interrupted. Economic policy had therefore to deal with the temporary consequences of the war and endeavour to remove the obstructions to production and trade which it left behind.

One of the most widespread and far-reaching of these difficulties was the disorganisation of public finances and the depreciation of currencies. At the time of the Brussels Conference [of 1920], only four European countries had succeeded in balancing their budgets. Now, nearly every country has established its budgetary equilibrium.

If this indispensable first stage of financial reconstruction is not yet quite complete, and if it would be too much to say that in each individual country financial stability is assured, it is at least true that, in general, a disorganised condition of public finances and fluctuations in the various currencies in relation to each other are not at the present moment a factor of primary importance in depressing trade and production.

Another difficulty which has played a great part in recent years has been the shortage of capital. The low level of production that followed the war left in Europe, at all events, no margin for saving. This situation has gradually changed. The recovery of production in Europe, together with a growing sense of security, has revived the process of saving and stimulated the international movement of capital. These developments have restored a more normal—though still inadequate—supply of capital, the evidence of which is the fall in the rate of interest from the excessive figures which at one time prevailed in several countries, particularly in Central Europe, to more normal levels. The rapidity with which rates have fallen is to a certain extent a reflection of the growing freedom of the movement of capital.

Similarly, in the case of international commerce, the conditions immediately succeeding the war did not permit of the immediate resumption of normal trading relations. Extreme forms of obstructions to trade were consequently imposed; but many of these have since been substantially removed, and liberty of trading, subject to the tariff and other barriers which are dealt with [later], has been largely restored.

But while the new economic situation of Europe since the war contains some features which are fortunately of a temporary character, there are others which we cannot hope to change for a considerable time to come, and others which must be regarded as permanent. The passing away of temporary financial and economic difficulties which have hitherto almost monopolised public attention now enable us to see more clearly and to study these more deeply rooted changes in the economic situation of the world. It is hopeless to try to solve such problems by striving after the conditions of 1913. In the face of a new situation new remedies must be found.

Some of these permanent changes, like the difficulties previously referred to, are the direct result of the war. For example, the belligerent countries of Europe have been left with financial difficulties which have extended to many other countries and will take many decades to remove. Not only is there in many countries a heavy annual charge for war debts, but also every belligerent country will for many years have to find the funds for war pensions. These burdens are in addition to the cost of current armaments, which still weigh heavily on the finances of the nations of the world. The level of taxation in relation to resources is therefore likely to remain very much higher in Europe for a long time to come than it was in 1913.

Moreover, the external obligations arising out of the war have an international economic significance. Taken in conjunction, on the one hand, with the loss of their foreign investments which certain nations have suffered, and, on the other, with the new loans which many of them have raised abroad, they have changed the balance of public and private indebtedness between nations as compared with the pre-war situation. This is one of the factors that ultimately involves a change in the distribution and direction of international trade; for the ultimate settlement of net balances due from one country to another must be made by means of goods and services—although not necessarily by the transfer of the debtor's goods and services direct to the creditor.

Another change which has an influence on the distribution of industry, on commercial policy and on trade is a reduction in the streams of emigration. This fact, taken in conjunction with the great differences in the natural increase of various nationals, is causing changes in the relative density of population. Those countries in which there is a rapidly increasing excess of population in relation to their territory and natural resources have consequently intensified their industrial activity, and attach particular importance to the adoption by other countries of a liberal policy in relation to raw materials. So far as Europe is concerned, the emigration problem has been partially and temporarily met by an abnormal amount of migration between the various continental countries.

Some of the changes, however, which our survey reveals are by no means entirely to be attributed to the effects of the war. European opinion is beginning to realise that the war has hastened changes in the world situation which had begun in the early years of the 20th century. After a whole century, during which other continents had been willing to supply Europe with raw products in return for the manufactures which Europe alone was in the position to make, a careful observer in 1905 or 1906—or possibly twenty years earlier in the case of the United States—could have perceived that a new chapter was opening in the history of these distant countries, the chief characteristic of which was the endeavour to establish manufacturing industries of their own. The war greatly stimulated this development by restricting and diverting foreign trade between Europe and the rest of the world.

But at the moment of facing this new situation, Europe finds herself severely handicapped. Some of her temporary difficulties have already been referred to. There are others which, in greater or less degree, affect the internal economy of various countries. Currency disorders have resulted in almost every country in a disproportion in the wage levels in various trades, in the prices of different commodities and in the relation between wages and prices, while the difficult adjustments which these conditions have involved have resulted in industrial disputes and sometimes in great social changes. These matters are outside our terms of reference, but they cannot be overlooked in an attempt to explain the causes of the present economic disequilibrium.

But Europe is also handicapped by problems of an international character. The effort to restore her economic position calls for the rationalisation of industry and a co-ordination between the economic efforts of various countries. It has to be recognised that the possibility of Europe being organised as an economic unit is more remote than before the war, partly because of excessive economic nationalism, which was the natural consequence of the war and is only now subsiding, and because of the economic consequences of retracing frontiers. This nationalisation and these territorial readjustments have resulted in the duplication of industrial plant and in a failure to apply the principle of division of labour between the various States of Europe. The normal process of interchange between the numerous units which constitute the new Europe has been seriously interrupted. The markets which certain areas had supplied before the war have been lost to them, and everywhere it has been necessary to seek new openings for trade.

Both in its trade relations with other continents and in its own internal intercourse, Europe, under the special circumstances of the day, urgently needs greater liberty for trade and commerce. In actual fact, this liberty is still substantially less than before the war. . . .

Whatever the particular subject under discussion, it became apparent, from the facts and evidence presented to the Conference, that each nation's commerce is to-day being hampered by barriers established by other nations resulting in a situation, especially in Europe, that is highly detrimental to the general welfare. . . .

The tendency to equalise the level of Customs protection in the various countries; the desire of each nation to improve its position pending trade negotiations; the impulse to take reprisals against particularly harmful foreign tariff measures; the tendency to retain for national consumption certain goods which have been rendered scarce by restrictive measures in the country of origin; the anxiety to maintain equal competitive conditions in matters of transport and credits; sometimes perhaps the mere contagious effect of example—all these circumstances cause each economic measure taken by one nation at a given time to react almost invariably on the policies of all other nations. . . .

The main conclusion to be drawn from the work of the Conference in the field of commercial policy is that the time has come to put a stop to the growth of Customs tariffs, and to reverse the direction of the movement by an effort made along three lines, viz.:

(1) Individual action by States with regard to their own tariffs;
(2) Bilateral action through the conclusion of suitable commercial treaties;
(3) Collective action, by means of an enquiry, with a view to encouraging the expansion of international trade on an equitable basis by removing or lowering the barriers to internationl trade which are set up by excessive Customs tariffs. . . .

Present Tariff Situation. The evidence before the Conference, which is contained in the documentation or in the statements made by the members of the Conference, shows that the recovery from the effects of the war has been unduly delayed and that the foreign commerce of all nations is in greater or less degree seriously hampered by existing obstacles to trade.

The Conference notes with satisfaction that some of the more injurious forms of obstruction that prevailed immediately after the war have been removed. To this fact must be attributed in part the recovery of world trade which has so far been achieved.

Tariffs, on the other hand, which in recent years have shown a tendency to rise, are for the most part higher than before the war, and are at present one of the chief barriers to trade. The increase in most countries is almost wholly due to higher duties on manufactured articles.

In Europe, the problem has been complicated by political readjustments which have changed many frontiers and increased the number of separate Customs units from 20 to 27, all of which strive for an independent national economy which they defend by means of tariff barriers.

The harmful effect of these tariffs upon trade has in many cases been increased through their constant changes, which have created an element of uncertainty and made it impossible to place long contracts. The nations have failed to deal with this situation by long-term treaties.

Causes. This state of affairs is largely due to a desire to meet the abnormal conditions arising out of the war. For example, many duties have been raised as a protection against an influx of goods from countries with a depreciating currency. Experience has proved that even the most rapid manipulation of tariffs is not an effective method of dealing with the still more rapid changes which are caused by monetary instability. Such attempts are a source of new difficulties for commerce and are themselves a source of uncertainty. Again, in the countries themselves whose currency has been depreciating, tariffs have been raised in order to check imports in the hope of stopping the depreciation. Finally, it has sometimes happened that, where depreciation has been followed by appreciation, Customs duties payable in paper money which had been raised during the inflation have not been correspondingly reduced when revalorisation occurred. These unstable currency

conditions have to a considerable extent passed away; but the tariff
and other measures which have been specially employed to deal
with them have not yet wholly disappeared.

A second reason for the present tariff situation both in
Europe and elsewhere is the desire of nations by means of tariffs to
keep existing or recently established industries in being by means of
tariffs on a scale which they would not otherwise be able to maintain. These industries have grown to their present extent, in some
cases as a result of abnormal expansion during the war, in others as
a result of the desire of certain nations to attain a degree of
economic independence which is not justified by their slender
resources, and again in others with a view to providing employment for surplus labour for which certain former outlets are at
present closed.

This increase in productive capacity has often outrun the capacity of the country to absorb the products either as regards its
material needs or its purchasing power. The result has been either
that the plant left idle has overweighted the costs of production,
particularly when borrowed capital is involved, or that, in order to
utilise the whole plant and to give some return to the capital
employed, it has been necessary to turn to the foreign market and
so to intensify international competition.

The desire to deal with the problem of excessive industrial
capacity has usually led to an attempt to reserve the home market
for home production by means of tariff barriers erected with a
view to creating an independent national economy capable of
producing, under the protection of the tariff wall, an increase of
invested wealth and a more satisfactory return for the work of the
nation. This effort to attain self-sufficiency cannot hope to succeed
unless it is justified by the size, natural resources, economic advantages and geographical situation of a country. There are very
few countries in the world which can hope to attain it. The
artificial increase of plant which is only partly employed has meant
not only uneconomical and costly production but also a wasteful
use of the world's reduced capital resources. It has thus been one of
the causes which has maintained an abnormally high rate of interest
in recent years. It should be added that, so long as unduly high
tariffs are maintained, this uneconomic use of capital continues and
creates an increasing number of vested interests which resist a
return to a sounder policy.

High tariffs of whatever system have, in many cases, also been imposed, in the first instance at all events, for bargaining purposes. But subsequent negotiations have in practice not resulted in adequate modifications, with the consequence that the Customs barriers have been left higher than before.

This evil has become accentuated in recent years by the postwar practice of enforcing the exaggerated rates of *tarifs de combat*, whether under the autonomous or any other system, even in advance of negotiations, with the result that vested interests have frequently grown up in the meantime which have made impossible the contemplated reductions. . . .

It is too often overlooked that the attempt to stimulate artificially industries which would not otherwise flourish in a country may check the development of those activities for which it is most naturally suited. Nations may determine, for political or other reasons, that it is essential to their safety to develop increased self-sufficiency, but it is appropriate for the Conference to point out that this has in most cases involved a sacrifice of material prosperity. In such cases, the loss is borne by consumers, who have to pay more for the products of the protected industry, and by those engaged in the industries that would otherwise have a larger possibility of export.

In analysing European commercial practices, it may be observed that the advocates of exaggerated protection have often made the mistake of imagining that it is always more advantageous to hinder imports than to increase exports; it may be observed that, if exports increase, production and national income are increased in a similar proportion; if, on the other hand, imports fall on account of tariff duties, the rise in the level of commodity prices reduces not only the possibility of export but also the consuming capacity of the country. A part only of the imports excluded by the Customs duties is replaced by home production. Excessive protection, which reduces national production and purchasing power, in the end defeats its own object.

In some cases excessive import duties, by permitting very high profits to be realised at home, give an uneconomic stimulus to exports, thus creating artificial competition on foreign markets. This practice is one of the most dangerous causes of market disorganisation and of economic conflicts between nations.

Such are some of the principal illusions and most dangerous practices which have impoverished certain nations or hindered their economic reconstruction. . . .

21. A Stagnating Industry: British Shipbuilding

Britain's economy, especially, suffered from the dislocations in world trade noted by the World Economic Conference. As early as 1924 the Labour Government, during its brief tenure in office, appointed a Committee on Industry and Trade to study the condition of British industry. This committee, frequently referred to as the Balfour Committee after its chairman, the industrialist Arthur Balfour, documented the depressed conditions of British industry, most notably in a four-volume *Survey of Industries* published in 1928 and in its final report presented in 1929. The following selection from the *Survey of Industries* concerns British shipbuilding, a classic example of how excess productive capacity and falling demand could inhibit recovery.

The Balfour Committee Report on Shipbuilding, 1928

SHIPBUILDING IS an industry notable for the large differences between the high and low points of production. Periods of "slump" alternate with periods of "boom," with the consequence that production in any given year is generally much above, or much below, the average annual production over a period. . . . During the fifteen year period 1900–14 the average production was 1,471,-000 gross tons, but the difference between the output in the best year (1913) and the worst (1908) was over 1,000,000 gross tons. Generally, the course of the fluctuations was, first, a fall in freight rates, followed by a falling-off in orders, particularly for "tramps"; competition ensued among shipbuilders for such orders as came forward, and, as most of the firms were independent, this competition became progressively more acute as the depression continued, and very low prices were quoted in an endeavour to keep the yards going; eventually demand for shipping space revived, freights rose, and a rush of orders resulted in a very high production point being reached. . . .

The total tonnage of vessels of 100 gross tons and over launched in the world in the period 1909–13 was 12,444,701, of which

Source: Committee on Industry and Trade, *Survey of Industries, Part IV: Survey of Metal Industries* (London: His Majesty's Stationery Office, 1928), pp. 371–395, with deletions.

7,608,746, or 61 per cent were launched in the United Kingdom. British shipbuilders held what may be termed the home market, as it was practically unknown for vessels to be built abroad for British owners, only a total of 24,679 gross tons being built abroad for the United Kingdom in the period 1909–13. The tonnage built by United Kingdom yards for foreign owners, on the other hand, was an important factor in the economics of the industry. In the period 1909–13 tonnage built in the United Kingdom for abroad averaged 340,749 gross tons per annum, or 22.4 per cent of the output, and the percentage did not vary much from this average in any year. Hence, as the total launchings were rising during the period so was the total of tonnage built for abroad, the tonnage of vessels of 100 tons gross and over launched for abroad in 1913 reaching 419,046. During the period the British share of all launchings for abroad, i.e. whether the vessels were built in the United Kingdom or elsewhere, averaged 26.1 per cent.

During the war the merchant shipping of the world sustained losses of the order of fifteen million gross tons.[1] In the years 1915–19 the launchings totalled 18,419,497 gross tons, of which 5,390,612 gross tons, or 29 per cent, were launched in the United Kingdom. The world's launchings of merchant tonnage in 1919 were more than twice as great as in the highest pre-war year, 1913; but, owing largely to special circumstances arising out of the war, launchings in the United Kingdom in 1919 were still below the 1913 figure by over 300,000 gross tons. The world increase was predominantly due to launchings in the United States, these (exclusive of tonnage launched on the Great Lakes) being no less than 3,352,000 gross tons greater in 1919 than in 1913, or over fourteen times as great. As to capacity, the highest world output ever achieved, 7,144,549 gross tons in 1919, was more than double the highest output before the war, that of 1913. The 1913 figure, as has been explained, was reached at a period when demand was strong, and may, consequently, be taken to represent something like the then full capacity; but, owing to the enormous amount of warship work undertaken during the war and to the abnormal steps then taken to meet an exceptional demand for merchant vessels, it is difficult to estimate what was the exact increase in the capacity of merchant shipbuilding yards between 1913 and 1919.

---

[1] The British merchant ship tonnage lost during the war by enemy action was 8,363,777 gross tons.

The total may have attained double the pre-war figure, but something like one-third of the total can be attributed to the United States. . . . The capacity of the yards of the United Kingdom also increased substantially during the war. This question is further dealt with later in discussing the post-war conditions. It is sufficient to say here that the capacity of the United Kingdom did not increase to double the pre-war capacity. In other words, in 1919 the capacity of the United Kingdom was a substantially lower proportion of world capacity than it had been in 1913, this again being mainly due to the huge increase in the capacity of the yards in the United States. . . .

Shipbuilding remained after the war one of the great British manufacturing industries, as it had been just prior to the war. It is impossible to give an exact measurement of its comparative size in the two periods. The Census of Production returns for the year 1924 show the total value of vessels completed and other work of construction in that year as approximately £34,573,000, and the value of repair work as £16,652,000, a total of £51,225,000 for Great Britain. The comparative figure from the Census of 1907 was £37,091,000; but this related to the United Kingdom, i.e. it included Belfast and there was also a considerable change in values between the two dates. As to the numbers [of workers] in the industry, there are no comparable statistics for dates prior to 1923. Since then the estimated numbers in the shipbuilding and ship repairing industry insured under the Unemployment Insurance Acts have been:

	Great Britain	Great Britain and Northern Ireland
1923 (July)	245,530	269,970
1924 "	232,760	254,230
1925 "	221,530	240,120
1926 "	208,510	223,100
1927 "	203,180	216,030

Thus, the numbers in the industry fell steadily from 1923 to 1926, and in the latter year were probably less than they had been before the war. There was a further fall in 1926-27, but it was markedly smaller.

There has been no important or lasting change in the organisation of the industry from that existing in the period 1909-14, as the industry still consists of numerous independent firms of varying size and still does the main bulk of its marketing by tendering. . . .

. . . The Booth Committee[2] drew attention to the possibilities of increased efficiency arising from improved mechanical appliances, from progressive standardisation, and from scientific research.

So far as the question of machine equipment is concerned, the importance of the adoption of new devices for rapid, efficient, and cheap production is of the highest importance in shipbuilding, as in almost all other industries. There is no reason to suppose that, generally speaking, the industry does not utilise the newest improvements so far as they can be afforded. . . . In the larger shipyards facilities for the erection of the material from the ground into place have already made some headway in recent years by the installation of modern crane equipment. The initial cost is, however, high, and unless the plant can be kept fully employed and thereby earn a reasonable dividend on the capital outlay, its installation may not be economically justified and overhead costs may become unduly high. . . .

The history of shipbuilding since the war falls into two distinct sections, first the period of the "boom," when the war losses of Great Britain and certain other countries were being replaced and, secondly, the period when, these losses having been replaced, the industry experienced a severe "slump." The first period may be taken as the years 1920 and 1921, the year 1919 being [treated as a war year]. . . . In 1920 the shipbuilding industry of the United Kingdom launched the greatest tonnage of merchant vessels ever reached, nearly 2,056,000 gross tons, or 124,000 gross tons more than in 1913, the "peak" year of the pre-war period. In the latter part of 1920 freights dropped, but the shipbuilding slump did not follow immediately, as, in spite of cancellations, there were the orders placed prior to the fall in freight to be met; and the launchings of 1921 amounted to 1,538,000 gross tons. Thus, in these two years the industry of the United Kingdom launched 3,594,000 gross tons, of which 2,156,000 gross tons were for the United Kingdom. The result of this new construction was that during 1921 the tonnage owned in the United Kingdom exceeded that owned in 1914, and the work of replacing war losses was com-

[2] A committee, headed by Sir Alfred A. Booth, appointed during the war by the Board of Trade to study the prospects of British shipbuilding after the war. Its report was issued in July, 1917.–Eds.

pleted. The same thing occurred in connexion with foreign fleets at the same time, the fleets of all those countries . . . having lost tonnage during the war having more than regained their pre-war size.

The consequence was that the second division of the period, i.e. the years 1922 to 1926, was one of almost continual depression in this country, marked by a distinct, if not very great, improvement during 1924, when the launchings in the United Kingdom reached nearly 1,440,000 gross tons. . . . The average annual output in the two divisions of the period was: In 1920–21, 1,797,000 gross tons, and in 1922–26, 968,000 gross tons, as against an annual average for the whole period of 1,205,000 gross tons. The significance of these figures will be realised if it is repeated that the annual average in the period 1909–13 was 1,522,000 gross tons.

The whole period, also, was one in which little warship work was available as compared with that being done in the period immediately preceding the war.

The greatest amount of tonnage under construction at any time in the United Kingdom was nearly 3,800,000 gross tons in March, 1921, which compares with an estimated pre-war maximum of about 2,600,000. The annual shipbuilding capacity of the United Kingdom in the post-war period may be placed at about 3 million gross tons, an increase of half a million tons over the pre-war figure. In no year has production approached 3 million tons, nor, as will be seen from the following paragraph dealing with demand, is it likely to do so in the near future. Since the end of 1921 the shipyards of the United Kingdom could have produced the whole of the new tonnage constructed in each year in the world and still not have exhausted their capacity. . . .

It was pointed out in an earlier section of this memorandum that a fall in ocean freights has always been the forerunner of a falling-off in demand for new vessels. Freights had been very high during the war, but they began to weaken in 1919 and fell suddenly and rapidly towards the middle of 1920. The monthly Index Number of Shipping Freights (average of year 1920 = 100) during that year was : January 123, March 141, June 112, September 84. In January, 1921, it was 45, and in March 37. The consequence was that demand instantly fell away, orders for over 300 vessels which had been contracted for in this country being cancelled. Ocean freights have remained low, the Index Number having fallen as low as 22, and never having risen above 40 between the middle of 1921 and the autumn of 1926. . . . Thus, the industry did not, during the period under consideration, experience the keen demand consequent upon a high or rising freight market.

Closely related to the question of freight rates is the amount of tonnage available in relation to the volume of the overseas trade of the world. No accurate figure of such tonnage is available. The figures of all tonnage of 100 gross tons and over amounted in June, 1914 to, approximately, 49,000,000 gross tons. In June, 1921, when the fleets of Great Britain and the other countries which had, on balance, lost tonnage during the war had been brought to their pre-war size, the world tonnage amounted to, approximately, 62 million gross tons, an increase of 13 million gross tons, or 26.5 per cent, over the 1914 figure. In 1922 the world's tonnage reached 64 million gross tons, and, in 1923, 65 million, a figure to which it still approximated in 1926, representing an increase of 16 million gross tons, or 32.6 per cent over the 1914 figure. These figures, however, represent more than the tonnage available for overseas trade, since they include vessels laid up and vessels employed in the coastal trade which, in the case of the U.S.A., represent a very considerable proportion. Nevertheless, even if the tonnage of the U.S.A. be disregarded in its entirety, the merchant fleet of the rest of the world increased from, approximately, 42 million gross tons in 1913 to 50 million gross tons in 1926, an increase of rather more than 19 per cent. Upon the whole, the volume of the world's overseas trade was smaller during the post-war years than in the period immediately preceding the war; and consequently the shipbuilding industry could not look for any demand arising from a world shortage of ships.

The effect of this would have been discouraging to shipbuilding even had anything like all the tonnage been employed, but, in fact, large numbers of vessels throughout the period were laid-up. . . .

Even if the laid-up tonnage is deducted from the world's total tonnage, the remainder throughout the post-war years was considerably larger than the 1914 figures. No doubt some of this laid-up tonnage was composed of old and, comparatively speaking, inefficient vessels, but much of it was not; and the effect upon demand was that any slight increase in freight rates merely reduced the amount of laid-up tonnage, instead of causing inquiries for new vessels.

There are three other points which require mention in connexion with demand. First, owing to the increased building capacity of the world, competition has become even keener than it was
before the war; secondly, warship construction, which, as has been
mentioned, accounted for something like a quarter of the work of
British yards before the war, has been very greatly reduced; and,
thirdly, the increased size of vessels results in a given amount of
freight being carried by fewer ships, while the increase of speed
means that these ships can make more voyages in a given time. All
these tendencies towards the restriction of demand operated
strongly upon the British shipbuilding industry, which is by far the
largest of any and which has been dependent to so large an extent
upon building for abroad. . . .

During the "boom" year of 1920, employment, of course, was
good, the percentage of insured workpeople unemployed averag-
ing under 4 per cent until the occurrence of the coal strike in the
autumn of that year. Since then, very serious unemployment has
been continual in the industry in spite of the fact that the numbers
employed in it have been steadily falling. In March, 1921, the percentage unemployed was 14, but, since then, it has seldom fallen
below 30 per cent and has on several occasions been well above 40
per cent. At the end of 1926, it was still 42 per cent. In numbers,
these figures imply that between March, 1921, and the end of 1926,
there were always between 75,000 and 120,000 persons unemployed in the shipbuilding industry. . . . As to wages, the following are the averages of the recognised time-rates in nine principal
centres, in December, 1920, the "peak"; in December, 1923, the
lowest point reached; and in December, 1925. . . .

	July, 1914		December, 1920		December, 1923		December, 1925	
	s.	d.	s.	d.	s.	d.	s.	d.
Shipwrights	41	4	91	3	48	7	55	7
Joiners	40	0	101	4	50	9	57	9
Labourers	22	10	70	5	38	5	38	5

. . . Disregarding the years 1920 and 1921 . . . during the
period 1922–26, 47 per cent of the total tonnage launched in the
world was launched in the United Kingdom, as compared with 61

per cent in the period 1909–13. This fall was due to a decrease of the average annual launchings in the United Kingdom from 1,522,-000 gross tons in 1909–13 to 968,000 gross tons in 1922–26 and to an increase in the average annual launchings abroad from 967,000 gross tons in 1909–13 to 1,077,000 gross tons in 1922–26. . . .

22. Cartelization of Industry

One method of dealing with excess capacity, overcapitalization, and low profits was for producers to form combinations that would limit competition, allocate markets, and support prices. Trusts and cartels were certainly not new in the 1920's, but their number and significance greatly increased in that decade, especially in Germany, where the government actively aided attempts to control competition. In 1923 a decree law was enacted there to regularize the activity of cartels, and their number was at that time officially estimated at 3,000. The cartelization movement was by no means confined to Germany, and manufacturers sought to introduce a measure of control in international as well as domestic markets. One of the most important international cartels was the International Steel Cartel, created in 1926 by producers in Germany, France, Belgium, Luxembourg, and the Saar Territory. In 1927, Czechoslovakia, Austria, and Hungary joined. The Cartel countries accounted for roughly 30 per cent of world steel production in the late 1920's, but for about two-thirds of world steel exports. The text of the agreement establishing the Cartel and a note on the quotas for production are given below.

The International Steel Agreement, 1926

ARTICLE 1. Each country shall pay 1 dollar monthly into a common fund for each ton of crude steel actually produced.

By the term "crude steel" is meant all the crude steel manufactured in the several countries by the Thomas, Bessemer, Siemens or Martin processes, by the electric crucible, or any other process. This sum shall be credited to the account of the country in question. . . .

Should the Government of one of the countries participating in the Agreement object to the transfer of all or any of the sums payable under the present Article, the actual payment might be replaced:

(1) By the guarantee of a bank approved by the Managing Committee; or

Source: League of Nations, Economic and Financial Section, *International* [World] *Economic Conference, Documentation: Memorandum on the Iron and Steel Industry* (Geneva: League of Nations, 1927), Annex VI, pp. 109–113.

(2) By a cash payment into a blocked account at a bank situated in the country in question and approved by the Managing Committee.

ARTICLE 2. The administration of the common fund shall be provided for by a Managing Committee of four members appointed respectively by each of the countries Parties to the Agreement, *i.e.* Germany, Belgium, France, and Luxemburg. . . .

In a general way, and in addition to the special provisions laid down in the Articles following, the Managing Committee shall make the necessary arrangements for carrying out the execution of the clauses of the present contract and for exercising the supervision which it entails. It shall also have full powers for the administration, handling, and custody of the monies paid into the common fund or held by it. The number of votes of the Managing Committee shall be allotted in accordance with the quotas.

ARTICLE 3. The Managing Committee shall fix the quota of each country for each quarter in accordance with the provisions of Article 4 not later than a fortnight before the beginning of that quarter, by applying coefficients—fixed once for all for each country—to the total tonnage representing the probable demand of the market.

ARTICLE 4. The coefficients allotted to the different countries can only be modified by unanimous consent.

The total quarterly tonnage, and accordingly the quotas of each country, shall be fixed by a two-thirds majority of the votes, each country commanding the number of votes proportional to its participation, with the proviso that unanimity of all the countries but one shall constitute a sufficient majority even if this latter country represents more than a quarter of the votes.

The Saar shall never vote individually; its votes shall be divided between France and Germany in their ratios of one-third and two-thirds.

ARTICLE 5. Every month each country's actual net production of crude steel during that month shall be ascertained, in relation to the figures indicated by the quotas.

ARTICLE 6. If the quarterly production of a country exceeds the quota which was fixed for it, that country shall pay in respect of each ton in excess a fine of 4 dollars, which shall accrue to the common fund, in addition to the payment provided for in Article 1.

ARTICLE 7. If the production of any country has been below the quota allotted to it, that country shall receive in compensation from the common fund the sum of 2 dollars per ton short.

The tonnage entitling to compensation may not, however, exceed 10 per cent of the quota fixed for the quarter in question. If a shortage of 10 per cent or more below the quota fixed continues during several successive quarters, the tonnage entitling to compensation shall be reduced by 2 per cent for each successive quarter, so that in the second quarter of such shortage of 10 per cent or more the compensation paid shall not exceed 8 per cent, and in the third quarter it shall not exceed 6 per cent, and so on. . . .

ARTICLE 8. . . . At the close of each half-year, the common fund shall be liquidated, after deduction of the general expenses; the remaining balance shall be distributed between the several countries:

(1) In proportion to the actual production during the accounting period, up to the limit of the payments made under Article 1;

(2) And, if any balance remains over from fines, in proportion to the participation figures of the accounting period concerned.

The first liquidation of the common fund shall take place on April 1st, 1927.

ARTICLE 9. The present Agreement shall terminate on April 1st, 1931. Up to May 1st, 1929, however, any country shall be entitled to give notice of withdrawal from the Agreement on October 31st, 1929, in which case the other countries shall be released from all obligations on the same date. . . .

ARTICLE 13. Any disputes arising between the Parties as to the interpretation and carrying out of the present Agreement shall be compulsorily settled by arbitration.

ARTICLE 14. It shall be open to steel manufacturers in the other European countries to join in the present Agreement. . . .

Note on Share Quotas in the Cartel

In fixing the share quotas of the individual countries in the International Steel Agreement, the basis taken was that of an aggregate annual production of raw steel of 25,278,000 tons and the annual quotas were fixed on this basis as follows:

Germany	40.45%
France	31.89
Belgium	12.57
Luxemburg	8.55
Saar Territory	6.54

These participation figures are changed if the total output rises by 1, 2, 3 or 4 million tons up to 29,278,000 tons. Above this figure the final quotas are as follows:

Germany	43.18%
France	31.18
Belgium	11.56
Luxemburg	8.30
Saar Territory	5.78

In the event of any further increase in output, these percentage quotas will remain unchanged. Belgium, however, on joining the International Steel Cartel, was granted a fixed quota of 295,000 tons per month irrespective of any restriction which might be imposed on output. As a consequence, the quotas of the other countries were somewhat reduced.

In November 1926, the total output of the International Steel Cartel for the fourth quarter of 1926 was fixed at 29,278,000 tons. In December 1926, by a resolution of the International Steel Cartel, it was decided to reduce the output for the first quarter of 1927 by 1.5 million tons. In March 1927 this reduced output was once more raised by 1.5 million tons for the second quarter of 1927.

At the beginning of 1927, Czechoslovakia, Austria and Hungary joined in the International Steel Agreement. These three countries together received a share of 7.272 per cent, or 2.14 million tons, annually on the basis of a total output by the International Steel Cartel of 27,278,000 tons. These three Central European countries having joined the Cartel as a single unit, the distribution of their quota between them is a matter to be settled by themselves.

PART V

Soviet Economic Policy in the 1920's

In the decade of the 1920's the economic history of the Soviet Union revolved around two closely interconnected problems: relations between agriculture and industry, and economic growth. The heart of the matter was a disequilibrium between the agricultural and industrial sectors, which had also existed before the Revolution. The industrial structure inherited from Czarist days was weighted toward heavy industry, an emphasis the Bolsheviks continued out of conviction. In the countryside the effect of the Revolution had been to enlarge the proportion of small, inefficient peasant holdings. In the first dozen years of Bolshevik rule there were a series of crises in which exchange between the industrial and agricultural sectors became seriously weakened. The first crisis was the period of War Communism (1918–21) during the Civil War. As a result of wartime conditions, and the nationalization of industry, foreign trade and banks, the transport and currency systems collapsed, and regular trade between city and countryside disappeared. Despite seizure of peasant crops, the cities starved, and the urban population fell by one-third to one-half. By 1921 total industrial production had fallen to one-fifth of the 1913 level, and Russia was in a state of spectacular economic collapse.

To end the economic chaos, Lenin introduced a New Economic Policy (NEP) in 1921. The key measure was directed at the peasant, who was allowed to sell his surplus on a free market. Around this free market a mixed economy grew up. The state retained control of heavy industry, transport, and banking—the so-called "commanding heights" of the economy—but allowed private enterprise in light industry and agriculture. Attempts were made to encourage foreign trade, and industrial concessions were granted to foreign companies. The NEP served to restore the economy. Except for grain, agricultural production recovered relatively rapidly, reaching the over-all 1913 level by 1925; industrial production reached the 1913 level in 1927. Recovery did not, however, provide a basis for sustained economic growth. Agriculture retained its peasant character and did not expand its output. Industrial recovery had been achieved by the restoration of pre-war equipment, and capital investment was inadequate even to cover depreciation, so that the capital of past years was being consumed.

In the mid-1920's there was much debate about how to accumulate capital for economic growth, the issue becoming enmeshed with the struggle for succession after Lenin's death in 1924. The Right argued that the key to creating sufficient capital lay in the improvement of agricultural production. Government policy should be to encourage the peasant to "enrich" himself, and, as rural productivity and income rose, NEP would evolve gradually and smoothly into industrial expansion and socialism. The Left, associated with Trotsky, insisted that a socialist Russia did not have time to wait for the gradual accumulation of capital, especially through the consumer-oriented NEP and that in any case economic growth was a discontinuous, not an evolutionary, process. It would be necessary to carry out rapid, planned industrialization financed by forced savings, a burden that would fall mainly upon the peasant majority. Stalin took a middle position in the debate, insisting only that Russia could build socialism by its own resources. He sided first with the Right, then in 1928 and 1929, after the Left was eliminated from power, adopted its solution in the extreme form of forced industrialization and collectivization of agriculture.

The first step was the decision, taken at the end of 1927, to embark upon rapid and planned industrial expansion. The First Five Year Plan called for a high rate of growth and sought to end the imbalance between agriculture and industry by creating larger agricultural units through collectivization and by modernizing agricultural production. But in 1928 and 1929 both industrialization and collectivization were accelerated, at least partly because of serious grain shortages. During the years of the First Five Year Plan (1928–32) industrial capacity was vastly enlarged. It was heavily weighted toward producer goods, especially traditional industries such as coal and steel, and was concentrated in extremely large production units, some so large as to be inefficient. Quality was poor and the planning system extremely unsophisticated and overcentralized. Control of agriculture was achieved only by forced collectivization. For the Soviet population the costs were high; real wages fell for industrial workers, and, in both city and village, standards of living declined. But sustained industrial growth had been achieved.

23. The New Economic Policy (NEP)

At the end of the period of War Communism the most pressing problem was peasant agriculture. Production had fallen sharply—by 1921 the sown area had decreased by 30 per cent compared with 1913—and the peasants refused to sell for worthless currency the crops they did raise. The New Economic Policy began as an emergency measure to decrease the pressure upon the peasant and thus to increase his incentive to produce—an approach Lenin called the "alliance" or "bond" of worker and peasant. The first step was the abandonment of grain seizures (the "surplus-grain appropriation system") and the introduction of a fixed tax on peasant production, first in kind and later in money. Such a tax implied a free market where the peasant could sell his surplus and, in turn, industrial production geared to the market. To those who objected that this amounted to a surrender to capitalism, Lenin replied that state control of heavy industry, transport, and banking assured a socialist core that would gradually expand and provide the means for transforming the Russian economy into an entirely socialist one. The first document below is the resolution, adopted in March, 1921, by the 10th Party Congress, establishing the tax in kind. The second is taken from a speech by Lenin, made a month later to a group of party functionaries, explaining the reasons for the new policy and his views on its evolution.

A. Resolution of the 10th Party Congress on the Tax in Kind, March, 1921

1. IN ORDER to assure proper and peaceful economic life on the basis of a freer use by the peasant of his economic resources, in order to strengthen the peasant economy and to raise its productivity, and also with the purpose of calculating precisely the peasants' obligation to the state, requisitioning, as a means of state procurement of foodstuffs, raw materials and fodder, shall be replaced by a tax in kind.

2. This tax must be less than that imposed up to this time by the requisition system of taxation. The total tax must be reckoned so as

Source: *Direktivy KPSS i sovetskogo pravitel'stva po khoziaistvennym voprosam*, Vol. I, 1917–28 (Moscow: Gosudarstvennoe Izdatel'stvo Politicheskoi Literatury, 1957), pp. 206–207, with deletions. Translated by the editors.

to cover the minimal requirements of the Army, the city workers, and the nonagricultural population. The total amount of the tax must be constantly diminished to the extent that the re-establishment of transport and industry will permit the Soviet Government to receive agricultural products by normal means, i.e., in exchange for the products of industry and the artisan.

3. The tax is to be in the form of a percentage or partial deduction from what is produced on a holding, taking into account the harvest, the number of eaters in the household, and the number of cattle.

4. The tax must be progressive, with a lower percentage established for the holdings of middle and poor peasants, of urban workers, etc. The holdings of the poorest peasants may be freed from some, and in exceptional cases from all, forms of the tax in kind. Industrious peasants who expand the amount of their holdings under crops and also those who increase the productivity of their holdings shall receive privileges in paying the tax in kind, either in the form of a lower tax rate or in the form of complete exemption from the tax.

5. The taxation law must be so framed, and published within such a time limit, that the peasants shall be informed as exactly as possible about the amount of their obligations before the beginning of spring planting.

6. The delivery to the state of the products listed for the tax shall end within definite time limits, precisely established by the law.

7. The sum due for the tax shall be calculated for the agricultural community (the *obshchestvo*). Within the community the tax shall be apportioned among the peasants, as they see fit, in accordance with the general norms set forth in paragraph 3. Measures to control application of the tax norms and for collection of the tax shall be worked out by elected organizations of local peasant taxpayers, divided according to the size of their tax.

8. All the reserves of foodstuffs, raw material, and fodder that remain with the peasants after the tax has been paid may be freely disposed of and may be used by them for improving and strengthening their holdings, for increasing their own consumption, and for exchange for the products of industry, of the artisan, and of agriculture. Exchange is permitted within the limits of local economic turnover. . . .

B. Lenin's Report on the Tax in Kind, April, 1921

COMRADES, ONE hears the most varied and highly confusing opinions on the question of the tax in kind and the change in our food policy, and also on the Soviet government's economic policy. . . .

The first question is: what has called forth this change, which many think to be too drastic and not sufficiently justified?

The fundamental and principal reason for the change is the extraordinarily acute crisis of peasant farming, and its very difficult condition, which has proved to be much harder by the spring of 1921 than could have been expected. On the other hand, its consequences have affected the restoration of our transport system and of our industry. I should like to point out that most mistakes on the question of substituting the tax in kind for the surplus-grain appropriation system, and on the significance of the change, are made because there is no effort to analyse the nature of the change and its implications. Here is a picture of peasant farming by the spring of 1921: an extremely severe crisis caused by the war-time ruin and aggravated by a disastrous crop failure and the resultant fodder shortage (for the failure also affected the hay crop) and loss of cattle; and the weakening of the productive forces of peasant farming, which in many places was doomed to utter ruin. And here we come to this question: what is the connection between this terribly acute crisis of peasant farming and the Soviet government's abolition of the surplus-grain appropriation system? I say that if we are to understand this measure we must ask ourselves: what is the transition we are making?

In the event of a workers' revolution in a country with a predominantly peasant population, with the factories, works and railways taken over by the working class, what, in essence, should be the economic relations between the working class and the peasantry? They should obviously be the following: the workers producing in the factories and works, which now belong to them, all that is necessary for the country—and that means also for the peasants, who constitute the majority of the population—should transport

Source: Excerpts from a speech delivered on April 9, 1921, to a meeting of party officials of the Moscow region, reprinted in V. I. Lenin, *Collected Works*, Vol. XXXII (Moscow: Progress Publishers, 1965), pp. 286–298.

all these things on their railroads and river vessels and deliver them to the peasants, in return for the surplus agricultural produce. . . . If peasant farming is to develop, we must also assure its transition to the next stage which must inevitably be one of gradual amalgamation of the small, isolated peasant farms—the least profitable and most backward—into large-scale collective farms. That is how socialists have always visualised it, and that is exactly how our own Communist Party sees it. I repeat, the greatest source of error and confusion is in appraising the tax in kind without making allowance for the specific features of the transitional measures which we must take, if we are to attain the goals which we can and must reach. . . .

You know that for several years after the victory of the workers' revolution in Russia, after the imperialist war, we had to endure a civil war, and it is now no exaggeration to say that Russia suffered more than any other country involved in the imperialist war, including those which had suffered because it was fought on their territory. For after four years of imperialist war we endured three years of civil war, which brought more havoc and industrial dislocation than any external war, because it was fought in the very heart of the country. This terrible devastation is the main reason why initially during the war—particularly when the Civil War cut us off from grain areas, like Siberia, the Caucasus and the whole of the Ukraine, and from our supplies of coal and oil, and reduced our possibilities of obtaining other types of fuel—we could hold out—in a besieged fortress—only through the surplus-grain appropriation system, that is, by taking from the peasant whatever surplus produce was available, and sometimes even a part of his necessaries, in order to keep the army in fighting trim and to prevent industry from going to pieces altogether. . . .

This was not an economic system or an economic plan for a policy, adopted from a number of possible choices. That was not the case at all. We could not think of restoring industry without ensuring a minimum of food and fuel. Appropriation of surpluses without remuneration—because you can't call paper currency remuneration—was the only answer to the task we set ourselves to preserve the remnants of industry, to keep the workers from dispersing altogether, and to maintain the army. We had no other way out. That is what we are discarding, and I have already told you what we are adopting. The tax is to help us make the transition. If it were possible to restore our industry faster, then perhaps, with a better harvest, we could make an earlier transition to the exchange of manufactured goods for agricultural products. . . .

Today I had a visit from Comrade Korolyov of Ivanovo-Voznesensk, our most industrial, proletarian, Red district. He gave me some facts and figures [on textile production]. In the first year [1920] only six factories were in operation, and not one of them ran for a month without stoppages. Industry was grinding down to a standstill. During the past year, 22 factories were started for the first time, some running for several months, others up to half a year, without stoppages. The planned target was set at 150 million arshins,[1] and according to the latest figures they produced 117 million arshins, getting only half the fuel they had been allocated. That is how production plans were disrupted, not only in Ivanovo-Voznesensk, but all over Russia. This was due to a large extent to the decline of peasant farming, to loss of cattle, and the impossibility of transporting a sufficient quantity of firewood to the railway stations and river wharves, all of which gave Ivanovo-Voznesensk less firewood, less peat, and less oil than it should have had. . . .

Now, why is peasant farming the focus? Because it alone can give us the food and the fuel we need. If the working class, as the ruling class exercising its dictatorship, wants to run the economy properly, it must say: the crisis of peasant farming is the weakest spot. It must be remedied, and another start made on the revival of large-scale industry, so that in Ivanovo-Voznesensk district, for instance, all 70 factories—and not just 22—are running again. These large factories will then satisfy national demand, and the working class will deliver the goods to the peasants in exchange for farm produce, instead of taking it in the form of a tax. That is the transition we are making, and the price is short rations all round, if we are to save those who alone can keep what is left of industry and the railways going, and the army in the field to fight off the whiteguards.

Our grain appropriations were maligned by the Mensheviks, who said that the Soviet power had given the population nothing but grain appropriations, want and destruction. They gloated over the fact that after the partial restoration of peace, after the end of the Civil War, the swift rehabilitation of our industry had proved to be impossible. But even the richest countries will take years to

[1] One *arshin* = 28 inches.—Eds.

get their industry going full blast again. Even a rich country like France will take a long time to revive her industry, and she did not suffer as much from the war as we did, because only a small part of her territory was devastated. The astonishing thing is that in the first year of a partial peace we were able to start 22 factories out of 70 in Ivanovo-Voznesensk, and to produce 117 million arshins of cotton goods out of an anticipated 150 million. The grain appropriations had once been inevitable, but now we have had to change our food policy: we have had to switch from the surplus appropriation system to the tax. This will undoubtedly improve the peasant's condition, and give him an assurance and a sense of certainty that he will be free to exchange all his available grain surplus at least for local handicraft wares. This explains why the Soviet government must conduct an economic policy on these lines.

Now, in conclusion, let me explain how this policy can be reconciled with the communist standpoint and how it has come about that the communist Soviet power is promoting a free market. Is it good from the standpoint of communism? To answer this question we must make a careful examination of the changes that have taken place in peasant farming. First, we witnessed the assault of the whole of the peasantry on the rule of the landowners. . . . We find the poor peasants organising to prevent the kulaks [richer peasants] from seizing the land taken away from the landowners. The Soviet government helped the Poor Peasants' Committees that sprang up in Russia and in the Ukraine. As a result, the middle peasants have become the predominant element in the rural areas. We know this from statistics, and everyone who lives in the country knows it from his own observations. The extremes of kulak and poor have been rounded off, and the majority of the population have come closer to the status of the middle peasant. If we want to raise the productivity of our peasant farming we must reckon chiefly with the middle peasant. The Communist Party has had to shape its policy accordingly.

Since the middle peasants now predominate in the rural areas, we must help them to improve their farming; moreover, we must make the same demands on them as we do on the workers. The principal question discussed at the last Party Congress was that of food propaganda: concentrate on the economic front; raise the productivity of labour and increase output! No progress is possible unless these tasks are fulfilled. If we say this to the worker, we must say as much to the peasant, but will demand in return that, after paying the tax, he should enlarge his farm, in the knowledge that no more will be exacted from him and that he will be free to use the whole of his surplus to develop his farm. Consequently, the change in policy in respect of the peasants is due to the change in their status. There are more middle peasants in the make-up of the rural areas and we must reckon with this, if we are to boost the productive forces.

. . . Large-scale industry is not back on its feet, and socialist factories are getting perhaps only one-tenth of what they should be getting. In consequence, small enterprise remains independent of the socialist factories. The incredible havoc, the shortage of fuel, raw materials and transport facilities allow small enterprise to exist separately from socialism. I ask you: What is state capitalism in these circumstances? It is the amalgamation of small-scale production. Capital amalgamates small enterprises and grows out of them. It is no use closing our eyes to this fact. Of course, a free market means a growth of capitalism; there's no getting away from the fact. And anyone who tries to do so will be deluding himself. Capitalism will emerge wherever there is small enterprise and free exchange. But are we to be afraid of it, if we have control of the factories, transport and foreign trade? Let me repeat what I said then: I believe it to be incontrovertible that we need have no fear of this capitalism. Concessions [to foreign firms] are that kind of capitalism.

We have been trying hard to conclude concession agreements, but, unfortunately, have not yet concluded a single one. Nevertheless, we are nearer to them now than we were several months ago, when we last discussed concessions. What are concessions from the standpoint of economic relations? They are state capitalism. The Soviet government concludes an agreement with a capitalist. Under it, the latter is provided with certain things: raw materials, mines, oilfields, minerals, or, as was the case in one of the last proposals, even a special factory (the ball-bearing project of a Swedish enterprise). The socialist state gives the capitalist its means of production such as factories, mines and materials. The capitalist operates as a contractor leasing socialist means of production, making a profit on his capital and delivering a part of his output to the socialist state.

Why is it that we badly need such an arrangement? Because it gives us, all at once, a greater volume of goods which we need but cannot produce ourselves. That is how we get state capitalism. Should it scare us? No, it should not, because it is up to us to determine the extent of the concessions. Take oil concessions. They will give us millions of poods of paraffin oil right away, and that is more than we produce ourselves. This is to our advantage, because in exchange for the paraffin oil—and not paper money—the peasant will give us his grain surplus, and we shall immediately be able to improve the situation in the whole country. That is why the capitalism that is bound to grow out of a free market holds no terrors for us. It will be the result of growing trade, the exchange of manufactured goods, even if produced by small industry, for agricultural produce.

. . . We do not shut our eyes to the fact that a free market entails some development of capitalism, and we say: This capitalism will be under the control and surveillance of the state. We need have no fear of it because the workers' state has taken possession of the factories and railways. It will help to stimulate the economic exchange of peasant produce for the manufactures of neighbouring craftsmen, who will satisfy some, if not all, of the peasants' requirements in manufactured goods. The peasant economy will improve, and that is something we need to do desperately. Let small industry grow to some extent and let state capitalism develop—the Soviet power need have no fear of that. We must face the facts squarely and call a spade a spade, but we must also control and determine the limits of this development.

Concessions are nothing to be afraid of. There is nothing terrible about giving the concessionaires a few factories and retaining the bulk in our own hands. . . . Growing capitalism will be under control and supervision, while political power will remain in the hands of the working class and of the workers' state. The capital which will exist in the form of concessions and the capital which will inevitably grow through the medium of the co-operatives and a free market, have no terrors for us. We must try to develop and improve the condition of the peasantry, and make a great effort to have this benefit the working class. We shall be able to do all that can be done to improve peasant farming and develop local trade more quickly with concessions than without them, while planning our national economy for a much faster rehabilitation of large-scale socialist industry. We shall be able to do this more quickly with the help of a rested and recuperated peasant economy than with the absolutely poverty-stricken peasant farming we have had up to now.

That is what I have to say on the communist appreciation of this policy, on why it was necessary, and why, if properly applied, it will bring improvement immediately, or, at all events, more quickly than if it had not been applied.

24. The Limits of the New Economic Policy

The NEP raised in a new form the question of the relationship between agriculture and industry. At the beginning of the period the situation in industry was especially difficult. Production recovered slowly, reaching only one-third of the 1913 level by 1923–24. Because of a shortage of working capital, equipment was under-utilized and production costs rose; from 1922 industrial prices began to climb sharply. At the same time, agricultural production recovered more rapidly, reaching three-quarters of the prewar level by 1923–24, and prices began to fall. As early as 1923, Trotsky noted the divergence of agricultural and industrial prices and invented the term "scissors" to describe the growing spread between them. He argued that although the very limitations of peasant agriculture made it resilient, heavy industry needed an extra push, and the scissors could be permanently closed only by an intense effort at planned industrial expansion to increase the supply and mix of products. Industrial expansion would impose heavy burdens upon the population, and he made popular the phrase "primitive socialist accumulation" of capital to describe this process.

Trotsky's Speech on the Problems of the NEP, 1923

In our country, the distribution of resources is directed first of all by the relationship between city and countryside. Agriculture is the predominant occupation of our population. Consequently . . . in Soviet Russia market relations must first of all regulate relations between city and village. This is the essential character of our New Economic Policy. So we must ask ourselves, has the NEP in the past two years resolved, or has it moved toward resolving, those tasks in the name of which we let loose the devil of market relations? Yes or no?

What are these tasks? The first and most basic "job" our party so to speak assigned to NEP was to nudge the productive powers of the country upward. The second job, one which we are the first in history to tackle, was to direct as far as possible these productive

Source: Excerpts from Trotsky's report to the 12th Party Congress, April, 1923, *Dvenadtsatyi s"ezd rossiiskoi kommunisticheskoi partii (bol'shevikov): Stenograficheskii otchet, 17–25 aprelia 1923 g.* (Moscow: Izdatel'stvo "Krasnaia Nov," 1923), pp. 282–322. Translated by the editors.

forces that were expanding or needed to be expanded into the channel of the workers' state, onto the socialist road. These two jobs, comrades, are definitely not the same thing. . . . At a certain stage of development, the market serves to raise the productive forces. But for us this is not the final nor the decisive fact. Where does our authentic and urgent work begin? *It begins when we direct these developing productive forces into the channels of socialist construction.* We must always keep these two sides of the problem clearly in view so as not to be deceived by the facts, data, and figures we extract from the imprecise reports on our economic life. And thus, if we raise the first question—in the last two years has the market served to raise the nation's productive forces?—without any hesitation we must reply affirmatively. Our statistics, as I have already said, are extremely incomplete. But, with the help of the Central Statistical Administration, I tried to work out summary figures for our economy. They cover all branches of the economy in 1913, 1921 and 1922. . . .

PRODUCTION IN PREWAR PRICES (rubles)

	Industry (value of finished product)				
	Heavy and medium industry	Handicraft and cottage industry	Total	Agriculture (gross product)	Grand total
1913	3,721	730	4,451	6,714	11,165
1921	669 } + 43%	260	929	3,535	4,464
1922	954	415	1,369	4,005	5,374

Here I draw your attention to a fact of extreme importance. The exchange of goods between city and countryside in the past year was mainly of a *consumer* character. That is, the city received from the village products of personal nourishment, and the peasant in his turn received from the city mainly articles of private consumption or household articles. That means that the so-called alliance—the economic exchange between city and countryside—is going through a primitive stage, that of the exchange of consumer goods. . . . The primitiveness of the recovery of our economy is reflected in two aspects: first, the consumer character of trade between city and village; and second, the disproportionately large role of handicraft and cottage industry. Handicraft and cottage industry, mainly peasant enterprise, produces 415 million gold rubles, and heavy and medium industry produces 954 million—that is, only a little over twice as much.

Here the full implication of the question is revealed: By what channels is trade between city and village developing and where do the odds lie? To speak clearly, do they lie on the side of capitalism or of socialism? The productive forces have indeed grown, and the country has become richer. But who has received the larger share of this increment, this augmentation, the workers' state or private capital? The NEP is, as is recognized by our legislation, an arena of struggle between us and private capital. We created that arena, and legalized that struggle which we must wage seriously for a long time. But it is necessary to carry out that struggle with calculation at every turn, at every stage—and not just at a party congress. The most important question is, who gets most out of the economic expansion, who grabs the lion's share? . . . How then do things stand in the area of the relations between state industry and the market? Are we successful here? And if we are, in what way? . . .

For the past year our state industry has had a net deficit. If we take light and heavy industry together—we can even add transport, or we can deal with it separately; it's all the same—then it turns out that state industry worked at a loss. That means that comparing the total material wealth the state had in the area of industry a year ago with today, we are poorer today than a year ago. It is necessary to be clearly aware of that. Separate branches of our economy, it is true, boast of profits. . . . But in general and on the whole, light and medium industry lived at the expense of public funds, at the expense of the peasant economy. I have already said that we had an increase of 43 per cent in all industrial production. But if we look just at mining, coal, and oil, the increase is insignificant. The biggest increase of all was in the cotton-fabric industry, from 86 million to 191 million prewar gold rubles. . . .

The whole apparatus of our industrial economy had become almost totally frozen, and, in order for the huge machine to thaw out and move, some extra fuel was necessary. The deficit consists of the extraordinary expense for firing up the engine, which was almost completely stiff with cold, reaching in some places, at some factories, to absolute zero and even well below that. Our loss represents those additional sacrifices demanded of us in order to get our industry into low gear. . . . Of our competitors, the peasant artisan and the traders are already working at a profit, and if we stand around gaping they will advance toward each other, not only to the detriment of the proletariat, but also of the peasant artisan. And against that you can't just shut the door with the monopoly of trade, for commercial capital and the peasant artisan are right in our midst, everywhere. We ourselves, in order that the revival of state industry should be possible, gave freedom—and had to give it—to the trader, the peasant craftsman, to the grain market. But if we are not able to control the process, a dangerous opponent can grow out of it.

We often say we occupy the commanding heights of industry, and that is absolutely correct. Transport is in our hands, metallurgy, fuel, the most important factories, banks—all of this constitutes the commanding heights. But these commanding heights, in contrast to geographical heights, either expand or diminish. . . . If we ask ourselves whether, over-all, our commanding heights are stronger, more powerful today than a year ago, then the answer is double-edged. Our industrial complexes are indeed beginning to get back to work, revealing their reviving vital energy, and that is a great step forward. But in terms of the total value of their inventories, they are poorer than they were a year ago. . . .

The second of the two questions posed by us was: "Who at present benefits from the economic revival?" We must answer that now the benefits go first of all to commercial capital and to petty and light industry, including the peasant artisan. Yet we are burning up a significant part of our basic capital as kindling for our big machines. . . .

Such is the balance sheet of the first period of NEP, and from that balance sheet emerge the tasks of the second period. I have, in fact, already indicated the general aspect of these tasks. We must do everything so that the general economic revival continues. We must have a conscious, skillful, and persistent policy of further development of industrial strength. In conformity with this, trade between city and village must take on more and more of a producer rather than a consumer character. Finally, it is vital for us as a workers' state that the revival is directed increasingly into state, socialist channels. By a skillful, purposeful policy and economic organization we must divert to the mill of socialism the maximum part of what we call surplus value, which is created by all the working population of our Union.

What are the ways of doing this? The first and most basic way we all know very well—the alliance of city and countryside. This alliance is a magnificent expression, but we use it so often that in fact we have almost forgotten its meaning. Therefore, it is necessary now to go into the question of the alliance somewhat more concretely. It bears first of all upon the exchange of the products of agriculture for the products of industry. . . . What kind of correlation of prices exists between agricultural and industrial products? Three months ago, the Commission of Internal Trade, headed by Comrade Lezhava, drew up these figures, which probably are known to you. For the bare quantities they are accustomed to use, peasants must now pay 267 per cent of what they paid in 1913 for textiles, soap, kerosene, leather goods, matches, salt, sugar, and oil. That is, where they once needed 1 pound of grain for a product, now they need 2.67 pounds, two and two-thirds times more, for the same thing. Yesterday, I asked Comrade Lezhava how things stood three months later. The answer: they had expected improvement, but things were worse, the coefficient had risen to 275 per cent. The peasant now pays for the products he needs from urban industry with two and three-quarters times the amount of grain he needed in 1913.

For clarity, comrades, I present this simple diagram. There is only one; I cannot make it bigger. It is very expressive. Three lines depict the movement of prices. The dotted and broken lines are the level of prices, the solid line is the general price level as of 1913. The dotted line expresses the price of industrial goods. In August last year [1922] they were lower than the 1913 level, then began to rise, quickly exceeded the prewar prices and continued to climb and climb. And here are agricultural prices, represented by the broken line. In August they were higher than in 1913, then sank to the prewar level, and down here we see them as of today. That— ugh!—is still called the "alliance." (Laughter) It is necessary to ponder hard over this chart. Two lines are going farther apart and that divergence, that scissors, is called the alliance. In itself it is the most immediate basic problem of Russian economic life. . . .

Relative prices have increased two and two-thirds times in comparison with prewar times, but industry works nonetheless at a loss. How is that explained? By the fact that industry is organized irrationally; paradoxical as it may seem, we suffer not from poverty but from "richness." We are too heavily armed for the struggle on the present weak market. We have preserved equipment if not for 100 per cent then for 75 per cent of prewar and wartime production, and we use 17 to 20 per cent of that equipment, 25 per cent at most. Incidentally, the cost of all nationalized equipment falls on us. . . .

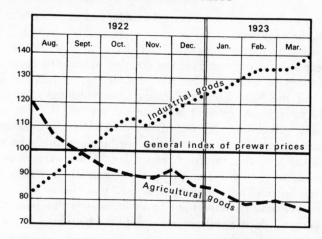

The first conclusion that follows from this is that there must be a *concentration of industry*. In the coming years we must concentrate production in those industries best-equipped and best-situated in geographical and commercial terms. . . . We face the necessity of dismissing workers—a very difficult nut our party must crack in the coming year. It cannot, however, be avoided. It would be the greatest cowardice on the part of the working class as a whole and of its party if they disguised unemployment, that is, retained an excessive number of workers in factories, whether fully employed, half employed or only one-third employed, merely in order not to doom them to open unemployment. There can be no doubt that hidden unemployment represents the worst, least effective and most expensive form of social security. . . .

Comrades, we are dreadfully poor, and our enemies are rich. At this point I went through a little arithmetical exercise, which I will share with you. If you compare the American United States with our Soviet United States—the total population is not significantly different from ours—you see a terrible contrast of wealth and poverty. Our annual national income is 5 billion gold rubles or slightly more; that of the United States is 130 billion gold rubles per year.[1] Per head, counting children, that comes to 1,300 rubles for America and 38 rubles for Russia. Capital invested in industry

[1] Trotsky's figures vastly inflate the difference between the national incomes of the Soviet Union and the United States in this period. According to Colin Clark, national income in the United States was somewhat more than six times that of the Soviet Union in 1922. See Colin Clark, *The Conditions of Economic Progress* (London: Macmillan, 1951), tables on pp. 46 and 188.

amounts in Russia to 2.5 billion gold rubles and in America to 90 billion, that is 36 times more. . . .

I pass now to the question I consider central at the present moment and for our congress, the question of *planned* economic work, without which we can have no success. . . . In the first period of the New Economic Policy some industrial executives pinned patently exaggerated hopes on the market. We can only gradually and slowly take out of dry dock—War Communism— our metallurgical, coal, oil, and machine-building industries and launch them on the waters of the market. If we were to doom heavy industry to the free play of the market, it would run aground because our heavy industry is too "heavy" for our market. We have to support our heavy industry with a budgetary jack so that it doesn't collapse and sink to the bottom. And that is just the approach to the plan. . . .

Comrades, I insist on this especially because the question of planning is in essence the question of management. We, too, generally speak of management of the economy, but really the management of the economy is first of all planning, i.e., *forecasting* and *coordinating*. There is no other way aside from planning, planning definitely not in the sense of the rigid administration of the economy as existed under War Communism, but planning first of all in the sense of maneuvering, i.e., forecasting and coordinating the conditions of the market on one side and the work and needs of the state on the other. . . . The question of planned management can in no way be identified with "plan mania," about which it is possible, of course, to make many jokes. We cannot tolerate grandiose and abstract planning. . . .

Gosplan [the State Planning Commission] is a very important organ for our development, and its significance will grow. In itself it does not give orders, does not operate things; rather it considers all elements involved in the operating, administration, direction, and guidance of the economy; it predicts, makes plans, coordinates, suggests, reminds, makes corrections—in other words, it does all the necessary staff work, coordinating operations with supply, transport, etc., for the economic command. Without such uninterrupted, preparatory, unifying coordination and accounting there can be no effective management of the economy. This is the great significance of Gosplan, and, I repeat, as time passes this will increase. . . . If we can expand the productivity of the country, consistently and firmly diverting it to the Soviet socialist mill, then the very significance of the planning organ in the general economic system will grow. . . .

We are about to go through the stage of *primitive socialist accumulation*. This apt expression was first used, it seems, by Comrade V. S. Smirnov who works for Gosplan. Primitive socialist accumulation! You remember what primitive capitalist accumulation is according to Marx, what kind of effort of the small entrepreneur it represents. That small exploiter appears as a miracle of heroism. He sleeps four hours a day, eats stale bread, energetically exploits his wife and children, skimps on every kopeck for himself. Thus passes the period of primitive capitalist accumulation. . . . We must fight with just this kind of passion, but for every Soviet socialist kopeck, a task worthy of all the heroism of the proletariat and of all the astuteness, energy, and will of our party. . . . The slogan of saving kopeck upon kopeck we now throw out to our party and to the entire country as the slogan of economic salvation and cultural revival. We must devote as much attention, as much ardent devotion as we once gave to [revolutionary work] . . . to every part of national property, augmenting and accumulating, preparing for full victory. And I, comrades, want to hope that, despite the heaviness of the present time for us [because of Lenin's illness], despite the fact that the party first of all is absorbed in the anxieties of revolutionary self-defense, I hope, I believe, that this congress is at the same time also the departure point for a more rapid, more concentrated economic offensive. . . . We say with unconquerable faith: despite our wretched, shameful poverty and lack of skill, we will all pull together as one and lead our country from poverty, from slavery, and we shall not surrender to capital!

25. Working Out the First Five Year Plan

During the 1920's planning had been carried out for specific state-owned industries, and there had been attempts to construct a plan for the entire national economy. From 1925 the State Planning Commission (Gosplan) published "control figures," setting approximate goals for the forthcoming economic year (which in this period began in October). These control figures, however, were largely forecasts of likely developments based on current trends, the Gosplan economists believing that the huge private sector of peasant agriculture prevented prescriptive planning. Nonetheless, by 1927 it was decided to work out a prescriptive plan for a five-year period. A number of agencies proposed plans, which were widely discussed. The Gosplan proposals retained the idea that planning was limited by the structure of the Soviet economy and stressed the need for several variants of the plan to allow for unfavorable circumstances. The issue was discussed at the 15th Party Congress in December, 1927, and Gosplan was formally instructed to draw up a Five Year Plan. The following speech to the Congress by the head of Gosplan, G. M. Krzhizhanovsky, discussing an early Gosplan draft, describes the history of planning work and reflects the daring yet relatively flexible attitude of Gosplan at the beginning of the Five Year Plan era.

The Development of Planning

Whenever we hear of attempts at planned economics in the capitalist countries, we must remember that although there have been critical moments, during wars for instance, in which capitalist countries have been forced to resort to a systematic conduct of economic life in order to utilize all forces for war purposes, in reality it is still money that rules in these countries, and any Socialism based on the reign of this yellow metal will be yellow Socialism, a transitory period of what might be named "yellow planned economics." These plans, as they are set up in the capitalist world, collapse as soon as they encounter a stronger capitalist group. We, however, are dependent solely on ourselves, and if unity of will is our highest trump, you may well imagine what a high degree of

Source: Speech of G. M. Krzhizhanovsky to the 15th Party Congress, *International Press Correspondence*, Vol. VIII (1928), No. 2, pp. 60–63, with deletions. Translation slightly modified by the editors.

unanimity and agreement of will is required if we are to commit ourselves to a program lasting five years from motives of actual conviction, and not merely because we are obliged to.

What has been the actual course of our planned development? As early as 1920 a rough outline of the ground plan of our economy was drawn up. Then the struggle against economic decline began. Comrade Lenin advised us—those comrades engaged on the elaboration of the plans—to set aside for the moment our general ground plan, and to tackle the most urgent questions of our economic life in this emergency. The State Planning Commission, organized in 1921, was at once engaged in a struggle against the crises in the food, fuel, and transport services. It took some time before we were gradually able to return from these questions to the actual lines being laid down for planned economy.

Let us take for instance state industry. At first glance it would seem as if it must be possible to introduce a planned régime here with special rapidity. But in reality it was not until 1925 that we had a comprehensive plan for all industry, including the techniques of production, the economic analysis, and the financial program.

The year 1925 terminated a certain stage of reorganization in our economic structure. Building activity increased, and industry made more rapid progress. A period began in which it became necessary to embrace in one comprehensive plan not only the plans for the various branches of industry, but at the same time the whole of the plans for the most important sectors of the national economy. Since 1925–26 we have been working out control figures for the national economy, furnishing the basis for the fulfillment of this task.

The first control figures of the State Planning Commission (1925–26) were compiled exclusively by the collaborators of the State Planning Commission itself. The Government could not make use of these figures for working out a plan of economic operations. In the following year (1926–27) a certain uniformity of system developed. For the first time the control figures contained general paragraphs referring to industrialization, etc.

Finally, the control figures for the economic year 1927–28 are at last the result of extensive collective compilation. These figures have not been worked out solely by the staff in the State Planning Commission and the corresponding commissions in the separate Soviet republics. They are the final result of the research of many thousands of economists all over our country. A number of congresses were called. At these congresses the general methods of dealing with the material have been laid down, and it may now be stated that, as a result of the work already accomplished, we have now material at our disposal comprising the budget, the financial plan for our industry, and our import and export plans, as constituents of a uniform and consistent plan of economy. This combination has been given a form enabling the Government to make immediate use of the control figures for 1927–28, since these already offer firm bases on which to set up all operative economic plans.

It is obvious that the Five Year Perspective Plan must not constitute any limit beyond which we must not go. The extent of our development is so great that we cannot come to a standstill at this stage. When we remember that our re-examination of the prospects of the coming five years confronted us at once with a series of burning questions—the question of unemployment, of the possibility of improving the prosperity of the working masses, and of the comparative strength of such huge branches of our economy as industry and agriculture—we see clearly that we must pass as speedily as possible from the five-year plan to the ten-year and fifteen-year plan, that is, to the general plan. The imperative necessity of special activity in the interests of the transport service urges us especially in this direction. . . .

What figures are proposed by us for the Five Year Plan? The congress of economists collaborating in the plan came to the conclusion that it was impossible to advance only one set of figures for the Five Year Plan. A plan extending several years into the future is a distant aim. We must proceed like the artillery man. He examines his mark through his glass and then adjusts his aim to two possibilities. The first adjustment is a careful and cautious estimate, taking as the basis the minimum of economic possibilities, guaranteeing the economy against unforeseen accidents. This is the *preliminary* adjustment. The second series of figures deals with more favorable chances, which may in certain circumstances offer the possibility of reaching our goal more rapidly. If this optimal estimate is not quite reached, it is no great misfortune. In spite of all difficulties, and in spite of our only breaking occasionally through the front of the elementary anarchy opposing us, we are advancing in the desired direction. The summing up of our economic possibilities under these two variations facilitates our economic maneuvers. . . .

After the scissors crisis of 1923 the policy toward the peasantry proposed by the Right was largely adopted. Industrial prices were lowered; in 1925 leasing of land and hiring of labor were authorized; taxation remained low. But the price scissors re-emerged as industrial production neared its limits within existing plant. In 1927 the amount of grain marketed began to fall off seriously at a time when the industrialization program was enlarging the urban population rapidly. The problem was that 85 per cent of Soviet grain was produced by poor and middle peasants who increasingly chose to consume rather than sell their products. Almost all the rest was supplied by richer peasants (widely called by their traditional peasant name of *kulak*, literally "fist"), who were able to hold back their grain until prices were high. In a departure from the policy of the Right, industrial prices were kept high, and emergency measures (increased taxation and confiscation of unmarketed surpluses) were directed against the *kulaks*. In the next two years the grain crisis became worse as production was cut back. At a meeting of the Central Committee of the party in July, 1928, Stalin bluntly argued that the grain crisis proved the urgent necessity of ending the disequilibrium between agriculture and industry. His optimism about the possibility of speedy voluntary collectivization was unrealistic, and his analysis of the problem foreshadowed the forced collectivization undertaken at the end of 1929.

Stalin on the Peasant and Industrialization, 1928

COMRADES, BEFORE I pass to the specific question of our difficulties on the grain front, allow me to deal with some general questions of theoretical interest which arose here during the discussion at the plenum.

First of all, the general question *of the chief sources of development of our industry*, the means of guaranteeing our present rate of industrialisation. . . .

I think that there are two chief sources nourishing our industry: firstly, the working class; secondly, the peasantry.

In the capitalist countries industrialisation was usually effected, in the main, by robbing other countries, by robbing colonies or

Source: Speech to the Plenum of the Central Committee of the Communist Party, given July 9, 1928, in J. V. Stalin, *Works*, Vol. XI (Moscow: Foreign Languages Publishing House, 1954), pp. 165-196, with deletions.

defeated countries, or with the help of substantial and more or less enslaving loans from abroad. . . .

One respect in which our country differs from the capitalist countries is that it cannot and must not engage in colonial robbery, or the plundering of other countries in general. That way, therefore, is closed to us.

Neither, however, does our country have or want to have enslaving loans from abroad. Consequently, that way, too, is closed to us.

What then remains? Only one thing, and that is to develop industry, to industrialise the country with the help of *internal* accumulations.

Under the bourgeois system in our country, industry, transport, etc., were usually developed with the help of loans. Whether you take the building of new factories or the re-equipment of old ones, whether you take the laying of new railways or the erection of big electric power stations—not one of these undertakings was able to dispense with foreign loans. But they were enslaving loans.

Quite different is the situation in our country under the Soviet system. We are building the Turkestan Railway, with a length of 1,400 versts,[1] which requires hundreds of millions of rubles. We are erecting the Dnieper Hydro-Electric Power Station, which also requires hundreds of millions of rubles. But have they involved us in any enslaving loans? No, they have not. All this is being done with the help of internal accumulations.

But what are the chief sources of these accumulations? As I have said, there are two such sources: firstly, the working class, which creates values and advances our industry; secondly, the peasantry.

The way matters stand with the peasantry in this respect is as follows: it not only pays the state the usual taxes, direct and indirect; it also *overpays* in the relatively high prices for manufactured goods—that is in the first place, and it is more or less *underpaid* in the prices for agricultural produce—that is in the second place.

This is an additional tax levied on the peasantry for the sake of promoting industry, which caters for the whole country, the peasantry included. It is something in the nature of a "tribute," of a supertax, which we are compelled to levy for the time being in order to preserve and accelerate our present rate of industrial

[1] One *verst* = 3,500 feet.—Eds.

development, in order to ensure an industry for the whole country, in order to raise further the standard of life of the rural population and then to abolish altogether this additional tax, these "scissors" between town and country.

It is an unpalatable business, there is no denying. But we should not be Bolsheviks if we slurred over it and closed our eyes to the fact that, unfortunately, our industry and our country cannot *at present* dispense with this additional tax on the peasantry.

Why do I speak of this? Because some comrades, apparently, do not understand this indisputable truth. They based their speeches on the fact that the peasants are overpaying for manufactured goods, which is absolutely true, and are being underpaid for agricultural produce, which is also true. But what do they demand? They demand the establishment of replacement prices for grain, so that these "scissors," these underpayments and overpayments, would be done away with *at once*. But what would be the effect of doing away with the "scissors" this year or next year, say? The effect would be to retard the industrialisation of the country, including the industrialisation of agriculture, to undermine our young industry which is not yet firmly on its feet, and thus to strike at our entire national economy. . . .

What, then, should our policy be? It should be gradually to close the "scissors," to diminish the gap from year to year, by lowering the prices for manufactured goods and improving agricultural technique—which cannot but result in reducing the cost of producing grain—and then, within the space of a number of years, to do away completely with this additional tax on the peasantry. . . .

The second question concerns the problem of the *bond with the middle peasant*—the problem of the aims of the bond and the means for effecting it.

It would follow from what some comrades say that the bond between town and country, between the working class and the main mass of the peasantry, is based *exclusively* on textiles, on satisfying the *personal* requirements of the peasantry. Is this true? It is quite untrue, comrades. Of course, it is of immense importance to satisfy the peasants' personal requirements for textiles. That is how we began to establish the bond with the peasantry in the new conditions. But to assert on these grounds that the bond based on textiles is the beginning and end of the matter, that the bond based on satisfying the peasants' personal requirements is the all-inclusive or chief foundation of the economic alliance between the working class and the peasantry, is to commit a most serious error. Actually, the bond between town and country is based not only on satisfying the peasants' *personal* requirements, not only on textiles, but also on satisfying the *economic* requirements of the peasants as *producers* of agricultural products. . . .

Hence, the bond is based not only on textiles, but also on metals. Without this, the bond with the peasantry would be insecure.

In what way does the bond based on textiles differ from the bond based on metals? Primarily in the fact that the bond based on textiles chiefly concerns the peasants' personal requirements, without affecting, or affecting to a comparatively small extent, the production side of peasant farming, whereas the bond based on metals chiefly concerns the production side of peasant farming, improving it, mechanising it, making it more remunerative and paving the way for uniting the scattered and small peasant farms into large socially-conducted farms.

It would be a mistake to think that the purpose of the bond is to preserve classes, the peasant class in particular. That is not so, comrades. That is not the purpose of the bond at all. The purpose of the bond is to bring the peasantry closer to the working class, the leader of our entire development, to strengthen the alliance of the peasantry with the working class, the leading force in the alliance, gradually to *remould* the peasantry, its mentality and its production, *along collectivist lines*, and thus to bring about the conditions for the abolition of classes. . . .

The third question is that of *the New Economic Policy (NEP) and the class struggle under NEP conditions.* . . .

Is it not obvious that our whole forward movement, our every success of any importance in the sphere of socialist construction, is an expression and result of the class struggle in our country?

But it follows from all this that the more we advance, the greater will be the resistance of the capitalist elements and the sharper the class struggle. . . .

It must not be imagined that the socialist forms will develop, squeezing out the enemies of the working class, while our enemies retreat in silence and make way for our advance, that then we shall again advance and they will again retreat until "unexpectedly" all the social groups without exception, both kulaks and poor peasants, both workers and capitalists, find themselves "suddenly" and "imperceptibly," without struggle or commotion, in the lap of a socialist society. Such fairy-tales do not and cannot happen in general, and in the conditions of the dictatorship of the proletariat in particular.

It never has been and never will be the case that a dying class surrenders its positions voluntarily without attempting to organise resistance. . . .

The fourth question concerns the problem of *emergency measures* against the kulaks and speculators. . . .

Was it a mistake to resort to emergency measures in the conditions of the grain procurement crisis? It is now recognised by all that it was not a mistake, that, on the contrary, the emergency measures saved the country from a crisis of our whole economy. What induced us to resort to these measures? The deficit of 128,000,000 poods of grain by January of this year, which we had to make good before the roads were spoiled by the spring thaws, at the same time ensuring a normal rate of grain procurement. . . . And what would have happened if we had not made good this deficit? We should now be having a most serious crisis of our entire national economy, hunger in the towns and hunger in the army. . . .

Allow me to pass now to the question *of the grain problem and the basic causes of our difficulties on the grain front.*

I think that a number of comrades have committed the error of lumping together different kinds of causes of our difficulties on the grain front, of confusing temporary and circumstantial (specific) causes with chronic and fundamental causes. There are two sets of causes of our grain difficulties: chronic, fundamental causes, the elimination of which will require a number of years, and specific, circumstantial causes, which can be eliminated now, if a number of necessary measures are adopted and carried out. To lump all these causes together is to confuse the whole question.

What is the underlying significance of our difficulties on the grain front? It is that they confront us squarely with the problem of grain, of grain production, with the problem of agriculture in general, and of cereal production in particular.

Do we have a grain problem at all, as an urgent question? We undoubtedly do. One must be blind to doubt that the grain problem is now harassing every aspect of Soviet social life. We cannot live like gypsies, without grain reserves, without certain reserves in case of harvest failure, without reserves with which to manoeuvre in the market, without reserves against the contingency of war, and, lastly, without some reserves for export. . . .

A reserve is absolutely essential to enable us to export grain. We have to import equipment for industry. We have to import agricultural machines, tractors and spare parts for them. But this cannot be done if we do not export grain, if we do not accumulate a certain reserve of foreign currency obtained by exporting grain. Before the war we used to export from 500,000,000 to 600,000,000 poods of grain annually. We were able to export so much because we went short ourselves. That is true. It should, however, be realised that all the same our marketable grain before the war was *double* what it is today. And it is just because we have now only half as much marketable grain that grain is ceasing to be an item of export. And what does ceasing to export grain mean? It means losing the source which enabled us to import—as we must import —equipment for industry and tractors and machines for agriculture. Can we go on living in this way—without accumulating grain reserves for export? No, we cannot. . . .

Can it then be denied that the grain problem is acute and that our difficulties on the grain front are serious?

But, because of our grain difficulties, we are also having difficulties of a political character. Under no circumstances must this be forgotten, comrades. I am referring to the discontent which was to be observed among a certain section of the peasantry, among a certain section of the poor peasants, and also of the middle peasants, and which created a certain threat to the bond. . . .

What is the *basis* of our grain difficulties, meaning by that the *chronic* and *fundamental* causes of the difficulties, and not the temporary, circumstantial ones?

The basis of our grain difficulties lies in the increasingly scattered and divided character of agriculture. It is a fact that agriculture, especially grain farming, is growing smaller in scale, becoming increasingly less remunerative and less productive of marketable surpluses. Whereas before the revolution we had about 15,000,000 or 16,000,000 peasant farms, now we have some 24,000,000 or 25,000,000; moreover, the process of division tends to become more marked.

It is true that our crop area today falls little short of pre-war, and that the *gross* output of grain is only some five per cent less than it was before the war. But the trouble is that, in spite of all this, our output of *marketable* grain is only *half*, that is, about 50 per cent, of pre-war. That is the root of the matter.

What is the point? The point is that small-scale farming is less remunerative, produces smaller marketable surpluses and is less stable than large-scale farming. The Marxist thesis that small-scale production is less profitable than large-scale production fully applies to agriculture also. That is why, from one and the same area, small-scale peasant farming yields much less marketable grain than large-scale farming.

What is the way out of this situation? . . .

1. The way out is to raise the productivity of small- and middle-peasant farming as far as possible, to replace the wooden plough by the steel plough, to supply small and medium machines, fertiliser, seed and agronomic help, to organise the peasantry into co-operatives, to conclude contracts with whole villages, supplying them with the best-grade seed on loan and thus ensuring the peasants collective credit, and, lastly, to place big machines at their disposal through machine-hiring stations. . . .

2. The way out, further, is to help the poor and middle peasants gradually to unite their scattered small farms into large collective farms based on new technical equipment and collective labour, as being more profitable and yielding larger marketable surpluses. I have in mind all forms of uniting small farms into large, socially-conducted farms, from simple co-operatives to artels, which are incomparably more productive and yield far larger marketable surpluses than the scattered small-peasant farms. . . .

3. The way out, lastly, is to strengthen the old state farms and to promote new, large state farms, as being the economic units that are the most remunerative and yield the largest marketable surpluses.

I am concluding, comrades. I think that the grain difficulties will not have been without their value for us. Our Party has learned and progressed by overcoming difficulties and crises of every kind. I think that the present difficulties will steel our Bolshevik ranks and induce them to tackle the solution of the grain problem in thorough fashion. And the solution of this problem will remove one of the biggest difficulties standing in the way of the socialist transformation of our country.

27. The Third Revolution

Two major drafts of the Five Year Plan were produced by Gosplan, a "minimal" draft, which took account of the possibility of unfavorable circumstances (crop failure, limited foreign trade and credit, poor quality in production, significant defense expenditures); and an "optimal" draft, which assumed there would be no unfavorable circumstances. In 1929 Stalin decided to break Russia's economic deadlock and, jettisoning all caution, had the "optimal" draft alone adopted. The Plan, whose official starting date was set back to October, 1928, called for vast increases in industrial output, with the annual growth to range from 16 per cent in the first year (1928–29) to 21 per cent in the last (1932–33). It was assumed that the capital required for growth could be found in industrial profits and in expanded foreign trade and credits. It was also assumed that agriculture would be substantially collectivized during the period by voluntary means. The assumptions all proved false. Industrial profits did not rise as expected, foreign credits were not forthcoming, world trade contracted with the Depression, and the peasantry refused to join state or cooperative farms. To obtain direct control of agricultural production and rural labor supply, forcible collectivization was undertaken in late 1929 and was largely completed by 1934. The costs were horrendous. Loss of life ran into millions, nearly half the livestock was destroyed, and agricultural production declined. Nonetheless, the peasant nation had been forced into industrial modernity and the adoption of the First Five Year Plan opened a new era in Soviet life. The following document is the resolution of the 16th Party Conference, held in April, 1929, which adopted the Plan.

Revision of the First Five Year Plan, 1929

I

HAVING HEARD the report on the Five Year Plan for the development of the national economy of the Union of Soviet Socialist Republics, the 16th All-Union Party Conference notes, first of all,

Source: Resolution of the 16th Conference of the All-Russian Communist Party, April, 1929, "O piatiletnem plane razvitiia narodnogo khoziaistva," *Direktivy KPSS i sovetskogo pravitel'stva po khoziaistvennym voprosam*, Vol. II, 1929–45 (Moscow: Gosudarstvennoe Izdatel'stvo Politicheskoi Literatury, 1957), pp. 26–32. Translated by the editors.

that the Five Year Plan calls for the following achievements in the over-all growth of the national economy:

1. While total capital investment during the five-year period 1923–24 to 1927–28 amounted to 26.5 billion rubles, for the five-year period 1928–29 to 1932–33 capital investment in the entire national economy is to reach 64.6 billion rubles. While in the past five-year period capital investment in industry amounted to 4.4 billion rubles, for the projected five-year period it is set at 16.4 billion rubles; the corresponding figures for agriculture are 15 billion and 23.2 billion rubles; for transport, 2.7 billion and 10 billion rubles; and for electrification, 0.9 billion and 3.1 billion rubles.

2. As a result of these investments the total fixed capital of the country will grow from 70 billion rubles in 1927–28 to 128 billion rubles in 1932–33, i.e., by 82 per cent. This will include an increase of the fixed capital of all industry from 9.2 billion to 23.1 billion rubles, of electrification from 1 billion to 5 billion rubles, i.e., a fivefold increase, of railroad transport from 10 billion rubles to 17 billion rubles, i.e., a 70 per cent increase, and of agriculture from 28.7 billion rubles to 38.9 billion rubles, ie., an increase of 35 per cent.

3. The huge amount of capital investment will be accompanied by a corresponding growth in total industrial production from 18.3 billion rubles in 1927–28 to 43.2 billion rubles in 1932–33, which is more than three times prewar industrial production. Agricultural production will increase from 16.6 billion to 25.8 billion rubles, exceeding prewar agricultural production by more than one and a half times. The work of railroads will grow from 88 billion ton kilometers to 163 billion. The net production of the entire national economy will grow from 24.4 billion rubles to 49.7 billion rubles.

4. In keeping with the general idea of the industrialization of the country, the strengthening of the defense capability of the Union, and liberation from dependency in relations with capitalist countries, 78 per cent of all capital investments in industry will be directed to industry *producing the means of production,* as a result of which the output of these branches of industry will grow significantly faster. While the value of the output of all planned industry will increase 2.8 times, the value of the output of those branches of industry producing the means of production will increase 3.3 times.

Electrification. The Plan envisages the construction of 42 regional power stations. . . . This huge construction will expand the amount of electrical energy produced from 5 billion kilowatt hours to 22 billion kilowatt hours at the end of the five year period.

Ferrous Metal Industry. New and powerful metallurgical factories will be constructed. . . . The construction of new factories and the reconstruction of existing ones will raise the production of pig iron from 3.5 million tons to 10 million tons in 1932–33.

Coal. Construction of extensive mining facilities is planned for the Don Basin and for the Urals, the Kuznetsk Basin and the Moscow coal basin, as a result of which output of coal will increase from 35 million tons in 1927–28 to 75 million tons in 1932–33.

Machine Building. Reconstruction and construction of new factories for machine building . . . will provide the opportunity to achieve an increase of 3.5 times in the value of the machine-building industry and an increase of four times in the output of agricultural-machine building.

Chemical Industry. The planned construction of chemical complexes . . . will increase the output of chemical fertilizers to more than 8 million tons in 1932–33 as against 175,000 tons in 1927–28.

5. The significant degree by which the projected rate of growth of the economy of the Soviet Union will exceed that of the capitalist countries will of necessity produce a change in the relative share of the U.S.S.R. in total world production even by the end of the five-year period. In pig iron the U.S.S.R. will move from sixth place to third place (after Germany and the United States), in coal from fifth place to fourth place (after the United States, Britain, and Germany).

Secondly, the Conference notes that the over-all growth of the national economy called for by the Five Year Plan is directed at the *decisive growth of the socialist sector* of the national economy in the city and countryside and at the expense of the capitalist element, as is evident from the following statistics:

1. The structure of fixed capital will change [in favor of the socialist sector]. . . .

2. There will be a corresponding change in the relative share of the socialist sector in the value of production of:

	1927–28	*1932–33*
Industry	80%	92%
Agriculture	2	15
Retail Trade	75	91

The construction program will improve particularly the socialized sector in agriculture (state and collective farms). The sown area in the socialized sector of agriculture by 1933 will expand to 26 million hectares, accounting for 17.5 per cent of all sown area. By 1933 this will guarantee 15.5 per cent of the value of agricultural production and 43 per cent of marketed grain. . . .

3. The most important indicators of the growth of the cooperative sector are given in the following comparisons:

	1927–28	*1932–33*
Share of collective farms in the value of production	1.0%	11.4%
Share of production of small-scale cooperative industry in total small-scale industrial production	19.4	53.8
Cooperative retail trade turnover	60.2	78.9
Number of peasant households united in agricultural cooperatives	9.5 million	25.58 million
Per cent of all peasant households	37.5	85.0

. . . This significant enlargement of the socialist element in the entire national economy, in production and trade turnover, given the development of a net of machine-tractor stations and broad use of contracted deliveries [of agricultural products at fixed prices], which, at the end of the five-year period, will embrace 85 per cent of the grain crop, will mean the strengthening of the guiding role of the working class and will create a new form of the alliance between city and countryside, leading to the massive reconstruction of agriculture on the basis of higher technique and of collectivization.

Thirdly, the Conference affirms that:

1. *National income* in constant prices will grow from 24.4 billion rubles in 1927–28 to 49.7 billion rubles, i.e., by 103 per cent.

This will produce an annual growth of national income of more than 12 per cent, i.e., a rate of growth markedly superior to that of capitalist countries.

2. *The social structure* of national income, first of all, will be characterized by a 71 per cent rise in the real wages of industrial workers by the end of the five-year period, resulting in an increase in the share of the entire working class in relationship to the entire income of the national economy from 32.1 per cent to 37 per cent. The income of the entire agricultural population will grow by the end of the five-year period by 67 per cent. But as a result of the expansion of industry, agricultural income will decline in relation to total national income from 49.8 per cent to 42.5 per cent of the total national income.

3. *Growth of the total state budget* (net) will be reflected in the fact that the sum total of the budget in the coming five-year period will be 51 billion rubles as against 19 billion rubles in the past five-year period (a growth of 166.7 per cent). Further, in 1932–33 the budget will comprise 30.9 per cent of national income as opposed to 25.9 per cent in 1928–29. This expansion of the budget will provide for the strengthening of the defensive capability of the country, for the expansion of investment in the national economy during the coming five-year period by almost four times (393 per cent) as compared with the past five-year period, and for the increase of social-cultural expenditures by almost three times (276 per cent).

4. The Five Year Plan envisages a significant growth in both *commodity and currency reserves.*

II

Proceeding from the facts about the Five Year Plan set out above, and keeping in mind that the Plan fully guarantees:

(1) maximum growth of production of the means of production as the basis of the industrialization of the country;

(2) decisive strengthening of the socialist sector in city and countryside at the expense of the capitalist elements in the national economy, drawing millions of peasants into socialist construction on the basis of the cooperative system and of collective labor, and giving every possible kind of help to the poor and middle individual peasants in their struggle against *kulak* exploitation;

(3) significant improvement in the material and cultural levels of the working class and the toiling mass of the peasantry;

(4) strengthening the leading role of the working class on the basis of the development of a new form of alliance with the masses of the peasantry;

(5) strengthening of the economic and political position of the proletarian dictatorship in its struggle with class enemies both within the country and abroad;

(6) economic and cultural development of the national [i.e., non-Russian] republics and backward regions and areas;

(7) significant strengthening of the capacity of the country for defense;

(8) a huge step forward in realizing the party slogan of overtaking and surpassing the leading capitalist countries in technological and economic development;

The Conference resolves to approve the Five Year Plan of the State Planning Commission in its optimal variant, approved by the Council of Peoples Commissars of the U.S.S.R., as a plan fully meeting the directive of the 15th Party Congress.

PART VI

The Depression

Weakness in the foundations of the prosperity of the 1920's was directly responsible for the Great Depression of the 1930's. More specifically, the origins of the Depression were twofold. The crash of the New York stock market in the fall of 1929 produced a financial crisis that, although delayed in Europe, was extremely severe. This, in its turn, worsened an already existing condition of overproduction in primary goods. Under the weight of both, international trade collapsed.

The burden of indebtedness, and particularly short-term indebtedness, that accumulated at a rapid rate during and after the war made European financial centers extremely sensitive to a large-scale withdrawal of funds. The United States and Great Britain were the chief capital exporters; it is estimated that between 1923 and 1929 Britain and the United States each had made net capital exports of more than $3 billion. When the stock market crash came, both these countries, but especially the United States, began calling in their exported capital. In Europe, Germany and Austria were the chief borrowers. In the 1923 to 1929 period Germany was a net capital importer to the amount of more than $4 billion, and Austrian borrowings reached $1.3 billion. Thus German and Austrian finance felt the withdrawal of funds most immediately, but the lines of capital movement were so tangled that few major centers escaped from the scramble to find gold and foreign exchange with which to meet foreign obligations. The result was that in 1931 the financial structure of all central Europe collapsed. Debt moratoria and suspension of debt service were declared, stock markets were closed, the gold standard was abandoned, and foreign-exchange controls were introduced.

The second major source of difficulty lay in the markets for primary goods. The boom period of the 1920's encouraged expansion of the production of food products and raw materials, frequently by means of borrowing at high rates. By the late 1920's surplus stocks were beginning to accumulate for many goods whose demand was relatively inelastic. When the financial crisis came, agricultural and raw-material commodity prices fell drastically, and commodity exporters could no longer afford to import the same quantities of manufactured goods.

Thus the crisis in finance and primary-goods production became a generalized depression characterized by falling prices and production in all spheres, mass unemployment, and severe social dislocation. In 1932 European industrial production stood at 80.1 (average for the years 1925 to 1929 = 100), and prices experienced a similar drop. Unemployment rose to unprecedented heights—over 6 million in 1932 in Germany, where it was greater than in any other European country.

Governments introduced a variety of measures designed to produce recovery or at least to limit the impact of the Depression until a natural revival set in, but many of these had only limited success. The prolonged character of the crisis and its severity, combined with the apparent inability of many governments to stimulate recovery effectively, shook the confidence of Europeans and caused many to turn to radical solutions.

28. The Agricultural Crisis

From the middle of the 1920's the terms of trade turned against primary products, and agricultural and raw materials prices were depressed. A "scissors crisis" on a world-wide scale began to emerge. When the full force of the financial crisis hit Europe, it brought a worsening of agrarian conditions as prices and foreign trade continued to decline and credit dried up. The European countries most severely shaken by the agricultural crisis were the economically underdeveloped food exporters of the East. By June, 1931, the Economic Committee of the League of Nations had prepared an extensive report on the situation. The selections that follow are taken from the introductory statement and the report on the conditions in Poland prepared for the League by the head of the Polish land bank.

League of Nations Report on Agrarian Conditions, 1931

1. Introduction

ALL COUNTRIES report the existence of a more or less accentuated agricultural crisis, even countries hitherto renowned for the prosperous situation ensured to their farmers by specialisation and by the diversification of their agricultural undertakings.

What is called the *agricultural crisis* is not, properly speaking, a crisis, that is to say, a fortuitous event rapidly occurring and disappearing as rapidly as it arises. We are confronted with a period of depression dating back a considerable time, and with every month that passes becoming more serious from the mere fact of its continuance.

Immediately after the world war, agriculture experienced a period of prosperity, but in most countries it passed through a crisis in 1920 and 1921; then a very real improvement took place in 1924 and 1925; finally, a marked depression occurred in the cultivation of cereals, and from 1928 spread throughout the entire world, after having also affected other branches of agricultural

Source: League of Nations, Economic Committee, *The Agricultural Crisis*, Vol. I (Geneva: League of Nations, 1931), pp. 7–8, 245–53, with deletions.

production, such as wool and cotton. Gradually, the situation became distinctly unfavourable. The year 1930 was a year of disappointment in every way, and it has left in the minds of farmers the memory of something approaching disaster. The stagnation is such that discouragement threatens to spread to every countryside in spite of the agriculturists' traditional quality of endurance, and the material difficulties are enhanced by the prevailing atmosphere of despondency. The complaints of the farmers are heard in almost every country. The difficulties have assumed a general international character, though there are certain aspects of them which are peculiar to particular countries. It is not merely a question of bad harvests caused by natural or atmospheric disorders, such as continuous rain or drought. The evil is deep-rooted and its progress may be traced throughout the world.

The crisis is universal; it does not merely affect the European market. It affects overseas States as well as the States of Europe. It operates with *unequal* intensity according to the economic development of the countries, their capacity for resistance and the relative advantages which they enjoy as agricultural producers. They do not suffer to the same extent from the same evils. The manifestations of the crisis vary according to the economc structure of States.

In agricultural exporting countries the economic organisation is more severely hit if the products of the soil are sold at a loss; and this fact explains the efforts undertaken since 1930 at successive conferences (Bucharest, Warsaw, Belgrade) by the States of Central and Eastern Europe, which are drawing together to establish between themselves positive economic collaboration, to reach an agreement as to a common defence of their interests and to find in common action a remedy for the situation.

It is the lowness of prices that constitutes the agricultural crisis. It is becoming difficult to sell products, and in many cases prices have reached a level at which they are scarcely, if at all, sufficient to cover the cost of production.

The reason for the crisis and for its continuance is to be found in the fact that agricultural prices are low in comparison with the expenditure which the farmer must meet. The profit-earning potentialities of agriculture are weakened. Agricultural products cost a lot to produce and then fetch very little in the market. In spite of the great technical progress achieved, operating costs remain implacably higher than selling prices, farmers obtain no longer a fair return on their labour or on their capital. Frequently the returns of agricultural undertakings are not enough to cover the necessary outlay for the purchase of the material or products necessary for continued operation or for the payment of wages and taxes and so forth.

This disproportion between the income and expenditue of agricultural undertakings, a condition due to a much more drastic fall of agricultural prices than of goods farmers buy for use in production and consumption, appears to constitute the dominant and decisive element of the prevailing agricultural depression.

Until 1929, prices were low as compared with prices of industrial products, but were above pre-war prices. The predominating tendency to a fall which was observed was not altogether general nor was it abnormally rapid. The general character of the price movement completely changed in 1930. A fall, sometimes catastrophic, spread with extreme violence to almost all agricultural produce. It was so rapid that at the end of the year, whilst some products reached the prewar level of prices, others fell as low as one-quarter or one-half below the 1913 level. In many countries, this fall in agricultural prices was the most abrupt experienced for half a century, and, save for the period 1920–21, modern economic history gives few instances of such a decline. Farmers throughout the world have suffered from it. This fall was more serious than that which occurred in retail prices or in the cost of living, and the inadequacy of agricultural prices is for the most part responsible for the agricultural depression.

The harm caused to farming by the relatively low level of prices is greatly aggravated by the *instability* of these prices. The fluctuations have pernicious results both for producers and consumers. They are incalculable and unforeseeable and increase the risks of producers and cause the income drawn by them from their harvest to vary greatly. They are particularly harmful during the months after the harvest, since many farmers are obliged to sell at any price to meet their obligations; and these sales *en masse* mean the collapse of prices. The violent fluctuations that have taken place in the prices of certain products completely nonplus consumers. The value of price stability to farmers cannot be over-estimated. . . .

2. Poland

. . . Poland is predominantly agricultural. Her arable land covers an area of 18,127,580 hectares—that is to say, 49 per cent of the total area of the country, and her rural population makes up 64 per cent of the total population. . . .

The part played by agricultural products in Poland's total trade balance is very considerable, as the following table will show.

Polish agriculture was very hard hit during the world war, much of the land being devastated by the belligerent armies, which destroyed 1,651,892 buildings, 70 per cent of which were agricultural buildings. It was the agricultural population which suffered most of the losses due to the war, which are estimated at 13,500,-000,000 gold francs, and were further increased in 1920 during the Soviet invasion.

The reconstruction of the devastated areas was effected with surprising rapidity in Poland. The peasants as well as the great landed proprietors were able to obtain the necessary funds to replenish their live-stock, reconstruct the necessary buildings and bring into cultivation the 3½ million hectares of land which had been allowed to lie fallow during the hostilities. This tremendous effort was made without any assistance in the form of reparations and payments with very small Government grants; almost entirely, that is to say, out of the resources of the population itself. These resources became, however, rapidly exhausted; the farmers had lost their working capital and were forced to depend on inadequate and often usurious loans; hence the financial weakening of the farmers and their sensitiveness to economic fluctuations abroad. It was impossible to remedy this state of affairs by granting the farmers long-term credits, as these were not available owing to the general impoverishment of the country and the collapse of the Polish currency, which was not finally checked until 1926.

It will be readily understood that in these circumstances the mortgage banks were unable to place their securities or find the money required to re-establish the credit disorganised during the war and successive inflation periods. At the present time, the long-term agricultural loans scarcely exceed 42 million dollars, whereas before the war they amounted to 410.4 million dollars.

The shortage of capital has placed the farmers at the mercy of usurers and forced them to sell their produce immediately after the harvest regardless of the disastrous consequences of the excessive supply and consequent fall in prices. This shortage of money has more than any other internal factor helped to aggravate the disastrous consequences of the agricultural depression in Poland.

Among other causes may be mentioned the high price of various

TOTAL EXPORTS AND EXPORTS OF AGRICULTURAL PRODUCTS
(in millions of zloty)

	1924–25	1925–26	1926–27	1927–28	1928–29	1929–30
Total exports	2,139	2,130	2,483	2,499	2,604	2,746
Percentage	100.0	100.0	100.0	100.0	100.0	100.0
Exports of agricultural products	1,005	1,254	1,310	1,503	1,482	1,547
Percentage	49.3	58.9	52.8	60.0	57.0	56.3
Vegetable products	162	332	194	201	278	327
Percentage	7.6	15.6	7.8	8.0	10.7	11.9
Animal products	367	392	426	559	577	599
Percentage	17.0	18.4	17.2	22.4	22.8	21.8
Industry working for agriculture	226	203	227	170	181	259
Percentage	10.5	9.5	9.1	6.4	7.0	5.8
Timber	303	326	463	573	448	365
Percentage	14.2	15.4	18.7	23.3	16.5	13.3
Exports of non-agricultural products	1,084	876	1,173	996	1,122	1,199
Percentage	50.7	41.1	47.2	40.0	43.0	43.7

industrial articles needed by agriculture and the discrepancy between the prices of these articles and those fetched by agricultural
products. This discrepancy is the result of the policy of protecting
Polish industry, which had also suffered great losses during the
hostilities and the German occupation and whose reconstruction
seemed urgently necessary on economic and social grounds.

The following are the general index numbers of wholesale prices
and those of agricultural and industrial products, calculated on the
basis of 100, for 1927, the year following the final stabilisation of
the zloty:

Year		General Index	Agricultural Products	Industrial Products
1922		71.3	58.2	82.4
1923		81.5	55.9	106.8
1924		102.6	86.3	114.9
1925		105.6	99.3	110.4
1926		88.7	81.7	93.7
1927		100.0	100.0	100.0
1928		101.0	97.2	104.2
1929		95.7	85.7	103.3
1930:	January	88.2	74.8	99.1
	February	84.9	69.3	98.2
	March	85.0	70.1	97.5
	April	85.0	71.3	96.5
	May	83.3	68.3	96.3
	June	83.1	68.9	95.2
	July	83.8	71.3	94.2
	August	81.8	68.2	93.2
	September	79.6	65.5	91.8
	October	78.4	64.3	90.6
	November	78.6	66.2	88.9
	December	76.6	63.2	87.8

These figures explain the unfavourable position of Polish agriculture as compared with that of industry prior to 1927, and the
aggravation of the present depression since last year.

Poland's commercial relations with the principal neighbouring
countries are not such as to improve the position of her agriculture
or to mitigate the evils due to the above-mentioned factors. They
are often hampered by indirect protectionism in the most varied
forms, such as restriction of the amount of foreign cereals allowed
to be ground, the requirement of marks of origin and other marks,

and disguised discrimination and restriction in the form of the arbitrary application of veterinary measures. Their stability is sometimes compromised by the fact that certain States apply a sliding scale of Customs duties. It is a matter of common knowledge that, against the sound advice of the Economic Conference in 1927, most of the industrial countries showing a deficit in agricultural products are constantly intensifying their agricultural protection, which was already excessive, and have resorted to "dumping" the foodstuffs produced by them. All this has helped to restrict markets and place further obstacles in the way of the free marketing of the surplus production of the agricultural countries.

Poland has not been able to settle her commercial relations with her two principal neighbours, Germany and Russia, in recent years. From 1925 until March 1930—that is to say, for nearly five years—Poland had been unable to conclude a commercial agreement with Germany, and the prolonged absence of an economic settlement between the two countries greatly reduced the possibility of placing Polish agricultural products in the nearest markets and, in addition, prevented their transit by rail to Western Europe. It is difficult to say whether this state of affairs will be remedied by the commercial agreement recently concluded, as the recent formidable increase in the German Customs duties on the principal agricultural products has had the effect of neutralising nearly all the advantages which Polish agriculture hoped to derive from the conclusion of the agreement. Even apart from this, the agreement by no means secures for Polish agricultural products free entry into Germany; imports of pigs and pork are strictly rationed and the import of other animals and meat products prohibited.

Nor are our commercial relations with Russia satisfactorily settled. Trade with Russia is becoming more and more uncertain, the export of Soviet products—which are a State monopoly—being sometimes reduced and sometimes increased for political reasons irrespective of economic considerations or necessities.

The present agricultural depression in Poland is further aggravated by the state of her trade in cereals and other products of the soil, which is less well organised than elsewhere and much poorer in privately owned working capital. Consequently, the agricultural syndicates and other commercial firms have to depend on inadequate credits granted at exorbitant rates. Their commercial operations thus become unduly costly and therefore necessarily restricted and the farmers are often forced to sell their produce to middlemen far below what would be regarded as a fair price in view of the price paid by the consumer. The margin between these two prices is too wide, far wider indeed than it would be if the producers' co-operatives and the consumers could deal direct with one another.

Another thing which greatly hampers trade in and marketing of agricultural products abroad is the shortage of warehouses, grain elevators and cold-storage apparatus.

It is owing to all these factors that the difference between the prices of agricultural produce in Poland and those on the principal world markets is often much greater than can possibly be justified.

The following table showing the prices of cereals will give an idea of this abnormal state of affairs:

AVERAGE PRICES OF WHEAT IN DOLLARS PER 100 KILOS

		Warsaw	Berlin	Prague	Paris	Liverpool	Chicago
1922–23		3.85	4.11	4.94	5.95	5.35	4.26
1923–24		3.77	3.80	5.10	5.03	4.70	4.10
1924–25		6.73	5.71	6.85	6.49	6.87	5.83
1925–26		4.69	5.89	5.94	5.94	6.46	6.05
1926–27		5.93	6.52	7.15	6.63	6.14	5.25
1927–28		6.04	6.02	6.76	6.38	5.81	5.07
1928–29		5.37	5.21	5.48	6.07	5.22	4.36
1929–30		4.58	6.05	5.30	5.46	4.78	4.27
1930–31:	August	3.71	5.96	4.92	6.55	4.17	3.34
	September	3.45	5.73	4.50	6.71	3.70	3.14
	October	3.15	5.40	4.09	6.61	3.34	2.94
	November	3.04	5.93	4.37	6.48	2.85	2.78
	December	3.08	5.91	4.42	6.57	2.80	2.90

. . . The present depression in Poland is not confined to agriculture, but is felt in other branches of production. Agriculture plays such an important part in the economic life of Poland that the effects of its depression cannot but be generally felt. The farmer who is deprived of his profits tends to restrict his own requirements and those of his business to a minimum. He only does what is strictly necessary and no longer devotes himself to the intense cultivation of his land. All this cannot but reduce purchasing power and restrict the home market.

The considerable decrease in the imports of various foreign commodities into Poland is without any doubt one of the consequences of the agricultural depression, as the interdependence of the various economic interests in all countries is an incontestable fact. The following figures speak for themselves:

IMPORTS IN THOUSANDS OF ZLOTY

1929		3,110,982	1930		2,245,973
1929:	August	226,535	1930:	August	188,491
	September	247,457		September	190,443
	October	257,247		October	202,201
	November	243,448		November	163,846
	December	214,381		December	158,907

29. The Financial Crisis

The financial crisis was delayed in Europe until the early summer of 1931. The first notable failure was that of the Austrian Creditanstalt, a bank deeply committed to capital investments throughout central Europe, in May, 1931. This sent a wave of panic throughout the area, producing large-scale withdrawals of credit, further bank closings, and emergency measures to prevent a complete collapse. Central European financial institutions appealed to their foreign creditors for assistance, and a number of emergency loans were granted. In 1929 the "Young Plan," put forth by an international committee headed by the American Owen D. Young, had created a Bank for International Settlements to deal simultaneously with transfers of reparation and war-debt payments. The Plan had diminished the total obligation of Germany while retaining the system of annual payments, but had allowed for part of an annual payment to be postponed in case of economic difficulties. But even this new system was unable to withstand the impact of the financial crisis, and on June 20, 1931, the President of the United States, Herbert Hoover, proposed a moratorium of reparation and war-debt payments. However, the Hoover Moratorium applied only to government debts, not to private ones, and further measures were needed. A series of international conferences met in the summer and fall of 1931, out of which came the "standstill" agreements, allowing a prolongation of credit to Germany and other European debtor states. These agreements greatly reduced the outward flow of short-term credit, but by no means eliminated the crisis. Conditions remained particularly serious in Germany, as was indicated in a report of experts for the Bank for International Settlements in December, 1931. The first document below is the text of the Hoover Moratorium proposal, the second is the report of the Special Advisory Committee of the Bank for International Settlements.

A. Hoover's Proposal for a Moratorium on War Debt and Reparation Payments, June, 1931

THE AMERICAN GOVERNMENT proposes the postponement during one year of all payments on intergovernmental debts, reparations and relief debts, both principal and interest, of course, not includ-

Source: William S. Myers, ed., *The State Papers and Other Public Writings of Herbert Hoover*, Vol. I: *March 4, 1929 to October 1, 1931* (Garden City, N.Y.: Doubleday, Doran and Co., 1934), pp. 591–593. Used by permission of the Herbert Hoover Foundation.

ing obligations of governments held by private parties. Subject to confirmation by Congress, the American Government will postpone all payments upon the debts of foreign governments to the American Government payable during the fiscal year beginning July 1 next, conditional on a like postponement for one year of all payments on intergovernmental debts owing the important creditor powers. . . .

The purpose of this action is to give the forthcoming year to the economic recovery of the world and to help free the recuperative forces already in motion in the United States from retarding influences from abroad.

The world wide depression has affected the countries of Europe more severely than our own. Some of these countries are feeling to a serious extent the drain of this depression on national economy. The fabric of intergovernmental debts, supportable in normal times, weighs heavily in the midst of this depression.

From a variety of causes arising out of the depression such as the fall in the price of foreign commodities and the lack of confidence in economic and political stability abroad there is an abnormal movement of gold into the United States which is lowering the credit stability of many foreign countries. These and the other difficulties abroad diminish buying power for our exports and in a measure are the cause of our continued unemployment and continued lower prices to our farmers.

Wise and timely action should contribute to relieve the pressure of these adverse forces in foreign countries and should assist in the reestablishment of confidence, thus forwarding political peace and economic stability in the world.

Authority of the President to deal with this problem is limited as this action must be supported by the Congress. It has been assured the cordial support of leading members of both parties in the Senate and the House. The essence of this proposition is to give time to permit debtor governments to recover their national prosperity. I am suggesting to the American people that they be wise creditors in their own interest and be good neighbors.

I wish to take this occasion also to frankly state my views upon our relations to German reparations and the debts owed to us by the allied Governments of Europe. Our government has not been a party to, or exerted any voice in determination of reparation obligations. We purposely did not participate in either general reparations or the division of colonies or property. The repayments of debts due to us from the Allies for the advances for war and reconstruction were settled upon a basis not contingent upon German reparations or related thereto. Therefore, reparations are necessarily wholly a European problem with which we have no relation.

I do not approve in any remote sense of the cancellation of the debts to us. World confidence would not be enhanced by such action. None of our debtor nations have ever suggested it. But as the basis of the settlement of these debts was the capacity under normal conditions of the debtor to pay, we should be consistent with our own policies and principles if we take into account the abnormal situation now existing in the world. I am sure the American people have no desire to attempt to extract any sum beyond the capacity of any debtor to pay and it is our view that broad vision requires that our government should recognize the situation as it exists.

This course of action is entirely consistent with the policy which we have hitherto pursued. We are not involved in the discussion of strictly European problems, of which the payment of German reparations is one. It represents our willingness to make a contribution to the early restoration of world prosperity in which our own people have so deep an interest.

I wish further to add that while this action has no bearing on the conference for limitation of land armaments to be held next February, inasmuch as the burden of competitive armaments has contributed to bring about this depression, we trust that by this evidence of our desire to assist we shall have contributed to the good will which is so necessary in the solution of this major question.

B. Report of the Special Advisory Committee of the Bank for International Settlements, December, 1931

THE GERMAN GOVERNMENT having, in accordance with article 119 of the Young plan, applied in a letter annexed to this report to the Bank for International Settlements on November 19, 1931, for the convocation of the Special Advisory Committee and having

Source: *Federal Reserve Bulletin*, Vol. XVIII, No. 1 (January, 1932), pp. 21–30, with deletions.

declared that "they had come to the conclusion in good faith that Germany's exchange and economic life might be seriously endangered by the transfer in part or in full of the postponable proportion of annuities," the board of the bank convened the committee in accordance with article 45 of its statutes. . . .

I

Present situation. The circumstances in which we have been called together are so well known that no lengthy recapitulation of events is necessary. The world depression, which started over two years ago, gradually gathered force until it broke in the credit crisis of the summer.

Every country has been shaken by that crisis, but its effects in Germany as well as in some other countries of central and eastern Europe were devastating. Sweeping withdrawals of foreign credits led to the crippling of the German banking system, strained the reserve and credit position of the Reichsbank to the uttermost, so that, in order to protect the currency, it was necessary to impose stringent measures of exchange control, which accentuated the already serious restrictions in the volume of economic activity. The pressure upon the whole structure of Germany culminated in the emergency decree of December 8, 1931, which includes measures without parallel in modern legislation. The following paragraphs sketch in brief outline the situation which these developments have created in Germany to-day.

Foreign debt. Germany was peculiarly susceptible to the credit crisis by reason of the large amount of her short-term foreign liabilities. In the first seven months of 1931, 2,900,000,000 reichsmarks ($690,780,000) of short-term credits were withdrawn, principally in June and July. A census taken by the German Government of the amount of foreign capital in Germany as on July 28 shows that the total commercial debt, and in particular the amount lent on short term, was even larger than was indicated in the available figures which were submitted to the bankers' committee early in August last.[1] This census indicates that the total of advances repayable by Germany at short term outstanding at the end of July

[1] "Report of the Committee Appointed on the Recommendation of the London Conference, 1931," *International Conciliation* (May, 1932).–Eds.

amounted to nearly 12,000,000,000 reichsmarks ($2,858,400,000). But this figure of 12,000,000,000 reichsmarks includes nearly 4,000,000,000 reichsmarks ($952,800,000) of nonbanking credits, which in all probability are not so likely to be withdrawn to the same extent as banking advances, and to a considerable extent are set off by direct counterassets. The Standstill Agreement, under which the banking creditors of Germany undertook not to call in their credits for six months as from September 1, 1931, applies to rather more than half of the 12,000,000,000 reichsmarks.

The Standstill Agreement, however, permitted the repayment of certain credits, and under these provisions sums estimated at 1,200,000,000 reichsmarks ($285,840,000) have been withdrawn during the period ending November 30, 1931.

Trade balance. Some set-off for the recent withdrawals has been found in the fact that they have coincided with a growing export surplus which began at the end of 1929. The figures are as follows:

(In millions)

	Imports		Exports		Surplus of Imports (−) or Exports (+)	
	Reichsmarks	Dollars	Reichsmarks	Dollars	Reichsmarks	Dollars
Monthly average:						
1925–1929	1,051	250	959	228	− 92	−22
1930	866	206	1,003	239	+137	+33
1931, January to June	634	151	794	189	+160	+38
July, 1931	562	134	827	197	+265	+63
August, 1931	454	108	803	191	+349	+83
September, 1931	448	107	835	199	+387	+92
October, 1931	483	115	879	209	+396	+94
November, 1931	482	115	749	178	+267	+64

The recent heavy export surplus is in part the result of certain abnormal factors, and it is doubtful if economic conditions will permit it to continue at the same high level. Exports have been maintained partly because the need for cash has put pressure on manufacturers to sell off stocks, in many cases at a loss, while some exceptional sales have been made to Great Britain in anticipation of tariffs. Imports have been reduced because unemployment, lower wages, and high taxation have reduced the consuming power of the country, and therefore the demand for imports of consumable commodities. The general reduction of industrial activity has curtailed the demand for imports of raw and semifinished material, and in any case the sharp reversal in the flow of foreign credit handicaps purchases abroad. The surplus has, moreover, been increased by the fact that up to now the world price level of the type of goods imported into Germany, viz., raw materials, foodstuffs, etc., has fallen much more than that of the type of goods exported by Germany, viz., finished products.

But it is impossible to disregard the existence of powerful general factors adverse to the continuance of this favorable development. Tariffs, exchange control measures in other countries, import restrictions and contingents, together with the enhanced competition Germany is likely to meet through the depreciation of sterling and other currencies, all tend to hamper German exports; on the import side it will be necessary for Germany to replenish her stocks of raw materials and to purchase food from abroad.

In any case, the surplus represented by the above figures has not become immediately available to Germany in the form of foreign exchange which can be utilized to repay debts. In view of the prevailing lack of confidence, there has been an increasing tendency to call upon Germany to pay cash for her imports, while she has had to give extended credits for her exports. In particular, German exports to Russia, which are running at about 80,000,000 reichsmarks ($19,056,000) a month, on the average of the last four months, have been made on very long credit terms. On the other hand, even exporters have been able, in spite of the legal restrictions, to keep abroad part of the foreign exchange resulting from exports. . . .

The Reichsbank. The Reichsbank reserve, which stood at 2,685,-000,000 reichsmarks ($639,567,000) at the end of 1930, and even at 2,576,000,000 reichsmarks ($613,603,200) at the beginning of June, 1931, had fallen to 1,610,000,000 reichsmarks ($383,502,-000) on July 31, 1931. Of this last amount, however, it owed at short-term 630,000,000 reichsmarks ($150,066,000) in respect of the rediscount credits granted to it by the Bank for International Settlements and the central banks, and to the Golddiskontbank by an American banking consortium. In order to insure that the necessary foreign exchange should be available to meet the service of Germany's long-term debt, for such repayment of short-term credits as is permissible under the standstill arrangements, and for the imports necessary to Germany, the Reichsbank has been forced to take or recommend a series of measures of increasing stringency, in order to limit to the greatest possible extent the other calls for foreign exchange which might be made upon it. Nevertheless, the reserve has fallen still further, until on December 15, 1931, it was no more than 1,161,000,000 reichsmarks ($276,550,200), of which 630,000,000 reichsmarks ($150,066,000) represent the amounts due under the rediscount credits referred to above.

The percentage cover for the note issue has thus fallen to 25.6 per cent, or if the 630,000,000 reichsmarks be excluded, to 11.7 per cent. The note circulation itself amounts to approximately 4,600,-000,000 reichsmarks ($1,095,720,000), which compares with a figure of 4,300,000,000 reichsmarks ($1,024,260,000) a year ago. In view of the reduction of business activity in the last year, as well as of certain measures taken to economize the use of currency, the present note circulation is high; this may be attributed to a decrease in the velocity of circulation and to a certain tendency on the part of the public to hoard notes. . . .

Production and employment. In order as far as possible to protect the external position—the reichsmark exchange and the export market—Germany has pursued a deliberate policy of stringent and sharp reduction of the level of wages and prices. The index figure of wholesale prices fell from 140 in November, 1928, to 106 in November, 1931, and prices are further to be reduced under the emergency decree of December 8, 1931, while wages are reduced under that decree to approximately the level prevailing at the beginning of 1927.

Taking 1928 as 100, the index of industrial production rose to 101 in 1929, fell to 86 in 1930, and for September, 1931 (the latest figure available), it had fallen to 66—in other words, one-third of the industrial life of Germany has stopped.

This gradual atrophy of industrial and commercial activity has further increased unemployment, which was already high before the crisis. The figure of unemployed (excluding part-time workers) on December 1, 1931, had reached a level of 5,000,000 out of approximately 21,000,000 employed persons.

The crisis has also seriously affected German agriculture, which in 1925 employed about 30 per cent of the working population of Germany. Having contracted debts at high rates of interest when prices were high, it now finds it difficult, if not impossible, to earn sufficient to meet the interest on these debts, and measures of protection and financial relief, amounting almost to a moratorium, have been taken in order to prevent a general collapse. . . .

The budget. The decline of economic activity, the fall of profits resulting from the fall in prices, and the lower yield of the taxes on wages due to increased unemployment and lower wage rates, have seriously reduced the yield of taxation. This fall (taken in conjunction with the cost of maintaining the growing army of the unemployed) has produced a critical situation in the public finances of Germany. In the five years preceding the depression the revenue and expenditure of the Reich, the Federal States and the communes showed a rapid increase. . . .

The revenue receipts for 1930–31 fell considerably short of the original estimates. The position in 1931–32, in which the revenue was expected to equal that actually received in the preceding year, has rapidly deteriorated. Fresh estimates made in September, 1931, showed an estimated fall in the total receipts from taxes collected by the Reich (including amounts subsequently transferred) of not less than 1,000,000,000 reichsmarks ($238,200,000). . . .

Apart from the increase in taxation . . . attempts are being made to meet the falling off in revenue by sweeping reductions in expenditure. So far as the Reich is concerned, expenditure on all objects other than service of the debt, transfers to the Federal States, external war burdens and emergency unemployment relief, has been reduced from 1929 to 1932 from 4,780,000,000 reichsmarks ($1,138,596,000) to 3,720,000,000 reichsmarks ($886,104,-000), that is, a reduction of 1,060,000,000 reichsmarks ($252,492,-000), or 22 per cent. . . .

III

In the course of its deliberations the committee had the opportunity of receiving a synopsis of the special measures taken by the German Government by form of emergency decrees, as from July, 1930, in order to meet the increasing difficulties of the situation.

The primary object of the German Government was to secure

the stability of the currency and in general the functioning of the German economy within the frame of the world economy. To this end they devoted all their efforts in securing the balance of the budget, not only in the Reich but also in the States and communes. Direct taxation was augmented by two increases in the income tax; indirect, by the imposition of further heavy duties on beer and tobacco, while finally the turnover tax has lately been increased from 0.85 to 2 per cent. Sweeping economies have been effected in the expenditure of the Reich; a series of cuts in the salaries of all public servants, reducing them by over 20 per cent, has been made in the last 18 months, so that salaries will be now on a lower level than at the beginning of 1927.

Similar measures have been taken with regard to the budgets of the Federal States and the communes. The latter have been authorized, and in certain cases compelled, to levy new and additional taxation in the form of a poll tax, a local beer duty, and a tax on beverages. The reductions in salaries apply also to officials employed by these bodies.

Contributions under the unemployment insurance scheme have been raised to 6.5 per cent of wages, while considerable reductions in the scope and scale of the benefits paid by the Insurance Institute have been made.

A further main point in the program of the Government was the reduction of prices and wages. Prices were generally reduced by 10 per cent. Rents are being reduced by a similar percentage. Even the rates of interest on long-term obligations must be reduced by about 25 per cent. In the sphere of wages, a general reduction to approximately the level prevailing at the beginning of 1927 has to take place.

The magnitude of the crisis forced the Government to emergency measures in the field of credit policy. Such measures have been taken for supporting a series of banking institutions and for strengthening the position of the money market. A system of general control of the banks has been set up, with a commissioner responsible to a board including representatives of the Reichsbank and of the competent Government authorities. New regulations have been made for the carrying on of the business of the savings banks and allied institutions, in particular limiting the extent to which they may finance the municipalities in future. For the time being they are not allowed to grant them new credits. The law governing public companies has been revised and the provisions regarding the responsibility of directors sharpened, while new regulations are made regarding the auditing of accounts.

Transactions in foreign exchange have been centralized in the Reichsbank with a view to limiting the purposes for which foreign exchange may be acquired, and all purchases of foreign exchange require prior authorization. All persons becoming possessed of foreign exchange, whether by exports or otherwise, are compelled to offer their holdings to the Reichsbank. It is no longer possible to remit abroad the proceeds of sales of securities on behalf of foreigners. Stringent provisions seek to limit the flight of capital. All the above-mentioned prescriptions are secured by heavy penalties (fines and prison). Repayment of foreign credits is regulated by the Standstill Agreement, or, if not covered by this agreement, under decree.

Finally, in order to prevent widespread collapse of agricultural credit, measures amounting practically to a moratorium for agricultural debts have been taken, chiefly for the eastern parts of Germany. Farmers suffering from special difficulties are allowed to appeal for protection against foreclosure or distraint on condition that they carry on their business under the supervision of trustees, pending approval of a scheme for relieving them of the immediate burden of their debts. Such schemes may provide for reduction of interest rates and the diminution of the capital debt, in certain cases even without the consent of the creditors.

The question how far the measures described above will be successful can not be answered at the present moment. But the committee considers that the steps taken to defend and to maintain the stability of the currency and the budget show, in their opinion, a resolute desire on the part of the German Government to meet the situation.

IV

It is evident from the facts outlined in the preceding chapters that Germany would be justified in declaring—in accordance with her rights under the Young plan—that in spite of the steps she has taken to maintain the stability of her currency, she will not be able in the year beginning in July next to transfer the conditional part of the annuity.

The committee, however, would not feel that it had fully accomplished its task and justified the confidence placed in it if it

did not draw the attention of the governments to the unprecedented gravity of the crisis, the magnitude of which undoubtedly
exceeds the "relatively short depression" envisaged in the Young
plan—to meet which the "measures of safeguard" contained therein
were designed.

The Young plan, with its rising series of annuities, contemplated
a steady expansion in world trade, not merely in volume but in
value, in which the annuities payable by Germany would become a
factor of diminishing importance. In fact, the opposite has been the
case. Since the Young plan came into effect, not only has the trade
of the world shrunk in volume, but the very exceptional fall in
gold prices that has occurred in the last two years has itself added
greatly to the real burden, not only of German annuities, but of all
payments fixed in gold.

In the circumstances the German problem—which is largely
responsible for the growing financial paralysis of the world—calls
for concerted action which the governments alone can take. . . .

30. Tariff Barriers

Everywhere, as foreign markets dried up and production and employment levels began to fall, nations struggled to preserve the home market. Tariffs were raised and import quotas introduced to prevent the importation of foreign goods. Sometimes this was done to create favorable bargaining positions for negotiation of tariff reductions with other states, but actual reductions were rare. By 1931 the tariff rates of some fifteen European nations had increased 64 per cent over the 1927 level. These measures acted to reduce international trade further—during the 1930's trade in manufactured products between Germany, Britain, and France fell to half the 1913 level—and to create greater disparities between domestic and world prices. The clearest indication of the pervasive pressures toward protection was the adoption of general import duties by Great Britain, the bastion of free trade. This historic step was announced on February 4, 1932, by Neville Chamberlain, the Chancellor of the Exchequer, in a speech to the House of Commons in which he surveyed the effects of the Depression on Britain's economy.

Chamberlain on Britain's Adoption of Protection, February, 1932

EVER SINCE this present House of Commons came together last year, the Members of the Government and, I am sure I may say, the whole body of our supporters, have been anxiously longing for the day on which we might settle down to the main business which had brought us to Westminster. That day has now come. I do not think that any reasonable man would say that the delay has been unduly protracted. Barely three months have elapsed since the most remarkable election in the whole of our political history[1] [An Hon. Member: "And the most corrupt!"]—when the National Government was formed with a mandate to apply an unprejudiced mind, free from all fetters, to the restoration of confidence in our financial stability, and to frame plans for ensuring a

Source: Great Britain, *Parliamentary Debates: House of Commons*, Fifth Series, Vol. 261, columns 279–296, with deletions.

[1] The election of October, 1931, which strengthened the majority of a "National Government" headed by Ramsay MacDonald, a Labourite, but dominated by Conservatives.—Eds.

favourable balance of trade. The Prime Minister, in his election manifesto, indicated some of the matters to which the Government would have to give their attention. He said:

> Tariffs, expansion of exports and contraction of imports, commercial treaties and mutual economic arrangements with the Dominions

were some of the matters with which the Government would have to concern themselves in deciding upon their programme, but nobody expected that immediately upon taking office it would be possible for the Government to lay down at once a permanent policy in all its details. Some interval was required in order that the various aspects of the problem might be thoroughly considered, and the consideration of those matters had to be examined in the light of new factors which had come into the situation. Our departure from the Gold Standard [in September, 1931] was still only recent, and we required some experience in order to see what its effects might be. The conditions of certain countries which have been among our most important customers were so critical that affairs required the most careful handling if we were not to pre-cipitate a crisis which might have had the most serious effects upon the trade and finances of our own country.

On the other hand, if we had simply waited until we were ready with our plans, the anticipation that we might introduce some material change in our fiscal system would certainly have tempted traders and exporters in other countries to forestall our intention and to flood this country with goods to an extent which would have completely disorganised our markets, and brought that ad-verse balance of trade, which was already mounting up at the rate of £2,000,000 a week, to large and, perhaps, even disastrous dimen-sions. What we had then to do at once was to keep the ring. Accordingly, we introduced two Measures, the Abnormal Impor-tations Act and the Horticultural Products Act with that purpose in view. . . . Behind the shelter of those two Acts, the Govern-ment have been able to pursue their examination with all the deliberation that was necessary, and they have now arrived, by a majority, at certain conclusions which I shall presently have to describe in detail.

Before I do so, I think, perhaps, it would be convenient if I were to draw attention to certain features in the situation. If we compare the position of the country to-day with what it was last November, I do not think that we have any cause for dissatisfaction. When my predecessor in my present office [Philip Snowden], with characteristic courage, framed his Budget so that by a series of drastic economies and severe increases in taxation the national accounts would balance, there were some who doubted whether it would be possible that his anticipations could be fulfilled. They doubted whether the economies which had been contemplated could actually be carried out, or whether the returns which were estimated from those taxes would produce the yield which he had expected. I am not yet in a position to affirm confidently to the Committee[2] that these melancholy forecasts will be falsified, but I can say that I do not believe you can find anywhere else in the world such an exhibition of self-sacrificing and devoted patriotism as has been shown by the British taxpayer during the last year.

Up to the end of last month the amount of Income Tax due and payable on 1st January collected by the officials of the Inland Revenue Department had reached a total of £105,000,000, as against £60,000,000 collected at the corresponding date last year, figures which, when allowance is made for the increase of rate and for the alteration in the allowances, indicate a collection at a rate 50 per cent higher than was the case last year. Similar results have been shown in the collection of Super-tax, which, in the same period, reached a total of £23,750,000, against £14,500,000 last year, and this at a time when these staggering increases of taxation coincide with a painful shrinkage of income which has been felt from one end to the other of the taxpaying class. No wonder that revenue authorities in "less happier lands" are left amazed at a spectacle which they surely must feel is the most remarkable demonstration that they have ever witnessed of that British eccentricity for which our country is notorious. . . .

I have dwelt at some length upon these favourable features in the situation, but we should be deceiving ourselves if we thought that we had yet really turned the corner, and I must ask the Committee to look for a moment at the other side of the picture. A great exporting country like ours is forced to look overseas for a great part of its trade. The catastrophic fall in the gold prices of commodities which has been taking place, and which as yet shows no signs of having reached bottom, has brought world trade into a truly deplorable condition. One of the first signs of this distress in

[2] The House of Commons, sitting as a Committee of the Whole.—Eds.

world trade is the extraordinary growth of trade restrictions. There is hardly any device, ranging from surtaxes to quotas, which has not been applied by one country or another; and there has sprung into existence in many places so-called systems of "devizen control"[3] planned on high Protection lines, which have raised almost impassable barriers to normal trading relations. Then there is that great problem which keeps Europe, or a great part of Europe, in a constant state of doubt and anxiety, the problem of Reparations and War Debts, still unsettled. Recent events in the Far East[3] have raised a new source of anxiety, and he would be a bold man who would prophesy to-day what may be the repercussions of those events in other countries far removed from their centre.

The figures of unemployment still remain of colossal dimensions, and we must naturally look forward to some increase in the figures in succession to the usual seasonal activities at Christmastime. The main industries of the country are very slow to move. Iron and steel remain in a stagnant condition; shipping and agriculture are still in the depths of depression. The effect of the depreciation of the pound, which at first seemed to hold out hopes of increased facilities for trading abroad, is being gradually whittled away as one country after another has departed from the Gold Standard, and although, as I have already pointed out, the pound has remained wonderfully steady over a long period, we cannot feel that confidence can be fully re-established while the trade balance remains so heavily against us. While we may admire and praise the public spirit of our taxpayers we must not suppose that they can indefinitely be called upon to make sacrifices of this extent, and that the State can go on extracting such vast sums from the pockets of the people without seriously crippling the resources from which industry must be fed if it is to maintain its vitality. . . .

. . . I am sorry to say that our investigations into the balance of trade have confronted us with disquieting results. The Committee is no doubt familiar with the way in which this balance of trade, or perhaps I should more properly call it this balance of payments, is calculated. There are three sets of figures in question. There are the figures of the imports of merchandise, the figures of the exports of merchandise, and then there are what are known as invisible exports, consisting of the income from shipping, the income from

[3] I.e., foreign exchange control.—Eds.
[4] Japanese occupation of Manchuria.—Eds.

foreign investments, the receipts from short interest and commissions, and some other minor items. The calculation is made by deducting the value of the exports from the value of the imports, leaving a surplus against which is set off the value of the invisible exports.

If I give figures to the Committee of two years, the years 1929 and 1931, they will see how rapid and how disastrous has been the change. I must say that the figures for 1931 are not yet absolutely final, but they may be taken as a very close approximation to the truth. In 1929 the value of imports less exports, that is, of the surplus of imports over exports, was £382,000,000. The value of the invisible exports was £482,000,000, leaving a favourable surplus of £100,000,000. In 1931 the surplus of imports over exports was £409,000,000, but the invisible exports were only £296,000,000, leaving an adverse balance in the neighbourhood of £113,000,000. In two years, therefore, the balance of payments had gone against us to the extent of over £200,000,000. . . .

. . . Before I come to the details of the Government's intended Measures, I think perhaps it would be convenient if I were to try to give to the Committee a very brief summary of the objects at which we are aiming, in order that they may perhaps get a better picture of the general scope and range of our intentions. First of all, we desire to correct the balance of payments by diminishing our imports and stimulating our exports. Then we desire to fortify the finances of the country by raising fresh revenue by methods which will put no undue burden upon any section of the community. We wish to effect an insurance against a rise in the cost of living which might easily follow upon an unchecked depreciation of our currency. We propose, by a system of moderate Protection, scientifically adjusted to the needs of industry and agriculture, to transfer to our own factories and our own fields work which is now done elsewhere, and thereby decrease unemployment in the only satisfactory way in which it can be diminished.

We hope by the judicious use of this system of Protection to enable and to encourage our people to render their methods of production and distribution more efficient. We mean also to use it for negotiations with foreign countries which have not hitherto paid very much attention to our suggestions, and, at the same time, we think it prudent to arm ourselves with an instrument which shall at least be as effective as those which may be used to discriminate against us in foreign markets. Last, but not least, we are going to take the opportunity of offering advantages to the countries of the Empire in return for the advantages which they now give, or in the near future may be disposed to give, to us. In that summary, under seven heads, we believe that we have framed a policy which will bring new hope and new heart to this country, and will lay the foundations of a new spirit of unity and cooperation throughout the Empire. . . .

The basis of our proposals is what we call a general *ad valorem* duty of 10 per cent upon all imports into this country, with certain exceptions to which I shall allude a little later. The purposes of that general duty are two-fold. We desire to raise by it a substantial contribution to the Revenue, and we desire also to put a general brake upon the total of the imports coming in here. . . . There are, however, certain exceptions to that general duty. Wherever there is an existing duty the article so dutiable will not be subject to the 10 per cent. . . .

I now pass to the superstructure which it is proposed to build upon the general *ad valorem* duties. That superstructure takes the form of additional duties which may be imposed upon non-essential articles. When I speak of non-essential articles, I mean either articles of luxury which are not essential to the individual, or articles which are not essential to the nation, in the sense that they either can be now or could be very shortly produced at home in substantial and sufficient quantity. We do not propose to specify these additional duties in the Bill; we propose that these duties may be imposed by Order of the Treasury after consultation with the appropriate Department, which will be the Board of Trade or the Ministry of Agriculture, or other Department concerned.

But the Treasury will not take the initiative in this matter. It would be extremely undesirable to put the selection of articles to be made dutiable, or the rates of duty to be levied, into the discretion of a single Minister. I am quite sure that his life would be very soon made intolerable by the demands which would be addressed to him, but, in addition to that, it might be thought that the decisions of such a Minister had been influenced by political considerations. Accordingly, it is proposed to set up an independent advisory committee consisting of a chairman and not less than two or more than five other members. This committee will be expected to give its whole time to its duties, and will be paid a salary which will be proportionate to the standing which we shall require of the members and to the sort of judicial attitude that we shall expect of them. It will be their function to consider the circumstances of those non-essential articles which are already subject to the duty of 10 per cent, and to recommend whether additional duties shall be placed on them. . . .

I now come to the position of the Empire countries in connection with this change in our fiscal system. The Committee is aware that next July the Imperial Conference is to be held in Ottawa, when the economic relations of the members of the British Commonwealth will be discussed. His Majesty's Government attach the utmost importance to that Conference, and they intend to approach it with a full determination of promoting arrangements which will lead to a great increase of inter-Imperial trade. I have no doubt that the Dominions would no more question our right to impose duties in our own interests, for the object either of raising revenue or of restricting imports, than we have questioned theirs to do the same, but considerations of that kind have to be weighed against the advantages to be obtained from preferential entry into Dominion markets, even though they should involve some surrender of revenue or some lessening of the reduction of imports; and since, until we meet the Dominion representatives, we shall not be in a position to estimate the advantages or the disadvantages on either side, and since we desire to mark at every stage our wish to approach this Conference in the true spirit of Imperial unity and harmony, we have decided that, so far as the Dominions are concerned—and in this arrangement we shall include India and Southern Rhodesia also—neither the general nor the additional duties shall become operative before the Ottawa Conference has been concluded. After the Conference, its results can be embodied in whatever modifications of these duties may have been agreed upon. I am confident that this decision of His Majesty's Government will be welcomed by the Dominions in the same spirit in which it has been made. . . .

31. The Impact of Unemployment

Mass unemployment overwhelmed Europe during the Depression. Although the worst period came at different times for different countries, the year 1932 was bad everywhere. During the first months of 1932 the number of people receiving unemployment benefits in Belgium rose to more than 21 per cent of those insured against unemployment, in Czechoslovakia to 15 per cent, in Germany to nearly 45 per cent, and in Britain to more than 18 per cent.[1] And these figures do not include the unemployed who did not qualify for unemployment benefits (professional people, some unskilled or non-unionized workers), those who had exhausted their benefits, and those who were only partially employed. The heavy burden of unemployment, much of it long-term, ate up unemployment funds, whether union, cooperative or public, so that benefits had to be reduced. Even those who remained at work often found their wages or salaries cut. The personal impact of the Depression cannot be conveyed by statistics. Homes, habits and hopes were washed away along with jobs, leaving anger or despair. The following selections were chosen to demonstrate the way the Depression bore down upon the unemployed. The first is an excerpt from a 1932 appeal by the unemployed in the British industrial cities of Manchester and Salford. The second, written in 1932, is from a statement by an unemployed British businessman. The third is an excerpt from an account by a German writer of the experience of spending a night in a public shelter for the unemployed.

A. Appeal of the Unemployed of Manchester
to the Public Authorities

IT IS WITH deep concern and profound feeling that I address you in the present circumstances. We have a deputation thoroughly representative of the unemployed; the patient, quiet, respectable, long-suffering, industrious people who, through our present economic chaos, have been thrust outside industry, and who, in consequence,

[1] *Monthly Labor Review*, Vol. 35, No. 6 (December, 1932), pp. 1275–1278.

Source: "Our Poverty—Your Responsibility," *Labour Magazine*, Vol. XI, No. 1 (May, 1932), pp. 29–31, with deletions. This was the official journal of the Labour Party.

are suffering from want and poverty, and all the pains and penalties of the damned. . . .

To-day we have more than 70,000 unemployed men and women in Manchester and Salford [a separate municipality but intimately connected with its neighboring city, Manchester], and nearly 300,-000 men, women and children suffering the most frightful distress in consequence; roughly 2,750,000 unemployed in Britain and more than a sixth of the entire population of this country suffering the most frightful distress in consequence. . . .

That responsibility rests largely upon you, my Lord Mayor, upon you and the Aldermen and City Councillors. You are here to safeguard, to maintain, and to foster the well-being, life, and happiness of the citizens of our community. That is the reason why you are what you are and where you are. Our poverty is your responsibility. You cannot escape from it.

We tell you that hundreds of thousands of the people whose interests you were elected to care for are in desperate straits. We tell you that men, women, and children are going hungry. We tell you that great numbers of your fellow citizens, as good as you, as worthy as the best of us, and as industrious as any of us, have been and are being reduced to utter destitution. We tell you that great numbers are being rendered distraught through the stress and worry of trying to exist without work. We tell you that the means of life are being denied to many of our fellow citizens. We tell you that unemployment is setting up a dreadful rot amongst the most industrious people in the body politic. We tell you that great measures of relief are needed, and that it is absolutely essential for you—our Public Authorities—to provide a vast amount of Public work. . . .

You will understand that we working people, and the unemployed whom we represent, are not bereft of all intelligence. Nor are we lacking in knowledge of the world about us. With that intelligence, with that knowledge, it is growing increasingly impossible to turn us off with tales of trade depression and fables about the need for economy. We know different. We know that we are being compelled to endure poverty in a world of plenty. We know that we are being compelled to suffer privation when the shops, stores, warehouses, are crammed to bursting point with all the things we need. We know that our folk are going short, going hungry, at a time when there are enormous gluts of wheat, tea, sugar, coffee, indeed of all the things necessary to satisfy that hunger. We have been made acquainted with these facts time and again in the public Press.

We know that the basic cause of unemployment is the very over-production of the things we need and our inability to buy back what we have produced. . . .

The necessary reorganisation and rehabilitation of Manchester and Salford would involve work in all the industries. In the matter of building (we refer to this as an example) many industries are involved—brickmaking, quarrying, timber, glass, metal and electrical, and so on. There are road-widening schemes needing to be done; bridge renovation and rebuilding schemes, the work of slum clearance; more parks and playgrounds, especially in the congested districts; cleansing and improving the Rivers Irwell and Irk, etc.; in short, the mighty complex task of getting Manchester and Salford into the mosaic of the present rather than leaving them to become derelicts of the past.

It will be impossible to beguile us with stories about the need for retrenchment, financial stringency, saving the rates, and so on. We know that these big wealthy cities of Manchester and Salford can, from all points of view, embark upon a vast scheme of necessary modernisation without harm to themselves and with infinite ultimate advantage. We are absolutely confident that there is capital enough and to spare for such purposes. Why, if to-morrow an appeal was made for subscriptions for a loan to some foreign power, or to finance some ruinous war, the treasure chests would open wide. . . .

If you do not do this—if you do not provide useful work for the unemployed—what we ask is your alternative? Do not imagine that this colossal tragedy of unemployment is going on endlessly without some fateful catastrophe. Hungry men are angry men. This unemployment, this hunger and want, privation and poverty, this heaping of worries and tribulations and sufferings on to increasing numbers of innocent people; this persistent hounding of men, women and children into the lowest depths of misery and degradation; this vile pauperisation of the workless by the Public Assistance Committees through the Means Test inquisition—are all going to produce—what? If the problem of existence is reduced to a beast-fight, the consequences will come back on you with boomerang effect. . . .

B. Unemployment in the Middle Class

FIVE YEARS ago, if anyone had told me I should be numbered amongst the unemployed I should probably have laughed at their gloomy prediction. My position appeared to be as safe as the Bank of England. (I assume that that institution is still "safe.") I had confidence in my own ability, a salary of £500 a year, and a staff of 28 really good, contented men under my control. I was able to report to the Board of Directors substantial increases in business turnover. . . .

Of course I knew that unemployment was increasing, but I did not connect it in the remotest degree with the sheltered position I then held. I did not know it would—and, in fact, was already—undermining my position. I did not know that this flood, like all uncontrolled forces, would sweep over me. I know to-day. I know that once the economic slide begins it accelerates with amazing rapidity.

I am but a very small unit in this increasing army of ruined men. What happens to me is unimportant. What is happening to thousands like me, and families like mine, constitutes a great social problem. You see, we are not counted amongst the unemployed, we are not carded and indexed: but our numbers are large, and they are increasing. I want to hammer that fact home. . . .

It is not so difficult whilst the savings last. One feels that courage and optimism will pull us through. "It is only for a short time; things will soon right themselves, and I shall obtain another position." Hope still springs! In the meantime, everything that we can possibly do without must go. A ruthless cutting down of expenditure shows how the weekly budget can be reduced. The telephone bill is heavy, therefore it must go; membership of various societies, library subscriptions, these, too, must go. The regular weekly meeting with a few friends must cease. (It is difficult to explain why you will not be one of the number who have been meeting regularly.) Concerts, theatres, an evening at the "pictures," picnics,

Source: An Unemployed Professional Man, "The Bitter Cry of the Black-Coated Worker," *Labour Magazine*, Vol. XII, No. 3 (July, 1933), pp. 109–111, with deletions.

which were such a joy to the family—these must be forgotten. The humble pipe, a real good friend to me—that must stay in the pipe rack. Until the need arises, one doesn't realise that an ounce of tobacco costs as much as two loaves of bread. . . .

The tradesmen are wondering why their orders are reduced. My wife has to reassure them that the reduction is not due to dissatisfaction with their supplies. The milkman's bill for a month is less than it used to be for one week. The grocer is the same. The butcher no longer calls. The amount of money we spent on meals for one day has now to provide us with food for a week. Buying clothes is out of the question—that is a thing of the past, and, of course, for the future. The whole whirl of problems has resolved itself into buying food and the payment of such accounts as rent, water, light, etc. At the moment all these accounts are due, and they are threatening to cut off supplies of light and water. What does one do when these essential supplies are cut off?

It is difficult to describe why these problems have assumed such tremendous proportions to me. . . . It is not so much a question of hope deferred; hope has been blasted, shattered; and whilst a new day used to bring its own stimulus and fresh encouragement, all days are now the same. There is no to-morrow for us. . . .

How long? I am now left with one decent suit of clothes. It is already showing the results of frequent pressing and sponging. I am afraid that when I obtain my next interview with a prospective employer my appearance will be so much against me that I shall not produce a favourable impression. Yes, it is like that. A smart appearance means a lot in our world. At the moment I look reasonably prosperous—even on two very carefully selected meals a day. "Black-coated" men cannot afford to look shabby. . . .

The tragedy is that some of the best brains at the disposal of British trade are being wasted. Brains and experience are for sale at a figure much below cost. Some of us are trying to keep body and soul together by selling silk stockings, vacuum cleaners, brushes, etc., from door to door. Yet we are men whose work remains effective long after our names have been removed from the salary list. We are denied access to the machine which in many cases we have created. Any moral obligation as to our future is forgotten. Business is business. . . .

C. German Unemployment and the Dole

AN ALMOST unbroken chain of homeless men extends the whole length of the great Hamburg-Berlin highway.

There are so many of them moving in both directions, impelled by the wind or making their way against it, that they could shout a message from Hamburg to Berlin by word of mouth.

It is the same scene for the entire two hundred miles, and the same scene repeats itself between Hamburg and Bremen, between Bremen and Kassel, between Kassel and Würzburg, between Würzburg and Munich. All the highways in Germany over which I traveled this year presented the same aspect.

The only people who shouted and waved at me and ran along beside my automobile hoping for a ride during their journey were the newcomers, the youngsters. They were still recognizable at once. They still had shoes on their feet and carried knapsacks, like the *Wandervögel*. . . .

But most of the hikers paid no attention to me. They walked separately or in small groups, with their eyes on the ground. And they had the queer, stumbling gait of barefooted people, for their shoes were slung over their shoulders. Some of them were guild members—carpenters with embroidered wallets, knee breeches, and broad felt hats; milkmen with striped red shirts, and bricklayers with tall black hats—but they were in a minority. Far more numerous were those whom one could assign to no special profession or craft—unskilled young people, for the most part, who had been unable to find a place for themselves in any city or town in Germany, and who had never had a job and never expected to have one. There was something else that had never been seen before—whole families that had piled all their goods into baby carriages and wheelbarrows that they were pushing along as they plodded forward in dumb despair. It was a whole nation on the march.

I saw them—and this was the strongest impression that the year 1932 left with me—I saw them, gathered into groups of fifty or a hundred men, attacking fields of potatoes. I saw them digging up the potatoes and throwing them into sacks while the farmer who

Source: An article by Heinrich Hauser originally published in *Die Tat*, a National Socialist monthly of Jena, here reprinted from *Living Age*, Vol. 344, No. 4398 (March, 1933), pp. 27–38, with deletions.

owned the field watched them in despair and the local policeman
looked on gloomily from the distance. I saw them staggering toward the lights of the city as night fell, with their sacks on their
backs. What did it remind me of? Of the War, of the worst period
of starvation in 1917 and 1918, but even then people paid for the
potatoes. . . .

I entered the huge Berlin municipal lodging house in a northern
quarter of the city. . . . Dreary barracks extended to the edge
of the sidewalk and under their dripping roofs long lines of men
were leaning against the wooden walls, waiting in silence and
staring at a brick structure across the street.

This wall was the side of the lodging house and it seemed to
blot out the entire sky. . . . There was an entrance arched by a
brick vaulting, and a watchman sat in a little wooden sentry box.
His white coat made him look like a doctor. We stood waiting in
the corridor. Heavy steam rose from the men's clothes. Some of
them sat down on the floor, pulled off their shoes, and unwound
the rags that were bound around their feet. More people were
constantly pouring in the door, and we stood closely packed together. Then another door opened. The crowd pushed forward,
and people began forcing their way almost eagerly through this
door, for it was warm in there. Without knowing it I had already
caught the rhythm of the municipal lodging house. It means waiting, waiting, standing around, and then suddenly jumping up.

We now stand in a long hall. . . . There under yellow lamps
that hang from the ceiling on long wires sit men in white smocks.
We arrange ourselves in long lines, each leading up to one of these
men, and the mill begins to grind. . . .

What does the man in the white smock want to know? All these
fellows in white smocks belong to a very special type of official.
The way they let the line flow by while they work so smoothly
together is facile, lazy, almost elegant. The way they say "Mr."
to the down-and-outers from the street is full of ironic politeness.
. . . The whole impersonal manner of the officials makes them as
incomprehensible as a cash register. . . .

Then come the questions. When and where were you born, and
where have you come from? Name of your parents? Ever been in
a municipal lodging house before? Where have you spent the last
three nights? Where did you work last? Have you begged? The
first impression that these questions and answers make on me is
that it is just like the army. . . .

My second impression is the helplessness of the men on my side of the bar and the shocking ruthlessness with which the men on the other side of the bar insult this helplessness. Eight out of each ten men on my side of the bar are young fellows and about a third of these are mere boys. . . .

The official presses a white card into my hand and tells me to go to the desk of another clerk that has the sign, "adjuster," over it. While waiting in line I look at my white card. It is divided into squares and has my name at the top and all kinds of mysterious symbols underneath. . . . I do not remember what the "adjuster" said to me—there was some inconsistency in my papers, I believe. . . . [He was sent on to a police examiner, but eventually was cleared.]

When I come out I am holding a check that has been given me for a night's sleep and food in the lodging house. . . . The bare walls of the room that we have entered are lined with iron bedsteads. There are no windows, but a sloping roof with skylights that reminds me of a factory. We sit down on the bedsteads along the middle of the room, closely packed together. A voice near me whispers, "What was the matter with you, buddy?"

"My papers."

"Say, you had luck to get out again. They kept the fellow that went in with you. He spent his dole of eighteen marks [about $4.30] in two days. Oh, boy, think of it! Eighteen marks! . . ."

I look at the clock again. Our reception ceremony lasted an hour and a half, and we now sit here another half hour, which makes two hours. They do not make it easy for you to get supper and a bed in a municipal lodging house. . . .

32. Unemployment Relief in Nazi Germany

Between 1930 and 1932 the governments of Germany had met the economic crisis with a series of emergency decrees designed primarily to keep the state solvent through deflationary measures. Wages, rents, pensions, and relief payments were drastically reduced (see document 29B, the Report of the Special Advisory Committee of the Bank for International Settlements). While it is understandable that, after the experience of 1923, the German government was concerned not to endanger the soundness of the currency by incurring large budgetary deficits, the measures taken did nothing to reduce unemployment or restore production. The National Socialist Government, which came to power early in 1933, adopted an entirely different, but now familiar, approach, expanding public expenditures to restore economic activity. The resources of the state were used to create jobs through public-works measures, subsidies, and tax concessions. The document that follows, the Law for the Reduction of Unemployment of June 1, 1933, was the first of a series of "pump-priming" measures put into effect by the Nazis.

Law for the Reduction of Unemployment, June, 1933

Part I: Providing Employment

1. (1) The Minister of Finance is empowered to allocate labor treasury notes to the amount of one billion Reichsmarks for the purpose of promoting the national employment, especially for the following purposes:
    1. repair and enlargement of administrative and residential buildings, bridges, and other construction works of states, municipalities, townships, and other such public bodies;
    2. repair of residential and farm buildings, the subdivision of dwellings, and the conversion into smaller units of other dwellings;
    3. development of suburban low-income housing;
    4. development of agricultural settlements;
    5. river control;
    6. providing for the needs of the population for gas, water, and electricity;

Source: *Reichsgesetzblatt* (Jahrgang 1933), Part I, No. 60, pp. 323–329, with deletions. Translated by the editors.

7. underground construction work in the states, municipalities, and townships;

8. material help for the needy.

(2) The measures designated in section (1), subsections 1, 3, 4, 5 and 6 shall be effected through the dispensing of loans. Only such works are to be undertaken as are economically worthwhile and which the proprietor could not carry out with his own financial resources in the foreseeable future.

(3) The measures specified in section (1), subsections 2, 7 and 8 should be carried out by the granting of subsidies:

1. to homeowners in the case of section (1), subsection 2;

2. to the states or municipalities and townships in the case of section (1), subsection 7;

3. to the district welfare organizations in the case of section (1), subsection 8.

2. For the granting of subsidies specified in section (1), subsection 7, for underground construction work, the following conditions hold:

1. subsidy may be granted only for work that is economically worthwhile and that could not possibly be carried out by those conducting the work with their own financial resources in the foreseeable future;

2. the work must begin not later than August 1, 1933;

3. all work is to be carried out by manual labor unless mechanical means are indispensable and no unduly high costs result from the use of manual labor;

4. insofar as the nature of the work does not require the employment of skilled workers who are not unemployed, only native unemployed workers may be hired;

5. unemployed workers hired under subsection 4 will not thereby establish a labor or service relationship in the sense of the labor law;

6. unemployed workers hired under subsection 4 are granted:

   a) the unemployment compensation (support from unemployment insurance, emergency relief, public relief) to which they would be entitled if their unemployment continued;

   b) an allowance of 25 reichsmarks for every four full work weeks in the form of maintenance certificates, made available by the Reich as a means of subsidy. These certificates may be used to procure clothing and laundry and household needs from shops that are prepared to accept them;

    c) a hot meal every workday from the employer or a suitable payment in cash.

3. The provision of section (1), subsection 8, is to be fulfilled by the presentation of maintenance certificates to the district welfare organizations. The maintenance certificates authorize the district welfare offices to procure clothing and laundry and household needs from shops that are prepared to accept them. The district welfare organizations are to make distributions among needy persons according to individual and family needs.

4. Other public works will be promoted through loans granted out of the donations to the Voluntary Fund for the Recovery of National Employment [*Freiwillige Spende zur Förderung der nationalen Arbeit*]. . . . The choice of the works to be undertaken rests with the Reich Minister of Labor in consultation with the Minister of Finance.

5. The labor treasury notes (paragraph 1) shall be redeemed, one-fifth each year in the fiscal years 1934, 1935, 1936, 1937, and 1938. The Minister of Finance is empowered to include the necessary sums in the budgets of these years.

6. In order to ensure the redemption of the labor treasury notes, a special sinking fund of the Reich is established, to be administered by the Reich Minister of Finance.

Part II: Tax Exemptions for Replacement of Equipment

In the determination of earnings for purposes of the income tax, corporation taxes, and taxes on commercial profits, the following exceptions to paragraph 16 of the income-tax law hold good, beginning June 30, 1933, and ending January 1, 1935:

Expenditures for the purchase or installation of machinery, equipment or similar objects of industrial or agricultural capital may be deducted in full from the tax returns if the four following conditions are met:

    1. the new equipment must be of domestic production;

    2. the taxpayer must purchase or install the new equipment after June 30, 1933, and before January 1, 1935;

    3. the new equipment must replace similar equipment hitherto operative;

    4. it must be shown that the use of the new equipment will not lead to a reduction of workers in the taxpayer's shop. . . .

Part V: Marriage Assistance

The Reich promotes the contracting of marriages with the following measures:

1. (1) When this law takes effect, German citizens who marry may receive, upon application, marriage loans up to the amount of one thousand Reichsmarks. The application for the granting of a loan may be made before the marriage takes place. The conditions for the granting of a marriage loan are:

a) that the future wife has held a job in the country for at least six months in the period between June 1, 1931, and May 31, 1933;

b) that a public declaration is made in the marriage-registration office by the future wife that she will give up her status as an employee not later than the time of the marriage, or that she has already done so when the application is made;

c) that the future wife is forbidden to resume employment so long as the future husband has an income (in the sense of the income-tax law) of more than 125 Reichsmarks per month and the marriage loan is not entirely redeemed.

The facts under a) are to be proven; those under b) are to be shown credible.

(2) No one employed in the household or the business of an immediate relative is to be considered an employee under section (1), a) above.

(3) The application for the granting of a marriage loan is to be made to the local authorities in the district in which the future husband legally or usually resides. This local authority will forward the recommendation to the proper finance office if it supports it. The finance office makes final decision on the application.

(4) The marriage loan is to be granted to the husband. In case of a division of property, each partner will receive half of the marriage loan.

2. (1) The marriage loan is noninterest-bearing. It is to be repaid, to the income-tax office of the husband, in monthly installments of 1 per cent of the original sum of the marriage loan. The monthly payments are due on the tenth day of every month. The obligation to make repayment begins at the start of the first calendar quarter following receipt of the marriage loan.

(2) The marriage partners are jointly responsible for the repayment of the marriage loan.

(3) The Reich tax regulations apply to the collection of repayments.

3. The marriage loans will be issued in the form of maintenance certificates. These are valid for the purchase of furniture and household articles in shops prepared to accept them. Maintenance certificates may be redeemed for cash by merchants at finance offices.

4. The funds allocated in paragraph 1 for the granting of marriage loans shall be raised by the creation of an *Ehestandshilfe* [Fund for the Aid of Marriage]. Contributions to the *Ehestandshilfe* will be made by all single persons with incomes, as defined in the income-tax law. The amount of the levy of the wage and salary earners to the *Ehestandshilfe* is determined by the type of their income. . . .

Part VI: Implementation

The Finance Minister, and in the case of Part 1, 4, the Minister of Labor, in consultation with the Finance Minister, are authorized to abrogate existing laws and ordinances in order to carry out and implement this law.

33. The Popular Front in France

France did not experience such depths of economic depression as did some other European countries or the United States. Partially this can be explained by her ability to provide for most of her own agricultural and industrial needs so that she was less dependent upon foreign trade than Britain or Germany and could maintain national production behind high tariff barriers. In addition, a conservative financial policy shielded France from the worst of the financial crisis of 1931. Nonetheless, by 1932 the impact of the Depression began to be felt in France. The problems it brought—unemployment, falling wages and prices, declining production—were combined with more fundamental weaknesses: a nearly stagnant population which grew by only two millions in the entire interwar period; a low level of investment in industry (except in the area of war devastation, which had been reconstructed at considerable cost); low productivity and consequently low per capita income. Furthermore, compared to other European countries, France had been slow to enact basic welfare and labor legislation.

From 1932 to 1936 French governments adopted a policy of retrenchment in response to the problems created by the Depression. State expenditures were cut by such means as reducing the salaries of public employees and lowering interest payments on the debt. But this deflationary policy, which did little to restore production and employment, was repudiated in 1936 by the parties of the Left (Radicals, Socialists and Communists) who combined in a Popular Front coalition headed by the Socialist leader Léon Blum. On a platform pledging a general reform and renewal of economic life, the Popular Front won a decisive majority in the parliamentary elections of May, 1936. Improving the conditions of labor became urgent as a series of sit-down strikes in early June threatened to paralyze much of French industry. During the summer of 1936 a vast amount of legislation was enacted. The reforms of the new government mark the real beginning of the welfare state in France, although some of the new policies did not come to fruition until after World War II. The broad scope of the reforms is indicated by the first document presented here, taken from the opening statement of the Blum government to the new legislature. The second reflects the Popular Front's repudiation of the deflationary policies of previous governments. The third and fourth documents concern the new pattern of labor-management relations created under the Popular Front. The Matignon Accords, an agreement for collective bargaining, was worked out during the sit-down strikes when Blum brought together representatives of employers and employees at his official residence, the Matignon Palace. The last document gives excerpts from the June 11 report of the legislature present-

ing the forty-hour work week bill to the Chamber; the bill was passed
as presented and promulgated on June 26.

A. Ministerial Declaration of the
Popular Front, June, 1936

GENTLEMEN, THE government comes before you following general
elections in which universal suffrage, the judge and master of us
all, delivered its judgment with greater force and clarity than at
any other moment in the history of the Republic.

The French people have indicated their resolute determination
to preserve against violent and cunning attacks the democratic
liberties they created and which remain their heritage. They have
voiced their determination to seek new remedies for the crisis which
crushes them, relief from the suffering and agony which has been
made even crueler by long duration, and to return to active, healthy
and confident life. Finally, they have proclaimed the desire for
peace which animates them all. . . .

The government does not need to formulate its program. Its
program is the common program accepted by all the parties making up the majority, and the sole problem will be to translate it
into law. These laws will be presented in rapid succession, for the
government believes that the moral and material changes demanded
by the country will be achieved through their combined effect.

From the beginning of the next week, we shall bring before the
Chamber a group of bills which we shall ask the two Houses to
act upon before adjournment. These bills will deal with:

A political amnesty; the forty-hour week; collective bargaining
contracts; paid vacations; a public works program to provide facilities for public health, science, sports and tourism; the nationalization of armament production; a wheat office which will serve as
a model price support system for other agricultural products such
as wine, meat and milk; the extension of the years of [compulsory]
schooling; a reform in the organization of the Bank of France that
will guarantee the predominance of national interests in its management; a first revision of the decree laws in favor of the most severely
affected categories of public service employees and of veterans.

As soon as these measures are disposed of, we shall present to

Source: *Journal Officiel de la République française, Debats parlementaires,
Chambre des Députés, Session ordinaire de 1936*, pp. 1315–1316, with deletions. Translated by the editors.

parliament a second series of bills dealing with national unemployment insurance, insurance against agricultural disasters, the regulation of agricultural debts, and a pension system guaranteeing the aged workers in the city and on the land protection against misery.

In a short time we shall present a comprehensive system of fiscal simplification and relief in order to ease the condition of industry and commerce, and, above all, to permit general recovery. The measures will require no new revenues, except out of wealth acquired through repression and fraud.

While we shall strive, with your full cooperation, thus to revitalize the French economy, to absorb the unemployed, to increase disposable income in general, and to provide well-being and security for those whose labor creates true riches, we must govern the country. We shall govern as republicans; we shall assure the republican order. We shall apply the laws of republican defense with quiet firmness. We shall show that we intend to instill the republican spirit throughout the entire administration and public services. If democratic institutions are attacked, we shall assure their integrity with the means appropriate to the danger or the resistance.

The government misapprehends neither the nature nor the seriousness of the difficulties that await it. As it has not deceived itself, neither will it deceive the country. In a few days it will present publicly a report on the economic and financial situation as it exists at the beginning of this legislative session. It realizes that for a country like France, accustomed by long usage to political liberty, one can speak the truth without fear, and that frankness of governments assures rather than impairs the necessary confidence of the nation. As for us, the immensity of the task we face, far from discouraging us, only increases our determination. . . .

B. Repudiation of Retrenchment

GENTLEMEN, AN examination of the consequences of the decree laws of the Doumergue and Laval Governments[1] regarding veterans,

Source: Resolution of June 6, 1936, proposing annulment of the decree laws, in *Journal Officiel de la République française*, *Chambre des Députés*, *Session ordinaire de 1936*, *Documents parlementaires*, *Annexés au procès verbaux des séances*, Part II, pp. 805–806. Translated by the editors.

[1] From the spring of 1932 French governments tried to balance the budget and keep the country on the gold standard by reducing government expenditures. Cuts were made by decree by the government of Gaston

war victims, and public servants shows that the laws have worsened the living conditions of an important segment of the population. Disabled veterans whose injuries were minor and therefore did not entitle them to full disability benefits, have been particularly affected, and there are many unemployed among them. Lesser officials, whose previously inadequate salaries were reduced by the decree laws, find themselves in a very difficult situation. Moreover, private industry, emulating the example of the State, has taken advantage of this situation by imposing on their employees new and important wage reductions.

This reduction of the purchasing power of wage earners has had disastrous consequences for small and medium merchants. Businesses fail more and more frequently, and farmers find the market price for agricultural products considerably reduced. As a result, the sale of government bonds has diminished, making budget estimates less reliable and thus putting the Treasury in difficulties.

In view of the fact that justice demands the restoration of the salaries of state and public service employees, and that to do so would be in the best interests of the entire country, we have the honor to propose the following resolution:

The Chamber requests the Government immediately to formulate a bill providing for:

1. Restoration of full rights to veterans and war victims by the suspension of the reductions adopted after June 1, 1932;

2. Annulment of the reductions made after June 1, 1932, in payments for public health and child care, as well as in welfare and social security payments;

3. Immediate suspension of all reductions in pension payments resulting from measures taken after June 1, 1932, and complete reorganization of the pension system so as to allow all the retired, both civilian and military, treatment that is equitable and that accords all categories satisfaction of their legitimate claims;

4. For all employees of the State, the departments, municipalities, public services, of Algeria, the colonies, protectorates and mandated territories, abolition of the salary reductions effected after June 1, 1932;

5. Restoration of the 10 per cent cut in interest imposed on government bonds held by small investors by the decree law of July 16, 1935.

Doumergue (February–November, 1934) and in particular by that of Pierre Laval (June, 1935–January, 1936), the last important government before the election of the Popular Front.

C. The Matignon Accords

ARTICLE 1. The representatives of the employers accept the immediate establishment of collective labor contracts.

ARTICLE 2. These contracts are specifically to include Articles 3 and 5 following.

ARTICLE 3. Observance of the law being the duty of all citizens, the employers acknowledge the freedom of opinion of workers as well as their right freely to join and belong to trade unions established in accordance with Book 3 of the Labor Code.

Employers undertake not to allow the fact of membership or nonmembership in a union to affect their decisions in matters of hiring, the conduct or the distribution of labor, disciplinary measures, or dismissal.

If one of the parties to the contract contests the motive for dismissal of a worker as having been in violation of the rights of organized labor indicated above, both parties will seek to gather the facts and in disputed cases to arrive at an equitable solution.

This action does not prejudice the right of the parties to obtain through the courts compensation for damages caused. The exercise of the rights of organized labor ought not to result in acts contrary to law.

ARTICLE 4. The real wages paid to all workers on May 25, 1936, will be, when work is resumed, raised on a descending scale beginning at 15 per cent for the lowest wages and declining to 7 per cent for the highest.

The total wages bill of any establishment must not in any case increase by more than 12 per cent. Wage increases agreed to after the above date are to be included in the adjustments specified. However, increases that exceed the above adjustments will remain.

The negotiations for collective contracts fixing minimum wages by region and by category, which are to begin immediately, ought to be concerned particularly with necessary adjustments in abnormally low wages.

The representatives of the employers pledge to proceed with any adjustments necessary to maintain a normal relationship between the earnings of wage earners and salaried employees.

Source: *Le Populaire* (June 8, 1936). Translated by the editors.

ARTICLE 5. Except for particular cases already regulated by law, in each establishment employing more than ten workers, after agreement with trade-union organizations or, in their absence, among the interested parties, there will be designated two (head) or several (head and assistant) workers' delegates according to the size of the establishment. These delegates are responsible for presenting to the management individual complaints not expressly met concerning the application of the laws, decrees, regulations of the Labor Code, the rates of wages, and measures of hygiene and safety.

All workers, male and female, above eighteen years of age, provided they have been employed in the establishment at least three months and that they have not been deprived of their civic rights, are qualified voters [for the workers' delegates].

Eligible [as delegates] are the voters as defined above who are French citizens, at least twenty-five years of age and who have been employed in the establishment continuously for one year, with the reservation that the duration of employment may be shortened if it reduces the number of those eligible to five.

Workers engaged in the retail trade, of whatever nature, whether conducted by themselves or by their spouses, are not eligible.

ARTICLE 6. The employers' representatives undertake not to employ sanctions against workers [now] on strike.

ARTICLE 7. The representatives of the labor confederation will request that striking workers return to the job as soon as the management of the establishment has accepted the general agreement arrived at, and as soon as discussions concerning its application have begun between management and labor in the establishment.

D. The Forty-hour Law

GENTLEMEN, THE proposed law on the forty-hour week is part of a century-long effort to reduce hours of work. It promotes at one and the same time both social and economic goals.

Source: Report of June 11, 1936, by the commission established to draft the forty-hours bill, in *Journal Officiel de la République française, Chambre des Députés, Session ordinaire de 1936, Documents parlementaires, Annexés aux procès verbaux des séances*, Part II, pp. 852–853, with deletions. Translated by the editors. The draft of the law as presented in this report was passed by both Houses without amendment.

The social goal: In the face of increased mechanization of industry, the law seeks to provide the individual with the increased leisure needed for the preservation of his personality.

The economic goal: In the face of unemployment, a good part of which arises from technological progress and increased mechanization, the law seeks to provide leisure for the workers and a general increase in their purchasing power.

Two questions have been raised. Will the forty-hour week serve to reabsorb the unemployed? Will it not result in price increases that will offset some of the advantages obtained?

Regarding the first point, we do not expect the reduction of hours of work to effect a miraculous and total elimination of unemployment. Nevertheless it remains probable that the reduction of hours of work will require the hiring of a very large number of additional workers, allowing the immediate reemployment of at least one-quarter to one-third of the unemployed.

Regarding the second point, it is undeniable that the reduction in working hours without wage reductions will increase production costs, but that increase should be much less than is feared by certain opponents of the law. It is difficult to establish with precision what place wages have in the total cost of production. The few statistics available indicate great variation from one industry to another. Wages represent, according to the case in question, from 20 to 60 per cent of the cost of production. The shift from a forty-eight-hour to a forty-hour week without reduction in wages thus is likely to produce an increase in costs of 4 to 12 per cent with the average being about 8 per cent. But living costs probably would not rise as much as wage costs, because a reduction in the working day will be accompanied by an increase in the productivity of the worker. . . .

Although increases in costs of production may have repercussions for wholesale prices in general, they are unlikely to produce a corresponding increase in retail prices. The experience of recent years has shown that in a period of depression the lowering of wholesale prices has not been followed by an equivalent reduction in retail prices—mainly because some important general costs (taxes, transportation, interest charges) have not been reduced in the same proportion. By the same token, an increase in wholesale prices resulting from the adoption of the law would not affect other elements in the general costs of production and would have only a

very limited effect on retail prices. These, we are convinced, would
not rise by more than 5 per cent.

In these circumstances reduction of the working day without
wage reductions would produce some temporary difficulties for
export industries which the Government ought to assist by means
of its tariff policy and by granting credits. In the domestic market,
by contrast, we expect that a minimal increase in the cost of living
will be offset by the increase in demand resulting from the increased purchasing power of the country. This increase in demand,
by permitting a distribution of general costs among a larger number of product units, is capable ultimately of reducing the cost of
living.

Several hundred thousand workers at present impoverished or
living stringently on unemployment benefits will receive regular
wages and will enter the market for goods. This demand will be
felt first in the market for food products where it will reinforce
recent price increases. It will also reach the markets for manufactured goods. . . .

For these reasons the commission believes that most of the fears
of the opponents of the forty-hour week law are unjustified.

After the failure of the deflationary policy, which lowered the
income of workers without improving matters and in fact aggravated the existing economic dislocation, the forty-hour week is
not to be seen as an isolated measure but as an essential part of a
broad policy directed toward the restoration of the purchasing
power of the masses and thereby general economic recovery.

Under these circumstances, the commission approved in general
terms the bill submitted to it by the Government. . . .

ARTICLE 1. Chapter II (Hours of Work) of Title I of Book II of
the Labor Code is amended as follows:

ART. 6. In industrial, commercial, handicraft and cooperative
establishments or in their subsidiaries, of whatever nature,
public or private, secular or religious . . . hours of labor of
workers or salaried employees of either sex and of any age are
not to exceed forty per week.

ART. 7. Decrees of the Council of Ministers, after consultation
with the professional section or sections of the National Economic Council, will determine . . . the means of applying the
preceding article. These decrees will be issued either on the initiative of the government or at the request of one or several of

the employer or worker organizations concerned. In either case, the employer and worker organizations concerned must be consulted; they must present their views no later than one month after these have been requested. These decrees will be revised in the same manner. They must take into consideration the agreements undertaken between employer and worker organizations, in cases where such agreements exist.

ART. 8. In underground work in mines the length of time each worker spends underground must not exceed thirty-eight hours and forty minutes a week.

ART. 9. A decree issued by the Council of Ministers under the same conditions as those indicated in Article 7 shall determine the means of applying the preceding article, specifically the means of calculating the length of time underground.

ART. 10. The application of the provisions of Articles 6 to 9 do not affect collective labor agreements which establish shorter hours of work.

ARTICLE 2. No reduction in the standard of living of workers may result from the application of the present law, which shall not be made a reason for reducing the remuneration of the worker (wages or fringe benefits).

ARTICLE 3. Articles 6 to 13 which presently constitute Chapter II (Hours of Work) of Title I of Book II of the Labor Code are abrogated. . . .

ARTICLE 4. The present law applies to Algeria. Decrees will determine the conditions of its application in colonies and protectorates. . . .

PART VII

The Economics of Fascism

In neither Nazi Germany nor Fascist Italy did radically new and comprehensive economic "systems" emerge. In each case the new régime came to power in a time of economic crisis and much of its attention was devoted to solving immediate problems, frequently by making more intensive use of practices that had already been employed elsewhere in similar situations. In Italy, the corporate system was put together piecemeal, and its doctrinal underpinnings were often formulated after the fact. Yet, if much was borrowed, if there was sometimes a disparity between doctrine and practice, and if economic policy clearly reflected the changing demands of domestic and foreign politics, Fascist economics is still to be distinguished by its special tone and emphases.

Fascist doctrine expressed a strong hostility to economic liberalism and socialism and instead emphasized the development of a national economic system, requiring harmony among the various productive forces. Increased production, especially of essential materials, was furthered in order to make the country less dependent on international trade. Finally, there was, in contrast to the liberal democratic states, no ideological restraint on government intervention in economic life in defense of these national interests as defined by the régimes.

The emphasis on the priority of the interests of the national community over those of the individual or any particular economic group resulted in measures to destroy independent labor organizations, to eliminate industrial conflicts, and to bring labor and, to a lesser extent, industry under the control of the state. Elaborate new organizations were created to take the place of the old and, within this system, provision was made for state-sponsored cultural, recreational, and welfare facilities.

In order to develop national economic strength and independence efforts were made to increase output and, especially in the case of Italy, to achieve what was regarded as a better balance in the economy between agriculture and industry. But in spite of various efforts, both Germany and Italy continued to depend on foreign supplies of many goods. Thus, control of foreign trade in the interest of national well-being was held to be essential. One of the aspirations of both states was to assure supplies of essential raw materials and to provide markets for their exports. Germany was reasonably successful in establishing (by means of bilateral trade agreements) a dominant position in the economies of the agricultural Balkan states, hard hit by the depressed international market for primary goods.

The record of the Fascist régimes in the economic sphere is difficult to assess because the experiment was disrupted by the Second World War. There is also much debate about the extent to which military production, especially in Germany, was responsible for economic recovery. It is certainly true that in the short run the Fascist governments in both Italy and Germany were able to restore a measure of economic order and to introduce a number of programs leading toward economic development. That these measures in the long run proved extremely costly is beyond question.

34. Regulation of Labor Relations

In the name of the social peace they claimed to establish, both the Italian and German Fascist régimes acted quickly to bring labor-management relations under their control. In Italy, after an initial period of competition between Fascist and independent labor organizations, a period marked by some industrial unrest, a Law on Corporations was enacted on April 3, 1926. This law brought to an end the independent unions and created a new set of organizations for labor and employers. The Law on Corporations constituted one of the major legislative pillars of the corporate system. In Germany the Nazis acted even more quickly to gain control of labor and industrial relations. There, a law of January 20, 1934, established the new system of regulation.

A. Italian Law on Corporations, April, 1926

Chapter I

ART. 1. Associations of employers and of workers, both intellectual and manual, may obtain legal recognition when they can prove that they comply with the following requirements:

1) in the case of associations of employers, that the employers who have voluntarily registered as members employ not less than one-tenth of the workers in the service of the concerns of the kind for which the association has been formed, existing in the district in which it operates; and in the case of associations of workers that the workers who have voluntarily registered as members number not less than one-tenth of those of the class for which the association has been formed, existing in the district in which it operates;

2) that besides the protection of the economic and moral interests of its members the association proposes to promote, and does actually promote, the assistance, instruction, and moral and patriotic education of its members;

3) that the director of the association affords guarantees of ability, morality, and sound national loyalty. . . .

ART. 6. The associations may be communal, district, provincial, regional, inter-regional, and national.

Source: Benito Mussolini, *Fascism: Doctrine and Institutions* (Rome: Ardita, [1935]), pp. 75–89, with deletions.

Recognition may also be granted, under the provisions of this Act, to federations or unions of several associations, and to confederations of several federations. The recognition of such federations or confederations implies the *ex officio* recognition of the several member associations or federations. The federations or confederations exercise disciplinary powers over their member associations, as well as over the individual members of same, these rights being exercised in accordance with the rules laid down in their respective statutes.

Legal recognition can only be granted to one association for each class of employers, workers, artists, or professional men. Similarly, legal recognition can only be given to one federation or confederation of employers or workers or artists or professional men, referred to in the preceding paragraph, for the class or classes of employers or workers represented within the district assigned to each.

If recognition be granted to a national confederation of all classes of employers or workers in agriculture, industry, or trade, or for all categories of artists or professional men, recognition cannot be granted to federations or associations which are not affiliated to the said Confederation.

In no case can associations be recognised which, without the preliminary consent of the Government, have contracted any ties of discipline or dependance with associations of an international character. . . .

ART. 10. Collective labour contracts drawn up by the legally recognised associations of employers, workers, artists, and professional men, are valid in respect of all employers, workers, artists, and professional men belonging to the category to which said contract refers and which the associations represent in accordance with the provisions of Art. 5 of this Act.

Collective labour contracts must be written under pain of nullity. They are also held null and void if they fail to state the period for which they hold good. . . .

A copy of the collective contracts . . . must be deposited with the local prefecture and published in the sheet of announcement of the Province in the case of communal, district, or provincial associations, and must be deposited with the Ministry of National Economy and published in the *Gazzetta Ufficiale* of the Kingdom in the case of the regional, inter-regional or national associations.

Employers and workers who fail to abide by collective contracts and general rules to which they are parties, are held civilly responsible for such failure both toward the association of workers and toward the association of employers who are parties to the said contract.

The other rules applying to the drawing up of collective labour contracts and concerning their validity will be promulgated by Royal Decree on the proposal of the Minister of Justice.

ART. 11. The provisions of this Act on the legal recognition of syndical associations are not applicable to associations of persons in the employ of the State, the Provinces, the Communes, or public charity institutions, for whom provisions will be made by separate measures. . . .

Chapter II

ART. 13. All disputes arising as to the regulation of collective contracts, or of other existing regulations, or the request for new conditions of labour, come within the jurisdiction of the Courts of Appeal acting as Labour Courts. Before delivering judgment the President of the Court must attempt conciliation.

Disputes referred to in the above provisions can be settled by arbitration. . . .

ART. 15. Each Court of Appeal will draw up a panel of experts on problems of production and labour, classified by groups and subgroups, according to the several kinds of business activities carried on within the jurisdiction of the court. This panel will be revised every two years. . . .

ART. 17. Only associations which are legally recognised may take action in disputes arising out of collective labour agreements and such action must be taken against legally recognised associations, when they exist; otherwise against a trustee specially appointed by the President of the Court of Appeal. In the latter case voluntary intervention in the case of private individuals is admitted. . . .

Chapter III

ART. 18. The lock-out and the strike are forbidden.

Employers who without justifiable motive, and for the sole purpose of obtaining from their dependents changes in existing labour agreements, suspend work in their factories, establishments, concerns, or offices render themselves liable to a fine of not less than ten thousand and not to exceed one hundred thousand lire.

Three or more employees or workers who, by preconcerted agreement, leave their work or perform it in such wise as to interfere with its continuity or regularity, with a view to obtaining from their employers different labour conditions render themselves liable to a fine of not less than one hundred and not to exceed one thousand lire. . . .

When the persons guilty of the offences foreseen under the above paragraphs are more [than three], the leaders, promoters, and organisers are liable to detention for not less than one year and not to exceed two years, besides the fine provided for under said paragraphs.

ART. 19. Persons in the employ of the State and of other public bodies or bodies performing essential public services who, in the number of three or more, by preconcerted agreement, leave their work or perform it in a manner likely to interfere with its continuity or regularity, render themselves liable to imprisonment for a period of not less than one month and not to exceed six months. . . . The leaders, promoters, and organisers are liable to imprisonment for a period of not less than six months and not to exceed two years, and to interdiction from public office for not less than three years.

Persons carrying on public services, or services essential to the public who suspend, without justifiable motives, work in their establishments, concerns, or offices, are liable to imprisonment for a period of not less than six months and not to exceed one year, and to a fine of from five thousand to one hundred thousand lire, besides temporary interdiction from public office.

When the action referred to in this article causes danger to personal safety the penalty incurred is that of imprisonment for a period of not less than one year. Should such action be the cause of death to one or more persons the penalty incurred is that of imprisonment for a period of not less than three years.

ART. 20. Persons in the employ of the State and of other public bodies, persons carrying on public services and services essential to the public, and their dependents, who in the event of strikes or locks-out fail to do all in their power to secure the regular working or the resumption of a public service essential to the public, are liable to detention for a period of not less than one month and not exceeding six months.

ART. 21. When the stoppage of work by employers or the act of leaving work or performing it irregularly by workers aims at coercing the will or influencing the decisions of a department or organ of the State, Provinces, or Communes, or of a Government official, the leaders, promoters and organisers render themselves liable to imprisonment for a period of not less than three and not to exceed seven years and to perpetual interdiction from public office, and the other persons concerned in such offence are liable to imprisonment for a period of not less than one and not to exceed three years and to the temporary interdiction from public office. . . .

B. German Law for the Organization of National Labor, January, 1934

Part I

1. In each establishment the owner of the undertaking as the leader (Führer) of the establishment and the salaried and wage-earning employees as his followers shall work together for the furtherance of the purposes of the establishment and for the benefit of the nation and the State in general.

2. (1) The leader of the establishment shall make decisions for his followers in all matters affecting the establishment in so far as they are governed by this Act.

(2) He shall promote the welfare of his followers. The latter shall be loyal to him as fellow-members of the works community.

3. (1) In incorporated associations and other bodies the statutory representatives shall be the leaders of the establishment.

(2) The owner of the undertaking (or in the case of incorporated associations and other bodies the statutory representatives) may appoint a person taking a responsible part in the management of the establishment to represent him (or them); this shall be done in cases where the establishment is not managed by the said owner or statutory representatives. They may also appoint another person to represent them in matters of minor importance.

(3) If the leader of an establishment is disqualified by an enforceable decision of the honour court under section 38 for the position of leader, another leader shall be appointed for the establishment.

4. (1) Managing offices shall be included among establishments for the purposes of this Act.

Source: International Labour Office, *Legislative Series*, Vol. XV (1934), Part II (Geneva: 1937), pp. 795–808, with deletions.

(2) Subsidiary establishments and departments of establishments which are linked with the principal establishment by being under the same management shall not be deemed to be independent establishments unless they are situated at a considerable distance from the principal establishment.

(3) The provisions of this Act, with the exception of sections 32 and 33, shall not apply to craft engaged in maritime, inland and aerial navigation, nor to their crews.

5. (1) In establishments which as a rule employ at least twenty persons, confidential men shall be appointed from among the followers to advise the leader. Together with him and under his presidency they shall constitute the confidential council of the establishment.

(2) For the purposes of the provisions respecting the confidential council, persons engaged in home industries shall also be included among the followers if they work as a rule for the same establishment either alone or with the help of members of their family.

6. (1) It shall be the duty of the confidential council to strengthen mutual confidence within the works community.

(2) It shall be the task of the confidential council to consider all measures directed towards the increase of efficiency, the formulation and carrying out of the general conditions of employment (especially the establishment rules), the carrying out and promotion of industrial safety measures, the strengthening of the ties which bind the various members of the establishment to one another and to the establishment, and the welfare of all members of the community. Further, the said council shall endeavour to settle all disputes within the works community. Its views shall be heard before penalties are imposed under the establishment rules.

(3) The confidential council may delegate the performance of certain tasks to particular confidential men.

7. (1) The number of confidential men shall be as follows:

in establishments employing   20 to   49 persons   2,
      ”   ”   ”   50 ”   99   ”   3,
      ”   ”   ”   100 ” 199   ”   4,
      ”   ”   ”   200 ” 399   ”   5.

(2) The above number shall be increased by one for each additional three hundred persons employed, and shall not exceed ten.

(3) An equal number of substitutes shall be appointed.

(4) Salaried employees, wage-earning employees and persons

engaged in home industries shall be duly taken into account in the selection of the confidential men.

8. A person shall not be appointed as a confidential man unless he has completed his twenty-fifth year, has belonged to the establishment or undertaking for at least one year and has worked in the same branch or related branches of employment or industry for at least two years. He must be in possession of civic rights, a member of the German Labour Front[1] characterised by exemplary human qualities, and guaranteed to devote himself unreservedly at all times to the National State. The requirement as to one year's membership of the establishment may be waived on the occasion of the first appointment of confidential men after the coming into operation of this Act.

9. (1) Every year in March the leader of the establishment shall draw up a list of confidential men and their substitutes in agreement with the chairman of the National Socialist establishment cell organisation. The followers shall then decide for or against the list by ballot.

(2) If the leader of the establishment and the chairman of the National Socialist establishment cell organisation fail to agree respecting the confidential men and substitutes to be nominated, or in case of failure to appoint a confidential council for any other reason, and in particular if the followers fail to approve the list, the labour trustee may appoint the requisite number of confidential men and substitutes.

10. (1) On National Labour Day (1st May) the members of the confidential council shall take a solemn oath before the followers to perform the duties of their office exclusively for the benefit of the establishment and of the nation as a whole, setting aside all private interests, and to set an example to the members of the establishment by the life which they lead and the way in which they perform their duties. . . .

11. The term of office of the confidential council shall begin when the oath has been taken (as a rule on 1st May) and shall end on 30th April of the next year.

12. The confidential council shall be convened when necessary by the leader of the establishment. It shall also be convened if half the confidential men so request.

13. (1) The office of confidential man shall be an honorary office, and remuneration shall not be paid for the performance of its

[1] The Nazi labor organization that superseded all independent trade union groups.—Eds.

duties. The customary wage shall be paid for any hours of work which must necessarily be lost by the performance of the said duties. Necessary expenditure shall be repaid by the management of the establishment.

(2) The necessary accommodation and office requisites for the due performance of the duties incumbent upon the confidential council shall be provided by the management of the establishment. The leader of the establishment shall be bound to give the confidential men the information necessary for the performance of their duties.

14. (1) The term of office of a confidential man shall expire on his leaving the establishment, as well as on his voluntary resignation. A confidential man shall not be dismissed unless this is necessitated by the closing of the establishment or of a department thereof, or is done for a reason which entitles the employer to terminate the employment without notice.

(2) The labour trustee may remove a confidential man from office on account of his unsuitability in circumstances or person. The term of office of a confidential man who is removed from office shall expire on the communication of the trustee's decision in writing to the confidential council. . . .

16. A majority of the confidential council of an establishment may lodge an appeal in writing with the labour trustee without delay against any decision of the leader of the establishment respecting the formulation of the general conditions of employment, and in particular, respecting the establishment rules, if the said decision appears incompatible with the economic or social situation of the establishment. The operation of the decision made by the leader of the establishment shall not be hindered by the appeal.

17. If two or more establishments which are economically or technically similar or have related purposes are under the control of one and the same owner, the said owner (or, if he himself does not manage the undertaking, the leader of the undertaking appointed by him) shall appoint an advisory council from the confidential councils of the separate establishments to advise him on social questions.

Part II

18. (1) Labour trustees shall be appointed for large economic areas, the boundaries of which shall be fixed by the Federal[2]

[2] In this document "Reich" (untranslated in previous documents) has been translated as "Federal." The national government is meant.—Eds.

Minister of Labour in agreement with the Federal Minister of Economic Affairs and the Federal Minister of the Interior. They shall be Federal officials and shall be under the service supervision of the Federal Minister of Labour. The Federal Minister of Labour in agreement with the Federal Minister of Economic Affairs shall fix their headquarters.

(2) The labour trustees shall be bound to observe the principles and instructions laid down by the Federal Government.

19. (1) The labour trustees shall ensure the maintenance of industrial peace. In order to achieve this task, they shall take the following action:

1. they shall supervise the formation and operations of the confidential councils, and give decisions where disputes occur;
2. they shall appoint confidential men for establishments and remove them from office in accordance with subsection (2) of section 9, subsection (2) of section 14 and section 15;
3. they shall decide respecting appeals from confidential councils in accordance with section 16; they may quash the decision of the leader of the establishment and themselves issue the necessary ruling;
4. they shall decide respecting proposed dismissals in accordance with section 20;
5. they shall supervise the observance of the provisions respecting establishment rules (sections 26 et seq.);
6. they shall lay down principles and collective rules under the conditions specified in section 32, and supervise their observance;
7. they shall co-operate in the exercise of jurisdiction by the social honour courts under sections 35 et seq.;
8. they shall keep the Federal Government supplied with information respecting social progress, in accordance with detailed instructions issued by the Federal Minister of Labour and the Federal Minister of Economic Affairs.

(2) The Federal Minister of Labour and the Federal Minister of Economic Affairs may assign further tasks within the scope of the law to the labour trustees. . . .

20. (1) Every owner of an establishment shall be bound to give notice in writing to the labour trustee in the following cases:

(a) in an establishment which as a rule employs less than 100 persons, before he dismisses more than nine persons;
(b) in an establishment which as a rule employs not less than 100 persons, before he dismisses ten per cent of the persons

usually employed in the establishment and before he dismisses more than fifty persons within four weeks.

(2) Dismissals of the prospect of which notice must be given under subsection (1) shall not become operative without the approval of the labour trustee until four weeks have elapsed since the sending to him of the notice; the labour trustee may grant retroactive approval. He may also give instructions that dismissals shall not become operative until at most two months after notice thereof is given. In cases where dismissals are not carried out within four weeks of the date as from which they are operative under the first or second sentence, it shall be held that the notice has not been given. The right to dismiss employees without notice shall not be affected hereby.

(3) If the owner of the undertaking is not in a position to keep his employees in full work until the date mentioned in subsection (2), the trustee may authorise him to introduce a reduction of the hours of work in his undertaking (spreading the work). Nevertheless, for this purpose the weekly hours of work of an employee shall not be reduced below twenty-four hours. Where the system of spreading the work is adopted, the owner of the undertaking shall be entitled to make a proportionate reduction in the wages or salary of the employees whose hours of work are reduced, provided that the reduction of pay shall not become operative until the date on which the employment would end under the general provisions of the law or the terms of the contract.

(4) In establishments which as a rule do more work at a particular time of year (seasonal establishments), or which as a rule do not work for more than three months in the year (temporary seasonal establishments), the provisions of subsections (1)–(3) shall not apply to dismissals occasioned by the special nature of the establishment.

21. The Federal Minister of Labour may appoint officers subordinate to a labour trustee in cases where the size and special economic conditions of his economic territory render this necessary; and the tasks incumbent upon the labour trustee in respect of a particular district or particular branches of industry may be delegated wholly or in part by the Federal Minister of Labour or the labour trustee to the said officers, or particular tasks may be delegated to them in this manner. The said officers shall be bound by the instructions of the Federal Minister of Labour and the labour trustee.

22. (1) If any person repeatedly and wilfully contravenes general

instructions issued by the labour trustee in writing in the performance of his duties, the said person shall be liable to a fine; in particularly serious cases the penalty of imprisonment may be imposed instead of the fine or in addition to it. The relevant criminal prosecution shall not be instituted unless the labour trustee requests it.

(2) If an offender is sentenced to a public penalty, this shall not constitute an obstacle to prosecution for the offence in question as an offence against social honour.

23. (1) The labour trustees shall appoint an advisory council of experts from the various branches of industry in their territory for consultation on questions within their jurisdiction which are of a general nature or involve a principle. Three-fourths of the experts shall be chosen from lists of candidates nominated by the German Labour Front, which shall put forward in the first instance a considerable number of suitable members of the confidential councils of the establishments in the district of the labour trustee in question, with due regard to the various occupational groups and branches of industry. Leaders of establishments and confidential men shall be included in the lists in approximately equal numbers. One-fourth of the experts required may be appointed by the trustees from among persons in their district who are otherwise suitable.

(2) In so far as the corporate organisation of separate branches of industry has been carried out by means of laws enacted by the Federal Government, the German Labour Front shall nominate the experts to be put forward by it in agreement with the special industrial organisations.

(3) The labour trustees may further appoint a committee of experts to advise them in individual cases.

24. The experts shall be sworn in by the labour trustees before beginning their work. They shall be called upon to swear that they will exercise their functions as experts impartially and conscientiously to the best of their ability, refrain from pursuing any private interests and strive only for the welfare of the nation. . . .

Part III

26. In every establishment employing as a rule at least twenty salaried and wage-earning employees, establishment rules shall be issued in writing by the leader of the establishment for the followers (section 1).

27. (1) The following conditions of employment shall be included in the establishment rules:

1. the beginning and ending of the normal daily hours of work and of the breaks;
2. the times for the payment of remuneration and the nature thereof;
3. the principles for the calculation of jobbing or bargain work, if work is done on a job or bargain basis in the establishment;
4. regulations for the nature, amount and collection of fines if provision is made for them;
5. the grounds on which an employment can be terminated without notice, in cases where this does not rest upon statutory grounds;
6. the utilisation of remuneration forfeited by the unlawful termination of an employment, in cases where the said forfeiture is prescribed in the establishment rules or contract of employment in pursuance of statutory provisions. . . .

32. (1) The labour trustee may lay down guiding principles for the tenor of establishment rules and individual contracts of employment after considering the matter in a committee of experts. . . .

Part IV

35. Every member of a works community shall be responsible for the conscientious performance of the duties incumbent upon him in consequence of his position in the said community. He shall conduct himself in such a manner as to show himself worthy of the respect due to his position in the works community. In particular, he shall devote all his powers to the service of the establishment and subserve the common good, always bearing in mind his responsibility.

36. (1) Gross breaches of the social duties based on the works community shall be dealt with by the honour courts as offences against social honour. Such offences shall be deemed to have been committed in the following cases:

1. when the owner of an undertaking, the leader of an establishment or any other person in a position of supervision abuses his authority in the establishment by maliciously exploiting the labor of any of his followers or wounding their sense of honour;

2. when a follower endangers industrial peace in the establishment by maliciously provoking other followers, and in particular when a confidential man wittingly interferes unduly in the conduct of the establishment or continually and maliciously disturbs the community spirit within the works community;

3. when a member of the works community repeatedly makes frivolous and unjustifiable complaints or applications to the labor trustee or obstinately disobeys instructions given by him in writing;

4. when a member of the confidential council reveals without authority any confidential information or technical or business secrets which have become known to him in the performance of his duties and have been specified as confidential matters.

(2) Public officials and soldiers shall not be under the jurisdiction of the social honour courts. . . .

35. Fascist Labor Recreation Organizations

One of the reasons Fascist régimes gave for intervening in matters of labor and industrial relations was that they sought to improve the social and moral well-being of the working class. Schemes to this end were developed in both Germany and Italy. In Germany the Strength Through Joy (*Kraft durch Freude*) and in Italy the *Dopolavoro* organizations provided a wide variety of leisure-time activites for workers. The following selection, an account prepared by the leadership of the *Dopolavoro* organization, provides some indication of the scope of these activities.

Report on the Organization and Development of the Italian *Dopolavoro*

THE VAST organization commonly known under the name of *Dopolavoro* (Leisure time) which promotes schemes for the better employment of the free time of workers of all classes, with the object of raising their intellectual, moral, physical and social status in accordance with the policy of enhancing national values promoted by Fascism, has assumed such proportions, especially recently, under the auspices of the General Secretary of the P.N.F. [National Fascist Party], that it may be considered as one of the most characteristic achievements of the Fascist revolution. The following notes give a brief summary of the history, organization and functioning of this institution, founded by Signor Mussolini.

The Dopolavoro passed through several phases before reaching its present organization. These may be divided into three different periods: in the first phase, it was an attempt due to private initiative; in the second, it was affiliated to the National Confederation of Fascist Syndicates; and in the third it assumed a State controlled and national character.

The first period dates from 1919 to the end of 1923.

The Dopolavoro Office proposed in the beginning to carry out a

Source: Tomaso Sillani, ed., *What Is Fascism and Why?* (New York: Macmillan, 1931), pp. 209–214, with deletions. The book is a semi-official propaganda piece, published with the support of Italian banking and industry.

work of propaganda, advice and assistance, with the object of encouraging employers' welfare schemes on behalf of their workers and also of promoting the spread of higher general education and of sport among the people.

When the National Confederation of Fascist Syndicates, with a view to the moral uplift of the masses, as understood by Fascism, added educational propaganda to its regular tasks, the Dopolavoro Office became its mouthpiece. It was then that the first lines of the movement began to be laid down, although in very rudimentary form, for it was impossible to attract those who were not connected with the syndicalist federations into the orbit of the institution.

With the creation of the *Opera nazionale Dopolavoro* (National Leisure-time Organization [O.N.D.]) by Act of Parliament on May 1, 1925, and the acceptance of its presidency by H. R. H. the Duke of Aosta, the Dopolavoro organization began to take definite form; its new status entitled it to federate thousands of clubs, societies, sporting, educational and artistic groups, and enabled it to extend its efforts into the ranks of the great State services by means of organizations in aid of railway and postal employees and those of the Tobacco Monopoly, in accordance with the Royal Decrees of October 25, 1925, July 9, 1926 and May 18, 1927.

The Secretary of the National Fascist Party, who took over the supreme direction of the organization after the resignation of the Duke of Aosta, has reorganized the entire administration of the Dopolavoro, as well as its programme, giving it an organic structure more in accordance with the aims and methods of the National Fascist Party. And on September 14, 1929, the work was officially recognized as a distinctively Fascist institution at the five-yearly Fascist Assembly, and included among the Government schemes.

The Leisure-time movement, as developed during recent years in Italy, has much in common with the welfare work in Anglo-Saxon countries, which embrace all the efforts of the greater firms for the assistance and future provision of their employees; and has also several points of analogy with other great organizations such as the Y.M.C.A., the Playground and Recreation Association of America, the Carnegie United Kingdom Trust, the National Education Association of the United Kingdom, the *Commission centrale des Loisirs des Ouvriers de l'Hainault* of Belgium, and other foreign organizations and associations that promote libraries, culture and artistic education for adults, sport, popular tours, and so on. In addition to these characteristics, however, the Italian movement has intrinsic features of its own which differentiate it from all organizations of the kind.

The Dopolavoro is a public institution which, by its technical, organizing and directive functions is able to deal directly with the problems of welfare, education and recreation of the working classes. Whereas in other countries—including those that have reached the highest degree of material civilization—the solution of the various problems of instruction, physical education, and the various forms of social aid for the working classes is left to private initiative, in Italy alone, thanks to the enterprising spirit of Fascism, these tasks have become an integral part of the State's activities, and in this field also the State asserts its position as the controlling force of the nation. . . .

The programme of the O.N.D. is divided into four great sections: *Instruction* (culture for the people and the teaching of trades); *Artistic education* (dramatic societies, music and chorus singing, cinematography, wireless, folklore); *Physical education* (Italian Excursion Federation and Central Sporting Commission); *Social welfare and hygiene* (dwellings, hygiene, provision for the future, leisure-time occupation for the various classes of workmen).

It will probably be of more interest to give a brief summary of the more important works, rather than a detailed explanation of the various services that correspond with the several branches of the above programme and with their many ramifications.

Extensive arrangements have been made in all the local Dopolavoro offices and societies federated to the O.N.D. for the higher education of the people; and the same measures have been taken in numberless industrial concerns, in the offices of the Railway Dopolavoro and those of the Postal Service and Tobacco Monopoly: libraries, reading rooms, evening instruction courses, lectures with lantern slides or cinematograph [motion picture] films, people's universities. The general management supports and subsidizes these undertakings, supervising them with a view to their co-ordination and consistent purpose. The Dopolavoro makes considerable use of the educational cinema. . . . It was the first to organize open-air cinemas in Italy. The O.N.D.'s programme of popular instruction has the approval and constant support of the Ministry of National Education. A measure has been passed providing that elementary and intermediary teachers who give their work for the benefit of the Dopolavoro's higher education for the people shall be entitled to a special order of merit, which will have preference over other documents in competitions and examinations for promotion. The National Institute also interests itself in promoting and assisting evening and Sunday vocational schools and courses in technical improvement.

In this important field, which is the index to the civilization of a country, out of the 1437 institutions controlled by the Dopolavoro in 1926, only 87 were promoting sections for higher education, folklore, and trade teaching, the number of such sections being 1249 altogether. In 1930, the number of institutions controlled had increased to 14,027, and of this number 5225 had promoted no less than 78,744 sections in the above mentioned branches. The Dopolavoro had 178 libraries open to its members in 1926, while in 1930 the number had increased to 2,388.

The Institution is endeavouring to encourage the revival of the love of drama by every means in its power: propaganda, theatrical schools, dramatic publications, artistic shows, the touring "Cars of Thespis," tours in the provinces; provincial, regional and national societies, reduced author's rights, and other forms of encouragement.

In the realm of sport a vast, fertile, and original work is being carried on. A truly imposing number of young men and women now go in for athletics and are being trained in all the soundest forms of sporting exercise, from gymnastics to fencing, swimming, rowing, cycling, running, and so on.

The Italian Excursion Federation has grouped together hundreds of sporting, alpine and excursion institutions, promoting very extensive patriotic pilgrimages to the battlefields and cemeteries of the war, joint tours of pleasure and instruction, and Sunday cruises and excursions, in which thousands and thousands of authentic workers have taken part. The institutions affiliated to the Dopolavoro have increased the 2538 sports and excursion sections that existed in 1926 to the very big number of 115,676 in 1930.

The Institution promotes exhibitions, matches, and competitions for the benefit of the welfare section and carries out an important work of propaganda and organization.

In 1927, the O.N.D., in collaboration with the "Ente Nazionale delle piccole industrie" (National organization of small industries) got up the exhibition of the "Three Venetias" for economic housefurnishing. They also arranged two other great competitions, in

1928, for the economic and rational furnishing and fitting out of the home, the competitions being held in every part of Italy. They constitute the biggest and most organic experiment of the kind that has yet been attempted anywhere.

Research and studies, popular campaigns and practical courses are now being organized to encourage the cultivation of allotments and kitchen gardens. After taking part in the International Congress for the organization of kitchen gardens, which was held at Luxembourg in June, 1927, the Dopolavoro has been endeavouring to unite together the manifold but disconnected efforts being made in outlying districts and by various local societies into a national organization.

In addition to the O.N.D.'s part in creating new hygienic conditions of life for the working classes: improved dwelling houses, kitchen gardens and flower gardens, factory restaurants, depots for the sale of foodstuffs, small-loan banks, etc.; the institution concerns itself with hygienic propaganda, collaborating, by its publications and lectures, in the campaigns against tuberculosis and cancer and drink, in the anti-malaria crusade, the propaganda for seaside hospices, alpine colonies and sanatoriums.

The progress of the Dopolavoro organization may be realized from the following figures concerning membership cards. In 1926, the O.N.D. controlled 1497 institutions with a total membership of 280,584; in 1929, the number of institutions controlled was 11,084 and the number of members 1,445,226. . . .

If such satisfactory results have been obtained already in the short existence of the institution—six years—it is mainly due to the fact that the heads of the Dopolavoro have always put into practice the fundamental principle of Fascist education, which consists in working with purpose, method and order. Before the advent of Fascism, people here were forever talking of social reforms, everyone was posing as apostle of the workers' redemption, but it all ended in words, for nothing practical was ever accomplished. To-day, little is said, but much is done. Improved organizations, better equipment, a broadening of functions, the growing number of members are all so many signs of the vitality of this work, which Fascism ranks among its finest achievements.

36. Land Reclamation in Italy

Fascist Italy was concerned with its dependence on imports of essential materials and with meeting as many of its needs as possible from domestic supplies. There was little that could be done in some spheres (coal and iron, for example), but the régime did seek to increase agricultural production in order to improve both the balance of payments and rural conditions. In June, 1925, Mussolini launched a "battle of grain," and this was followed in 1928 by a comprehensive land-reclamation scheme. The results of the program are rather difficult to assess because success varied considerably from one project to another, and work on many sites was not completed before the war. However, millions of acres were involved in the scheme in one way or another, and the projects provided work for thousands during the period of the Depression. At the same time, both the area under cultivation and grain production were increased slightly. The selection that follows is a report on land reclamation written in 1931 by the director of the program, Arrigo Serpieri.

Report on the Progress of Land Reclamation in Italy, 1931

I. *Integral Land Reclamation*. The integral reclamation of the land is one of the fundamental enterprises of the Régime. It is the outcome of the conditions of Italian economics and of the will of Fascism.

A dense population confined within a circumscribed territory, poor in natural resources; a Nation desirous of growing in power and of spreading Italian ideals throughout the world, must of necessity create new centres of intensified rural life, in order to increase the revenues of the Nation and fortify the healthy and prosperous family life of the country against the destructive forces of the towns.

It is this that the reclamation of the land aims at. Hence the necessity of providing the land with a permanent equipment without which it cannot be made ready to receive, together with a better use of the land and the water supplies, intensive systems of

Source: Tomaso Sillani, ed., *What Is Fascism and Why?* (New York: Macmillan, 1931), pp. 72-87, with deletions.

land production, and offer a living to a denser population, firmly attached to the land.

Works of all kinds are necessary for the achievement of the ends in view, both in cases of joint ownership and of single ownership: engineering works and technical forest and agricultural works, for the recovery of the land, for hygienic protection, for the formation of centres of rural population and buildings, for the upkeep of the roads, for the protection of the water supply and the utilization of water-energy, for reforestation and other work, for agricultural settlement and the improvement of the land.

But it matters not what combinations it has been necessary to have recourse to for these works on the land, which are all characterized by the investment of capital at long term; they are only a means towards the attainment of the purpose mentioned above.

Land reclamation becomes *integral* reclamation when the whole of the enterprises necessary for the new order of land production demanded by the economic, moral and political aims of the Nation, have been carried out. . . .

III. *The Importance of the Mussolini Act.* The most important contribution to the development of the rural policy of the Régime was the Act of December 24, 1928, relating to the integral reclamation of the land, which law represents the greatest effort of the State towards the full development of the land and the greater efficiency of rural life.

The peculiar merit of this law, which is called after the Duce, is that it sums up previous legislation and makes of it a more efficacious instrument for favouring the resettlement of the country: the basis of the moral and economic renewal of the Nation.

It crowns the legislative program by tackling the problems connected with the supply of drinking water, the building of roads for farming purposes, rural constructions and hamlets, all of which had been greatly neglected by former legislation, which inclined towards the towns.

In order to encourage the rational distribution of population, not neglecting those regions generally shunned by the farmers owing to the lack of comforts indispensable to civilized life, the law assures a contribution of 75% of the total cost of works for conveying drinking water to isolated rural buildings or to groups of rural buildings, even if they are outside the districts subject to reclamation; it also provides for contributing 40% of the total cost of works destined to collect and gather water, in the interest of several farms.

At the same time it authorizes the building, in Southern Italy and the Islands, under the reclamation law, of roads which though not serving formerly marshy lands, promote the culitivation, or the more intense cultivation, of districts in backward agricultural conditions. It also allows for a subsidy of 40% all over Italy towards the cost of building and reconditioning roads used for carrying products to market with less loss of time. . . .

A second class of provisions relating to the Act of December 24, 1928 (No. 3134) aims at drawing up a plan to regulate the operating of the great enterprise for the full development of national lands. By means of new appropriations of considerable value to be entered in the State Budget for the payment of State subsidies, the law provides for carrying out, in the shortest time allowed for by technical possibilities and by the availability of manual labour, of a number of new works to the amount of *seven billions*. . . .

VI. *The results obtained in the last four years, taking into special consideration the first year of the enforcement of the Mussolini Act.* Let us give a rapid glance to what has already been accomplished towards the reclamation and improvement of the land.

On a surface of 31 million hectares Italy has over 2,300,000 liable to drainage.

Over 700,000 hectares have been reclaimed. Half of these, however, still call for the building of roads, houses and water conduits, to guarantee the results of drainage and to permit a more profitable cultivation of the soil.

Some 1,200,000 hectares are being drained, and drainage operations have still to be begun on another 1,485,000 hectares. . . .

The direct execution of reclamation works by the State has been gradually decreasing while, on the contrary, concessions have been steadily increasing: so much so, that in these last years the direct intervention of the State has been restricted to the upkeep of the works and to a few other enterprises. . . .

In less than 10 months' activity, the Under-Secretaryship for integral land reclamation has granted concessions for drainage enterprises amounting to L. 386,494,973, while there are other works in progress for over one and a half billions. . . .

The special legislation for the Agro Romano, which has sub-

jected a territory of about 20,000 hectares to obligatory reclamation on the part of the owners, whom it aids and encourages,
continues to be enforced more and more strictly and has been
extended over other districts.

In the five years from 1925 to 1930, some 219 obligatory
reclamation schemes have been elaborated and enforced on land
owners. They cover 81,000 hectares of land on which there have
been built and are still being built farmhouses, barns, silos, farm
roads, drinking water plants and plants for irrigation purposes. For
the financing of these works 273 accommodation loans, amounting
to 243 millions lire, have been granted and 212 millions have
already been disbursed.

Special mention should be made of the formations of new
centres of land settlement around the Capital, comprising the cultivation of almost 3000 hectares of ground. . . .

It is by this powerful effort that Fascist Italy carries on her great
battle for reclaiming the land, and makes big immediate sacrifices
for a better future.

37. Nazi Commercial Policy

The abandonment of the gold standard and the introduction of foreign-exchange controls and import quotas, measures taken before the Nazis assumed power, required a reorganization of German commercial policy. In 1934 a so-called New Plan was developed under the direction of Hjalmar Schacht, then Director of the Reichsbank and Minister of Economic Affairs. The Plan was essentially a system of bilateral trade agreements worked out on a semibarter basis; Germany purchased products from countries that would agree to purchase German products in exchange. The scheme was extremely complicated— Schacht himself noted in a speech that at a trade fair a German exporter had decorated his booth with the more than forty forms he had to fill out in the conduct of his business. But the system allowed Germany to make purchases abroad in the absence of adequate gold or foreign-exchange reserves. Beyond that, it became the vehicle for greater economic penetration of the states of southeastern Europe and an instrument of German domination in that region in the years before the war. The first of the documents below is the German anaysis of the implications of the 1934 commercial treaty with Yugoslavia; the two following documents, relating to the German-Rumanian trade agreement of March 23, 1939, demonstrate the expansion of the mechanism of German penetration by the eve of the Second World War.

A. Economic Significance of the German-Yugoslav Commercial Treaty of May, 1934

SUBJECT: THE political and economic significance of the Commercial Treaty with Yugoslavia.

With reference to our despatch of June 11. . . .

For your personal and confidential information only.

The German-Yugoslav Commercial Treaty transmitted in the despatch under reference, which will apply provisionally as from June 1 next, represents a fundamental remodelling of trade relations between Germany and Yugoslavia.

The object of the negotiations was to place the mutual exchange of goods on a broader basis and to keep opportunities of develop-

Source: Secret dispatch of the German Foreign Ministry to the Embassy in Italy, June 21, 1934, *Documents on German Foreign Policy, 1918–45*, Series C, Vol. III (Washington, D.C.: U.S. Government Printing Office, 1959), pp. 54–56.

ing the Yugoslav market open to Germany in future, besides providing us with an economic foothold in Yugoslavia and thus also in the Little Entente,[1] from which it would be possible to prevent or at least render very difficult Yugoslavia's becoming economically bound up with other countries contrary to our wishes.

The German concessions suffice to make the German market indispensable to Yugoslavia's exports should the Treaty remain in force for a prolonged period, since even under the German system of monopoly management it has proved possible to make substantial allowance for Yugoslavia's export interests in her most important products (plums, eggs, apples, wheat, maize and lard), and under the agreed rebate system, which is tantamount to a disguised preference system, Yugoslavia is assured of far-reaching export possibilities on the German market, which would be virtually non-existent without this system. In the case of eggs, it is true that the 30,000 dozen conceded fall short of Yugoslavia's demands, but sufficiently substantial Yugoslav interests are established through centralized purchasing. The question of maize has been settled. With regard to wheat, we shall probably be unable to avoid, next year too, having to help Yugoslavia in disposing of her products on the world market.

Given the economic importance of these concessions, the various possibilities for terminating the agreement place us in the position of being able, if required, to exert adequate pressure on Yugoslavia.

The economic advantages accorded to us by Yugoslavia not only provide an economic counterpart but, in addition, will probably work out to Germany's advantage.

Germany obtains, through the unrestricted most-favoured nation treatment and release from all future quota measures, an open door in Yugoslavia which, taken together with numerous tariff concessions, may be expected to lead to a favourable development for our exports. Moreover, the Yugoslav Government's promise about the promotion of imports from Germany, especially in connexion with public works, opens up further opportunities of development for German exports.

As regards the value of goods to be exchanged, the object was not to try and strike a balance but rather to aim at the largest possible trade surplus in Germany's favour whilst providing adequate transfer facilities. A surplus of this kind would correspond, in

[1] Interwar alliance among Yugoslavia, Czechoslovakia and Rumania.—Eds.

Yugoslav opinion also, to the normal proportions of the exchange of commodities between the two countries. Transfer facilities for this surplus are provided by the general clearing agreement, by the agreement on tourist traffic, by the inclusion of the 7.7 million marks secret refund payable by us, and by foreign exchange obtained from the export of wheat to third markets.

The possibilities indicated in the Treaty are to be further developed in future. Responsibility for this will devolve on the Government Committees which are, if only for this purpose, indispensable. Furthermore, they provide a means of ensuring that in allocating quotas and concessions the actions of the Yugoslav authorities shall correspond to Germany's interests. The Government Committees will, in particular, also have to deal with the adjustment of Yugoslavia's agricultural production to Germany's import requirements, a question of special importance for the future, but which is only settled in principle in the Treaty. The further expansion of the Treaty will largely depend upon the cooperation of the Government Committees.

There is no necessity to inform other Governments, especially as it would be politically undesirable for the economic significance and corresponding political implications of the Treaty to be picked upon and magnified abroad and made the subject of public discussions. But should the Embassy consider it appropriate to inform the Italian Government in broad outline of the outcome of the negotiations, reference should be made to the text of the Treaty as published in the *Reichsanzeiger* of May 11, 1934; it should further be explained that the reason for those agreements which contain concessions going beyond the scope of the Treaty (which may have become known to the Italian Government and which they may bring up), is that during the course of the negotiations it became necessary to make certain changes in the previous agreements to safeguard mutual interests over export. Such explanations should, as far as possible, avoid conveying to the Italian Government the impression that the Treaty also serves political purposes and is not exclusively designed to promote reciprocal trade relations. . . .

B. Discussions Leading to German-Rumanian Trade Agreement, 1939

PROMPTLY UPON his arrival Ministerialdirektor Wohlthat was received by the King, who made reference to his conversation with Field Marshal Göring in Leipzig. The possibilities of close economic cooperation were discussed at great length. The King declared himself as favoring an extensive reliance on Germany for Rumanian economic development. It developed that the outlines of an economic program had been prepared by Foreign Minister Gafencu, Economics Minister Bujoiu, Minister of Armaments Slavescu and Finance Minister Constantinescu, with the King presiding.

In Wohlthat's further conversation with the Foreign Minister and the Minister of Economics the intention to undertake long-range collaboration with Germany was again confirmed: "Germany generally shall regain the position of economic predominance in Rumania which she had before 1914." In view of such Rumanian willingness the following economic program should be drawn up in an "agreement for the promotion of economic relations between the two countries":

I. For the purpose of promoting and securing German imports from Rumania

    1. the authorities and commercial organizations on both sides shall establish regular contacts for adapting Rumanian production to German requirements, especially in the agricultural field;

    2. investments and capital participation shall be undertaken to develop a German-Rumanian petroleum industry;

    3. Rumanian mineral resources shall be explored and exploited in common;

    4. a timber management plan shall be drawn up and Germany shall participate in the exploitation of forests (elimination of Jews from the lumber business).

II. Rumania is prepared

    1. to expand Rumanian industry and cooperate with German industry while respecting German export interests;

Source: Telegram from German Legation in Rumania to the Foreign Ministry, February 14, 1939, *Documents on German Foreign Policy, 1918–1945*, Series D, Vol. V (Washington, D.C.: U.S. Government Printing Office, 1953), pp. 392–394.

2. to expand and standardize Rumanian armament, especially of the air force, with German aid;

3. to develop her armament industry along German lines;

4. to cooperate in matters of communication, especially in the construction of roads and waterways.

Germany would be reimbursed from export proceeds.

If this goal is attainable, Germany will indeed achieve predominance in Rumania. Since the Government commission is aware of this fact and therefore considers the attainment of this goal in the interest of the country, such a favorable opportunity of tying this country to us should, in our opinion, be exploited. By such a close economic association between the two countries Rumania will be more and more removed from the influence of the Western powers and the Soviets, and thereby from the Jews, and the general atmosphere between us will be improved.

I request prompt consideration and instruction as to whether Wohlthat may prepare and sign an agreement on the basis given.

C. German-Rumanian Trade Agreement, March, 1939

ARTICLE I. With a view to collaboration between the contracting parties there is arranged, as a completion of the present regulations for Rumanian-German economic exchanges, an economic plan of several years' duration, having as its basic principle a balance of reciprocal economic exchanges. The economic plan will take into account, on the one hand, Germany's needs for imports, and, on the other, the possibilities of increasing Rumanian production, of Rumania's internal necessities, and of Rumania's need for economic trade with other countries. The plan will comprise in general:

1. (a) An increase and orientation of Rumanian agricultural production. In this sphere, after a preliminary exchange of experience by the competent bodies of both countries, the cultivation of new agricultural produce, as well as the intensification of production, especially of fodder and oleaginous and textile plants, will be introduced.

    (b) An increase of existing agricultural industries, and the creation of new agricultural industries.

Source: Royal Institute of International Affairs, *Documents on International Affairs, 1939–1946*, Vol. I (London: Oxford University Press, 1951), pp. 117–118. Used by permission.

2. (a) The development of Rumanian forestry and wood economy.

   (b) The introduction of forest exploitation and measures for the defence of forests.

3. (a) The delivery of machines and plant for the exploitation of mines in Rumania.

   (b) The foundation of mixed Rumanian-German companies for the opening up and exploitation of calceo-pyrites in Dobruja, chromium ores of the Banat, and manganese ores in the Vatra Dornei and Bresteni region. Moreover, the exploitation of the bauxite deposits and the eventual creation of an aluminum industry will be studied.

4. The setting up of a mixed Rumanian-German company to work petroleum and arrange the distribution of its products.

5. Collaboration in the industrial sphere.

6. The creation of a free zone containing industrial and commercial undertakings, and the construction in this free zone of equipment for transshipments between the two countries.

7. The delivery of armaments and equipment for the Rumanian Army, Navy, and Air Force, and the armaments industry.

8. The development of communications by land and water.

9. The construction and installation of public utility concerns.

10. Collaboration between Rumanian and German banks in the interests of both countries, in particular for the financing of these various undertakings.

ARTICLE II. In the carrying out of this Treaty a Governmental Commission under the terms of Article 32 of the Treaty of stabilization, commerce and navigation of March 23, 1935, between the Rumanian and German Governments, will be set up.

ARTICLE III. These two Governmental Commissions will communicate with each other on their intentions in connexion with this Treaty. They will arbitrate on the carrying out of the various projects. Both Governments will grant the necessary means for the organization of the firms which will concern themselves with the preparation and carrying out of the projects contemplated in Article I and will assure the carrying through of projects approved by the Governmental Commissions in accordance with their powers, which are necessarily in conformity with their laws.

ARTICLE IV. The payments to be effected by Germany and Rumania respectively by virtue of this Treaty will conform to the general terms of the existing Payments Agreement between Rumania and Germany. The Governmental Commissions will have power to allocate a percentage of the counter-value of deliveries stipulated in Sections 7–9 of Article I, or the counter-value of other deliveries of goods, to finance the projects contemplated in Article I.

ARTICLE V. The Treaty will enter into force a month after the exchange of deeds of ratification, which will take place in Berlin as soon as possible. The contracting parties will apply it provisionally from the date of signature. The Treaty remains in force until March 31, 1944. If it is not denounced a year before that date it will be indefinitely prolonged, but in such case may be denounced at any time providing a period of notice of one year is given, at the end of any calendar quarter.

PART VIII

The Second World War

The second great European war of the twentieth century had an economic impact even larger than the first. Its duration—six years—was longer; the destructive capability of military force was more extensive; and German occupation of large areas in both East and West disrupted the lives of a far larger number of people. Yet many of the economic measures adopted by the belligerent powers and many of the difficulties that had to be dealt with were similar to those of the First World War. The shortages, the controls, the manpower problems remained basically the same.

There were, however, major differences between the economic requirements and consequences of the two conflicts. In contrast to the trench warfare of 1914 to 1918, the fighting in the second war was characterized on both sides by the rapid movement of armies over great distances. There was no one area so thoroughly devastated as northern France had been, but damage extended over much greater areas.

Initial victories allowed Germany to dominate a large part of the European continent and to draw upon its resources. "Occupied Europe" was exploited in any number of ways ranging from looting and confiscation to the manipulation of finance and commerce for Germany's advantage. The domination of large areas certainly eased some of Germany's shortages of strategic materials, especially metals and food products, and plant and equipment could be set to work on German orders. At first, looting and confiscation provided a number of windfalls, but much of this had no great significance for the German war effort. However, foreign occupation brought the war directly into the lives of the civilian populations. The Dutch, for example, found their country stripped of consumer durables within a few months of the German occupation. More serious was the seizure of raw materials, gold reserves, and transport facilities.

The most significant advantage gained by Germany was the huge reserve of labor of the occupied territory. By 1945 millions of foreign workers had been drawn into the service of German war production. According to an estimate of the International Labour Office, there were more than 8.6 million foreign workers in Germany in January,

1944, of whom about 2.2 million were war prisoners, the remainder civilian workers. And these figures do not take into account those employed on German orders in their own countries.

A second factor that distinguished the Second World War from the First was the use of long-range aerial bombardment. Strategic bombing brought the war for the first time directly to cities and industrial complexes far behind the front lines. There has been debate about the effectiveness of strategic bombing as a means of destroying productive capacity, and the estimates are that no more than about 20 per cent of Germany's industrial plant was destroyed from all causes during the war. But there can be little doubt that strategic bombing brought tremendous devastation to major urban centers. Housing was most severely affected; in Germany nearly 10 million dwellings were destroyed or severely damaged, a figure representing about 40 per cent of the total, and destruction to housing was great in other countries as well.

In the course of the First World War, the United States had become a major supplier of strategic materials to the Allies, and the same situation developed in the Second. But it happened more quickly and the means employed—Lend-Lease—had the advantage of avoiding many of the problems of interallied indebtedness that had plagued Europe after 1918. Under this system the United States supplied material to the Allies free of charge for the duration of the war. Britain was the major recipient, although some aid went to the Soviet Union as well. During the war the net amount (there was some reverse Lend-Lease from Britain to the United States) of aid Britain received under Lend-Lease was slightly more than $20 billion.

When the six years of fighting had ended, the European economy was thoroughly disrupted. Many cities lay in ruins; agricultural and industrial production stood at only a fraction of the prewar levels; and the transportation system had completely broken down. Yet the damage to Europe's productive capacity was not so great as might have been expected. Shortages of raw materials and physical exhaustion were frequently the chief impediments to increased producton. However, with much of her industry idle, Europe was in no position to pay for the purchases abroad that were necessary for recovery. Far more than after the First World War foreign assistance was needed. Another difficulty lay in the fact that political changes growing out of the war disrupted old economic patterns. Soviet domination in eastern Europe cut off traditional supplies of food and raw materials to western Europe and forced fundamental changes on eastern European countries as well. Similarly, the political division of Germany ruled out a return to former economic patterns there. However, in spite of these problems, Europe experienced a remarkable recovery in the next twenty years, in part because of substantial foreign aid, but also because of the determination of Europeans to avoid the difficulties that had oppressed Europe for so long after the First World War.

38. British Mobilization

The extraordinary effort made by the British during the Second World War is only partially revealed by the two documents that follow, the first relating to manpower, the second to industrial plant. Relying on foreign supplies of many nonmilitary goods, the British devoted a huge amount of their productive capacity to wartime production. Between 1941 and 1944 more than half of British production went to meet the needs of war.

A. General Review of Wartime Mobilization of Labor in Britain

Responsibilities of the Ministry

THE WORK of the Ministry of Labour and National Service during the period covered by this Report was dominated by problems of man-power.

The Government had made full plans for setting up immediately on the outbreak of war a Ministry of National Service. While the decision to add these obligations to the duties of the Ministry of Labour was not reached until August, 1939, the Ministry was the parent Department for planning purposes on man-power problems throughout the long period of preparation. In addition to its responsibilities for compiling from 1937 onwards the Schedule of Reserved Occupations and for conducting during 1939 the National Service Campaign, it was given Departmental responsibility for the detailed administration of the Military Training Act, 1939. When the title of the Ministry was enlarged in September, 1939, a considerable range of national service duties was already embodied within the structure of its departments.

On the outbreak of war the Ministry became responsible for calling up men, and later for calling up women, to meet the requirements of the Armed Forces and the Women's Auxiliary Services, and also for supplying man-power for Civil Defence and for expanding the munitions and other vital industries and services.

Source: Ministry of Labour and National Service, *Report for the Years 1939–1946* (Cd. 7225) (London: His Majesty's Stationery Office, 1947), pp. 1–4.

Wide powers for these purposes were given to the Minister by the National Service Acts, 1939 to 1942, and by the Orders and Regulations made under the Emergency Powers (Defence) Acts of 1939 and 1940. The fundamental aim of the Ministry's policy was to mobilise the nation's resources in such a way and at such a speed that our naval, military and air forces and our war production reached their highest point at the time when maximum impact on the enemy was required. Even after the peak period of general mobilisation had been reached in September, 1943, the Ministry was continuously engaged in strengthening the fighting Forces and the industries essential to military operations.

Mobilisation of Man-Power Resources

The man-power problem involved not only building up the "working population" to the maximum possible but also its proper allocation between the Forces, Civil Defence and the essential industries, and its most economical use in industry.

To build up the working population it was possible to draw on two main sources, namely, the "non-industrial" classes (that is, persons outside industry and the Services) and persons over the normal working age.

From the non-industrial classes large numbers of men and women not normally employed in industry, including housewives and domestic servants, were drawn into industry or the Services. About half a million men and 2½ million women were thus mobilised. Owing to household responsibilities many of the women were able to take only part-time industrial employment. This form of employment increased rapidly from 1942 onwards and eventually about 900,000 women were so employed. In the statistics which follow two part-time workers are counted as one unit.

In addition, men and women over the normal working age remained in or returned to employment. The number of men aged 65 and over and women aged 60 and over in industrial employment at the peak was about one million, representing a very substantial increase since 1939. . . .

The number at work was further increased by the absorption of the unemployed. In the years preceding the outbreak of war the numbers in employment had been rising from the depression level of 1931–1932, and in 1939 this movement was accelerated by the large scale Government expenditure on the re-armament programme. Nevertheless, at mid-1939 there were in Great Britain about 1¼ million insured persons registered as unemployed, comprising a million men and a quarter of a million women. The immediate effect of the dislocation caused by the outbreak of war was a rise in the number of unemployed, but as the war effort got under way, the unemployed were steadily absorbed into the Forces or into the expanding munitions industries, or into other industries to replace those withdrawn for more vital work. By mid-1942 the total number of unemployed had been reduced to less than 100,000 and it did not rise above that figure until after the end of hostilities in Europe.

The overall mobilisation of men in the Forces and in war occupations was virtually completed at an early stage of the war even though a considerable volume of transfers between duties continued as demands changed. By mid-1941 about 1½ million men of working age had been added to the numbers employed in the Forces, Civil Defence and industry. After that date casualties in the Armed Forces brought about a decline in the total number of employed men. The full mobilisation of women was not completed until later, although nearly 1¼ million women of working age were added to the numbers employed by mid-1941, when recruitment of women was still on a voluntary basis. The registration of women under the Registration for Employment Order, and the application to women of the National Service Acts, further stimulated recruitment, and by mid-1943 the number of women in industry and the Services had increased by 2,400,000, that is, an increase of 50 per cent over the number employed before the war.

When the peak of mobilisation was reached about September, 1943, out of approximately 15,920,000 men of working age domiciled in Great Britain, nearly 15 millions were in the Forces, Civil Defence or industry, the balance being mainly students or invalids or men otherwise unfit for industrial employment. Of approximately 16,020,000 women of working age, about 7¼ millions were in the Forces, Civil Defence or industry. About 80 per cent of the single women aged 14 to 59 (approximately 90 per cent of those aged 18 to 40) and about 80 per cent of the married women and widows aged 18 to 40 with no young children, were so employed.

At this stage men and women up to the age of 50 had been registered for employment in industry or the Services and the employed population was composed to a substantial extent of women who would not have entered industry except under the pressure of war-time needs and for whom industrial employment raised acute domestic problems. The substantial increase in the number of marriages, accompanied by a rise in the birth rate, was bound to lead to the retirement of many such women and as the available reserves had been exhausted those retiring could not be replaced in sufficient numbers to prevent a decline in the total labour force.

The amplitude of the changes is indicated by the following figures which relate to Great Britain and show the numbers of men aged 14 to 64 and women aged 14 to 59 in H.M. Forces, Civil Defence or industrial employment at mid-1939, September, 1943, and mid-1945:

	Mid-1939	Sept. 1943	Mid-1945
Total	18,480,000	22,245,000	21,506,000
Men	13,643,000	14,987,000	14,786,000
Women	4,837,000	7,258,000	6,720,000

Thus, the numbers of men and women in the Forces, Civil Defence or industry had by September, 1943, increased by rather more than 3¾ millions over the mid-1939 figure, but by mid-1945 the increase had fallen away to about 3 millions.

Distribution of Man-Power

Concurrently with the building-up of the total man-power there was the problem of its distribution between the Forces, Civil Defence and the industries and services supplying the Forces and essential civilian needs. The experience of the first world war had shown the folly of indiscriminate recruiting for the Forces, and considerable attention was given from 1937 onwards to the proper distribution of man-power in the event of war, especially of the types of skilled labour which would be scarce in war-time.

The allocation of individuals was determined in the first place by means of the Schedule of Reserved Occupations, which fixed for a large number of occupations age limits at and above which men were ineligible for acceptance into the Armed Forces or for the full-time Civil Defence Services. As the war progressed and the shortage of man-power became more acute, the system of block reservation under the Schedule of Reserved Occupations was replaced by individual deferment of call-up and the proper allocation of the limited supply of man-power available became the subject of careful planning. . . .

The broad outline of the redistribution of labour brought about by the mobilisation to meet war needs is indicated in the following Table which shows the number of men and women of "working age" in certain categories of employment at mid-1939, September, 1943, and mid-1945:

	Mid-1939	Sept. 1943	Mid-1945
Forces and Auxiliary Services	480,000	4,841,000	5,090,000
Civil Defence, National Fire Service and Police	80,000	311,000	127,000
Manufacture of Equipment and Supplies for the Forces	1,270,000	5,121,000	3,830,000
Total of above	1,830,000	10,273,000	9,047,000
Home Civilian Manufacture and Services and Export	16,650,000	11,972,000	12,459,000
Total	18,480,000	22,245,000	21,506,000

Extent of Mobilisation of Man-Power

The aggregate numbers of men and women in the Forces and Civil Defence, or engaged in the manufacture of munitions, equipment and supplies for the Forces, thus increased in about four years by approximately 8½ millions. This increase was achieved by a reduction of about 4¾ millions in the number of persons engaged in manufacture and services for home civilian needs and export, by the absorption of nearly 1¼ million from the unemployed and of about 2½ million persons (counting two half-time workers as one unit) from the non-industrial classes.

In addition to the paid employment which is covered by the above figures, large numbers of women with household responsibilities undertook voluntary unpaid work at canteens and nurseries, and men and women were called upon to perform additional duties, outside their normal occupations, in Civil Defence or in the Home Guard.

The extent of the mobilisation was considerably greater than was achieved during the first world war. Greater mechanisation of the Armed Forces and the larger programmes of factory building, airfield and camp construction and repair of air-raid damage, made it necessary to retain a greater proportion of men in industry. On the other hand women were brought directly into the war effort to a far greater extent. Compulsory national service was applied to women, and the high degree of mobilisation attained was largely due to the contribution of women to the national effort.

This vast mobilisation of the nation's man-power for war purposes was brought about by various measures which together formed a carefully timed plan. The policy of the Ministry was to consult the employers' and work-people's organisations on proposed changes. On all major issues involving labour legislation or changes in policy the Minister sought the advice of the National Joint Advisory Council (consisting of representatives of the Trades Union Congress General Council and of the British Employers' Confederation) or its Joint Consultative Committee. So far as possible it was the practice to inform the public of the reasons for new measures by announcements in Parliament, in the Press and by wireless. In the detailed administration at the Ministry's Local Offices of the schemes involving registration, interviewing and placing, consideration was given to the particular circumstances of each case and adequate opportunities were given for appeal to independent tribunals. The relative ease with which the labour controls operated was largely due to this policy, but even more to the willingness with which men and women accepted restrictions and hardships in order that the war might be brought to a successful conclusion.

B. Official Statement on Mobilization and Rationalization of British Industry, 1941

THE PRESIDENT of the Board of Trade explained to the House of Commons on the 6th March that the Government's economic policy in war-time is to facilitate the fullest possible transfer of resources to war production while maintaining exports as far as

Source: Board of Trade, *Concentration of Production, Explanatory Memorandum* (Cd. 6258) (London: His Majesty's Stationery Office, 1941). This brief statement is here reproduced in its entirety.

practicable. This policy demands the severe cutting down of civil consumption and the release of labour, materials and factory space for more essential purposes.

If they consulted only their own interests, the industries concerned might wish that all their component firms should carry on with their remaining share of the trade in the hope that conditions might improve. From the point of view of the national interest, however, it is most undesirable that the reduced production for civil needs should be met by large-scale part-time working. A spread-over of this kind results in an uneconomical use of certain types of labour. It does not free the factory and storage space which will, in many cases, be needed for Government use. The effect of a diminished turnover on costs may, in some instances, have serious repercussions on prices which the Government cannot ignore. Finally, it would be against the long-term interest of the firms themselves to allow their working capital to be eaten up in the vain hope that the position might become easier; many smaller firms might be forced into bankruptcy during the war and all would be gravely hampered in the period of post-war reconstruction.

The policy of the Government must, therefore, be to concentrate production in a reduced number of factories working full time. These factories should be able to produce the output required for Government orders, the greatest practicable export trade and the minimum needs of our population, while at the same time preserving the goodwill of the factories closed down. The closed factories should be kept ready to start up again as soon as possible after the war. The Departments concerned will then take all measures open to them to assist their speedy re-opening; meanwhile the Board of Trade will keep a record of factories closed down and the Ministry of Labour will keep a record of transferred workers so that their return to their old employment after the war may be facilitated.

The Government will facilitate this concentration by granting to groups of undertakings which fulfil the necessary conditions—"nucleus" firms, as they are to be called—special help to safeguard their requirements of labour and of raw materials. Loses due to the war assume various forms and His Majesty's Government regret that they cannot contemplate the use of public funds to relieve the position and provide compensation. In this matter the Government's policy remains as stated by the Prime Minister in his statement on the War Situation on the 5th September last. The "nucleus" firms have a clear duty to provide a measure of compensation for the firms whose factories are closed down. The Government feel confident that those concerned will carry through these voluntary group arrangements in a manner that will mitigate the hardships inevitable in the process of contraction.

The industries affected by this policy are in general those covered by the Limitation of Supplies (Miscellaneous) Order and also include certain industries subject to Raw Material Control.

In deciding the methods by which their policy was to be carried out, the Government were faced with a choice of means. They might themselves select the "nucleus" firms in each industry; they might ask an industry through its Association or representative body to prepare a scheme to cover all its members; or they might, by laying the essential facts clearly before the industries concerned, encourage individual firms to initiate the desired changes in industrial structure. The Government have chosen this last means for several reasons. First, it promises speedy results. Secondly, it ensures the greatest possible degree of flexibility and variety in the devices that may be applied in each trade. Thirdly, it permits firms to adjust themselves to the exceptional circumstances of war and at the same time will permit their rapid return to a structure appropriate to peace-time conditions. Finally, it reconciles most completely traditional British economic policy with the requirements of a war-time economy.

An essential feature of the policy is that individual firms in each industry will be expected to make arrangements with one another that will provide for the required degree of concentration. The degree of concentration required in every industry will be indicated by the Board of Trade, and a procedure, which will differ in detail from industry to industry, will be suggested for attaining it.

It will be for each individual firm which wishes to qualify as a "nucleus" firm to make arrangements with others that permit it to "run full" or to approach as nearly to that condition as circumstances permit. For some of the industries the rate of production in a previous period may be appropriate; in other cases a firm may arrange to close down a prescribed amount of machine capacity in other firms and to run its own machinery full-time. Where a firm owns several factories it may achieve the condition of running full if it closes one or more of them. These arrangements can and should be made among small firms as well as among larger organisations, and every help will be given to the smaller firms in overcoming their special problems.

A firm which wishes to qualify as a "nucleus" firm is also required to satisfy certain other conditions. These are:

(*a*) it must provide for the complete closing down of the factory or works whose output is to be transferred to the protected firm;

(*b*) the "nucleus" firm must make its own financial arrangements to compensate the firm or firms whose works are to be closed as a result of the scheme;

(*c*) the arrangement must provide for the plant of the closed firm to be kept intact, unless the premises should be requisitioned;

(*d*) the arrangement must provide for the maintenance of the production for export and for the Government which was previously undertaken by the firm closed down;

(*e*) the arrangements for dealing with the workers affected by the scheme must be satisfactory.

In order to comply with condition (*e*) of paragraph 9, firms will be required by the Board of Trade and Ministry of Labour to ensure that:

(*a*) production is concentrated, so far as possible, in areas where the competing demands of the munitions industries are least severe;

(*b*) the labour released is adaptable and of a type likely to be readily absorbed in the new employment;

(*c*) labour which is displaced from factories closed down and which cannot be absorbed into the war industries should, as far as possible, be taken on in the factories remaining in production; and

(*d*) the time for the release of labour should be, as far as possible, regulated to the demand.

The objectives are two-fold: first, to obtain the labour required for the war industries and, secondly, to avoid unnecessary unemployment. Thus it is necessary to keep in production factories in areas where alternative employment is not available and to time the release of workers so that they can be immediately transferred to war work. Firms remaining in production should be prepared to release their younger and more adaptable workers so as to make room for elderly workers displaced from other factories.

There are many urgent demands for labour that must be filled and it is not possible to suspend the existing method of filling them, in part, by the transfer of workers from less essential industries. It is therefore very desirable that schemes for concentration should be settled as early as possible so that the withdrawal of labour from these industries may be made to conform with the plans for concentration.

Firms are advised to obtain from the Divisional Controllers of the Ministry of Labour information relevant to the conditions set out in this paragraph at an early stage of their arrangements.

Firms which qualify as "nucleus" firms will enjoy certain advantages. These are:

(a) the firm will be eligible for inclusion on the list of protected firms. This will result in a lower age of reservation for its workers than if it were not, and the fact that it is on the list will be taken into consideration in dealing with applications for deferment;

(b) the Ministry of Labour will safeguard the labour requirements of these firms in appropriate cases upon the recommendation of the Board of Trade;

(c) Government orders will as far as possible be given to these firms;

(d) the Board of Trade will as far as possible prevent the factories from being requisitioned;

(e) help will be given to these firms to safeguard as far as possible their supplies of raw materials.

Firms which do not qualify as "nucleus" firms will not enjoy these advantages.

In order to help the Board in carrying out their task, the scope of the Export Council is being expanded and it has been renamed the Industrial and Export Council. A Committee of the Council has been formed under the Chairmanship of the President of the Board of Trade, which includes Lord Portal, the Parliamentary Secretary for Raw Materials of the Ministry of Supply, and Mr. G. Tomlinson, Parliamentary Secretary of the Ministry of Labour. The membership also includes men experienced in business who will advise the firms in carrying through the work of reorganisation.

39. Lend-Lease

Two American laws shaped the economic relations of other countries with the United States at the beginning of the Second World War: the Johnson Act of 1934 prohibited loans to governments that had defaulted on First World War loans; and the Neutrality Act of 1937 prohibited the sale of arms to belligerents and required that strategic materials be fully paid for before export and that they be carried in non-American ships. After the fall of France in the spring of 1940, these "cash and carry" provisions placed heavy burdens on British dollar reserves, particularly because of the need for aircraft. By December, 1940, the reserves were exhausted, and massive United States assistance was required. The Lend-Lease Act of March 11, 1941, reversed previous American policy and allowed the British build-up to continue.

The Lend-Lease Act, March, 1941

Be it enacted by the Senate and House of Representatives of the United States of America in Congress assembled, That this Act may be cited as "An Act to Promote the Defense of the United States."

SEC. 2. As used in this Act—

(a) The term "defense article" means—

(1) Any weapon, munition, aircraft, vessel, or boat;

(2) Any machinery, facility, tool, material, or supply necessary for the manufacture, production, processing, repair, servicing, or operation of any article described in this subsection;

(3) Any component material or part of or equipment for any article described in this subsection;

(4) Any agricultural, industrial or other commodity or article for defense.

Such term "defense article" includes any article described in this subsection: Manufactured or procured pursuant to section 3, or to which the United States or any foreign government has or hereafter acquires title, possession, or control.

(b) The term "defense information" means any plan, specification, design, prototype, or information pertaining to any defense article.

Source: *United States Statutes at Large*, Vol. LV, Part I, pp. 31-33.

SEC. 3. (a) Notwithstanding the provisions of any other law, the President may, from time to time, when he deems it in the interest of national defense, authorize the Secretary of War, the Secretary of the Navy, or the head of any other department or agency of the Government—

(1) To manufacture in arsenals, factories, and shipyards under their jurisdiction, or otherwise procure, to the extent to which funds are made available therefor, or contracts are authorized from time to time by the Congress, or both, any defense article for the government of any country whose defense the President deems vital to the defense of the United States.

(2) To sell, transfer title to, exchange, lease, lend, or otherwise dispose of, to any such government any defense article, but no defense article not manufactured or procured under paragraph (1) shall in any way be disposed of under this paragraph, except after consultation with the Chief of Staff of the Army or the Chief of Naval Operations of the Navy, or both. The value of defense articles disposed of in any way under authority of this paragraph, and procured from funds heretofore appropriated, shall not exceed $1,300,000,000. The value of such defense articles shall be determined by the head of the department or agency concerned or such other department, agency or officer as shall be designated in the manner provided in the rules and regulations issued hereunder. Defense articles procured from funds hereafter appropriated to any department or agency of the Government, other than from funds authorized to be appropriated under this Act, shall not be disposed of in any way under authority of this paragraph except to the extent hereafter authorized by the Congress in the Acts appropriating such funds or otherwise.

(3) To test, inspect, prove, repair, outfit, recondition, or otherwise to place in good working order, to the extent to which funds are made available therefor, or contracts are authorized from time to time by the Congress, or both, any defense article for any such government, or to procure any or all such services by private contract.

(4) To communicate to any such government any defense information, pertaining to any defense article furnished to such government under paragraph (2) of this subsection.

(5) To release for export any defense article disposed of in any way under this subsection to any such government.

(b) The terms and conditions upon which any such foreign government receives any aid authorized under subsection (a) shall be those which the President deems satisfactory, and the benefit to the United States may be payment or repayment in kind or property, or any other direct or indirect benefit which the President deems satisfactory.

(c) After June 30, 1943, or after the passage of a concurrent resolution by the two Houses before June 30, 1943, which declares that the powers conferred by or pursuant to subsection (a) are no longer necessary to promote the defense of the United States, neither the President nor the head of any department or agency shall exercise any of the powers conferred by or pursuant to subsection (a); except that until July 1, 1946, any of such powers may be exercised to the extent necessary to carry out a contract or agreement with such a foreign government made before July 1, 1943, or before the passage of such concurrent resolution, whichever is the earlier.

(d) Nothing in this Act shall be construed to authorize or to permit the authorization of convoying vessels by naval vessels of the United States.

(e) Nothing in this Act shall be construed to authorize or to permit the authorization of the entry of any American vessel into a combat area in violation of section 3 of the Neutrality Act of 1939.

SEC. 4. All contracts or agreements made for the disposition of any defense article or defense information pursuant to section 3 shall contain a clause by which the foreign government undertakes that it will not, without the consent of the President, transfer title to or possession of such defense article or defense information by gift, sale, or otherwise, or permit its use by anyone not an officer, employee, or agent of such foreign government.

SEC. 5. (a) The Secretary of War, the Secretary of the Navy, or the head of any other department or agency of the Government involved shall, when any such defense article or defense information is exported, immediately inform the department or agency designated by the President to administer section 6 of the Act of July 2, 1940, of the quantities, character, value, terms of disposition, and destination of the article and information so exported.

(b) The President from time to time, but not less frequently than once every ninety days, shall transmit to the Congress a report of operations under this Act except such information as he deems incompatible with the public interest to disclose. Reports provided for under this subsection shall be transmitted to the Secretary of the Senate or the Clerk of the House of Representatives, as the case may be, if the Senate or the House of Representatives, as the case may be, is not in session.

SEC. 6 (a) There is hereby authorized to be appropriated from time to time, out of any money in the Treasury not otherwise appropriated, such amounts as may be necessary to carry out the provisions and accomplish the purposes of this Act.

(b) All money and all property which is converted into money received under section 3 from any government shall, with the approval of the Director of the Budget, revert to the respective appropriation or appropriations out of which funds were expended with respect to the defense article or defense information for which such consideration is received, and shall be available for expenditure for the purpose for which such expended funds were appropriated by law, during the fiscal year in which such funds are received and the ensuing fiscal year; but in no event shall any funds so received be available for expenditure after June 30, 1946.

SEC. 7 The Secretary of War, the Secretary of the Navy, and the head of the department or agency shall in all contracts or agreements for the disposition of any defense article or defense information fully protect the rights of all citizens of the United States who have patent rights in and to any such article or information which is hereby authorized to be disposed of and the payments collected for royalties on such patents shall be paid to the owners and holders of such patents.

SEC. 8. The Secretaries of War and of the Navy are hereby authorized to purchase or otherwise acquire arms, ammunition, and implements of war produced within the jurisdiction of any country to which section 3 is applicable, whenever the President deems such purchase or acquisition to be necessary in the interest of the defense of the United States.

SEC. 9. The President may, from time to time, promulgate such rules and regulations as may be necessary and proper to carry out any of the provisions of this Act; and he may exercise any power or authority conferred on him by this Act through such department, agency, or officer as he shall direct.

SEC. 10. Nothing in this Act shall be construed to change existing law relating to the use of the land and naval forces of the United States, except insofar as such use relates to the manufacture, procurement, and repair of defense articles, the communication of information and other noncombatant purposes enumerated in this Act.

SEC. 11. If any provision of this Act or the application of such provision to any circumstance shall be held invalid, the validity of the remainder of the Act and the applicability of such provision to other circumstances shall not be affected thereby.

40. Strategic Bombing and the German War Economy

The Second World War provided the first major test of strategic bombing as a means of destroying a nation's ability to produce the goods necessary for modern warfare. In theory Germany was a good target for strategic bombing—a highly capitalized country with large concentrations of industrial plant. Between 1942 and the end of the war the Allies delivered an unprecedented bomb tonnage over Germany. By 1945 the average monthly delivery of combined British and American forces had risen to 170,000 tons. Yet the effects of this massive bombing were not clear at the time. After the war a thorough investigation undertaken by the United States Strategic Bombing Survey revealed that strategic bombing had not been so effective as had been hoped. The selection that follows is taken from the summary and conclusions of this exhaustive study.

The Effects of Strategic Bombing

The German War Economy

THE OUTSTANDING feature of the German war effort is the surprisingly low output of armaments in the first three years of the war—surprisingly low as measured not only by Germany's later achievement, but also by the general expectations of the time and by the level of production of her enemy, Britain. In aircraft, trucks, tanks, self-propelled guns, and several other types of armaments, British production was greater than Germany's in 1940, 1941, and 1942.

For these early years the conclusion is inescapable that Germany's war production was not limited by her war potential—by the resources at her disposal—but by demand; in other words, by the notions of the German war leaders as to what was required for achieving their aim. The Germans did not plan for a long war, nor were they prepared for it. Hitler's strategy contemplated a series of separate thrusts and quick victories over enemies that were even less prepared than Germany; he did not expect to fight a prolonged war against a combination of major world powers. . . .

Source: The United States Strategic Bombing Survey. Overall Effects Division, *The Effects of Strategic Bombing on the German War Economy* (Washington, D.C.: n.p., 1945), pp. 6-14, with deletions.

The defeat before Moscow, and the entry of the United States into the war [both] in December 1941, brought the German leaders for the first time face to face with the prospect of a prolonged war with the three greatest powers ranged against them. From that time onward limitations of demand no longer played a role in restricting armaments production; Germany's leaders called for an all-out effort. Yet, measured by the standards of other belligerents, there was no "total mobilization" and no long-term planning to bring the war effort to its attainable maximum. The production of civilian goods was restricted only to a moderate extent; there was no further mobilization of women and no large scale transfer of labor from nonessential to essential industries.

In February 1942, Albert Speer, Hitler's personal architect, was appointed Minister of Armament Production with wide powers; and the production history of the following two and a half years bears the stamp of the "Speer Period." Speer set about replacing the existing machinery of control with a new organization (the "Rings" and "Committees"), manned by people selected from among the production managers and technicians of industry. They were charged with the task of increasing production by rationalizing German war industry; that is, by simplifying designs, standardizing components, concentrating production in the most suitable plants, reducing the number of different armaments orders given to a single firm, exchanging patents and secret processes, and generally adopting, throughout industry, the most efficient processes of production. The result of this policy was a more than threefold increase in Germany's munition production. . . .

Within two and a half years Germany's military output in aircraft, weapons and ammunition was raised more than threefold, in tanks nearly sixfold—an achievement for which Speer and his associates take most of the credit. One may ask, however, whether this expansion represents the full utilization of the potentialities of the German economy.

There can be no doubt that Germany started the conversion of her economy to a wartime footing far too late. Had Germany's leaders decided to make an all-out war effort in 1939 instead of 1942, they would have had time to arm in "depth"; that is, to lay the foundations of a war economy by expanding their basic industries and building up equipment for the mass production of munitions. Starting their armament program as late as 1942, they could only arm in "width"; that is, accept their equipment and material base as given and expand munitions production on the basis of available capacity.

But, to ask the next question, was Germany able to make full use of her existing capacity? It will be shown below that she was not. While the German economy was approaching its basic limitations in mid-1944, it never attained its full war potential. Production capacity, except in a few special cases, of which oil was the most notable, was never really short; machinery capacity was never fully utilized. Manpower—particularly woman power—was never fully mobilized. Raw material stocks of the most important categories, such as steel, were rising up to mid-1944. The output of civilian consumption goods, after the restriction of the first two years of the war (which still left the civilian standard of living at a fairly comfortable level and above that of the depression years in the early thirties), was maintained virtually stable until the second quarter of 1944. . . .

To assess the effects of strategic bombing on the German economy, one must analyze the extent to which Germany utilized her resources, and the extent to which she could afford losing industrial capacity or divert resources to the restoration of destroyed capacity. The basic resources of an economy are the capital equipment of its industries, its industrial manpower, and its supply of raw materials. Of these three, capital equipment alone is directly vulnerable by aerial attack; and the strategic bomber offensive mounted against Germany aimed primarily at lowering military output by destroying equipment in the armament industries, in the industries supplying basic materials and components, and in the transportation system. The supply of raw materials can only be affected indirectly by bombing, through the destruction of equipment in the raw material extracting and manufacturing industries. Similarly, in the bombing of Germany, industrial manpower could only be affected indirectly by strategic bombing, insofar as it affects morale, causes absenteeism, and diverts labor to anti-aircraft defense and to debris clearance and reconstruction.

The German economy does not appear to have suffered from shortages of machine tools, general machinery, or plant facilities—except temporarily in a few isolated cases. On the contrary, machine tool and machinery capacity was generally in excess of needs. Detailed inventories of industrial equipment are not available, but the total inventory of machine tools suggests that on the whole, machine tool capacity was more than sufficient. This view is also confirmed by the fact that apart from the aero-engine industry and a few other exceptions, the German armament industries worked only a single shift throughout the war, and the great capacity reserve that would have been available from double or triple shift operations was largely unutilized. Furthermore, the German machine tool industry hardly expanded during the war, worked on a single shift basis throughout, and converted almost 30 per cent of its capacity to direct munitions production.

Germany's easy machine tool position is in striking contrast with the experience of the United States and Great Britain, where machine tools were kept working 24 hours a day seven days a week, and the machine tool industry was very much expanded and strained to the utmost to supply requirements. One reason for Germany's strong position was her large machine tool industry which, being an important exporter, had a capacity greatly in excess of Germany's domestic peace time requirements. Secondly, Germany started the war well stocked with machine tools which, unlike the American inventory, consisted mainly of universal machines and could therefore easily be converted to war production. In any case, Germany's war production was not limited by her machinery equipment. The important exceptions to this rule occurred in the synthetic oil and chemical industries, in the electric power system, and in the manufacture of high grade steel. Germany had ample capacity also in plant facilities. Statistics of factory floor space are lacking; but it appears that new factory construction was moderate during the war, while the large industrial dispersal programs occasioned by the Allied air offensive were carried out without being handicapped by a shortage of factory space. . . .

With the progress of the war, the mobilization of manpower increased both in Great Britain and in the United States; but not so in Germany, where the total employment of Germans (including those called up for the Wehrmacht and not deducting casualties) remained practically unchanged throughout the war and reductions in the civilian labor force due to military draft were not completely offset by the employment of foreigners.

The increase, from September 1939 to September 1944, in the number of German men and women employed (including the armed forces) was less than one million, and it fell short of the natural growth of the working age population over the period. The armed forces mobilized 11 ½ million men from the outbreak of the war up to September 1944; and their place in the civilian labor force was but partially filled by 7 million foreign workers and prisoners of war and the 1 million newly mobilized Germans, resulting in a net loss of 3½ million (10 per cent) to the civilian labor force.

This decline in civilian manpower is the more remarkable, because Germany did not exhaust her reserves of manpower in the course of the war. She began the war with about the same proportion of occupied women (outside agriculture) as Britain. But while in Britain the number of women in full- or part-time work increased 45 per cent in the course of the war, the number of German women mobilized remained practically unchanged. In Britain, the number of domestic servants was cut from 1.2 to 0.5 millions in the course of the war; in Germany it fell only from 1.5 million to 1.3 million. There were also other sectors of the economy that had large reserves of labor which could have been utilized for war work. Among them were the public administration system employing some 3.5 million workers, which Speer attempted unsuccessfully to reduce; and civilian industry which had a considerable cushion until the last stages of the war. . . .

Germany's dependence on imported raw materials was always regarded as the main weakness of her war potential. The Four Year Plan of 1936, which was designed to mitigate this weakness, secured her a certain degree of independence in critical war materials —chiefly through the synthetic production of rubber, oil, textile fibers and fats, the development of domestic iron ores in central Germany and through increasing the capacity of aluminum and magnesium production. These steps, however, did not render Germany self-sufficient—not even in the limited field of materials that could be synthetically produced. At the outbreak of the war, Germany still depended on foreign sources for 70 per cent of her iron ore, 90 per cent of her copper, and for all of her manganese, chrome, nickel, wolfram, tungsten and a host of other raw materials. Apart from nitrogen and coal, in no war material of importance could German production cover peacetime consumption, still less any additional requirements of war.

Germany managed, however, at least until late in 1944, to avoid any serious embarrassment to her war effort from the shortage of imported materials. When the war started, stocks of copper, iron ore, lead and magnesium were adequate for less than nine months' consumption and only in the case of manganese was there a supply sufficient for 18 months. In the case of copper and ferro-alloys, the Germans found that consumption could be drastically cut without real detriment to the quality of armaments; and they were able to reclaim considerable stocks from scrap. The annual consumption of copper, wolfram, molybdenum and cobalt was reduced by more than one-half. The victories of 1939 and 1940–41 led to the capture of considerable stocks of these materials and also to new sources of current supply, such as chromium from Bulgaria and Greece, nickel and molybdenum from Finland and Norway, copper from Yugoslavia, Norway and Finland, manganese from Russia, mercury from Italy and Spain, and bauxite from Hungary, France, Yugoslavia and Italy.

Synthetic capacity for rubber and oil was increased during the war, or at least until 1944, when it was reduced by bombing. Synthetic rubber production was raised from 5,000 tons in 1938 to an annual rate of 117,000 tons by the beginning of 1944. Synthetic oil production was raised from 1.6 million tons in 1938, to an annual rate of 6 million tons by early 1944, and crude oil production was expanded from 0.6 million tons to 2 million tons. Together with the Rumanian and Hungarian imports of about 2.5 million tons, oil supplies were considered adequate for the type of strategy adopted. It is to be noted, however, that this strategy was itself adjusted to the oil supply. Means of warfare involving heavy oil consumption—such as a fully motorized army or a large force of heavy bombers—were and perhaps had to be foregone.

The supplies of normally home-produced materials, such as steel and coal, were likewise adequate or more than adequate for the armament program, at any rate up to the middle of 1944. . . .

The supply of power, despite a considerable expansion of capacity, became tight early in the war. The curtailment of less essential uses began in October 1941. By the winter of 1943–44 the shortage had become so serious that from time to time temporary cuts were made in the allocation of power to the aluminum, nitrogen and other chemical industries, the main consumers of power.

An economy such as that just analyzed is peculiarly unsusceptible to damage to its finished goods industries. Destroyed capital equipment can be replaced out of reserves, destroyed factory space can be made good by drawing on empty factory space, lost man-hours can be made good by making working hours temporarily longer and by taking on more labor. Each and all of these methods

were, of course, resorted to by the Germans to offset the effects of
air raids. . . .

Over-All Effects of the Air Offensive

Prior to the summer of 1943, air raids had no appreciable effect
either on German munitions production or on the national output
in general. The area attacks of the RAF did considerable damage to
buildings and caused local delays in production by diverting labor
to repair work and debris clearance, and by causing absenteeism
and local disorganization. The first big raid on Kiel, for instance,
seems to have caused a three weeks' delay in submarine production;
and similar small delays were caused by the late 1942 and early
1943 campaigns against submarine production. But considering the
nature of the German economy during this period, it is impossible
to conclude that either submarine production or munitions output
as a whole was any smaller as a result of air raids than it would
have been otherwise. The only important bottlenecks at this time
occurred in certain sectors of the parts and components industries;
and there is no evidence that these industries suffered through air
raid damage.

The effects of air raids became more noticeable from the summer
of 1943 onward. This was partly due to the heavier weight of the
RAF attacks and partly to the appearance of the AAF in major
strength. Area raids on the Ruhr caused an estimated 8 per cent loss
of steel output, but adequate stocks in the hands of industrial users
prevented the loss from affecting armament output. The same attacks also created a bottleneck in crankshafts, which may have
slowed down the output of tanks and motor vehicles. Raids on the
aircraft industry caused an estimated 13 per cent loss of total
production for the period July through December. The loss from
direct damage, however, was less important than the sacrifice in
output caused by dispersal and other defensive measures taken as a
result of the intensification of the air war. These latter factors
explain the relatively great loss of output following the early raids
on the aircraft industry compared with the smaller effect of the
much heavier later raids. Ball bearing production fell 5 per cent
below the preraid average as a result of attacks in the fall of 1944,
but the presence of large supplies forestalled any effect on armament output. The total loss of German armament output from air
raids in the latter part of 1943 is estimated at 5 per cent.

For the first four months of 1944 the AAF, capable for the first time of carrying out repeated attacks deep into Germany, concentrated its strength on aircraft and ball bearing targets. During the attacks beginning in February, about 90 per cent of German fighter production capacity was attacked and 70 per cent destroyed. Production fell during the first month of the attack but rose phenomenally in succeeding months, despite the continuance of the offensive. The total number of aircraft produced rose from 1,525 in January to 2,475 in July; single-engine fighter output rose from 381 to 1,050. This large increase in output is explained by the adoption of energetic rationalization measures, by drawing on the pipe line of components, and by the fact that a large scale expansion of the industry had been planned previously. To what extent bombing prevented the realization of these plans is difficult to decide. It is possible that production would have been 15–20 per cent higher in the absence of bombing.

As a result of continued attacks, the production of ball bearings in the second quarter of 1944 fell to 66 per cent of the preraid average. An energetic dispersal policy, however, made it possible for production to reach almost the preraid average in the third quarter of the year. In the meantime, careful use of stocks, substitution of plain bearings for antifriction bearings, and redesign of equipment to eliminate the previously luxurious use of bearings, enabled the Germans to prevent the fall in bearing production from affecting the output of finished munitions.

The only other measurable effect of air raids on munitions production was a 5 per cent loss in panzer output caused mainly by the RAF attack on Friedrichshafen and a small loss of ammunition output mostly due to area raids. In the absence of these losses, total armament production in the first half of 1944 would have been almost 10 per cent higher than it actually was.

The campaigns which carried the promise of decisive results began after D-day. The offensives that started against oil and nitrogen plants in May and June, against the German transportation system in September, and against the Ruhr steel producing area in October, all achieved results fully up to expectations or above them. In addition to these major campaigns, the raids on aircraft plants were continued and attacks were made also against motor vehicle and panzer production.

The attack on oil was concentrated against Germany's synthetic plants. They produced 90 per cent of her aviation gasoline and 30 per cent of her motor gasoline. Synthetic production (hydrogenation and Fischer-Tropsch) fell from an average of 359,000 tons in the four months preceding the attacks to 134,000 tons in June and 24,000 tons in September. The aviation gasoline output of these plants fell from 175,000 tons in April to 5,000 tons in September. In the same period stocks of motor and aviation gasoline fell by two-thirds, and only drastic curtailments in consumption kept them from falling still further. As in the case of ball bearings and aircraft, the Germans took the most energetic steps to repair and reconstruct oil plants. As many as 350,000 men were engaged in reconstruction projects and the building of underground plants, but these measures proved of little value. Reconstructed plants were soon reattacked, while underground plants even at the end of the war produced but a fraction of Germany's then minute oil supply.

The attacks on the synthetic oil plants were found to have cost Germany a considerable part also of her synthetic nitrogen, methanol and rubber supply. These products were either produced in conjunction with synthetic oil or their manufacture required by-products of oil production. By the end of the year synthetic nitrogen output was reduced from a preraid level of over 75,000 tons to 20,000 tons monthly. The Germans were forced to curtail the use of nitrogen in agriculture, and then to cut supplies used for the production of explosives. Methanol production also necessary for explosives manufacture was similarly cut. These shortages were largely responsible for the 20 per cent loss of ammunition production in the last half of 1944.

By the end of 1944 synthetic rubber production had been reduced to approximately 15 per cent of the January–April average. Had the war continued, Germany's rubber position would have become critical. No indication was found, however, that the rubber shortage was a limiting factor on German war production or on the movement of the German army before the war ended. . . .

The heavy attack on the Ruhr area in the last quarter of 1944 reduced its steel output by 80 per cent. Total German steel production (including that of the occupied territories) declined from 2 million tons in September to 1 million tons in December. Approximately 80 per cent of this decline was due to air attack. Although production continued to fall to the end of the war, the steel shortage—overshadowed by the transportation breakdown—was not a significant causal factor in the decline of munitions output.

The attack on transportation beginning in September 1944 was the most important single cause of Germany's ultimate economic collapse. Between August and December freight car loadings fell by approximately 50 per cent. The progressive traffic tie-up was found to have first affected commodities normally shipped in less than full trainload lots—finished and semifinished manufactured goods, components and perishables. The effects of the attack are best seen, however, in the figures of coal transport, which normally constituted 40 per cent of rail traffic. Shipments by rail and water fell from 7.4 million tons in August to 2.7 million tons in December. By March coal shipments were scarcely adequate even for the needs of the railroads. The operation of Germany's raw material industries, her manufacturing industries, and her power supply were all dependent on coal. By January their stocks were becoming exhausted and collapse was inevitable.

The index of total munitions output reached its peak in July 1944 and fell thereafter. By December it had declined to 80 per cent of the July peak, and even this level was attained only by using up stocks of components and raw materials. Air raids were the main factor in reducing output, which in their absence would probably have risen. A loss of armaments output somewhat above 15 per cent can be credited to bombing in the last half of 1944. This compares with a 5 per cent loss for the last half of 1943 and a 10 per cent loss for the first half of 1944.

By the third quarter of 1944 bombing had succeeded in tying down a substantial portion of the labor force. This diversion amounted to an estimated 4.5 million workers, or nearly 20 per cent of the nonagricultural labor force. This estimate includes 2½ million workers engaged in debris clearance, reconstruction and dispersal projects and in other types of activity necessitated by bombing, 1 million workers engaged in replacing civilian goods lost through air raids, and slightly less than 1 million workers in the production and manning of antiaircraft weapons. Air raid casualties were not numerous. By the middle of 1944 they had reduced the labor force by not more than 250,000 or less than one per cent. Late in 1944 the diversion of laborers due to bombing began to lose importance because the disintegration of the economy had reached a point at which the full utilization of the total labor force was no longer possible.

As to the effects of bomb damage on the civilian economy, there is no evidence that shortages of civilian goods ever reached a point where the German authorities were forced to transfer resources from war production in order to prevent disintegration on the home front. It was not until the end of 1943 that the area raids of the RAF had caused important shortages in certain segments of the civilian economy; and even for the whole of 1944, the output of manufactured consumer goods was only slightly below that of 1943. The most that can be said is that bombing destroyed a substantial part of the consumer goods cushion and thereby prevented the further conversion of the civilian economy to war production in 1944.

From December 1944 onwards, all sectors of the German economy were in rapid decline. This collapse was due to the results of air raids working in combination with other causes. The armament index fell from 322 in July to 263 in December and to 145 in March (the last month for which records are available).

These figures fail to show, however, the full extent to which the situation had deteriorated. During the process of contraction the shrinkage in final output always lags behind the shrinkage in productive activity. Some production of finished munitions could be temporarily maintained because of the relatively large stocks of semifinished products, at least for as long as the minimum coal and power requirements of the munitions industries could be covered. After the end of March this was no longer possible. Even in February 1945, coal deliveries, partly through the loss of Silesia and the Saar, fell to 25 per cent of normal. In March they fell to 16 per cent and, by the end of the month, to only 4 per cent of normal. . . . Even if the final military victories that carried the Allied armies across the Rhine and the Oder had not taken place, armament production would have come to a virtual standstill by May; the German armies, completely bereft of ammunition and motive power, would almost certainly have had to cease fighting by June or July.

In the actual case—as in most other cases in the history of wars—the collapse occurred before the time when the lack of means would have rendered further resistance physically impossible.

41. Postwar Economic Problems

Even during the war attention had been given to planning for the relief of war-torn areas of Europe. A United Nations Relief and Rehabilitation Administration was created in 1943, the financial burden of relief to be shared by United Nations members whose countries had not been subjected to war damage, in proportion to their national incomes. UNRRA was conceived as an organization to provide only temporary relief. The major part of its assistance went to the devastated regions of central and eastern Europe and significantly reduced suffering there. But in spite of the efforts of UNRRA and of other limited relief measures, European recovery stalled in 1947. It became clear that more than temporay relief was required. In June, 1947, the United States Secretary of State, George C. Marshall, in a now famous speech at Harvard University, proposed that the European nations jointly survey their needs and formulate a program of recovery upon which American assistance could be based. The following selection on the problems of European recovery is taken from the report prepared in response to Secretary Marshall's invitation.

Report of the Committee of European Economic Cooperation, 1947

The industrial structure of Western Europe was based upon coal, steel and chemicals; its output of these products in the period just before the war was slightly greater than that of the United States. Every part of this machine depended upon the efficient working of the other parts and none of the Western European countries was in a position to organise its industry effectively without the support of the others.

A high level of agricultural production was attained based in some cases on the specialised cultivation of high quality products, and in other cases on intensive farming techniques depending on the use of fertilisers and imports of feeding stuffs. The density of agricultural population was many times greater than that of North America, and among the countries with the most efficient agriculture were those which made most use of imported supplies.

Source: Committee of European Economic Cooperation, *General Report*, Vol. I (London: His Majesty's Stationery Office, 1947), pp. 3–8, with deletions.

The exceptional degree of specialisation in the industry and agriculture of the participating countries and Western Germany was responsible for their high standard of living, but it contained certain elements of weakness. The machine was highly developed and delicate. It depended for its efficient working upon the smooth working of international trade and the uninterrupted flow of goods and services. The war of 1939–45 destroyed this process, and a breakdown occurred which altered the whole basis of the economy of Europe. As time passed, it also became apparent that, even when the war had come to an end, the vital flow could not immediately be resumed. Allied victory had been obtained at the price of the temporary destruction of some of the centres of production and the dislocation of the transport system; and by the sacrifice of shipping and foreign investments, upon which the essential imports had so heavily depended.

These losses and sacrifices had weakened the economic structure of the sixteen countries[1] and their effect was aggravated by many other factors. The agriculture, trade and industry of European countries had been twisted out of shape by their own war effort or by policies imposed by armies of occupation. Great numbers of workers were displaced or deported. Overseas importers, deprived of the normal flow of supplies from Europe, transferred an increased part of their trade to the United States. Many of the main sources of supply of these sixteen countries were laid waste; the devastation in Eastern Europe and the Soviet Union cut off a major source of food and timber; the extension of the war into South-East Asia upset Europe's trade balance with the United States, which was partly financed by exports from South-East Asia, and in addition led to a double loss to the European food supply; for the countries of South-East Asia not only became incapable of sending their normal share of food exports to Europe but required and obtained food which would normally have come to Europe.

In 1945 Europe was perhaps more denuded of resources than at any time in modern history. There was a shortage of all basic

[1] That is, those responding to Marshall's invitation: Austria, Belgium, Denmark, France, Greece, Iceland, Ireland, Italy, Luxembourg, The Netherlands, Norway, Portugal, Sweden, Switzerland, Turkey, and the United Kingdom. West Germany, then still under military government, was associated with the sixteen. In 1948 these nations formed the Organization for European Economic Cooperation.—Eds.

materials: of fertilisers to renovate the soil, of raw materials and equipment to quicken production, and in most countries of available labour. Some industries began to run down for lack of facilities for all but temporary repair.

After the shortage of food, the decline in the production of coal and steel was perhaps the hardest blow to the economy of Europe. Immediate rehabilitation was made difficult; urgent domestic needs pushed aside the claims of the export trade thereby further reducing capacity to buy vital industrial equipment abroad. Except in Germany, European forests were generally overcut—particularly in the occupied countries and the United Kingdom. Timber exports from North-Eastern Europe fell off sharply, with serious consequences for the basic industries of Western Europe.

Meanwhile prices had risen and, although no inflation comparable to that of 1914–18 had occurred, the problem of unbalanced budgets and rising prices was serious in many countries—in some it was catastrophic. The shortage of gold and dollars in a large number of European countries brought about the development of bilateral agreements, which promoted a limited revival of trade, but could not provide the steady and universal growth which would have taken place if conditions had allowed a return to the normal multilateral system.

To sum up, the difficulties of the participating countries at the end of a war fought over three continents were due to the following main causes:

(i) Physical devastation and disruption in Western Europe and in the principal food and timber-producing zones of Eastern Europe which, together with the dislocation of the European transport system, caused a temporary paralysis of production in Western Europe, including Germany;

(ii) Prolonged interruption of international trade, which occurred simultaneously with the loss of income from merchant fleets and foreign investments, led to the exhaustion or diminution of dollar funds in the sixteen countries at a moment when many vital needs could be met only from dollar sources;

(iii) Human strain and exhaustion resulting from six years of war or enemy occupation;

(iv) Internal financial disequilibrium which is the inevitable result of a long war;

(v) In South-East Asia, the shortage in the supply of food and
raw materials which were vital to the European economy,
both for direct consumption and as earners of dollars;

(vi) The abnormal increase of population in certain areas resulting from the war-time movement of peoples.

The scale of destruction and disruption of European economic
life was far greater than that which Europe had experienced in the
first World War. Industrial production in Belgium, France and the
Netherlands was reduced to between 30 and 40 per cent of pre-
war, and in Italy to only 20 per cent; production of bread grains
fell to only two-thirds of pre-war; 300,000 freight cars had been
destroyed out of a total of 2,000,000, and 800,000 freight cars were
damaged. The devastated countries had to start again almost from
the beginning.

Nevertheless recovery proceeded well—indeed, much faster
than after the first World War. Eighteen months after the end of
fighting in Europe, industry and transport were moving again
vigorously and the work of reconstruction was getting under way.
This was made possible by the efforts of the European countries
themselves, with generous assistance from the United States and
other countries and from U.N.R.R.A. So successful were these
efforts that by the end of 1946 industrial production in Belgium,
France and the Netherlands had recovered to between 85 and 95
per cent of the pre-war level, whilst Italian industrial production
was back to 60 per cent of pre-war level. In the United Kingdom
the process of demobilisation of the war economy had been accomplished smoothly, and the pre-war level of national output had
been fully restored. In the Scandinavian countries production was
steadily rising. In the case of agricultural production which,
though hard hit by the war, had not declined to the same extent as
industrial production the beginning of recovery was evident in all
countries in 1946. Indeed, the participating countries as a whole
had made a good and resolute start on their task.

This improvement was not maintained in the winter of 1946–47.
The European economy, still at the convalescent stage, suffered a
most serious setback as a result of the continued shortage of coal,
the increased cost of primary products and the prolonged world
shortage of food and other essential commodities. This crisis was
intensified by the exceptionally severe winter and the drought
which followed. Further advance from the levels of autumn 1946
would, in any case, have been difficult in view of the continued

inability of the German economy to supply the coal and other products upon which so much of Europe's economic life depends. But the failure of production to recover in other devastated parts of the world, the consequent development of further shortages, and further price increases, created additional problems for Europe which threatened the whole basis of the recovery which had been made so far. The credits which many countries had obtained in the early post-war period were becoming exhausted, and the upsurge of recovery had used up the stocks which countries had managed to retain or acquire after the Liberation.

Early in 1947 it became clear that the effect of the war had been to upset the balance between the productive power and resources of the Western Hemisphere and those of the rest of the world. The effect of this disequilibrium was shown most clearly in the surplus in the United States' balance of payments which was then running at the rate of $10,000 millions a year. In order to maintain the progress which had so far been achieved, the European countries were bound to maintain the volume of their imports from the American continent at increasing cost. This process inevitably led to a rapid depletion of gold and dollar reserves. The effects of this process reach far beyond Europe and threaten the foundations of the world economy. But Europe was affected most acutely and urgently because of the dissipation of her financial and physical resources during the war.

By the early summer of 1947, the earlier hopes of a rapid and sustained recovery from the effects of the war had receded. Agricultural recovery was halted by frost damage. It became apparent in May that the prolonged winter and the spring drought would lead to poor harvests. The later droughts have caused a further deterioration in crop prospects. In fact, industry in most European countries recovered well from the winter crisis, and the levels of the previous autumn had been generally restored by the middle of the year. But this improvement was being maintained only at the cost of depletion of financial reserves. When these were exhausted, the peoples of Europe would be threatened with an indefinite prolongation of insecurity and lower standards of living. Unless drastic steps were taken to arrest the process, European production could never play its proper part in redressing the growing unbalance of the world economy.

On 5th June, 1947, Mr. Marshall, the United States Secretary of State, delivered a speech at Harvard University. He said:

Europe's requirements for the next three or four years of foreign food and other essential products—principally from America—are so much greater than her present ability to pay that she must have substantial additional help or face economic, social and political deterioration of a very grave character. . . . Before, however, the United States can proceed much further in its efforts to alleviate the situation and help start the European world on its way to recovery, there must be some agreement among the countries of Europe as to the requirements of the situation and the part these countries them-selves will take in order to give proper effect to whatever action might be undertaken by this Government. It would be neither fitting nor efficacious for this Government to undertake to draw up uni-laterally a programme designed to place Europe on its feet economi-cally. . . . The initiative . . . must come from Europe. The role of this country should consist of friendly aid in the drafting of a European programme and of later support of such a programme, so far as it may be practical for us to do so. The programme should be a joint one agreed to by a number, if not all, European nations.

On 12th June, Mr. Marshall explained that he had in mind the entire continent west of Asia—and including both the United Kingdom and the Soviet Union.

On 16th June, Mr. Bevin, the British Foreign Secretary, visited M. Bidault, the French Foreign Minister, in Paris. They agreed to seek to associate the Soviet Government with their initiative in framing a reply to Mr. Marshall, and discussion between Mr. Bevin, M. Bidault and Mr. Molotov started in Paris on 27th June. Much to the regret of the Governments of France and the United Kingdom, agreement could not be reached.

On 3rd July, Mr. Bevin and M. Bidault decided themselves to issue invitations to all other European countries (except Spain) to attend a conference in Paris in order to prepare a report for presen-tation to Mr. Marshall in response to his Harvard Speech. . . .

The Conference opened in Paris on 12th July, under the chair-manship of Mr. Bevin. Within four days the Conference ad-journed, having set up a Committee of Economic Co-operation and Technical Committees covering food and agriculture, fuel and power, iron and steel and transport to prepare a Report. . . .

As the work of the Committee of Co-operation was proceeding the foreign exchange crisis continued to gather momentum. There was a rapid increase in the rate of exhaustion of Europe's financial reserves. On 20th August, the United Kingdom was forced tempo-rarily to suspend the convertibility of sterling into United States dollars; on 28th August, the Government of France announced the suspension of all dollar imports except cereals, coal and certain other supplies of similar essentiality; at the beginning of September, the Italian Government was obliged to suspend purchases of coal, oil and other basic supplies. Action on similar lines has been taken, or is likely to become necessary in the near future, in most of the participating countries.

At the moment at which this Report is published many of the participating countries have already reached the point at which they are forced by lack of foreign exchange to restrict their imports of the fuel and raw materials which are indispensable for their industrial and agricultural production and to cut their imports of food to a point at which industrial efforts can no longer be sustained at the level required to enable recovery to take place. From the devastation of war Europe recovered well. But that recovery is now halted; the crisis is deepening, and its repercussions are spreading to every corner of the world economy.

In this critical situation, the participating countries and Western Germany have examined their prospective requirements and resources over the next four years and have in common formulated a recovery programme. The various countries handle their economic affairs by diverse means; some work to a long-term plan, and others follow relatively unrestricted private enterprise. The means of carrying out this programme will therefore vary from country to country, but each will be able fully to play its part in the programme, and all are determined to do so.

The recovery programme is based upon four points:

(i) A strong *production effort* by each of the participating countries, especially in agriculture, fuel and power, transport, and the modernisation of equipment;

(ii) The creation and maintenance of *internal financial stability* as an essential condition for securing the full use of Europe's productive and financial resources;

(iii) The development of economic *co-operation* between the participating countries;

(iv) A *solution* of the problem of the participating countries' *deficit with the American continent*, particularly by increased exports.

The production expansion which is envisaged by 1951 is similar in general scale to that achieved by the United States in the mobilisation years 1940 to 1944. [In the United States from 1940 to

1944 coal output increased by 34 per cent, steel output by 31 per cent, electric power output by 61 per cent. The European coal output is planned to increase by 33 per cent from 1947 to 1951, steel output (excluding Germany) by 60 per cent, and power output by 39 per cent.]² It calls for an unprecedented peace-time effort of work by the whole population of all the participating countries. It is the maximum self-help which each country can accomplish; it will restore agricultural production to the pre-war level; and it will carry with it a significant expansion of mining and manufacturing production beyond the levels which were ruling in 1938.

The production programme provides for mutual help between the participating countries over a wide field, and for a number of practical steps for specific action, such as the International Power Project. In addition broader proposals are made for the reduction of trade barriers and the removal of financial obstacles to intra-European trade.

The creation of internal financial stability in certain countries is necessary in order to get their entire productive and distributive systems into effective operation, and in order to secure the full use of internal and external financial resources. While the necessary economic and financial reforms can be initiated without external assistance, such assistance will be required to make them fully effective.

In order to carry out their production effort, and after making full allowance for the supplies which they can obtain from each other, the participating countries need food, raw materials, fuel and capital equipment from overseas. There are two difficulties to be overcome: the inadequate supplies of certain key commodities available in the world, and the lack of means of paying for them. In this Report, it is estimated that available supplies to the participating countries, assuming complete achievement of their agricultural programmes, will be insufficient to permit even the restoration of the pre-war standard of food consumption by the end of 1951. Moreover, in the immediate future, the lack of supplies from normal sources in Eastern Europe and South-East Asia increases the urgency of the need for supplies from the American continent. The financial counterpart of the unbalanced flow of goods and

² The sentences in brackets were a footnote in the original.—Eds.

services from the American continent is the dollar deficit of the participating countries.

The European recovery programme cannot get fully under way until the immediate dollar problem is solved. Failure to solve it would destroy the basis of production and internal confidence in Europe; a descending spiral of production and consumption would become inevitable. Immediate and fully adequate aid in 1948 is therefore necessary as a first step for the fulfilment of the programme of production, stabilisation and co-operation. If the initial stages of the programme can be successfully accomplished, a momentum will be created that will ease the task in the following years.

The productive effort which is generated in 1948 can be sustained and developed further only if the participating countries can obtain and pay for the necessary supplies from overseas. There will still be a large deficit in the following years. The purpose of the European recovery programme is to reduce this deficit as fast as possible. There will be some deficit in 1951; the participating countries have always depended on dollar earnings from the rest of the world to meet their deficit with the American continent, and will do so in the future. But by the end of 1951, given reasonably favourable external conditions, the deficit should be of dimensions which will be manageable through normal means without special aid.

This is a fundamental problem which cannot be solved quickly. The effects of the war, which are so clearly illustrated by the lack of balance in the world's trading pattern, cannot be cured in a few months. Nevertheless the participating countries are confident that in four years considerable and decisive progress can be made to overcome them. This recovery programme can break the back of the problem. But continuing constructive action by the European countries and by the rest of the world will be needed in order to keep the trading position balanced, and to prevent the re-appearance of the international maladjustment which is the root of Europe's present difficulties.

In order to ensure that the recovery programme is carried out, the sixteen participating countries pledge themselves to join together, and invite other European countries to join with them, in working to this end. This pledge is undertaken by each country with respect to its own national programme, but it also takes into account similar pledges made by the other participating countries. In particular, each country undertakes to use all its efforts:

   (i) to develop its production to reach the targets, especially for food and coal;

  (ii) to make the fullest and most effective use of its existing productive capacity and all available manpower;

 (iii) to modernise its equipment and transport, so that labour becomes more productive, conditions of work are improved, and standards of living of all peoples of Europe are raised;

 (iv) to apply all necessary measures leading to the rapid achievement of internal financial, monetary and economic stability while maintaining in each country a high level of employment;

  (v) to co-operate with one another and with like-minded countries in all possible steps to reduce the tariffs and other barriers to the expansion of trade both between themselves and with the rest of the world, in accordance with the principles of the Draft Charter for an International Trade Organisation;

 (vi) to remove progressively the obstacles to the free movement of persons within Europe;

(vii) to organise together the means by which common resources can be developed in partnership.

By these means, and provided the necessary supplies can be obtained from overseas, European recovery can be achieved.

PART IX

The New Europe

Within a decade after the end of the Second World War the economic face of Europe had changed vastly. Reconstruction merged with transformation in such a way that economic growth became one of the central features of European society, both East and West. Large numbers of people were brought into industrial employment, and investment rates were sustained at high levels. In western Europe this growth, associated with only limited structural change, was most remarkable for the steadiness of expansion, for universal participation in a new prosperity, and for an increasing degree of economic co-operation among nations. In eastern Europe the most important aspects of economic development were radical structural change and the rapid expansion of heavy industry, but until the later 1950's growth was achieved at the expense of both the agricultural sector and living standards. In both West and East some kind of state planning became a permanent feature of economic life.

The war and the demands of reconstruction significantly disrupted prewar economic patterns. Immediately after the war there was a wave of nationalization. All the eastern European states nationalized industry; in Britain the new Labour Government nationalized the Bank of England and many basic industries, beginning with coal in 1946; in that year, too, the French nationalized major banks, many insurance companies, and the coal, gas, and electrical industries. Perhaps more important than nationalization was the way in which the war broke the hold of tradition upon the minds of European leaders and seemed to dissolve the pessimism that had prevailed during the Depression. Numerous plans were put forward to renew rather than just restore the economy after the war. These stressed the importance of redistributing or enlarging national income in order to improve the conditions of life. The most obvious example of the new attitude was the commitment of all major states to extensive systems of public welfare and to ensuring full employment. Of equal importance was the emphasis upon continuing governmental responsibility for managing the conditions for economic growth and for stimulating technical advance.

The years of reconstruction in western Europe began an unprecedented period of stable economic growth. By the end of the 1940's prewar levels of production generally had been surpassed, but the economies of the major industrial countries continued to boom during the 1950's. At the beginning, this growth was greatly stimulated by large quantities of American aid, mainly through the Marshall Plan; it was sustained by various systems of economic "management"—in which government power was used to even out business cycles, and to ensure high rates of capital formation and full employment—and by a high rate of technological progress..

Economic expansion was also stimulated by greater economic co-operation. The idea of cooperation had received wide support during the war, but American pressure was significant in pushing the western European states into forming the Organization for European Economic Cooperation. A number of other institutions for cooperation were created in the next decade. Finally, in 1957, a European Economic Community—the Common Market—was established by Belgium, France, Italy, Luxembourg, The Netherlands, and West Germany. Its main feature was a customs union that succeeded in greatly increasing trade among its members. But the purposes of the Community went beyond the elimination of trade barriers to broader economic integration.

In eastern Europe, except in the Soviet Union, the postwar years were marked by a sharp break with the prewar economic system, and, in contrast to western Europe, by depressed standards of living. During the war losses of manpower had been extremely heavy, and the Nazi occupation policies of confiscating key industrial concerns and dispossessing Jews had undermined property relations. When Soviet economic domination replaced German, the already strained resources of eastern Europe were pumped into Soviet recovery. At the same time the eastern European economies underwent deep structural transformation in three main stages. In the reconstruction stage, immediately after the war, a large part of industry was nationalized and land reforms were carried out. Then, starting at the end of the 1940's, the Soviet pattern of forced industrialization was imposed, including full nationalization, centralized planning, rapid development of capital goods industries, collectivization of agriculture, and a drive for virtual autarchy. By the early 1950's Soviet-type industrialization was being achieved, but at the expense of living standards. In the third stage, which opened with Stalin's death in 1953 but took full shape only in 1956, there began an irregular process of moderating the imbalance between heavy industry on the one hand and consumer industries and agriculture on the other. Standards of living began to rise, and some of the worst inefficiencies of the Stalinist system were removed. In this period there were attempts at economic integration—in contrast to Soviet domination—but in comparison with the Common Market they had had limited success by the end of the 1950's.

42. The Welfare State

A minister in Churchill's War Cabinet had responsibility for reconstruction problems. He appointed, in June, 1941, an Interdepartmental Committee on Social Insurance and Allied Services, headed by Sir William Beveridge. In November, 1942, Beveridge presented a report based upon the work of the Committee. It concluded that "in a system of social security better on the whole than can be found in almost any other country there are serious deficiencies which call for remedy." Beveridge argued that "the purpose of victory is to live into a better world than the old world,"[1] and that the provision of security against want, of medical care, and of employment for all citizens should become the central purpose of government economic policy. The report offered in some detail a plan for social insurance, which received a warm popular reception and was accepted by both the Conservative and Labour Parties as a central plank of postwar policy. The main points of his proposal are presented in the following excerpts from the report.

The Beveridge Report, 1942

IN PROCEEDING from this first comprehensive survey of social insurance [carried out by the Beveridge Committee] to the next task—of making recommendations—three guiding principles may be laid down at the outset.

The first principle is that any proposals for the future, while they should use to the full the experience gathered in the past, should not be restricted by consideration of sectional interests established in the obtaining of that experience. Now, when the war is abolishing all landmarks of every kind, is the opportunity for using experience in a clear field. A revolutionary moment in the world's history is a time for revolutions, not for patching.

The second principle is that organisation of social insurance should be treated as one part only of a comprehensive policy of social progress. Social insurance fully developed may provide in-

[1] Sir William Beveridge, *Social Insurance and Allied Services* (Cd. 6404) (London: His Majesty's Stationery Office, 1942), pp. 6 and 171.

Source: Sir William Beveridge, *Social Insurance and Allied Services* (Cd. 6404) (London: His Majesty's Stationery Office, 1942), pp. 5–20 and 153–172, with deletions.

come security; it is an attack upon Want. But Want is only one of five giants on the road of reconstruction and in some ways the easiest to attack. The others are Disease, Ignorance, Squalor and Idleness.

The third principle is that social security must be achieved by co-operation between the State and the individual. The State should offer security for service and contribution. The State in organising security should not stifle incentive, opportunity, responsibility; in establishing a national minimum, it should leave room and encouragement for voluntary action by each individual to provide more than that minimum for himself and his family.

The Plan for Social Security set out in this Report is built upon these principles. It uses experience but is not tied by experience. It is put forward as a limited contribution to a wider social policy, though as something that could be achieved now without waiting for the whole of that policy. It is first and foremost, a plan of insurance—of giving in return for contributions benefits up to sub-sistence level, as of right and without means test, so that individuals may build freely upon it. . . .

The plan is based on a diagnosis of want. It starts from facts, from the condition of the people as revealed by social surveys between the two wars. It takes account of two other facts about the British community, arising out of past movements of the birth rate and the death rate, which should dominate planning for its future. . . . The first of the two facts is the age constitution of the population, making it certain that persons past the age that is now regarded as the end of working life will be a much larger proportion of the whole community than at any time in the past. The second fact is the low reproduction rate of the British community today; unless this rate is raised very materially in the near future, a rapid and continuous decline of the population cannot be prevented. The first fact makes it necessary to seek ways of post-poning the age of retirement from work rather than of hastening it. The second fact makes it imperative to give first place in social expenditure to the care of childhood and to the safeguarding of maternity. . . .

The main feature of the Plan for Social Security is a scheme of social insurance against interruption and destruction of earning power and for special expenditure arising at birth, marriage or death. The scheme embodies six fundamental principles: flat rate of subsistence benefit; flat rate of contribution; unification of admin-istrative responsibility; adequacy of benefit; comprehensiveness;

and classification. . . . Based on them and in combination with national assistance and voluntary insurance as subsidiary methods, the aim of the Plan for Social Security is to make want under any circumstances unnecessary. . . .

The main provisions of the plan may be summarised as follows:

(i) The plan covers all citizens without upper income limit, but has regard to their different ways of life; it is a plan all-embracing in scope of persons and of needs, but is classified in application.

(ii) In relation to social security the population falls into four main classes of working age and two others below and above working age respectively, as follows:

I. Employees, that is, persons whose normal occupation is employment under contract of service.

II. Others gainfully occupied, including employers, traders and independent workers of all kinds.

III. Housewives, that is married women of working age.

IV. Others of working age not gainfully occupied.

V. Below working age.

VI. Retired above working age.

(iii) The sixth of these classes will receive retirement pensions and the fifth will be covered by children's allowances, which will be paid from the National Exchequer in respect of all children when the responsible parent is in receipt of insurance benefit or pension, and in respect of all children except one in other cases. The four other classes will be insured for security appropriate to their circumstances. All classes will be covered for comprehensive medical treatment and rehabilitation and for funeral expenses.

(iv) Every person in Class I, II or IV will pay a single security contribution by a stamp on a single insurance document each week or combination of weeks. In Class I the employer also will contribute, affixing the insurance stamp and deducting the employee's share from wages or salary. The contribution will differ from one class to another, according to the benefits provided, and will be higher for men than for women, so as to secure benefits for Class III.

(v) Subject to simple contribution conditions, every person in Class I will receive benefit for unemployment and disability, pension on retirement, medical treatment and funeral expenses. Persons in Class II will receive all these except unemployment benefit and disability benefit during the first thirteen weeks of disability. Persons in Class IV will receive all these except unemployment and disability benefit. As a substitute for unemployment benefit, training benefit will be available to persons in all classes other than Class I, to assist them to find new livelihoods if their present ones fail. Maternity grant, provision for widowhood and separation and qualification for retirement pensions will be secured to all persons in Class III by virtue of their husbands' contributions; in addition to maternity grant, housewives who take paid work will receive maternity benefit for thirteen weeks to enable them to give up working before and after childbirth.

(vi) Unemployment benefit, disability benefit, basic retirement pension after a transition period, and training benefit will be at the same rate, irrespective of previous earnings. This rate will provide by itself the income necessary for subsistence in all normal cases. There will be a joint rate for a man and wife who is not gainfully occupied. Where there is no wife or she is gainfully occupied, there will be a lower single rate; where there is no wife but a dependant above the age for children's allowance, there will be a dependant allowance. Maternity benefit for housewives who work also for gain will be at a higher rate than the single rate in unemployment or disability, while their unemployment and disability benefit will be at a lower rate; there are special rates also for widowhood as described below. With these exceptions all rates of benefit will be the same for men and for women. Disability due to industrial accident or disease will be treated like all other disability for the first thirteen weeks; if disability continues thereafter, disability benefit at a flat rate will be replaced by an industrial pension related to the earnings of the individual subject to a minimum and a maximum.

(vii) Unemployment benefit will continue at the same rate without means test so long as unemployment lasts, but will normally be subject to a condition of attendance at a work or training centre after a certain period. Disability benefit will continue at the same rate without means test, so long as disability lasts or till it is replaced by industrial pension, subject to acceptance of suitable medical treatment or vocational training.

(viii) Pensions (other than industrial) will be paid only on retirement from work. They may be claimed at any time after the minimum age of retirement, that is 65 for men and 60 for women. The rate of pension will be increased above the basic rate if retirement is postponed. Contributory pensions as of right will be raised to the full basic rate gradually during a transition period of twenty years, in which adequate pensions according to needs will be paid to all persons requiring them. The position of existing pensioners will be safeguarded.

(ix) While permanent pensions will no longer be granted to widows of working age without dependent children, there will be for all widows a temporary benefit at a higher rate than unemployment or disability benefit, followed by training benefit where necessary. For widows with the care of dependent children there will be guardian benefit, in addition to the children's allowances, adequate for subsistence without other means. The position of existing widows on pension will be safeguarded.

(x) For the limited number of cases of need not covered by social insurance, national assistance subject to a uniform means test will be available.

(xi) Medical treatment covering all requirements will be provided for all citizens by a national health service organised under the health departments and post-medical rehabilitation treatment will be provided for all persons capable of profiting by it.

(xii) A Ministry of Social Security will be established, responsible for social insurance, national assistance and encouragement and supervision of voluntary insurance and will take over, so far as necessary for these purposes, the present work of other Government Departments and of Local Authorities in these fields.

Under the scheme of social insurance, which forms the main feature of this plan, every citizen of working age will contribute in his appropriate class according to the security that he needs, or as a married woman will have contributions made by the husband. Each will be covered for all his needs by a single weekly contribution on one insurance document. All the principal cash payments—for unemployment, disability and retirement will continue so long as the need lasts, without means test, and will be paid from a Social Insurance Fund built up by contributions from the insured persons, from their employers, if any, and from the State. . . .

Social security as used in this Report means assurance of a certain income. The Plan for Social Security set out in the Report is a plan to win freedom from want by maintaining incomes. But sufficiency of income is not sufficient in itself. Freedom from want is only one of the essential freedoms of mankind. Any Plan for Social Security in the narrow sense assumes a concerted social policy in many fields, most of which it would be inappropriate to discuss in this Report. The plan proposed here involves three particular assumptions so closely related to it that brief discussion is essential for understanding of the plan itself. . . .

The first of three assumptions underlying the Plan for Social Security is a general scheme of children's allowances. This means that direct provision for the maintenance of dependent children will be made by payment of allowances to those responsible for the care of those children. . . .

As to the source of children's allowances, the view taken here is that they should be non-contributory, provided wholly out of taxation, and not to any extent out of insurance contributions. . . .

The second of the three assumptions [comprehensive health and rehabilitation services] has two sides to it. It covers a national health service for prevention and for cure of disease and disability by medical treatment; it covers rehabilitation and fitting for employment by treatment which will be both medical and post-medical. . . .

The first part of Assumption B is that a comprehensive national health service will ensure that for every citizen there is available whatever medical treatment he requires, in whatever form he requires it, domiciliary or institutional, general, specialist or consultant, and will ensure also the provision of dental, ophthalmic and surgical appliances, nursing and midwifery and rehabilitation after accidents. Whether or not payment towards the cost of the health service is included in the social insurance contribution, the service itself should

(i) be organised, not by the Ministry concerned with social insurance, but by Departments responsible for the health of the people and for positive and preventive as well as curative measures;

(ii) be provided where needed without contribution conditions in any individual case.

Restoration of a sick person to health is a duty of the State and the sick person, prior to any other consideration. . . .

Assumption C [maintenance of employment] does not imply complete abolition of unemployment. In industries subject to seasonal influences, irregularities of work are inevitable; in an economic system subject to change and progress, fluctuations in the fortunes of individual employers or of particular industries are inevitable; the possibility of controlling completely the major alternations of good trade and bad trade which are described under the term of the trade cycle has not been established; a country like Britain, which must have exports to pay for its raw materials, cannot be immune from the results of changes of fortune or of economic policy in other countries. The Plan for Social Security provides benefit for a substantial volume of unemployment. In the industries now subject to unemployment insurance, the finance of the Unemployment Fund has been based by the Unemployment Insurance Statutory Committee on the assumption of an average rate of unemployment through good years and bad of about 15 per cent. In framing the Social Security Budget . . . it has been assumed that, in the industries now subject to insurance, the average rate of unemployment will in future be about 10 per cent and that over the whole body of insured employees in Class I unemployment will average about 8½ per cent. It is right to hope that unemployment can be reduced to below that level, in which case more money will be available in the Social Insurance Fund either for better benefits or for reduction of contributions. But it would not be prudent to assume any lower rate of unemployment in preparing the Security Budget. Assumption C requires not the abolition of all unemployment, but the abolition of mass unemployment and of unemployment prolonged year after year for the same individual. In the beginning of compulsory unemployment insurance in 1913 and 1914, it was found that less than 5 per cent of all the unemployment experienced in the insured industries occurred after men had been unemployed for as long as 15 weeks. Even if it does not prove possible to get back to that level of employment, it should be possible to make unemployment of any individual for more than 26 weeks continuously a rare thing in normal times. . . .

The argument of this section can be summed up briefly. Abolition of want cannot be brought about merely by increasing production, without seeing to correct distribution of the product; but correct distribution does not mean what it has often been taken to mean in the past—distribution between the different agents in production, between land, capital, management and labour. Better distribution of purchasing power is required among wage-earners themselves, as between times of earning and not earning, and between times of heavy family responsibilities and of light or no family responsibilities. Both social insurance and children's allowances are primarily methods of re-distributing wealth. Such better distribution cannot fail to add to welfare and, properly designed, it can increase wealth, by maintaining physical vigour. It does not decrease wealth, unless it involves waste in administration or reduces incentives to production. Unemployment and disability are already being paid for unconsciously; it is no addition to the burden on the community to provide for them consciously. Unified social insurance will eliminate a good deal of waste inherent in present methods. Properly designed, controlled and financed, it need have no depressing effect on incentive.

Want could have been abolished in Britain just before the present war. It can be abolished after the war, unless the British people are and remain very much poorer then than they were before, that is to say unless they remain less productive than they and their fathers were. There is no sense in believing, contrary to experience, that they will and must be less productive. The answer to the question whether freedom from want should be regarded as a post-war aim capable of early attainment is an affirmative. . . .

43. Planning and Economic Growth: The Example of France

At the beginning of 1946 the French government established a Planning Commission, headed by the businessman Jean Monnet. It brought together representatives of capital and labor, and technicians to draft a four-year plan for reconstruction and to modernize and develop the French economy. The plan, generally called the Monnet Plan, was completed in the fall of 1946. It represented a break with traditional French attitudes in its proposal to merge reconstruction into general economic growth by concentrating investment at key points and by substantial government direction. It set as a goal for 1952 a 14 per cent increase in the gross national product above the 1929 level, to be achieved by planned investment in six key industrial sectors. The system of planning developed in France by the technicians of the Planning Commission was not a centralized production program but rather "indicative planning." It set production goals and then used the weapons of government investment and fiscal policy to encourage private enterprise to work toward those goals. By the mid-1950's France had emerged from its prolonged economic stagnation and had entered upon steady yet venturesome growth. The followng documet is an excerpt from Parts I and II of the Monnet Plan.

The Monnet Plan, 1946

I

Two WARS and a prolonged economic crisis between them have caused our country to lose a large part of the accumulated reserves that permitted it to enjoy a standard of living greater than its [economic] activity and the product of its labor would merit.

On the eve of the second world conflagration nearly one-third of our industrial capacity was idle. The spirit of enterprise was weakened to the point where investment scarcely covered replacement needs. In agriculture as well as in industry the productivity of labor was generally lower than in countries with modern plant and equipment.

As a result of our reduced efficiency and of unemployment, real

Source: *Rapport général sur le Premier Plan de Modernisation et d'équipement* (Paris: Commissariat général du Plan de modernisation et d'équipement, 1947), pp. 9–34, with deletions. Translated by the editors.

wages and living conditions in France were noticeably inferior to those in other countries. Although mediocre, this standard of living was not earned by actual production; the income from our foreign investments was used to pay for from 20 to 25 per cent of our purchases abroad. In other words, we were living on the savings of earlier generations.

The conflict that has just ended destroyed part of our fixed capital and required us to liquidate the greater part of our liquid assets in gold and currency. In the years to come France will have nothing to live on but the product of its labor. A number of resources of vital necessity are lacking in our country, and we must export the useful in order to procure the indispensable. The labor of Frenchmen, after the short respite that foreign credits and the utilization of our last reserves will give us, will become their only resource. In order to prevent an unacceptable lowering of the standard of living, their effort must be made as efficient as possible; that is to say, each hour of labor in France must create the maximum of production, both in agriculture and industry.

As regards its productivity, France, which was already outdistanced before the war, has fallen even farther behind because of the conflict. While the destruction, the privations of the population, the failure to renew plant and equipment, the break of communications with the outside world aggravated the weakness of its productivity, that of other countries continued to progress at a tempo accelerated by the very requirements of war. Most notably, in the United States an industrial revolution has taken place that is even more extensive than that of the First World War. Of course, these improvements have had as yet only limited effects on peacetime production, but the expansion of economic power is gigantic. Finally, the Second World War has accelerated the industrialization of the new nations that was initiated by the First.

This is why it is essential to increase our productivity and, in order to do that, to modernize and mechanize our economy. Certainly, we would not attempt to increase it overnight to the level of the most advanced countries, but the distance that separates us from them is only partially a result of natural factors. It is in our power to come considerably closer to them. By taking advantage of the technological progress these countries have made and by adapting our activities more to our aptitudes, French agriculture and industry could become competitive in world markets. Thus a durable equilibrium in our balance of payments could be re-established—one that would correspond to the realities of our new situation, but would nevertheless permit an increasing improvement in living conditions.

In view of the prime need to increase productivity, the modernization we must undertake should not consist solely of a renovation of the means of production. In a great many cases, it is the methods that have to be rejuvenated, eventually by a transformation of the economic structure. Following the example of what has for a long time been the case abroad in both agriculture and industry, closer relations must in particular be established between scientific research and its practical applications. But if our country does not itself participate in the work of discovery that is being carried out in the world, its equipment, even modernized on the basis of present techniques, will rapidly become obsolete once more.

In general, efficiency must be a primary concern throughout the economy. Modernization is not a condition of things; it is a condition of mind.

Such a renovation of our methods and of our means of production is not an enterprise that France can adopt or reject as it chooses. It is a necessity for which there is no alternative but decadence. . . .

The War of 1939 to 1945 spread its ravages across the entire country. Of 90 departments, 79 have been classified as damaged, and none of the remaining 11 has been entirely spared. By contrast, from 1914 to 1918 only one-sixth were devastated. Also a comparison of the balance sheet of the two wars shows that twice as many buildings were damaged [in the second]. . . .

In quantity and in value the losses are relatively even higher. Whereas the damages of 1914 to 1918, with the exception of the coal mines and certain cities of the North, were primarily to old buildings in rural areas, the military operations of 1940 and 1944 and 1945, as well as aerial bombardments, affected urban centers principally. It is clear that France has had its economic equilibrium more severely disrupted by destruction in the majority of its important centers, which hit its essential industries and centers of communication with such precision, than by the blind but limited destruction of a war of position. . . .

Only by modernizing and developing the construction industry and those industries that govern its activity (metallurgy, building materials, transportation) will it be possible to construct more, better, more quickly, and at lower cost. If this is done, we may hope to repair all of the war-damaged buildings in seven or eight years and, at the same time, to broaden the work of reconstruction into a general policy of expansion and renovation of French dwellings, in the countryside as well as in the cities. The modernization of the means of production is thus not only the indispensable condition of rapid reconstruction, but also the remedy for one of the most serious social liabilities of the interwar period. . . .

Another fundamental task is to provide an uninterrupted improvement in the living conditions of the population, at first in comparison with the prewar standard, but later in such a way that all Frenchmen can share, thanks to an equitable distribution of income, in the material advantages enjoyed by the populations of the most progressive countries. . . .

Technical capacity and the industry of French workers is in every way equal to that of foreign workers. But, as has been demonstrated by the work of the Modernization Commissions, capital in the form of agricultural and industrial equipment has been insufficient in France since before the war and the organization of production only too often archaic. This has not permitted the labor force to operate with as much effectiveness or efficiency as in Great Britain or the United States. As a result, a French worker produces in the same unit of time about three times less than an American worker and one and one-half times less than a British worker (of course, these comparisons are only averages). This is why the real per capita income, which measures the standard of living, places France far behind many other countries. . . .

France, a country with an aging population, has seen its birth rate climb since 1942, so that in 1945, for the first time in half a century, it equaled the mortality rate. If this recovery continues, the active population, diminished by the war, will have to support at the same time more aged and more children. For at least a score of years our country will have to bear not only the consequences of its previous population decline, which kept the French population perceptibly below the optimum level—that is, the level that would have allowed to everyone a maximum of well-being—but also the increased burdens implied in the reversal of that trend. There is in particular a need to educate a more numerous group of young people in order to prepare them for later increases in productivity. . . .

Before the war our exports abroad paid for only two-thirds of

Country	Last Year for which Figures Available	Per Capita Income[1]
New Zealand	1937	1,702
United States	1937	1,485
Canada	1936	1,352
Great Britain	1937	1,275
Australia	1937	1,212
Switzerland	1936	1,036
Germany	1937	828
Sweden	1938	804
Norway	1937	705
Denmark	1933	679
Netherlands	1934	662
France	1934	641

our imports. If our country succeeded in covering the chronic deficit in its trade balance, that was largely due to foreign investments. Nearly two-thirds of the deficit was met by the income from foreign investments, of which the greater part had been made before 1914.

But we had to liquidate our public holdings in gold and foreign exchange, with the exception of the minimum deposits necessary to avoid jolts in our foreign payments. The mobilization of private holdings would bring us only a brief respite, and with their liquidation the income they produce would disappear as well.

Within a brief period, then, we shall no longer be able to pay for imports except by means of exports (the income from tourism roughly corresponds to shipping costs and noncommercial accounts). . . .

The assistance of foreigners is essential until we arrive at the point where our exports pay for our imports entirely and until the income from tourism returns to the level of the best prewar years. But that point must be reached as soon as possible, or we shall

[1] Expressed in international units (the average amount of goods and services that a dollar would purchase in the United States during the period 1925 to 1934). The authors of the Plan point out that the gap between France and Britain was not so great as the figures suggest; 1937 was a relatively good year in Britain, but 1934 represented the depth of the Depression for France.—Eds.

acquire a massive indebtedness, which would threaten us with servitude.

For France, in its new situation of debtor nation, "economic independence" means therefore the export of a quantity of merchandise sufficient to pay for our imports. . . .

This is all the more true because, contrary to a generally held belief, our luxury exports, for which considerations of price are less important, play only a secondary role in our foreign trade. In 1938 they represented less than 10 per cent of the total value of our exports.

Our large export industries, textiles and manufactured products in particular, must lower their costs of production to the international standard. An increase in the productivity of labor is the sole means of achieving this, even while progressively raising real wages. . . .

In conclusion, it cannot be said that France has a choice to make, because there is no choice for her except between a gradual decadence and immediate action.

The only way open to us is that of modernization and mechanization; the only question to be answered is how rapidly we will undertake it. . . .

II

The French economy, being limited by its resources, must immediately undertake the necessary action to develop the economy according to a coherent plan; must make the best use possible of the means available; must increase key resources to the maximum; must utilize its disposable national resources in an order of priority that reflects the exigencies of the situation.

Because of the straining of all its essential activities, which make demands on common and limited resources (power, steel, foreign exchange, labor), the work of modernization cannot be properly carried on by isolated and unco-ordinated efforts. If the French are to succeed, they must undertake modernization with a common perspective, in order that each can be assured of the support of others and that inadequacies in one sector or another will not retard general progress. We must therefore act on the basis of a plan that the entire nation fully accepts.

Such a plan (and it is in this spirit that the first plan for modernization here proposed was formulated) is essentially *a method of unifying our activity* and the means by which each can relate his effort to the whole. In an economy like ours, which contains both a nationalized sector and a large free-enterprise sector, the plan must apply at the same time to services of the state and to private enterprises and consequently must be *as much a plan of guidance as of prescription*. What is most important is to permit both [sectors] to give their maximum effort.

This plan is not to be merely a simple collection of partial plans. It will integrate their objectives and means in a general scheme. In this it differs from previous programs of public works as well as from certain partial plans developed since the Liberation. Both kinds were technical and considered only one sector of industry or communications.

In a time of scarcity such as the present, it appears to be increasingly indispensable to co-ordinate [state and private enterprise] and also to view them from the point of view of the whole. In fact they are at once competing and complementary. We must assure that a satisfactory balance is maintained between the limited resources available and the needs of all the interested parties. By establishing objectives that will serve as guides to the efforts of all, and by coordinating the means to be employed to attain them, the plan will be as it should the instrument of co-ordinating activity. . . .

Above all, when the first imperative is to produce and to produce rapidly, it is necessary to make the most of existing potential. This is also the way to achieve quickly a higher level of productivity and well-being. The activities that have been previously developed in France, save a few exceptions, are best suited to the natural and human conditions of the country. One of the essential conclusions of the Modernization Commissions is *that there are in France few industries in the broad sense of the term that could not, by means of continued but short-term effort, be made competitive in world markets*. This is especially true of agriculture, which is and will remain by far the largest French industry. . . .

Inasmuch as modernization consists in large part in a renovation not only of production techniques but also of managerial methods, in both public and private sectors, the mass of equipment required in the form of machines, of plant, and of public works will necessarily be very great. At the outset we will benefit from the importation of machinery that will permit us to spread the effort over the longest number of years and to lighten its burden. But, at best, we cannot hope that foreign aid will substantially exceed 10 per cent of the total necessary investment.

We must count primarily on ourselves. The drafting of an investment plan is thus required as part of a vigorous production plan, in order that the French economy can provide at the same time both the capital goods of which it has need and the increasing supply of consumer goods essential to the production effort. . . .

That is why the Planning Council [*Conseil du Plan*] recognized, at its opening session, that it was imperative to increase the volume of French production in 1950 to an average level higher than the maximum achieved in the past, that is, the 1929 level.

The following stages have been suggested: that the 1938 level be attained by the end of 1946; that toward the middle of 1948 the 1929 level, which was about one-quarter higher than in 1938, be reached; and finally to surpass the 1929 level by 25 per cent in 1950.

There may be debate over whether it is preferable to develop or create one industry sooner than some other, what levels should be proposed for various agricultural products, how rapidly to proceed with reconstruction, etc. . . . , but it is obvious that the expansion of production, no matter what its orientation, will require considerably increased quantities of coal, electricity, steel, and cement, an agriculture sufficiently mechanized to assure the population adequate nourishment, and, finally, appropriate transportation facilities. The maximum development of these key resources, without which no general economic development is possible, must be the primary objective of the plan. . . .

In spite of the general expansion of domestic production that will take place in the coming years, availability of resources will remain limited throughout the entire period, as much because of the delays resulting from the development of basic industry as because of the extent of our needs. As a result, between now and 1950 these resources must be employed according to an order of priorities that corresponds to the hierarchy of tasks. The French economy will live and develop under a system of priorities demanding constant arbitration.

The fundamental tasks of the French economy and the particular requirements of the next few years dictate the specific goals to be attained and the function of the first modernization plan. Everything cannot be done at once. The tasks and requirements indicated in the plan are to be implemented according to the following scheme:

(a) To modernize the six basic sectors: *coal, electricity, metallurgy, cement, agricultural machinery, and transportation* and to increase considerably their production or activity, on which the life of the nation depends and which determines the development of the entire economy.

(b) To undertake and to promote the modernization of *agriculture* in order to improve the nutritional level of the population as rapidly as possible and to ease our foreign balance of trade. . . .

(c) To make maximum use of available resources in order to accelerate *reconstruction* and, to that end, to modernize the construction industry and to increase the production of building materials. . . .

Establishing priorities in reconstruction will, nevertheless, be inevitable. Priority must be given to providing lodgings for the homeless and to all that is vital for the national economy. That includes not only industrial and agricultural buildings but also the housing necessary to the growth of production, especially in the basic sectors. In several essential industries (coal, metallurgy, textiles, etc.) the rapid construction of workers' housing is essential to solving the labor problem, which is the most critical of all those that the French economy must face during the next four years.

(d) To develop our exports, at first by taking advantage of the exceptional shortage of goods existing in the world, later by the lowering of production costs through modernization and increased output. The *export industries*, especially those sections of manufacturing and textiles whose activity is directed toward foreign markets, must likewise enjoy a very high priority in the distribution of available resources.

(e) To increase to the maximum, through modernization, the production of *industries that provide the equipment* for the above-mentioned activities, as well as for those that produce essential consumer goods. . . .

The plan for modernization and mechanization for 1947 to 1950 submitted to the Council has as its essential objectives to assure a rapid rise in the standard of living of the population and especially its nourishment; to modernize and mechanize basic industry (coal, electricity, metallurgy, cement, agricultural machinery, and transportation); to modernize agriculture; to make available the maximum resources for reconstruction while, nevertheless, not losing sight of the needs of basic industry and the need for modernizing the building-materials and construction industries; to modernize and to develop export industries in order to assure equilibrium in the balance of payments in 1950. The point of departure will thus be established for undertaking, in a second stage, the transformation of living conditions, especially housing.

The implementation of the plan presented requires:

(a) Fixing the *goals* of production or activity for 1950 in the principal branches of the economy, including reconstruction. The goals of this first plan are based essentially on the limits imposed by the resources that can be made available between the present and 1950;

(b) Adopting immediately the programs of production and modernization for each of the years 1947, 1948, 1949, and 1950 for the six basic industries, coal, electricity, metallurgy, cement, agricultural machinery, and inland transport, and putting them into practice immediately for the period as a whole by granting them from now on the means they require;

(c) Continuing or initiating the necessary measures, in France as well as abroad, to secure in the course of the next few years the essential resources (power, ferrous metals, foreign exchange, manpower) in quantities sufficient to achieve the goals set for 1950;

(d) Determining in due time, each year for the following year (as is now the case for 1947) the *annual programs* of production, modernization, reconstruction, investment, imports, etc. These programs established within the framework of the goals set for 1950 depend upon material means (whose availability can be reasonably predicted), on the progress of the basic programs, on the results obtained in practice (the necessary complement to the common resources of all spheres of activity), on experience, and on the progress of modernization and productivity in the various sectors;

(e) Putting into practice the *methods* that will permit the continued development of the plan and its adaptation to circumstances, as well as those methods that will assure its execution. These methods must be inspired by those adopted to establish the proposals made in the present report. A collective endeavor must have a collective organization and constant collective consultations.

44. European Economic Cooperation

The first step toward postwar European economic cooperation was the "Benelux" customs union among Belgium, The Netherlands, and Luxembourg, created in 1944. Four years later the Organization for European Economic Cooperation, composed of sixteen (later eighteen) nations, cut quota restrictions on trade and set up a European Payments Union to facilitate transfers. Then in 1951 Belgium, France, Italy, Luxembourg, The Netherlands, and West Germany signed a treaty (ratified in 1952) joining them together in a European Coal and Steel Community. It was created in response to an apparent overcapacity in steel, but, rather than restricting production as was done in the 1920's, it sought to utilize production fully and even to expand it by eliminating trade barriers and co-ordinating production. By 1955, the success of the ECSC in increasing trade in steel led to discussions between the member nations for further cooperation. The Treaty of Rome, signed in March, 1957, created a European Economic Community, generally called the Common Market. Its first goal was to create a large trading area through a customs union, free of internal tariffs and presenting a uniform tariff to nonmember states. But it also provided for broader economic cooperation in the shape of free movement of capital and labor and in uniform institutions and integrated economic policies. Although there remained differences in economic interest among the member states, the detailed and binding clauses of the Treaty reflect how far Europe had advanced along the road to economic integration. There follow some of the most important clauses of the Treaty.

Excerpts from the Treaty of Rome, 1957

Article 1

BY THE present Treaty, the High Contracting Parties [Belgium, West Germany, France, Italy, Luxembourg and The Netherlands] establish among themselves a EUROPEAN ECONOMIC COMMUNITY.

Article 2

It shall be the aim of the Community, by establishing a Common Market and progressively approximating the economic policies of

Source: *Treaty Establishing the European Economic Community* (Brussels: Secretariat of the Interim Committee for the Common Market and Euratom, 1957), pp. 17–183, with deletions.

Member States, to promote throughout the Community a harmonious development of economic activities, a continuous and balanced expansion, an increased stability, an accelerated raising of the standard of living and closer relations between its Member States.

Article 3

For the purposes set out in the preceding Article, the activities of the Community shall include, under the conditions and with the timing provided for in this Treaty:

(a) the elimination, as between Member States, of customs duties and of quantitative restrictions in regard to the importation and exportation of goods, as well as of all other measures with equivalent effect;

(b) the establishment of a common customs tariff and a common commercial policy towards third countries;

(c) the abolition, as between Member States, of the obstacles to the free movement of persons, services and capital;

(d) the inauguration of a common agricultural policy;

(e) the inauguration of a common transport policy;

(f) the establishment of a system ensuring that competition shall not be distorted in the Common Market;

(g) the application of procedures which shall make it possible to co-ordinate the economic policies of Member States and to remedy disequilibria in their balances of payments;

(h) the approximation of their respective municipal law to the extent necessary for the functioning of the Common Market;

(i) the creation of a European Social Fund in order to improve the possibilities of employment for workers and to contribute to the raising of their standard of living;

(j) the establishment of a European Investment Bank intended to facilitate the economic expansion of the Community through the creation of new resources; and

(k) the association of overseas countries and territories with the Community with a view to increasing trade and to pursuing jointly their effort towards economic and social development.

Article 4

1. The achievement of the tasks entrusted to the Community shall be ensured by: AN ASSEMBLY, a COUNCIL, a COMMISSION, a COURT OF JUSTICE.

Each of these institutions shall act within the limits of the powers conferred upon it by this Treaty. . . .[1]

Article 6

1. Member States, acting in close collaboration with the institutions of the Community, shall co-ordinate their respective economic policies to the extent that is necessary to attain the objectives of this Treaty.
2. The institutions of the Community shall take care not to prejudice the internal and external financial stability of Member States.
. . .

Article 8

1. The Common Market shall be progressively established in the course of a transitional period of twelve years.

The transitional period shall be divided into three stages of four years each; the length of each stage may be modified in accordance with the provisions set out below.

2. To each stage there shall be allotted a group of actions which shall be undertaken and pursued concurrently.

3. Transition from the first to the second stage shall be conditional upon a confirmatory statement to the effect that the essence of the objectives specifically laid down in this Treaty for the first stage has been in fact achieved and that, subject to the exceptions and procedures provided for in this Treaty, the obligations have been observed.

This statement shall be made at the end of the fourth year by the Council acting by means of a unanimous vote on a report of the Commission. The invocation by a Member State of the non-fulfilment of its own obligations shall not, however, be an obstacle to a

---

[1] The Assembly is the deliberative body of the Community, composed of delegates appointed by the legislatures of member states, with greatest representation going to the larger states. The Council is the executive of the Community, composed of one representative appointed by the government of each member state, but on crucial matters it votes by "qualified majority" (the votes of Germany, France, and Italy counting as four, those of Belgium and The Netherlands as two, and that of Luxembourg as one). The Commission is, in effect, the civil service of the Community. The Court has the power of review over actions of member states falling under the Treaty.—Eds.

unanimous vote. Failing a unanimous vote, the first stage shall automatically be extended for a period of one year.

At the end of the fifth year, the Council shall make such confirmatory statement under the same conditions. Failing a unanimous vote, the first stage shall automatically be extended for a further period of one year.

At the end of the sixth year, the Council shall make such a statement acting by means of a qualified majority vote on a report of the Commission. . . .

Article 9

1. The Community shall be based upon a customs union covering the exchange of all goods and comprising both the prohibition, as between Member States, of customs duties on importation and exportation and all charges with equivalent effect and the adoption of a common customs tariff in their relations with third countries. . . .

Article 12

Member States shall refrain from introducing, as between themselves, any new customs duties on importation or exportation or charges with equivalent effect and from increasing such duties or charges as they apply in their commercial relations with each other.

Article 13

1. Customs duties on importation in force between Member States shall be progressively abolished by them in the course of the transitional period. . . .
2. Charges in force between Member States having an effect equivalent to customs duties on importation shall be progressively abolished by them in the course of the transitional period. . . .

Article 14

1. In respect of each product, the basic duty which shall be subject to the successive reductions shall be the duty applied on 1 January 1957.
2. The timing of the reductions shall be as follows:

(*a*) in the course of the first stage, the first reduction shall be made one year after the date of the entry into force of this Treaty; the second reduction shall be made eighteen months later; the third, at the end of the fourth year after the date of the entry into force of this Treaty;

(*b*) in the course of the second stage, a reduction shall be made eighteen months after the beginning of that stage; a second reduction, eighteen months after the preceding one; a third reduction shall be made one year later; and

(*c*) the reductions which still remain to be made shall be carried out in the course of the third stage; the Council, acting by means of a qualified majority vote on a proposal of the Commission, shall fix their timing by means of directives. . . .

6. Member States shall . . . endeavour to ensure that the reduction applied to the duties on each product shall amount: at the end of the first stage to at least 25 per cent of the basic duty; and at the end of the second stage to at least 50 per cent of the basic duty. . . .

Article 18

Member States hereby declare their willingness to contribute to the development of international commerce and the reduction of barriers to trade by entering into reciprocal and mutually advantageous arrangements directed to the reduction of custom duties below the general level which they could claim as a result of the establishment of a customs union between themselves.

Article 19

1. . . . The duties under the common customs tariff shall be at the level of the arithmetical average of the duties applied in the four customs territories covered by the Community.

2. The duties taken into account for calculating this average shall be those applied by Member States on 1 January 1957. . . .

Article 30

Quantitative restrictions on importation and all measures with equivalent effect shall . . . hereby be prohibited between Member States. . . .

Article 38

1. The Common Market shall extend to agriculture and trade in agricultural products. Agricultural products shall mean the products of the soil, of stock-breeding and of fisheries as well as products after the first processing stage which are directly connected with such products. . . . .

4. The functioning and development of the Common Market in respect of agricultural products shall be accompanied by the establishment of a common agricultural policy among the Member States.

Article 39

1. The common agricultural policy shall have as its objectives:

(*a*) to increase agricultural productivity by developing technical progress and by ensuring the rational development of agricultural production and the optimum utilisation of the factors of production, particularly labour;

(*b*) to ensure thereby a fair standard of living for the agricultural population, particularly by the increasing of the individual earnings of persons engaged in agriculture;

(*c*) to stabilise markets;

(*d*) to guarantee regular supplies; and

(*e*) to ensure reasonable prices in supplies to consumers.

2. In working out the common agricultural policy and the special methods which it may involve, due account shall be taken of:

(*a*) the particular character of agricultural activities, arising from the social structure of agriculture and from structural and natural disparities between the various agricultural regions;

(*b*) the need to make the appropriate adjustments gradually; and

(*c*) the fact that in Member States agriculture constitutes a sector which is closely linked with the economy as a whole.

Article 40

1. Member States shall gradually develop the common agricultural policy during the transitional period and shall establish it not later than at the end of that period.

2. With a view to achieving the objectives set out in Article 39, a common organisation of agricultural markets shall be effected.

This organisation shall take one of the following forms according to the products concerned:

(*a*) common rules concerning competition;

(*b*) compulsory co-ordination of the various national market organisations; or

(*c*) a European market organisation.

3. The common organisation in one of the forms mentioned in paragraph 2 may comprise all measures necessary to achieve the objectives set out in Article 39, in particular, price controls, subsidies as to the production and marketing of various products, arrangements for stock-piling and carry-forward, and common machinery for stabilising importation or exportation. . . .

Article 48

1. The free movement of workers shall be ensured within the Community not later than at the date of the expiry of the transitional period.

2. This shall involve the abolition of any discrimination based on nationality between workers of the Member States as regards employment, remuneration, and other working conditions.

3. It shall include the right, subject to limitations justified by reasons of public order, public safety and public health:

(*a*) to accept offers of employment actually made;

(*b*) to move about freely for this purpose within the territory of Member States;

(*c*) to stay in any Member State in order to carry on an employment in conformity with the legislative and administrative provisions governing the employment of the workers of that State; and

(*d*) to live, on conditions which shall be the subject of implementing regulations to be laid down by the Commission, in the territory of a Member State after having been employed there. . . .

Article 52

Within the framework of the provisions set out below, restrictions on the freedom of establishment of nationals of a Member State in the territory of another Member State shall be progressively abolished in the course of the transitional period. Such progressive abolition shall also extend to restrictions on the setting up of agencies, branches or subsidiaries by nationals of any Member State established in the territory of any Member State. . . .

Freedom of establishment shall include the right to engage in and carry on non-wage-earning activities, and also to set up and manage enterprises and, in particular, companies within the meaning of Article 58, second paragraph, under the conditions laid down by the law of the country of establishment for its own nationals, subject to the provisions . . . relating to capital. . . .

Article 59

. . . Restrictions on the free supply of services within the Community shall be progressively abolished in the course of the transitional period in respect of nationals of Member States who are established in a State of the Community other than that of the person to whom the services are supplied.

The Council, acting by means of a unanimous vote on a proposal of the Commission, may extend the benefit of the provisions . . . to cover services supplied by nationals of any third country who are established within the Community.

Article 60

Services within the meaning of this Treaty shall be deemed to be services normally supplied for remuneration, to the extent that they are not governed by the provisions relating to the free movement of goods, capital and persons.

Services shall include in particular: (a) activities of an industrial character; (b) activities of a commercial character; (c) artisan activities; and (d) activities of the liberal professions.

Without prejudice to the provisions . . . relating to the right of establishment, a person supplying a service may, in order to carry out that service, temporarily exercise his activity in the State where the service is supplied, under the same conditions as are imposed by that State on its own nationals. . . .

Article 67

1. Member States shall, in the course of the transitional period and to the extent necessary for the proper functioning of the Common Market, progressively abolish as between themselves restrictions on the movement of capital belonging to persons resident in Member States and also any discriminatory treatment based on the nation-

ality or place of residence of the parties or on the place in which such capital is invested. . . .

Article 74

The objectives of this Treaty shall, with regard to the subject covered by this Title, be pursued by the Member States within the framework of a common transport policy [for rail, road and inland water transport]. . . .

Article 79

1. Any discrimination which consists in the application by a carrier, in respect of the same goods conveyed in the same circumstances, of transport rates and conditions which differ on the ground of the country of origin or destination of the goods carried, shall be abolished in the traffic within the Community not later than at the end of the second stage. . . .

Article 81

Charges or dues collected by a carrier, in addition to the transport rates, for the crossing of frontiers, shall not exceed a reasonable level, due account being taken of real costs actually incurred by such crossing.

Member States shall endeavour to reduce these costs progressively.

The Commission may make recommendations to Member States with a view to the application of this Article. . . .

Article 85

1. The following shall be deemed to be incompatible with the Common Market and shall hereby be prohibited: any agreement between enterprises, any decisions by associations of enterprises and any concerted practices which are likely to affect trade between the Member States and which have as their object or result the prevention, restriction or distortion of competition within the Common Market, in particular those consisting in:

(a) the direct or indirect fixing of purchase or selling prices or of any other trading conditions;

(b) the limitation or control of production, markets, technical development or investment;

(*c*) market-sharing or the sharing of sources of supply;

(*d*) the application to parties to transactions of unequal terms in respect of equivalent supplies, thereby placing them at a competitive disadvantage; or

(*e*) the subjecting of the conclusion of a contract to the acceptance by a party of additional supplies which, either by their nature or according to commercial usage, have no connection with the subject of such contract.

2. Any agreements or decisions prohibited pursuant to this Article shall be null and void. . . .

Article 92

1. Except where otherwise provided for in this Treaty, any aid, granted by a Member State or granted by means of State resources, in any manner whatsoever, which distorts or threatens to distort competition by favouring certain enterprises or certain productions shall, to the extent to which it adversely affects trade between Member States, be deemed to be incompatible with the Common Market. . . .

3. The following may be deemed to be compatible with the Common Market:

(*a*) aids intended to promote the economic development of regions where the standard of living is abnormally low or where there exists serious under-employment;

(*b*) aids intended to promote the execution of important projects of common European interest or to remedy a serious disturbance of the economy of a Member State;

(*c*) aids intended to facilitate the development of certain activities or of certain economic regions, provided that such aids do not change trading conditions to such a degree as would be contrary to the common interest. Any aids to shipbuilding existing on 1 January 1957 shall, to the extent that such aids merely offset the absence of customs protection, be progressively reduced under the same conditions as apply to the abolition of customs duties, subject to the provisions of this Treaty relating to the common commercial policy in regard to third countries. . . .

Article 99

The Commission shall consider in what way the law of the various Member States concerning turnover taxes, excise duties and other forms of indirect taxation, including compensatory measures applying to exchanges between Member States, can be harmonised in the interest of the Common Market. . . .

Article 100

The Council, acting by means of a unanimous vote on a proposal of the Commission, shall issue directives for the approximation of such legislative and administrative provisions of the Member States as have a direct incidence on the establishment or functioning of the Common Market. . . .

Article 103

1. Member States shall consider their policy relating to economic trends as a matter of common interest. They shall consult with each other and with the Commission on measures to be taken in response to current circumstances.
2. Without prejudice to any other procedures provided for in this Treaty, the Council may, by means of a unanimous vote on a proposal of the Commission, decide on measures appropriate to the situation.
3. The Council, acting by means of a qualified majority vote on a proposal of the Commission, shall, where necessary, issue any requisite directives concerning the particulars of application of the measures decided upon under the terms of paragraph 2.
4. The procedures provided for in this Article shall apply also in the event of difficulties arising in connection with the supply of certain products.

Article 104

Each Member State shall pursue the economic policy necessary to ensure the equilibrium of its overall balance of payments and to maintain confidence in its currency, while ensuring a high level of employment and the stability of the level of prices.

Article 105

1. In order to facilitate the attainment of the objectives stated in Article 104, Member States shall co-ordinate their economic policies. They shall for this purpose institute a collaboration between the competent services of their administrative departments and between their central banks. . . . .

Article 110

By establishing a customs union between themselves the Member States intend to contribute, in conformity with the common interest, to the harmonious development of world trade, the progressive abolition of restrictions on international exchanges and the lowering of customs barriers. . . .

Article 117

Member States hereby agree upon the necessity to promote improvement of the living and working conditions of labour so as to permit the equalisation of such conditions in an upward direction.

They consider that such a development will result not only from the functioning of the Common Market which will favour the harmonisation of social systems, but also from the procedures provided for under this Treaty and from the approximation of legislative and administrative provisions.

Article 118

Without prejudice to the other provisions of this Treaty and in conformity with its general objectives, it shall be the aim of the Commission to promote close collaboration between Member States in the social field, particularly in matters relating to: employment, labour legislation and working conditions, occupational and continuation training, social security, protection against occupational accidents and diseases, industrial hygiene, the law as to trade unions, and collective bargaining between employers and workers. . . .

Article 123

In order to improve opportunities of employment of workers in the Common Market and thus contribute to raising the standard of living, a European Social Fund shall hereby be established . . . : it shall have the task of promoting within the Community employment facilities and the geographical and occupational mobility of workers. . . .

Article 125

1. At the request of a Member State, the Fund shall . . . cover 50 per cent of expenses incurred after the entry into force of this

Treaty by that State or by a body under public law for the purpose of:

(*a*) ensuring productive re-employment of workers by means of: occupational re-training, resettlement allowances; and

(*b*) granting aids for the benefit of workers whose employment is temporarily reduced or wholly or partly suspended as a result of the conversion of their enterprise to other productions, in order that they may maintain the same wage-level pending their full re-employment. . . .

Article 129

A European Investment Bank having legal personality shall hereby be established.

The members of the European Investment Bank shall be the Member States. . . .

Article 130

The task of the European Investment Bank shall be to contribute, by calling on the capital markets and its own resources, to the balanced and smooth development of the Common Market in the interest of the Community. For this purpose, the Bank shall by granting loans and guarantees on a non-profit-making basis facilitate the financing of the following projects in all sectors of the economy:

(*a*) projects for developing less developed regions;

(*b*) projects for modernising or converting enterprises or for creating new activities which are called for by the progressive establishment of the Common Market where such projects by their size or nature cannot be entirely financed by the various means available in each of the Member States; and

(*c*) projects of common interest to several Member States which by their size or nature cannot be entirely financed by the various means available in each of the Member States. . . .

45. The Eastern European Experience: The Example of Poland

At the end of the war Poland faced the dual problem of reconstructing and transforming her economy. In the interwar period the largely agrarian economy had stagnated—on the eve of the war output per capita (and in some cases output on an absolute basis) was below the 1913 level—and private enterprise proved weak. Wartime devastation was extensive, estimated at 7 per cent of the total 1938 national wealth, and about 20 per cent of the population killed. The tremendous demands of reconstruction drew the state deeply into economic life. In January, 1946, a large part of Polish industry was nationalized, partly to take over former German assets, including those in the extensive territories annexed from Germany, but also with the purpose of pursuing a program of development. During the 1946 to 1948 period the mixed Polish economy recovered rapidly, although agricultural production remained low.

The character of economic development, however, was determined by the fact of Soviet domination. In 1949 and 1950, Sovietization of the Polish economy began in earnest with a Six Year Plan. As a result, growth in capital goods was rapid; by 1952 the proportion of national income produced by industry had risen from the 1939 level of 23 per cent to 43 per cent. The movement of labor from agriculture to industry was accelerated, but at the cost of both efficiency and the standard of living (which probably fell as much as 15 per cent by 1953). But by the early 1950's the worst phase of industrialization had passed. In July, 1956, the Central Committee of the Communist party surveyed the condition of the economy, concluded that the Stalinist pattern of development since 1949 had included serious "disproportions," and proposed to eliminate these in a new Five Year Plan. The first of the documents below includes the key sections of the 1946 law nationalizing industry. The second document is taken from the resolution of the Central Committee meeting in 1956.

A. Polish Law Nationalizing Industry, 1946

ARTICLE I. For the purpose of planned reconstruction of the national economy, in order to assure the economic sovereignty of

Source: Law Concerning the Nationalization of Basic Branches of the National Economy, January 3, 1946, in Samuel L. Sharp, *Nationalization of Key Industries in Eastern Europe* (Washington, D.C.: Foundation for Foreign Affairs, 1946), pp. 75–81, with deletions. Used by permission.

the State and raise the level of general welfare, the State takes over the ownership of undertakings on the basis of this law.

ARTICLE II. A. The State takes over, without compensation, industrial, mining, transportation, banking, insurance and commercial undertakings of:

1. the German Reich and the former Free City of Danzig;
2. citizens of the German Reich and of the former Free City of Danzig with the exception of persons of Polish nationality and of any other [nationality] persecuted by the Germans;
3. German and Danzig legal persons with the exception of legal persons of public law;
4. corporations controlled by German citizens or citizens of Danzig or by the German or Danzig administration;
5. persons who fled to the enemy. . . .

D. An undertaking defined under *A* is not taken over by the State or legal persons of public law provided:

1. it was seized and confiscated by the former occupation authorities, unless it had previously belonged to the Treasury or the above-mentioned legal persons or if the seizure or confiscation applied to undertakings of persons or corporations listed under *A* and *C* [referring to legal persons], or
2. it was ceded to persons and corporations mentioned under *A* and *C* after September 1, 1939, under the influence of threats so that the owner of the undertaking may claim nullification of the cession. . . .

ARTICLE III. A. The State takes over with compensation:

1. Mining and industrial undertakings in the following branches of the national economy:
   a. mines and mining rights subject to the regulations of the Mining Law;
   b. the petroleum industry including mines, refineries, gasoline plants and other processing works, pipe lines and the synthetic fuel industry;
   c. undertakings producing, processing, transmitting or distributing electric energy for gainful purposes or servicing public means of transportation using electric energy;
   d. undertakings producing, processing, transmitting, or distributing gas for industrial and household purposes;
   e. waterworks extending to more than one community (district waterworks);
   f. iron and light metal foundries;

g. plants of the armament, airplane and explosives industries;

h. cokeries;

i. industrial mills and refineries;

j. industrial distilleries, refineries of alcohol, and vodka factories;

k. breweries with a yearly production capacity over 15,000 hectolitres;

l. yeast factories;

m. corn mills with a capacity over 15 tons daily, calculated on the basis of the surface of the millstones;

n. oil plants with a yearly productive capacity over 500 tons and all refineries of edible fats;

o. cold storage establishments;

p. large and medium-sized textile industries;

q. printing establishments. . . .

2. Industrial undertakings not mentioned under 1, if they are capable of employing more than 50 employees per shift.

   a. Building construction and contracting enterprises regardless of the number of persons which they are capable of employing are exempted from the provision of this rule.

   b. An ordinance of the Council of Ministers may raise the lower limit of 50 employees in industries producing articles not considered of common use, or in little mechanized industries or [those] of a pioneer or seasonal character.

3. Transportation undertakings (normal and narrow-gauge railroads, electric railroads, air transportation).

4. Tele-communication undertakings (telephone, telegraph, radio).

B. Undertakings listed under *A-1* and belonging to municipalities, unions of municipalities, cooperatives or unions of cooperatives, are not taken over by the State. If the municipalities or cooperatives own only part of an undertaking or part of an interest in it, only the remaining part is taken over by the State.

C. A decision of the Council of Ministers, on the recommendation of the interested minister, may exempt individual undertakings or certain categories or groups of undertakings from the application of the provisions of sec. *A-1*.

D. Individual undertakings existing on the date of promulgation of this law and not subject to the provisions of sec. *A-1* may be taken over by the State on the basis of a decision of the Council of Ministers taken at the recommendation of the interested minister, if they hold an actual production monopoly on important branches of the national economy; in the same way may be taken over by the State banking establishments and special storage and transshipment installations, especially in harbors or connected with railroads and waterways. . . .

F. The decision to nationalize under the provisions of this article may be taken only up to December 31, 1946.

ARTICLE IV. The formation of new undertakings in the branches of industry and transportation, to which the provisions of Art. *III*, *A-1*, *3* and *4* apply, has as a condition precedent the granting of a concession by the appropriate minister, the Chairman of the Central Planning Office concurring.

ARTICLE V. A. The State may administer directly the nationalized undertakings or transfer them to municipalities or cooperatives or their unions on the basis of a decision of the Council of Ministers made on the recommendation of the appropriate minister. . . .

ARTICLE VII. A. The owner of an undertaking transferred to the State (Art. III) will receive from the Treasury compensation within one year from the day of the receipt by the owner of notification of the final determination of the amount of compensation awarded.

B. Compensation will in principle be paid in securities, and in exceptional, economically justified, cases may also be paid in cash or other values.

C. The amount of compensation will be determined by special commissions. Interested persons will have the right to participate in the proceedings of the commissions. Whenever necessary and at any rate at the request of interested persons, the commission will call appropriate experts. . . .

E. In the determination of compensation the following will be taken under consideration:

1. general decrease in value of the national wealth;
2. net value of the assets of the undertaking on the day of its transfer to the State;
3. decrease in value of the undertaking as a result of war losses and losses suffered in connection with the war and occupation in the period between September 1, 1939, and the time of transfer to the State;
4. the amount of investments made after September 1, 1939;
5. special factors affecting the value of the undertaking (duration of concessions, licenses, etc.).

F. An ordinance of the Council of Ministers will determine the detailed principles of calculating compensation, of taking into consideration the special factors mentioned under *E*, as well as the way of paying compensation and of redeeming the securities. . . .

ARTICLE VIII. A. Whoever removes, conceals or damages property subject to transfer to the State (Art. *II* and *III*) or undertakes other acts in order to prevent the transfer, will be punished by imprisonment to five years and fine up to 10 million zloty or one of these penalties.

B. The court will also decree confiscation of the object of the crime. . . .

B. Excerpts from a Resolution of the Polish Communist Party, July, 1956

THE PARTY should become aware and bring home to the entire community the true economic situation of Poland, the nature of our difficulties, and the realistic possibilities and means of improvement and further economic development of the country.

As a result of the selfless effort of millions of working people during the period of the Six-Year Plan [1950 to 1955], important tasks outlined by the Party and Government have been carried out, and powerful foundations have been laid for the industrialization and socialist transformation of Poland. The regained territories have been rehabilitated; the capital has been rebuilt; an appreciable production and defense potential has been created in our country; the ranks of the working class have doubled; the social structure and the balance of class forces in the country have altered.

In the realization of the Six-Year Plan a great part was played by the assistance of the U.S.S.R. and cooperation with the people's democracies. Poland has become an important link in the world socialist system. These are undeniable historical achievements accompanied by profound cultural transformations and by progress in many fields of life—achievements that provide powerful testimony to the superiority of socialism over capitalism.

Source: Resolution Adopted by the Central Committee of the Polish United Workers Party at its Seventh Plenary Session, July 18 to 28, 1956, in Paul E. Zinner, ed., *National Communism and Popular Revolt in Eastern Europe* (New York: Columbia University Press, 1956), pp. 150–165, with deletions. Translation amended. Used by permission.

However, the implementation of these tasks, particularly in the first phase of the implementation of the Six-Year Plan—before the Second Party Congress[1]—have absorbed too many resources and means of our economy at the expense of neglecting other tasks of the Six-Year Plan, and, in particular, of the substantial increase in the living standards of the masses called for in the plan. The explosive increase of industrial employment and the expansion of many social services were accompanied, however, by only negligible increases of real wages. The situation of a part of the working class did not improve at all, and in the case of some groups it even deteriorated.

In the course of the implementation of the Six-Year Plan several disproportions occurred in our national economy. They have made it impossible to achieve the increase in living standards of the nation envisaged by the plan.

A serious disproportion arose between the pace of development of industry and the pace of development of agriculture, the base for the food supply of the population and the raw material base for light industry. This disproportion resulted from the underestimation of the production needs of agriculture, and from the weakening of the material incentives of the peasants, both individual farmers and members of cooperatives, owing to distortion of the principles of the worker-peasant alliance and owing to violation of the rule of law in relations between the state and the peasants. Attempts to deal with these distortions after the Second Party Congress and concentration of efforts upon increasing agricultural production—despite the fact that they have already brought about tangible results—have not eliminated this excessive disproportion.

A considerable disproportion occurred between the insufficiently developed raw-material base and the needs of the processing and building industries. Inadequacy of raw materials and other materials and the lack or inadequacy of reserves is a main cause of difficulties in the plan. It has led to difficulties in coordination: lack of steady implementation of plans, idleness of machinery, failure to exploit production capacity in many enterprises, and so forth, all of which have very painful effects.

A considerable disproportion occurred between the excessive

---

[1] The Second Congress of the Party was held in March, 1954. It eased some of the most extreme Stalinist pressures, particularly on private farmers, reflecting the "New Course" adopted in the Soviet bloc after Stalin's death.—Eds.

size and costs of capital investments—as a matter of fact, frequently there were widely scattered investments that were not always fully justified economically—and the possibilities of the national economy. This has caused an excessive proportion of the national revenue to be tied up in investments, the freezing of important resources in investments that realize returns slowly, and at the same time, the neglect of the modernization and exploitation of the production potential of old enterprises.

The burden of investments and of defense expenditure was considerably increased in the years 1951 to 1953, during the period of growing international tension in connection with the war in Korea, when the necessity arose for a speedy expansion of the defense industry. This entailed costly investments and the mobilization of skilled cadres, frequently at the expense of the development of civilian industry.

As a result of the wrong policy toward craftsmen and the particularly faulty fiscal and supply policy, a completely unjustified and detrimental restriction of the output of crafts and of small industry has occurred, as well as a hampering of the development of servicing points. This has rendered difficult the increase of mass-consumption goods, the widening of their range, and a better meeting of the demands of the population.

In the course of the implementation of the Six-Year Plan, an excessive centralization of the planning and administration of the economy has taken place, as well as an excessive growth of the state apparatus and of the administrative and economic apparatus and the bureaucratization of the methods of the leadership. These phenomena have hampered the initiative of the masses and of the economic workers directly in charge of the enterprises, have caused waste, and have retarded technical progress and economic expansion in general. . . .

Contrary to the Six-Year Plan in which the fundamental achievement was the great step made along the road leading to the industrialization of the country, accompanied, however, by an inadequate increase of living standards, the new Five-Year Plan [1955 to 1960] should, with the support of the production potential already created, yield such an increase of industrial and agricultural production as would allow the achievement of a considerably speedier growth of the living standard of the masses.

The fundamental premises of the Five-Year Plan should be:

(a) the stepping up of the real wages of workers and employees by 30 per cent, with the proviso that the wages of the lower paid workers would increase above this average, and the stepping up of the average income per capita of the rural population by 30 per cent;

(b) the improvement of housing conditions for the urban population through the building of houses, amounting to 1.2 million rooms during the five-year period.

These tasks are difficult but fully realistic, provided we are able to exploit and rationally develop the production capacity created during the Six-Year Plan and to set in motion the great reserves existing both in agriculture and in industry.

The guarantee of the realistic character of these tasks is:

First: The fact that several large investments from the period of the Six-Year Plan will only now and in the next few years be in full production, and it will be possible to achieve further increase of production with considerably smaller financial and material outlays. . . .

Second: The fact that we possess large cadres of skilled workers, technicians, and engineers who have been trained during the past period, and that the influx of unskilled labor into industry and the cost of their training can be considerably lower under the Five-Year Plan than during the Six-Year Plan. . . .

Third: The fact that in agriculture, owing to the liquidation of several distortions since the Second Congress and owing to the greater assistance of the state, and to the effectiveness of the material incentives, a production increase is taking place. . . .

The implementation of the program for the improvement of the living standards of the working masses, the principal premise of the Five-Year Plan, calls for a consistent and bold change of the methods and directions of our economic policy.

1. The indispensable condition for mobilizing the internal reserves of our national economy is the execution of profound changes in the existing system of management.

The general direction of these changes spells the deepening and widening of the democratic traits of our system, *liquidation of excessive centralization of planning and management, and further widening of the prerogatives of socialist enterprises,* creating foundations for wide social initiative and economic control on the part of the working masses. . . .

2. The fundamental condition for the exploitation of the reserve existing in the socialist enterprises is *the raising of the direct*

*material interest of the staff in the economic results of the enter-
prise. . . .*

3. One of the decisive conditions for the improvement of the
work of industry is the *streamlining of the management of materials, the systematic improvement of supplies of materials, the
systematic improvement of supplies to enterprises, and interenter-
prise cooperation. . . .*

4. *The strictest possible discipline is indispensable, both in financial and real investments.*

Investments should be concentrated on projects that are in the
process of building and on projects that allow rapid achievement of
maximum economic returns, combating all symptoms of squandering, squandering at the planning stage, and construction of projects
according to the requirements of modern technology. . . .

5. It is necessary to expand and deepen economic research considerably, and to insure the practical exploitation of the results of
that research and the participation of scientists and economists in
planning current and long-term economic policy. . . .

6. In regard to agriculture and relations with the peasantry, *it is
necessary to continue with all consistency the policy outlined by
the Second Congress. . . .* The 25 per cent increase in agricultural
production, called for in the Five-Year Plan, can be achieved only
if increased machinery, credit, and investment assistance are accompanied by increased material incentives, both for individual
peasant farmers and for producer cooperatives, through the development of free market purchases, contracting and so on. . . .

7. Considerable reserves for the growth of production and services for the needs of the population and, at the same time, for
increase in employment, *exist in the expansion of small industry,
work cooperatives, crafts, and cottage industry. . . .*

An improvement in the living conditions of the working class is
already being attained, within our economic possibilities, and will
be systematically implemented in the coming years as well. . . .

Bibliography

The material for the study of twentieth-century European economic history is vast. A great wealth of statistical information has been regularly published by national governments and international agencies. Government inquiries and studies by special committees are too numerous to specify. League of Nations reports on conditions in the 1920's and 1930's, especially those prepared in connection with the World Economic Conference of 1927 and those dealing with the Depression, are extremely valuable. The same can be said for publications of the International Labour Organization. The United Nations Economic Commission for Europe publishes annual economic surveys as well as special studies. In addition, a variety of nongovernmental groups have sponsored the publication of economic studies. Worthy of special mention are the numerous volumes dealing with economic problems relating to war published by the Carnegie Endowment for International Peace. The brief bibliography that follows, therefore, makes no claim to completeness. It merely indicates a few of the books to which a reader might turn for further information.

General

Paul Alpert, *Twentieth Century Economic History of Europe.* New York: Henry Schuman, 1951.

Colin Clark, *The Conditions of Economic Progress.* London: Macmillan, 1951.

Folke Dovring, *Land and Labor in Europe, 1900–1950.* The Hague: Nijhoff, 1956.

Alexander Gerschenkron, *Economic Backwardness in Historical Perspective.* Cambridge, Mass.: Harvard University Press, 1962.

Ervin Hexner, *The International Steel Cartel.* Chapel Hill, N.C.: University of North Carolina Press, 1943.

Henry V. Hodson, *Slump and Recovery, 1929–37*. London: Oxford University Press, 1938.

John Maynard Keynes, *The Economic Consequences of the Peace*. New York: Harcourt, Brace and Howe, 1920.

Eugene M. Kulischer, *Europe on the Move: War and Population Changes, 1917–47*. New York: Columbia University Press, 1948.

League of Nations, *Industrialization and Foreign Trade*. Geneva: League of Nations, 1945.

W. Arthur Lewis, *Economic Survey, 1919–1939*. London: Allen and Unwin, 1949.

Lionel C. Robbins, *The Great Depression*. London: Macmillan, 1936.

Andrew Shonfield, *Modern Capitalism: The Changing Balance of Public and Private Power*. New York: Oxford University Press, 1965.

Ingvar Svennilson, *Growth and Stagnation in the European Economy*. Geneva: United Nations, 1954.

United Nations: Economic Commission for Europe, *Some Factors in Economic Growth in Europe During the 1950's* (Part 2 of *Economic Survey of Europe in 1961*). Geneva: United Nations, 1964.

Ingo Walter, *The European Common Market, 1958–65*. New York: Praeger, 1966.

Regional and National Studies

Great Britain

W. K. Hancock and M. M. Gowing, *British War Economy*. London: His Majesty's Stationery Office, 1949.

Keith Hutchison, *The Decline and Fall of British Capitalism*. New York: Charles Scribner's Sons, 1950.

Sidney Pollard, *The Development of the British Economy, 1914–1950*. London: Edward Arnold, 1962.

France

Warren C. Baum, *The French Economy and the State*. Princeton, N.J.: Princeton University Press, 1958.

Henry W. Ehrmann, *Organized Business in France*. Princeton, N.J.: Princeton University Press, 1957.

Charles P. Kindleberger, *Economic Growth in France and Britain, 1851–1950*. Cambridge, Mass.: Harvard University Press, 1964.

Germany

Robert A. Brady, *The Rationalization Movement in German Industry*. Berkeley, Calif.: University of California Press, 1933.

Gerald D. Feldman, *Army, Industry and Labor in Germany, 1914–1918*. Princeton, N.J.: Princeton University Press, 1966.

Frank D. Graham, *Exchange, Prices, and Production in Hyper-Inflation: Germany, 1920–1923*. Princeton, N.J.: Princeton University Press, 1930.

C. W. Guillebaud, *The Economic Recovery of Germany from 1933 to . . . 1938*. London: Macmillan, 1939.

Burton H. Klein, *Germany's Economic Preparations for War*. Cambridge, Mass.: Harvard University Press, 1959.

Arthur Schweitzer, *Big Business in the Third Reich*. Bloomington, Ind.: Indiana University Press, 1964.

Gustav Stolper, *The German Economy, 1870–1940: Issues and Trends*. New York: Reynal and Hitchcock [1940].

Italy

Shepard B. Clough, *The Economic History of Modern Italy*. New York: Columbia University Press, 1964.

George H. Hildebrand, *Growth and Structure in the Economy of Modern Italy*. Cambridge, Mass.: Harvard University Press, 1965.

Fausto Pitigliani, *The Italian Corporative State*. New York: Macmillan, 1934.

Carl T. Schmidt, *The Corporate State in Action: Italy Under Fascism*. New York: Oxford University Press, 1939.

Eastern Europe

Thad P. Alton, *The Polish Postwar Economy*. New York: Columbia University Press, 1955.

Michael Kaser, *Comecon: Integration Problems of the Planned Economies*. London: Oxford University Press, 1965.

Henry L. Roberts, *Rumania: Political Problems of an Agrarian State*. New Haven, Conn.: Yale University Press, 1951.

Nicolas Spulber, *The Economics of Communist Eastern Europe*. New York: John Wiley and Sons, 1957.

Doreen Warriner, *Revolution in Eastern Europe*. London: Turnstile Press, 1950.

Soviet Union

Alexander Baykov, *The Development of the Soviet Economic System*. New York: Macmillan, 1947.

Maurice Dobb, *Soviet Economic Development Since 1917*. New York: International Publishers, 1948.

Alexander Erlich, *The Soviet Industrialization Debate, 1924–1928*. Cambridge, Mass.: Harvard University Press, 1960.

Alec Nove, *The Soviet Economy: An Introduction*. Revised edition. New York: Praeger, 1966.

Index

Selected titles: revised June, 1967

hARPER ⚡ ToRchBOOKS

HUMANITIES AND SOCIAL SCIENCES

American Studies: General

HENRY STEELE COMMAGER, Ed.: The Struggle for Racial Equality   TB/1300

CARL N. DEGLER, Ed.: Pivotal Interpretations of American History   TB/1240, TB/1241

A. S. EISENSTADT, Ed.: The Craft of American History: Recent Essays in American Historical Writing
Vol. I TB/1255; Vol. II TB/1256

CHARLOTTE P. GILMAN: Women and Economics. ‡ *Ed. with an Introduction by Carl N. Degler*   TB/3073

MARCUS LEE HANSEN: The Atlantic Migration: 1607-1860. *Edited by Arthur M. Schlesinger*   TB/1052

MARCUS LEE HANSEN: The Immigrant in American History   TB/1120

JOHN HIGHAM, Ed.: The Reconstruction of American History △   TB/1068

ROBERT H. JACKSON: The Supreme Court in the American System of Government   TB/1106

JOHN F. KENNEDY: A Nation of Immigrants. △ *Illus.*
TB/1118

LEONARD W. LEVY, Ed.: American Constitutional Law: *Historical Essays*   TB/1285

LEONARD W. LEVY, Ed.: Judicial Review and the Supreme Court   TB/1296

LEONARD W. LEVY: The Law of the Commonwealth and Chief Justice Shaw   TB/1309

RALPH BARTON PERRY: Puritanism and Democracy
TB/1138

ARNOLD ROSE: The Negro in America   TB/3048

American Studies: Colonial

BERNARD BAILYN, Ed.: The Apologia of Robert Keayne: *Self-Portrait of a Puritan Merchant*   TB/1201

BERNARD BAILYN: The New England Merchants in the Seventeenth Century   TB/1149

JOSEPH CHARLES: The Origins of the American Party System   TB/1049

CHARLES GIBSON: Spain in America†   TB/3077

LAWRENCE HENRY GIPSON: The Coming of the Revolution: 1763-1775. † *Illus.*   TB/3007

PERRY MILLER: Errand Into the Wilderness   TB/1139

PERRY MILLER & T. H. JOHNSON, Eds.: The Puritans: *A Sourcebook* Vol. I TB/1093; Vol. II TB/1094

EDMUND S. MORGAN, Ed.: The Diary of Michael Wigglesworth, 1653-1657: *The Conscience of a Puritan*
TB/1228

EDMUND S. MORGAN: The Puritan Family   TB/1227

RICHARD B. MORRIS: Government and Labor in Early America   TB/1244

KENNETH B. MURDOCK: Literature and Theology in Colonial New England   TB/99

WALLACE NOTESTEIN: The English People on the Eve of Colonization: 1603-1630. † *Illus.*   TB/3006

JOHN P. ROCHE: Origins of American Political Thought: *Selected Readings*   TB/1301

JOHN SMITH: Captain John Smith's America: *Selections from His Writings. Ed. with Intro. by John Lankford*
TB/3078

LOUIS B. WRIGHT: The Cultural Life of the American Colonies: 1607-1763. † *Illus.*   TB/3005

American Studies: From the Revolution to 1860

JOHN R. ALDEN: The American Revolution: 1775-1783. † *Illus.*   TB/3011

MAX BELOFF, Ed.: The Debate on the American Revolution, 1761-1783: *A Sourcebook* △   TB/1225

RAY A. BILLINGTON: The Far Western Frontier: 1830-1860. † *Illus.*   TB/3012

EDMUND BURKE: On the American Revolution. ‡ *Edited by Elliott Robert Barkan*   TB/3068

WHITNEY R. CROSS: The Burned-Over District: *The Social and Intellectual History of Enthusiastic Religion in Western New York, 1800-1850*   TB/1242

GEORGE DANGERFIELD: The Awakening of American Nationalism: 1815-1828. † *Illus.*   TB/3061

CLEMENT EATON: The Growth of Southern Civilization: 1790-1860. † *Illus.*   TB/3040

LOUIS FILLER: The Crusade Against Slavery: 1830-1860. † *Illus.*   TB/3029

WILLIAM W. FREEHLING, Ed.: The Nullification Era: *A Documentary Record‡*   TB/3079

FELIX GILBERT: The Beginnings of American Foreign Policy: *To the Farewell Address*   TB/1200

FRANCIS GRIERSON: The Valley of Shadows: *The Coming of the Civil War in Lincoln's Midwest: A Contemporary Account*   TB/1246

JAMES MADISON: The Forging of American Federalism. *Edited by Saul K. Padover*   TB/1226

BERNARD MAYO: Myths and Men: *Patrick Henry, George Washington, Thomas Jefferson*   TB/1108

JOHN C. MILLER: Alexander Hamilton and the Growth of the New Nation   TB/3057

RICHARD B. MORRIS, Ed.: The Era of the American Revolution   TB/1180

R. B. NYE: The Cultural Life of the New Nation: 1776-1801. † *Illus.*   TB/3026

FRANCIS S. PHILBRICK: The Rise of the West, 1754-1830. † *Illus.*   TB/3067

TIMOTHY L. SMITH: Revivalism and Social Reform: *American Protestantism on the Eve of the Civil War*
TB/1229

ALBION W. TOURGÉE: A Fool's Errand. ‡ *Ed. by George Fredrickson*   TB/3074

A. F. TYLER: Freedom's Ferment   TB/1074

GLYNDON G. VAN DEUSEN: The Jacksonian Era: 1828-1848. † *Illus.*   TB/3028

LOUIS B. WRIGHT: Culture on the Moving Frontier
TB/1053

American Studies: The Civil War to 1900

W. R. BROCK: An American Crisis: *Congress and Reconstruction, 1865-67* ° △   TB/1283

---

† The New American Nation Series, edited by Henry Steele Commager and Richard B. Morris.
‡ American Persectives series, edited by Bernard Wishy and William E. Leuchtenburg.
* The Rise of Modern Europe series, edited by William L. Langer.
** History of Europe series, edited by J. H. Plumb.
¶ Researches in the Social, Cultural, and Behavioral Sciences, edited by Benjamin Nelson.
§ The Library of Religion and Culture, edited by Benjamin Nelson.
Σ Harper Modern Science Series, edited by James R. Newman.
° Not for sale in Canada.
△ Not for sale in the U. K.

1

W. A. DUNNING: Reconstruction, Political and Economic: 1865-1877 TB/1073

HAROLD U. FAULKNER: Politics, Reform and Expansion: 1890-1900. † Illus. TB/3020

ROBERT GREEN MC CLOSKEY: American Conservatism in the Age of Enterprise: 1865-1910 TB/1137

ARTHUR MANN: Yankee Reformers in the Urban Age: Social Reform in Boston, 1880-1900 TB/1247

CHARLES H. SHINN: Mining Camps: A Study in American Frontier Government. ‡ Ed. by R. W. Paul TB/3062

VERNON LANE WHARTON: The Negro in Mississippi: 1865-1890 TB/1178

American Studies: 1900 to the Present

A. RUSSELL BUCHANAN: The United States and World War II. † Illus. Vol. I TB/3044; Vol. II TB/3045

FOSTER RHEA DULLES: America's Rise to World Power: 1898-1954. † Illus. TB/3021

JOHN D. HICKS: Republican Ascendancy: 1921-1933. † Illus. TB/3041

SIDNEY HOOK: Reason, Social Myths, and Democracy TB/1237

WILLIAM E. LEUCHTENBURG: Franklin D. Roosevelt and the New Deal: 1932-1940. † Illus. TB/3025

ARTHUR S. LINK: Woodrow Wilson and the Progressive Era: 1910-1917. † Illus. TB/3023

GEORGE E. MOWRY: The Era of Theodore Roosevelt and the Birth of Modern America: 1900-1912. † TB/3022

RUSSEL B. NYE: Midwestern Progressive Politics: 1870-1958 TB/1202

JACOB RIIS: The Making of an American. ‡ Edited by Roy Lubove TB/3070

PHILIP SELZNICK: TVA and the Grass Roots: A Study in the Sociology of Formal Organization TB/1230

IDA M. TARBELL: The History of the Standard Oil Company: Briefer Version. ‡ Edited by David M. Chalmers TB/3071

GEORGE B. TINDALL, Ed.: A Populist Reader ‡ TB/3069

Anthropology

JACQUES BARZUN: Race: A Study in Superstition. Revised Edition TB/1172

JOSEPH B. CASAGRANDE, Ed.: In the Company of Man: Portraits of Anthropological Informants TB/3047

W. E. LE GROS CLARK: The Antecedents of Man: Intro. to Evolution of the Primates. ° △ Illus. TB/559

CORA DU BOIS: The People of Alor. New Preface by the author. Illus. Vol. I TB/1042; Vol. II TB/1043

DAVID LANDY: Tropical Childhood: Cultural Transmission and Learning in a Puerto Rican Village TB/1235

L. S. B. LEAKEY: Adam's Ancestors: The Evolution of Man and His Culture. △ Illus. TB/1019

ROBERT H. LOWIE: Primitive Society. Introduction by Fred Eggan TB/1056

EDWARD BURNETT TYLOR: The Origins of Culture. Part I of "Primitive Culture." § Intro. by Paul Radin TB/33

EDWARD BURNETT TYLOR: Religion in Primitive Culture. Part II of "Primitive Culture." § Intro. by Paul Radin TB/34

W. LLOYD WARNER: A Black Civilization: A Study of an Australian Tribe. ¶ Illus. TB/3056

Art and Art History

WALTER LOWRIE: Art in the Early Church. Revised Edition. 452 illus. TB/124

EMILE MÂLE: The Gothic Image: Religious Art in France of the Thirteenth Century. § △ 190 illus. TB/44

MILLARD MEISS: Painting in Florence and Siena after the Black Death. 169 illus. TB/1148

ERICH NEUMANN: The Archetypal World of Henry Moore. △ 107 illus. TB/2020

DORA & ERWIN PANOFSKY: Pandora's Box: The Changing Aspects of a Mythical Symbol TB/2021

ERWIN PANOFSKY: Studies in Iconology: Humanistic Themes in the Art of the Renaissance △ TB/1077

ALEXANDRE PIANKOFF: The Shrines of Tut-Ankh-Amon. Edited by N. Rambova. 117 illus. TB/2011

JEAN SEZNEC: The Survival of the Pagan Gods △ TB/2004

OTTO VON SIMSON: The Gothic Cathedral △ TB/2018

HEINRICH ZIMMER: Myths and Symbols in Indian Art and Civilization. 70 illus. TB/2005

Business, Economics & Economic History

REINHARD BENDIX: Work and Authority in Industry TB/3035

GILBERT BURCK & EDITORS OF FORTUNE: The Computer Age: And Its Potential for Management TB/1179

ROBERT DAHL & CHARLES E. LINDBLOM: Politics, Economics, and Welfare TB/3037

PETER F. DRUCKER: The New Society: The Anatomy of Industrial Order △ TB/1082

EDITORS OF FORTUNE: America in the Sixties: The Economy and the Society TB/1015

ROBERT L. HEILBRONER: The Great Ascent: The Struggle for Economic Development in Our Time TB/3030

ROBERT L. HEILBRONER: The Limits of American Capitalism TB/1305

FRANK H. KNIGHT: The Economic Organization TB/1214

FRANK H. KNIGHT: Risk, Uncertainty and Profit TB/1215

ABBA P. LERNER: Everybody's Business TB/3051

PAUL MANTOUX: The Industrial Revolution in the Eighteenth Century ° △ TB/1079

HERBERT SIMON: The Shape of Automation: For Men and Management TB/1245

PERRIN STRYKER: The Character of the Executive: Eleven Studies in Managerial Qualities TB/1041

Contemporary Culture

JACQUES BARZUN: The House of Intellect △ TB/1051

CLARK KERR: The Uses of the University TB/1264

JOHN U. NEF: Cultural Foundations of Industrial Civilization △ TB/1024

NATHAN M. PUSEY: The Age of the Scholar: Observations on Education in a Troubled Decade TB/1157

PAUL VALÉRY: The Outlook for Intelligence △ TB/2016

Historiography & Philosophy of History

JACOB BURCKHARDT: On History and Historians. △ Intro. by H. R. Trevor-Roper TB/1216

J. H. HEXTER: Reappraisals in History: New Views on History & Society in Early Modern Europe △ TB/1100

H. STUART HUGHES: History as Art and as Science: Twin Vistas on the Past TB/1207

ARNALDO MOMIGLIANO: Studies in Historiography ° △ TB/1288

GEORGE H. NADEL, Ed.: Studies in the Philosophy of History: Essays from History and Theory TB/1208

KARL R. POPPER: The Open Society and Its Enemies △ Vol. I: The Spell of Plato TB/1101; Vol. II: The High Tide of Prophecy: Hegel, Marx and the Aftermath TB/1102

KARL R. POPPER: The Poverty of Historicism ° △ TB/1126

G. J. RENIER: History: Its Purpose and Method △ TB/1209

W. H. WALSH: Philosophy of History △ TB/1020

History: General

L. CARRINGTON GOODRICH: A Short History of the Chinese People. △ Illus. TB/3015

DAN N. JACOBS & HANS H. BAERWALD: Chinese Communism: Selected Documents TB/3031

BERNARD LEWIS: The Arabs in History △ TB/1029

BERNARD LEWIS: The Middle East and the West ° △ TB/1274

History: Ancient

A. ANDREWES: The Greek Tyrants △ TB/1103

ADOLF ERMAN, Ed.: The Ancient Egyptians TB/1233

MICHAEL GRANT: Ancient History ° △ TB/1190

SAMUEL NOAH KRAMER: Sumerian Mythology TB/1055

NAPHTALI LEWIS & MEYER REINHOLD, Eds.: Roman Civilization. Sourcebook I: The Republic TB/1231; Sourcebook II: The Empire TB/1232

2

History: Medieval

P. BOISSONNADE: Life and Work in Medieval Europe △ TB/1141
HELEN CAM: England before Elizabeth △ TB/1026
NORMAN COHN: The Pursuit of the Millennium △ TB/1037
G. G. COULTON: Medieval Village, Manor, and Monastery TB/1022
CHRISTOPHER DAWSON, Ed.: Mission to Asia △ TB/315
HEINRICH FICHTENAU: The Carolingian Empire: The Age of Charlemagne △ TB/1142
GALBERT OF BRUGES: The Murder of Charles the Good. Trans. with Intro. by James Bruce Ross TB/1311
F. L. GANSHOF: Feudalism △ TB/1058
DENO GEANAKOPLOS: Byzantine East and Latin West △ TB/1265
W. O. HASSALL, Ed.: Medieval England: As Viewed by Contemporaries △ TB/1205
DENYS HAY: Europe: The Emergence of an Idea △ TB/1275
DENYS HAY: The Medieval Centuries ○ △ TB/1192
J. M. HUSSEY: The Byzantine World TB/1057
ROBERT LATOUCHE: The Birth of Western Economy: Economic Aspects of the Dark Ages ○ △ TB/1290
FERDINAND LOT: The End of the Ancient World and the Beginnings of the Middle Ages TB/1044
MARSILIUS OF PADUA: The Defender of the Peace. Trans. with Intro. by Alan Gewirth TB/1310
G. MOLLAT: The Popes at Avignon: 1305-1378 △ TB/308
CHARLES PETIT-DUTAILLIS: The Feudal Monarchy in France and England ○ △ TB/1165
HENRI PIRENNE: Early Democracies in the Low Countries TB/1110
STEVEN RUNCIMAN: A History of the Crusades. △
  Volume I: The First Crusade and the Foundation of the Kingdom of Jerusalem. Illus. TB/1143
  Volume II: The Kingdom of Jerusalem and the Frankish East, 1100-1187. Illus. TB/1243
  Volume III: The Kingdom of Acre and the Later Crusades TB/1298
FERDINAND SCHEVILL: Siena: The History of a Medieval Commune. Intro. by William M. Bowsky TB/1164
HENRY OSBORN TAYLOR: The Classical Heritage of the Middle Ages TB/1117
F. VAN DER MEER: Augustine the Bishop: Church and Society at the Dawn of the Middle Ages △ TB/304
J. M. WALLACE-HADRILL: The Barbarian West: The Early Middle Ages, A.D. 400-1000 △ TB/1061

History: Renaissance & Reformation

JACOB BURCKHARDT: The Civilization of the Renaissance in Italy. △ Illus. Vol. I TB/40; Vol. II TB/41
JOHN CALVIN & JACOPO SADOLETO: A Reformation Debate. △ Edited by John C. Olin TB/1239
FEDERICO CHABOD: Machiavelli and the Renaissance △ TB/1193
EDWARD P. CHEYNEY: The Dawn of a New Era, 1250-1453. * Illus. TB/3002
G. CONSTANT: The Reformation in England: The English Schism, Henry VIII, 1509-1547 △ TB/314
G. R. ELTON: Reformation Europe, 1517-1559 ** ○ △ TB/1270
WALLACE K. FERGUSON et al.: Facets of the Renaissance TB/1098
WALLACE K. FERGUSON et al.: The Renaissance: Six Essays. Illus. TB/1084
JOHN NEVILLE FIGGIS: The Divine Right of Kings. Introduction by G. R. Elton TB/1191
JOHN NEVILLE FIGGIS: Political Thought from Gerson to Grotius: 1414-1625: Seven Studies TB/1032
MYRON P. GILMORE: The World of Humanism, 1453-1517.* Illus. TB/3003
FRANCESCO GUICCIARDINI: Maxims and Reflections of a Renaissance Statesman (Ricordi) TB/1160
J. H. HEXTER: More's Utopia TB/1195
HAJO HOLBORN: Ulrich von Hutten and the German Reformation TB/1238

JOHAN HUIZINGA: Erasmus and the Age of Reformation. △ Illus. TB/19
JOEL HURSTFIELD, Ed.: The Reformation Crisis △ TB/1267
ULRICH VON HUTTEN et al.: On the Eve of the Reformation: "Letters of Obscure Men" TB/1124
PAUL O. KRISTELLER: Renaissance Thought: The Classic, Scholastic, and Humanist Strains TB/1048
PAUL O. KRISTELLER: Renaissance Thought II: Papers on Humanism and the Arts TB/1163
NICCOLÒ MACHIAVELLI: History of Florence and of the Affairs of Italy △ TB/1027
ALFRED VON MARTIN: Sociology of the Renaissance. Introduction by Wallace K. Ferguson △ TB/1099
GARRETT MATTINGLY et al.: Renaissance Profiles. △ Edited by J. H. Plumb TB/1162
J. E. NEALE: The Age of Catherine de Medici ○ △ TB/1085
ERWIN PANOFSKY: Studies in Iconology: Humanistic Themes in the Art of the Renaissance △ TB/1077
J. H. PARRY: The Establishment of the European Hegemony: 1415-1715 △ TB/1045
J. H. PLUMB: The Italian Renaissance: A Concise Survey of Its History and Culture △ TB/1161
A. F. POLLARD: Henry VIII. ○ △ Introduction by A. G. Dickens TB/1249
A. F. POLLARD: Wolsey. ○ △ Introduction by A.G.Dickens TB/1248
CECIL ROTH: The Jews in the Renaissance. Illus. TB/834
A. L. ROWSE: The Expansion of Elizabethan England. ○ △ Illus. TB/1220
GORDON RUPP: Luther's Progress to the Diet of Worms ○ △ TB/120
FERDINAND SCHEVILL: The Medici. Illus. TB/1010
FERDINAND SCHEVILL: Medieval and Renaissance Florence. Illus. Volume I: Medieval Florence TB/1090
  Volume II: The Coming of Humanism and the Age of the Medici TB/1091
G. M. TREVELYAN: England in the Age of Wycliffe, 1368-1520 ○ △ TB/1112
VESPASIANO: Renaissance Princes, Popes, and Prelates: The Vespasiano Memoirs: Lives of Illustrious Men of the XVth Century TB/1111

History: Modern European

FREDERICK B. ARTZ: Reaction and Revolution, 1815-1832. * Ilus. TB/3034
MAX BELOFF: The Age of Absolutism, 1660-1815 △ TB/1062
ROBERT C. BINKLEY: Realism and Nationalism, 1852-1871. * Illus. TB/3038
ASA BRIGGS: The Making of Modern England, 1784-1867: The Age of Improvement ○ △ TB/1203
CRANE BRINTON: A Decade of Revolution, 1789-1799. * Illus. TB/3018
D. W. BROGAN: The Development of Modern France. ○ △ Volume I: From the Fall of the Empire to the Dreyfus Affair TB/1184
  Volume II: The Shadow of War, World War I, Between the Two Wars. New Introduction by the Author TB/1185
J. BRONOWSKI & BRUCE MAZLISH: The Western Intellectual Tradition: From Leonardo to Hegel TB/3001
GEOFFREY BRUUN: Europe and the French Imperium, 1799-1814. * Illus. TB/3033
ALAN BULLOCK: Hitler, A Study in Tyranny ○ △ TB/1123
E. H. CARR: German-Soviet Relations Between the Two World Wars, 1919-1939 TB/1278
E. H. CARR: International Relations Between the Two World Wars, 1919-1939 ○ △ TB/1279
E. H. CARR: The Twenty Years' Crisis, 1919-1939 ○ △ TB/1122
GORDON A. CRAIG: From Bismarck to Adenauer: Aspects of German Statecraft. Revised Edition TB/1171
DENIS DIDEROT: The Encyclopedia: Selections. Ed. and trans. by Stephen Gendzier TB/1299
FRANKLIN L. FORD: Robe and Sword: The Regrouping of the French Aristocracy after Louis XIV TB/1217

Intellectual History & History of Ideas

Literature, Poetry, The Novel & Criticism

4

Myth, Symbol & Folklore

JOSEPH CAMPBELL, Editor: Pagan and Christian Mysteries. *Illus.*   TB/2013
MIRCEA ELIADE: Cosmos and History: *The Myth of the Eternal Return* § △   TB/2050
MIRCEA ELIADE: Rites and Symbols of Initiation: *The Mysteries of Birth and Rebirth* § △   TB/1236
THEODOR H. GASTER: Thespis: *Ritual, Myth & Drama in the Ancient Near East* △   TB/1281
DORA & ERWIN PANOFSKY: Pandora's Box: *The Changing Aspects of a Mythical Symbol.* △ *Revised Edition. Illus.*   TB/2021
HELLMUT WILHELM: Change: *Eight Lectures on the I Ching* △   TB/2019

Philosophy

G. E. M. ANSCOMBE: An Introduction to Wittgenstein's Tractatus. *Second edition, Revised* o △   TB/1210
HENRI BERGSON: Time and Free Will o △   TB/1021
H. J. BLACKHAM: Six Existentialist Thinkers o △   TB/1002
CRANE BRINTON: Nietzsche   TB/1197
ERNST CASSIRER: The Individual and the Cosmos in Renaissance Philosophy △   TB/1097
FREDERICK COPLESTON: Medieval Philosophy o △   TB/376
F. M. CORNFORD: Principium Sapientiae: *A Study of the Origins of Greek Philosophical Thought*   TB/1213
F. M. CORNFORD: From Religion to Philosophy §   TB/20
WILFRID DESAN: The Tragic Finale: *An Essay on the Philosophy of Jean-Paul Sartre*   TB/1030
A. P. D'ENTRÈVES: Natural Law △   TB/1223
MARVIN FARBER: The Aims of Phenomenology: *Husserl's Thought*   TB/1291
MARVIN FARBER: Phenomenology and Existence: *Towards a Philosophy Within Nature*   TB/1295
PAUL FRIEDLÄNDER: Plato: *An Introduction* △   TB/2017
J. GLENN GRAY: The Warriors: *Reflections on Men in Battle. Intro. by Hannah Arendt*   TB/1294
W. K. C. GUTHRIE: The Greek Philosophers: *From Thales to Aristotle* o △   TB/1008
G. W. F. HEGEL: The Phenomenology of Mind o △   TB/1303
F. H. HEINEMANN: Existentialism and the Modern Predicament △   TB/28
EDMUND HUSSERL: Phenomenology and the Crisis of Philosophy   TB/1170
IMMANUEL KANT: The Doctrine of Virtue, *being Part II of the Metaphysic of Morals*   TB/110
IMMANUEL KANT: Groundwork of the Metaphysic of Morals. *Trans. & analyzed by H. J. Paton*   TB/1159
IMMANUEL KANT: Lectures on Ethics §   TB/105
IMMANUEL KANT: Religion Within the Limits of Reason Alone. § *Intro. by T. M. Greene & J. Silber*   TB/67
QUENTIN LAUER: Phenomenology   TB/1169
GABRIEL MARCEL: Being and Having △   TB/310
GEORGE A. MORGAN: What Nietzsche Means △   TB/1198
MICHAEL POLANYI: Personal Knowledge △   TB/1158
WILLARD VAN ORMAN QUINE: Elementary Logic: *Revised Edition*   TB/577
WILLARD VAN ORMAN QUINE: From a Logical Point of View: *Logico-Philosophical Essays*   TB/566
BERTRAND RUSSELL et al.: The Philosophy of Bertrand Russell   Vol. I TB/1095; Vol. II   TB/1096
L. S. STEBBING: A Modern Introduction to Logic △ TB/538
ALFRED NORTH WHITEHEAD: Process and Reality: *An Essay in Cosmology* △   TB/1033
PHILIP P. WIENER: Evolution and the Founders of Pragmatism. *Foreword by John Dewey*   TB/1212
WILHELM WINDELBAND: A History of Philosophy
    Vol. I: *Greek, Roman, Medieval*   TB/38
    Vol. II: *Renaissance, Enlightenment, Modern*   TB/39
LUDWIG WITTGENSTEIN: The Blue and Brown Books o   TB/1211

Political Science & Government

JEREMY BENTHAM: The Handbook of Political Fallacies. *Introduction by Crane Brinton*   TB/1069
KENNETH E. BOULDING: Conflict and Defense   TB/3024
CRANE BRINTON: English Political Thought in the Nineteenth Century   TB/1071
ROBERT CONQUEST: Power and Policy in the USSR: *The Study of Soviet Dynastics* △   TB/1307
ROBERT DAHL & CHARLES E. LINDBLOM: Politics, Economics, and Welfare   TB/3037
F. L. GANSHOF: Feudalism △   TB/1058
G. P. GOOCH: English Democratic Ideas in Seventeenth Century   TB/1006
SIDNEY HOOK: Reason, Social Myths and Democracy △   TB/1237
DAN N. JACOBS & HANS BAERWALD, Eds.: Chinese Communism: *Selected Documents*   TB/3031
HANS KOHN: Political Ideologies of the 20th Century   TB/1277
KINGSLEY MARTIN: French Liberal Thought in the Eighteenth Century △   TB/1114
BARRINGTON MOORE, JR.: Soviet Politics—The Dilemma of Power ¶   TB/1222
BARRINGTON MOORE, JR.: Terror and Progress—USSR ¶   TB/1266
JOHN B. MORRALL: Political Thought in Medieval Times △ TB/1076
KARL R. POPPER: The Open Society and Its Enemies △
    Vol. I: *The Spell of Plato*   TB/1101
    Vol. II: *The High Tide of Prophecy: Hegel, Marx, and the Aftermath*   TB/1102
BENJAMIN I. SCHWARTZ: Chinese Communism and the Rise of Mao   TB/1308
PETER WOLL, Ed.: Public Administration and Policy: *Selected Essays*   TB/1284

Psychology

ALFRED ADLER: The Individual Psychology of Alfred Adler △   TB/1154
ARTHUR BURTON & ROBERT E. HARRIS, Eds.: Clinical Studies of Personality
    Vol. I TB/3075;   Vol. II   TB/3076
HADLEY CANTRIL: The Invasion from Mars: *The Psychology of Panic*   TB/1282
HERBERT FINGARETTE: The Self in Transformation ¶   TB/1177
SIGMUND FREUD: On Creativity and the Unconscious § △ TB/45
WILLIAM JAMES: Psychology: *Briefer Course*   TB/1034
RICHARD M. JONES, Ed.: Contemporary Educational Psychology: *Selected Readings*   TB/1292
C. G. JUNG: Symbols of Transformation △
    Vol. I: TB/2009;   Vol. II   TB/2010
JOHN T. MC NEILL: A History of the Cure of Souls   TB/126
KARL MENNINGER: Theory of Psychoanalytic Technique   TB/1144
ERICH NEUMANN: Amor and Psyche △   TB/2012
ERICH NEUMANN: The Origins and History of Consciousness △   Vol. I *Illus.* TB/2007; Vol. II   TB/2008
JEAN PIAGET, BÄRBEL INHELDER, & ALINA SZEMINSKA: The Child's Conception of Geometry o △   TB/1146
JOHN H. SCHAAR: Escape from Authority: *The Perspectives of Erich Fromm*   TB/1155
MUZAFER SHERIF: The Psychology of Social Norms   TB/3072

Sociology

JACQUES BARZUN: Race: *A Study in Superstition*   TB/1172
BERNARD BERELSON, Ed.: The Behavioral Sciences Today TB/1127
LEWIS A. COSER, Ed.: Political Sociology   TB/1293
ALLISON DAVIS & JOHN DOLLARD: Children of Bondage ¶ TB/3049
ST. CLAIR DRAKE & HORACE R. CAYTON: Black Metropolis
    Vol. I TB/1086;   Vol. II   TB/1087
ALVIN W. GOULDNER: Wildcat Strike ¶   TB/1176

5

7

NATURAL SCIENCES
AND MATHEMATICS

Biological Sciences

Chemistry

Communication Theory

Geography

History of Science

Mathematics

Philosophy of Science

Physics and Cosmology

8